P9-DNP-107

the BOOKS of MAGIC

vertigo / dc comics

WRITER
neil gaiman

ILLUSTRATORS
john bolton

scott hampton

charles vess

paul johnson

LETTERER
todd klein

the Books of Magic

West Chester Public Library
415 N. Church St.
West Chester, PA 19

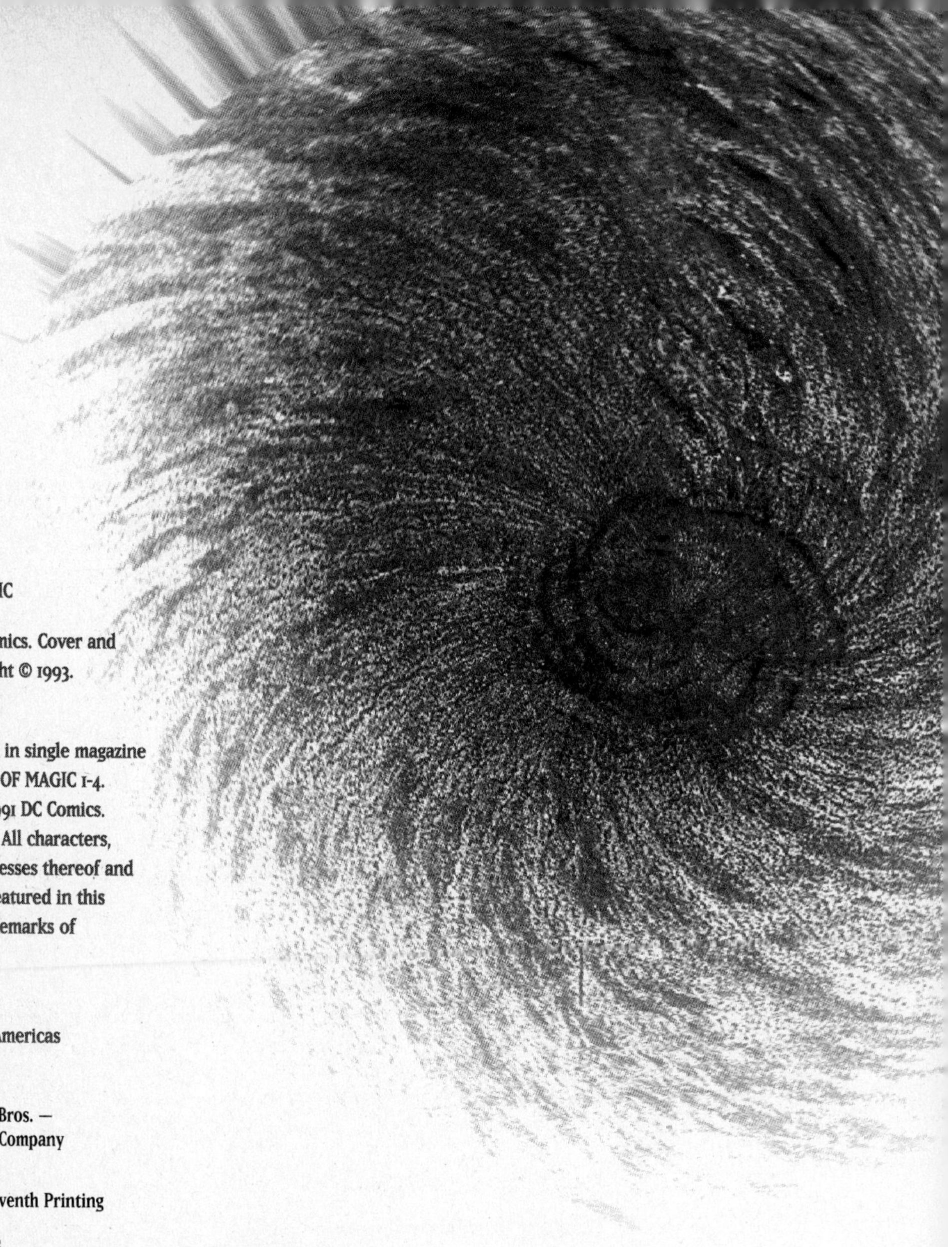

THE BOOKS OF MAGIC

Published by DC Comics. Cover and
compilation copyright © 1993.
All Rights Reserved.

Originally published in single magazine
form as THE BOOKS OF MAGIC 1-4.
Copyright © 1990, 1991 DC Comics.
All Rights Reserved. All characters,
the distinctive likenesses thereof and
all related indicia featured in this
publication are trademarks of
DC Comics.

DC Comics
1325 Avenue of the Americas
New York, NY 10019

A division of Warner Bros. —
An AOL Time Warner Company

Printed in Canada. Seventh Printing

ISBN # 1-56389-082-8

Logo, cover and publication design by
Richard Bruning/Brainstorm Unltd.

"MOOD INDIGO"
Words and music by D. Ellington,
I. Mills and A. Bigard. © 1931 (renewed
1958) Mills Music, Inc. & Famous Music
Corp. Used by permission of
CPP/Belwin, Inc., Miami, FL 33014.
All Rights Reserved. International
copyright secured.

This is a work of fiction.
Any resemblance to any real people
(living, dead, or stolen by fairies),
or to any real animals, gods, witches,
countries and events (magical or
otherwise), is just blind luck,
or so we hope.

DC COMICS

Jenette Kahn
President & Editor-in-Chief

Paul Levitz
Executive Vice President &
Publisher

Karen Berger
Executive Editor and Editor —
original series

Bob Kahan
Editor — collected edition

Georg Brewer
Design Director

Robbin Brosterman
Art Director

Richard Bruning
VP-Creative Director

Patrick Caldon
Senior VP-Finance & Operations

Dorothy Crouch
VP-Licensed Publishing

Terri Cunningham
VP-Managing Editor

Joel Ehrlich
Senior VP-Advertising &
Promotions

Alison Gill
Executive Director-Manufacturing

Lillian Laserson
VP & General Counsel

Jim Lee
Editorial Director-WildStorm

John Nee
VP & General Manager-WildStorm

Cheryl Rubin
VP-Licensing & Merchandising

Bob Wayne
VP-Sales & Marketing

Dedication

To Diana Wynne Jones, Jane Yolen,
Ellen Kushner and Terri Windling: four witches.

Acknowledgments

In my school holidays, when I was much younger, I would
spend whole days at our local library, reading my way through
the children's section. It was a magical journey, or rather, a
succession of journeys, in a small room full of books.

Writing this tale I found myself greatly indebted to that nine-
year-old me, sitting somewhere with a book; and to the people
who took me to wonderlands.

I owe a huge debt to all those arcane practitioners and master
magicians: Edith Nesbitt and P.L. Travers and Edward Eager, C.S.
Lewis and Andrew Lang, Margaret Storey and Noel Langley,
Lewis Carroll and J.P. Martin, Nicholas Stuart Gray and
J.B.S. Haldane and Clive King and T.H. White — and the rest:
there are many others, many of whose names I have by now
forgotten or never knew. They were the first to tell me that
there was magic, and where it was to be found.

Rachel Pollack gave me Tarot advice, Marv Wolfman explained
Baron Winter, and Bob Greenberger kibitzed on continuity.
The late Arthur Waley's translations of oriental poems helped
to assemble the tale of the Wu woman, and Karen Berger,
editor extraordinary, forgave me for sneakily writing a novel
when I should have been working on this.

So to them, and to John Bolton, Scott Hampton, Charles
Vess,and Paul Johnson, and also to Mike Dringenberg, Tom
Yeates, Paul Chadwick, John Ridgway, Ron Randall, Todd Klein
and the mysterious Mister Zed: my thanks.

—Neil Gaiman

Introduction

I once stopped in an odd little establishment in Ensenada, down in Baja, where a Hindu gentleman was selling tiny gold-plated orchids. He explained that they were real flowers, and that a process existed for plating them with that shiny metal without ruining their forms. Unable to resist, I said, "Sort of like gilding the lily, huh?" But his knowledge of the language had not progressed to the point of catching bad deadpan humor, and he responded, "No! No! Is not lily! Is orchid!"

Neil Gaiman does not really need an introduction. It would sort of be like—never mind.

He writes the award-winning SANDMAN series and is co-author with Terry Pratchett of the novel **Good Omens** which I have recommended to many and do yet again.

I first met Neil at an autographing session in Dallas. Most recently, I spent a pleasant evening with him and Steven Brust at the World Fantasy Convention in Phoenix, where we spoke of many things and I was reminded of something an older writer had told me long ago—namely, that editors only think that they're buying stories, that what they're really buying is the way a story is told. Look at Nick Bantock's fascinating **Griffin & Sabine**, where the medium is 95% of the enchantment.

Neil Gaiman is such a medium specialist. While his tales are gripping, moving, there is in particular the *way* of his stories to consider. I'm always fascinated by his point of attack and by the angles from which he views his people, settings, situations, actions. It's his approach that I study as much as the ideas he employs. And in the case of **The Books of Magic** I am again fascinated. This time he has chosen for his subject the tale of initiation, the story of the magician's journey from innocence along the road to power.

The four volumes of **The Books of Magic**, herein gathered, are a wonderful romp which I have read both backwards and forwards. In that they worked well for me in either direction, as well as in several odd shufflings of the deck, I feel free to talk about them in a variety of ways—none of which can really "give away the plot," because it's not that sort of story. While there is a storyline from which events depend, it is also a thematic tale, and I can talk about it at this level, choosing examples from wherever I would, without doing harm to anyone's reading pleasure.

by Roger Zelazny

Opening Joseph Campbell's **Hero with a Thousand Faces** to the Table of Contents and skipping over the Prologue wherein he will speak of the monomyth in general terms, we come to Part I, "The Adventure of the Hero," which is divided into four chapters: "Departure," "Initiation," "Return," and "The Keys." In that Campbell is examining the archetypes of all mythology here, and looking to describe a rhythm common to heroic fiction, I thought to hold it up next to **The Books of Magic** to see how Neil's story compares with the hero's journey in world mythology at large.

Looking at the first volume as representing "The Departure," we see that it is indeed characterized by the five features Campbell discussed. The "Call to Adventure" comes simply enough in the midst of Timothy's mundane activity, skateboarding. The "Refusal of the Call" follows immediately, as Timothy flees the Stranger, Dr. Occult, and Mr. E — whereupon Constantine stops him, offering the classical "Supernatural Aid" by turning his yo-yo into an owl/familiar. "The Crossing of the First Threshold" then takes him on a journey back through time to beginnings. Then comes "The Belly of the Whale," the return to the center of things — the self-sacrificial experience, the learning of the price — which begins in the theater.

Looking on Book II as a continuation of "The Belly of the Whale," let us hold Book III up against the "Initiation" chapter. Campbell's breakdown here is "The Road of Trials," "The Meeting with the Goddess," "Woman as the Temptress," "Atonement with the Father," "Apotheosis," and "The Ultimate Boon."

All of these are encountered in Fairyland, with Titania as the goddess and the temptress, the father as the sleeping king under the mountain, and the apotheosis of sorts occurring on the receipt of the boon.

I won't even try to match things up for the final **Book of Magic**. I will simply point out for homework that Campbell's next chapter, "The Return," contains the following sections: "Refusal of the Return," "The Magic Flight," "Rescue from Without," "The Crossing of the Return Threshold," and "Freedom to Live."

This is one way to look at it. Sure, all of those things are there. It does not matter one whit, though, whether Neil cleverly synthesized the piece out of Campbell or whether he crafted a tale drawing upon similar sources so that such a thoroughgoing analysis must necessarily apply. Either way, the result is a work worthy of respect.

One might remark on the sense of humor exhibited in Book III, where the hero and his companions are hanging around Baba Yaga's house, or the tangential nature of the future according to Book IV, or the blackness at the beginning of the universe, or at its end, view everything between as a cosmic day, and reduce all of the action to a solar myth; or, as I did earlier, one might play the sequence backwards, beginning with the playing-card archetypes and winding up regarding the Fall as an Ascension; or —

From a mundane standpoint, one might merely observe that Neil has arranged appearances here by every major occult figure in DC's history, to the possible end of introducing a new series character. And I do wonder whether Timothy will be back.

It is more than a clever story, however. It is rich and it is resonant. Like all good writing it causes the mind to wander off down byways by arousing speculations and leaving them to simmer. Why is Dr. Occult's female side so strong? What wonders will emerge from the mundane egg? What lock will Timothy's key one day fit? I like this allusiveness, this sense of depth. It entertains and engages me to see so much contained between these covers.

And Neil is fortunate here in having such interesting and talented colleagues as John Bolton, Scott Hampton, Charles Vess, and Paul Johnson rendering his visions into vivid images. And while people seldom comment on lettering because its job is generally to be unobtrusive, they also, for the same reason — habit — may not always note its subtle shifts in such places as the Museum of Ghosts sequences or Zatara's poem or the dialogue at Baba Yaga's or its alteration in various of the future sections — or simply not wonder why certain words get the bold-face treatment. Todd Klein's sure hand is a definite part of the magic here.

Neil Gaiman is a writer I have resolved to watch, and so far the effort has never failed to return more than the price of admission to his worlds. Yes, I have enjoyed this story in many ways. It has been a journey worth taking. To say more would be to dip it in molten metal. Sweet dreams.

— Roger Zelazny

I

The Invisible Labyrinth

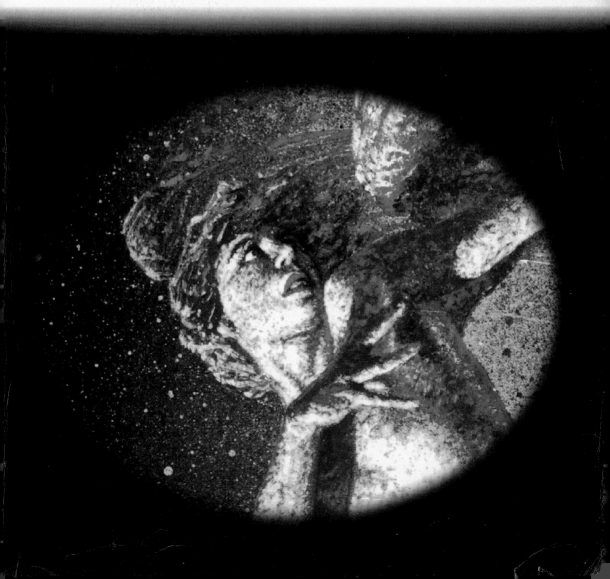

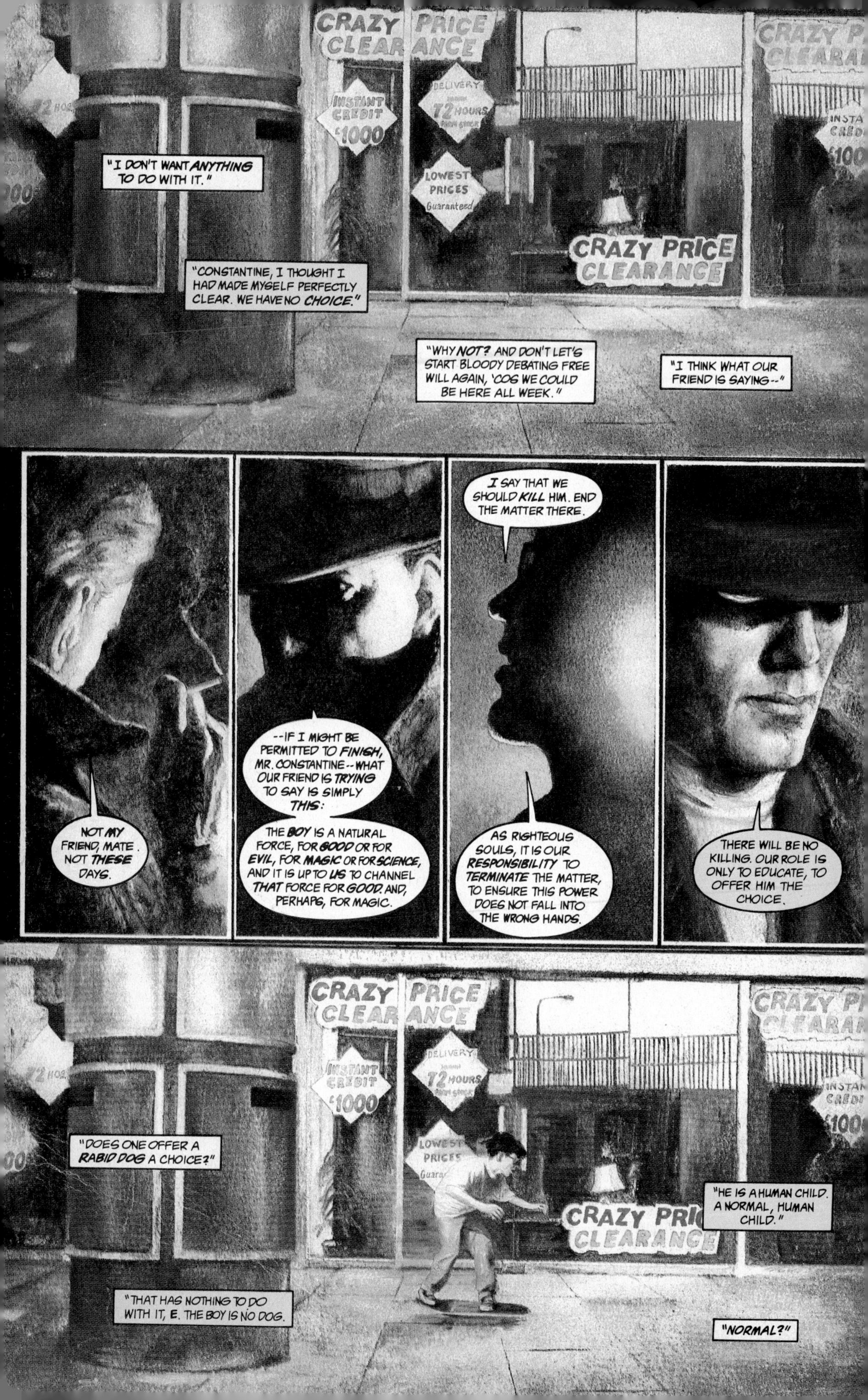

CRAZY PRICE CLEARANCE
INSTANT CREDIT £1000
DELIVERY 72 HOURS
LOWEST PRICES Guaranteed
"I DON'T WANT ANYTHING TO DO WITH IT."
"CONSTANTINE, I THOUGHT I HAD MADE MYSELF PERFECTLY CLEAR. WE HAVE NO CHOICE."
"WHY NOT? AND DON'T LET'S START BLOODY DEBATING FREE WILL AGAIN, 'COS WE COULD BE HERE ALL WEEK."
"I THINK WHAT OUR FRIEND IS SAYING--"
NOT MY FRIEND, MATE. NOT THESE DAYS.
--IF I MIGHT BE PERMITTED TO FINISH, MR. CONSTANTINE--WHAT OUR FRIEND IS TRYING TO SAY IS SIMPLY THIS:
THE BOY IS A NATURAL FORCE, FOR GOOD OR FOR EVIL, FOR MAGIC OR FOR SCIENCE, AND IT IS UP TO US TO CHANNEL THAT FORCE FOR GOOD. AND, PERHAPS, FOR MAGIC.
I SAY THAT WE SHOULD KILL HIM. END THE MATTER THERE.
AS RIGHTEOUS SOULS, IT IS OUR RESPONSIBILITY TO TERMINATE THE MATTER, TO ENSURE THIS POWER DOES NOT FALL INTO THE WRONG HANDS.
THERE WILL BE NO KILLING. OUR ROLE IS ONLY TO EDUCATE, TO OFFER HIM THE CHOICE.
"DOES ONE OFFER A RABID DOG A CHOICE?"
"THAT HAS NOTHING TO DO WITH IT, E. THE BOY IS NO DOG.
"HE IS A HUMAN CHILD. A NORMAL, HUMAN CHILD."
"NORMAL?"

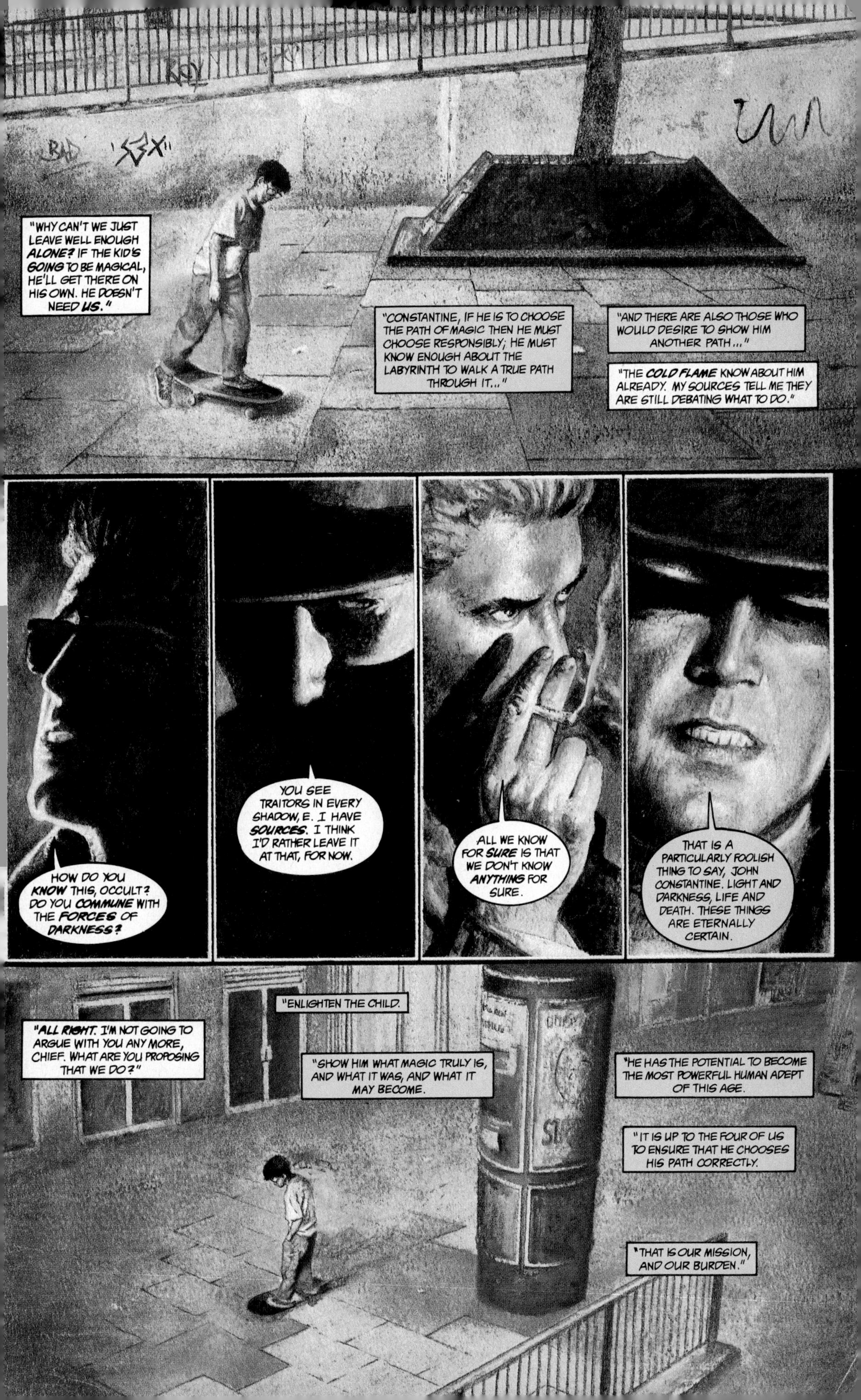
"WHY CAN'T WE JUST LEAVE WELL ENOUGH ALONE? IF THE KID'S GOING TO BE MAGICAL, HE'LL GET THERE ON HIS OWN. HE DOESN'T NEED US."
"CONSTANTINE, IF HE IS TO CHOOSE THE PATH OF MAGIC THEN HE MUST CHOOSE RESPONSIBLY; HE MUST KNOW ENOUGH ABOUT THE LABYRINTH TO WALK A TRUE PATH THROUGH IT..."
"AND THERE ARE ALSO THOSE WHO WOULD DESIRE TO SHOW HIM ANOTHER PATH..."
"THE COLD FLAME KNOW ABOUT HIM ALREADY. MY SOURCES TELL ME THEY ARE STILL DEBATING WHAT TO DO."
HOW DO YOU KNOW THIS, OCCULT? DO YOU COMMUNE WITH THE FORCES OF DARKNESS?
YOU SEE TRAITORS IN EVERY SHADOW, E. I HAVE SOURCES. I THINK I'D RATHER LEAVE IT AT THAT, FOR NOW.
ALL WE KNOW FOR SURE IS THAT WE DON'T KNOW ANYTHING FOR SURE.
THAT IS A PARTICULARLY FOOLISH THING TO SAY, JOHN CONSTANTINE. LIGHT AND DARKNESS, LIFE AND DEATH. THESE THINGS ARE ETERNALLY CERTAIN.
"ALL RIGHT. I'M NOT GOING TO ARGUE WITH YOU ANY MORE, CHIEF. WHAT ARE YOU PROPOSING THAT WE DO?"
"ENLIGHTEN THE CHILD.
"SHOW HIM WHAT MAGIC TRULY IS, AND WHAT IT WAS, AND WHAT IT MAY BECOME.
"HE HAS THE POTENTIAL TO BECOME THE MOST POWERFUL HUMAN ADEPT OF THIS AGE.
"IT IS UP TO THE FOUR OF US TO ENSURE THAT HE CHOOSES HIS PATH CORRECTLY.
"THAT IS OUR MISSION, AND OUR BURDEN."

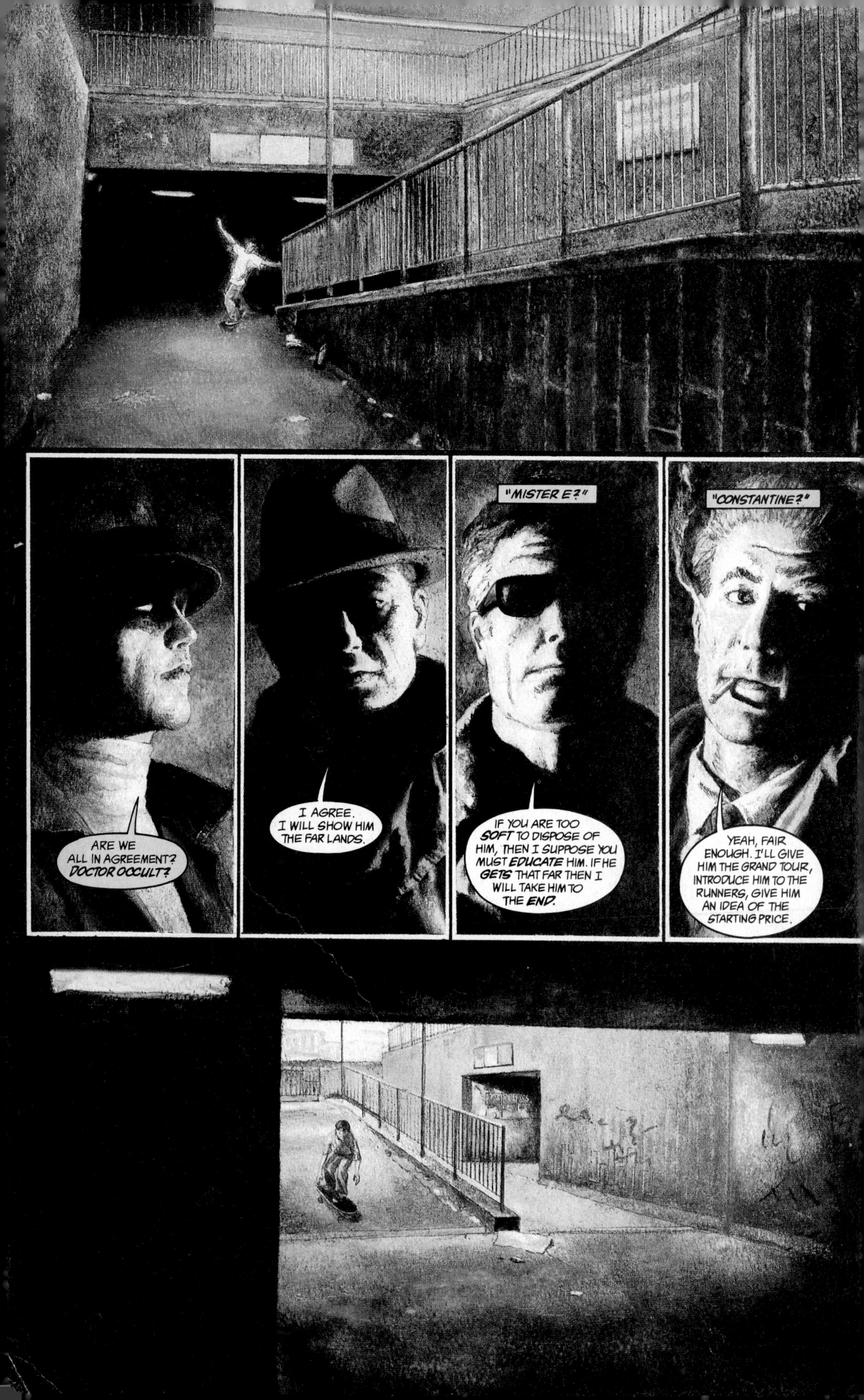
ARE WE
ALL IN AGREEMENT?
DOCTOR OCCULT?
I AGREE.
I WILL SHOW HIM
THE FAR LANDS.
"MISTER E?"
IF YOU ARE TOO
SOFT TO DISPOSE OF
HIM, THEN I SUPPOSE YOU
MUST EDUCATE HIM. IF HE
GETS THAT FAR THEN I
WILL TAKE HIM TO
THE END.
"CONSTANTINE?"
YEAH, FAIR
ENOUGH. I'LL GIVE
HIM THE GRAND TOUR,
INTRODUCE HIM TO THE
RUNNERS, GIVE HIM
AN IDEA OF THE
STARTING PRICE.

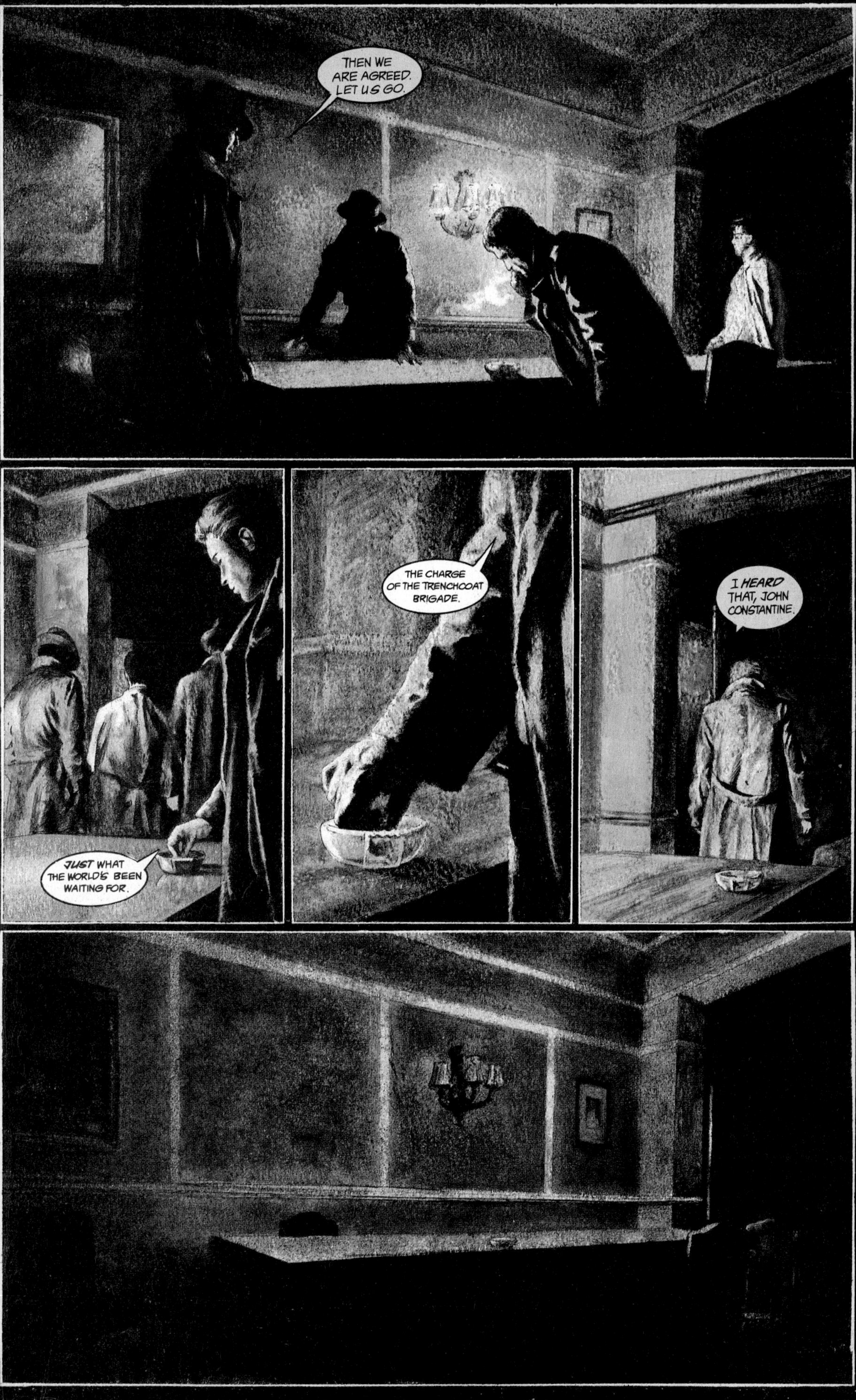
THEN WE ARE AGREED. LET US GO.
JUST WHAT THE WORLD'S BEEN WAITING FOR.
THE CHARGE OF THE TRENCHCOAT BRIGADE.
I HEARD THAT, JOHN CONSTANTINE.

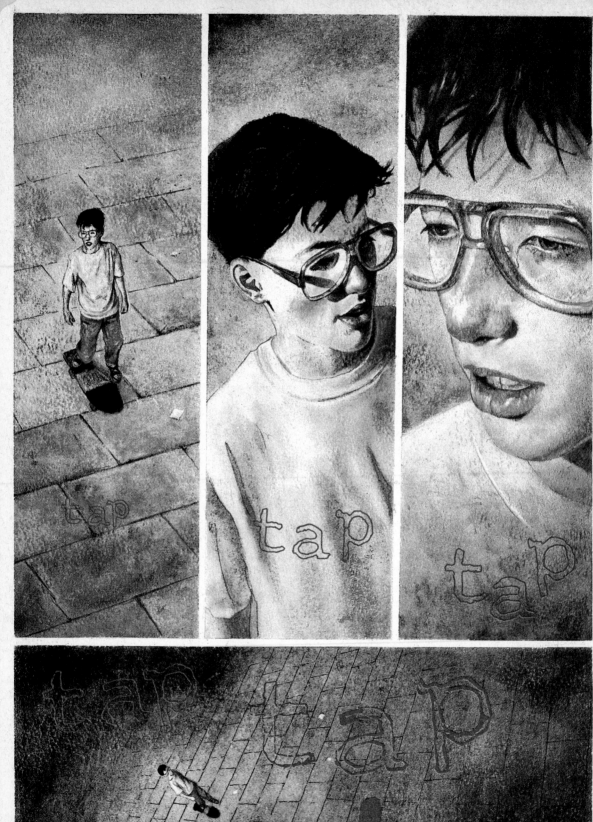

EVERYWHERE. IT'S COMING FROM EVERYWHERE.

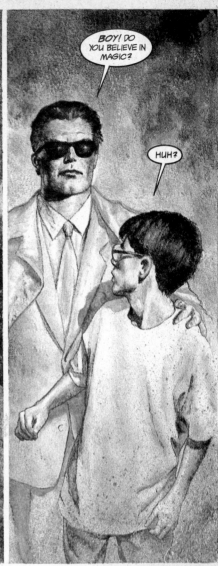

BOY! DO YOU BELIEVE IN MAGIC?

HUH?

WHO THE HELL WAS THAT? A WEIRDO? A PERVERT? I NEARLY JUMPED OUT OF MY SKIN.

STILL, LOST HIM NOW.

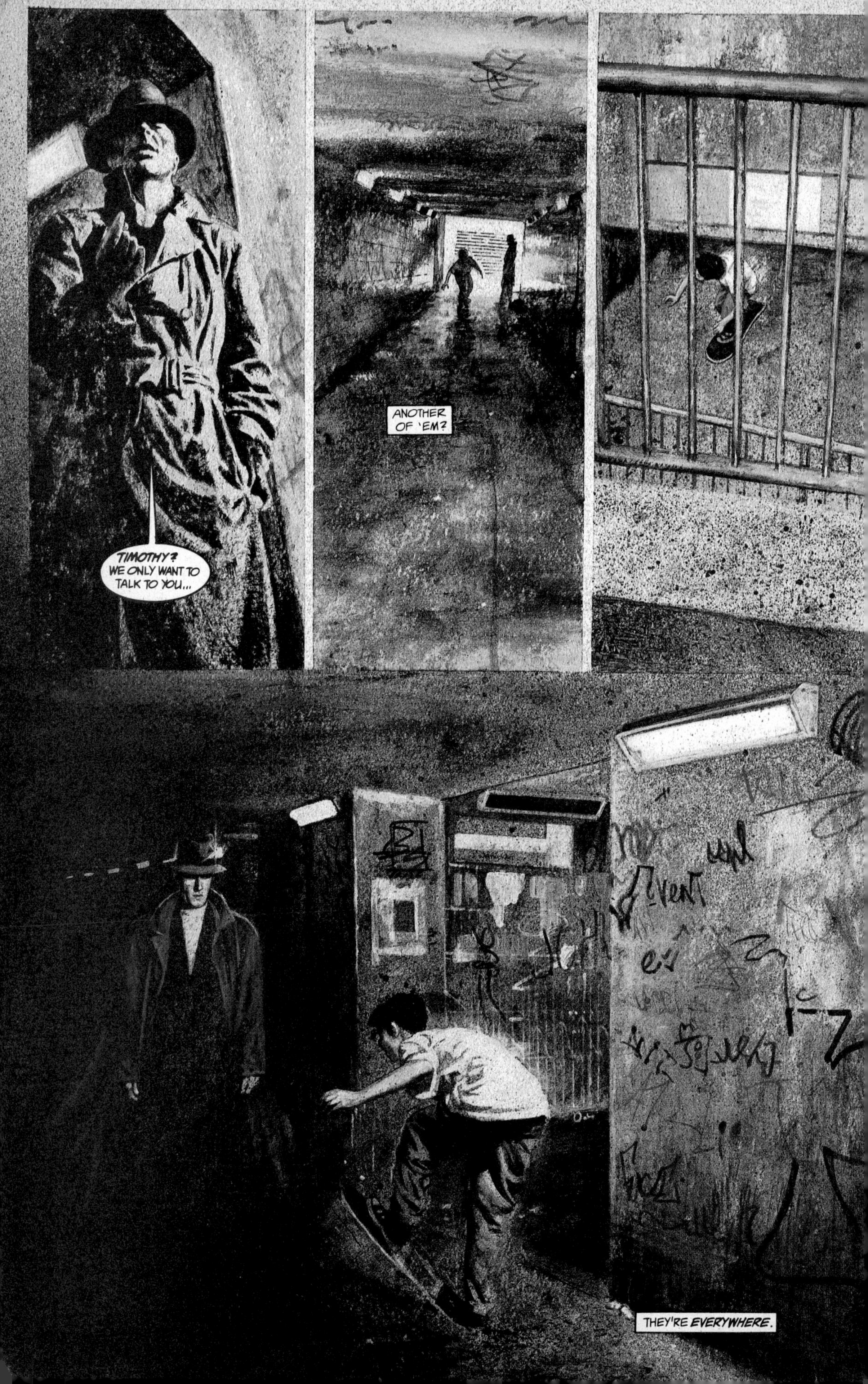
TIMOTHY? WE ONLY WANT TO TALK TO YOU...
ANOTHER OF 'EM?
THEY'RE *EVERYWHERE*.

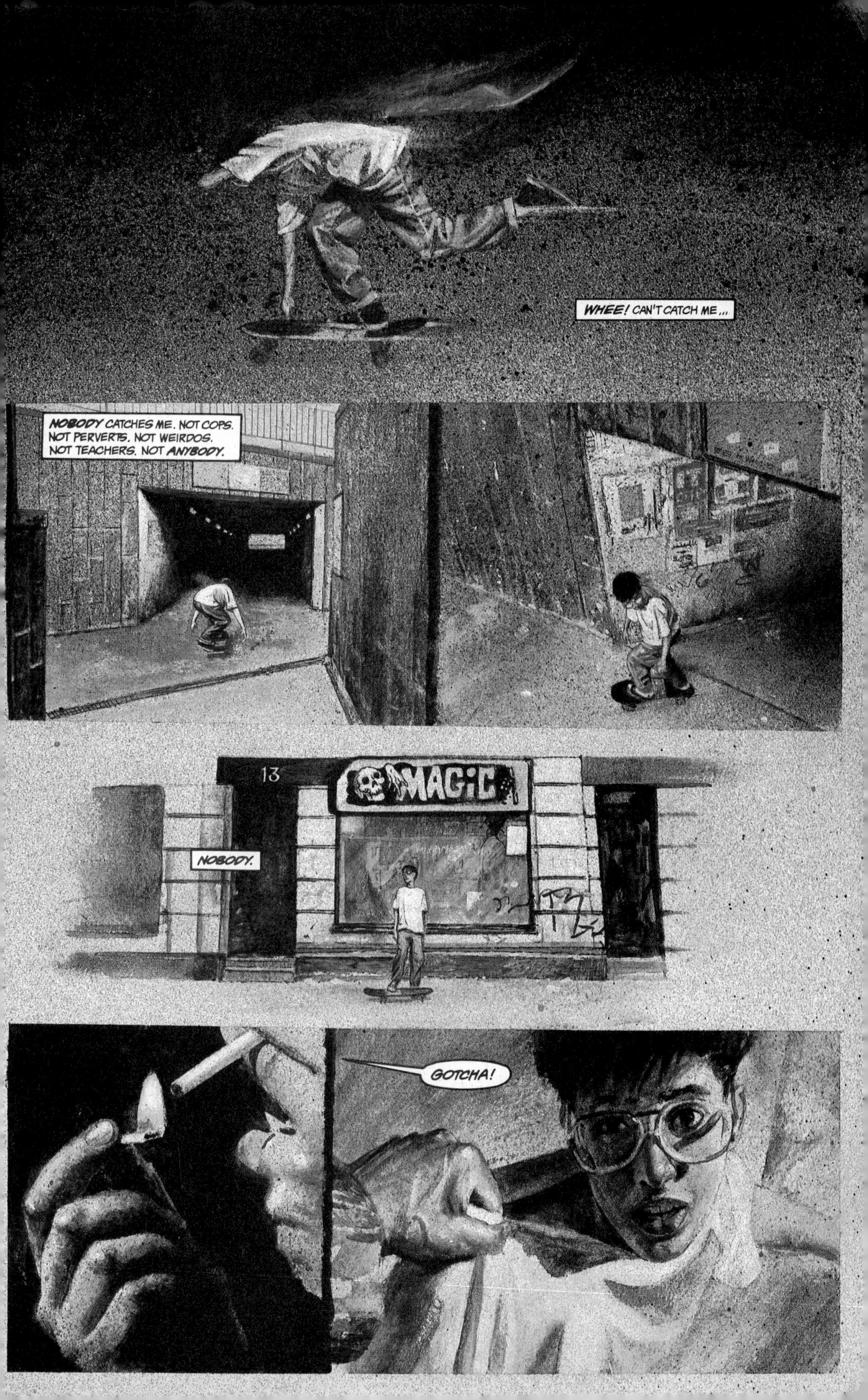
WHEE! CAN'T CATCH ME...
NOBODY CATCHES ME. NOT COPS. NOT PERVERTS. NOT WEIRDOS. NOT TEACHERS. NOT ANYBODY.
13
MAGIC
NOBODY.
GOTCHA!

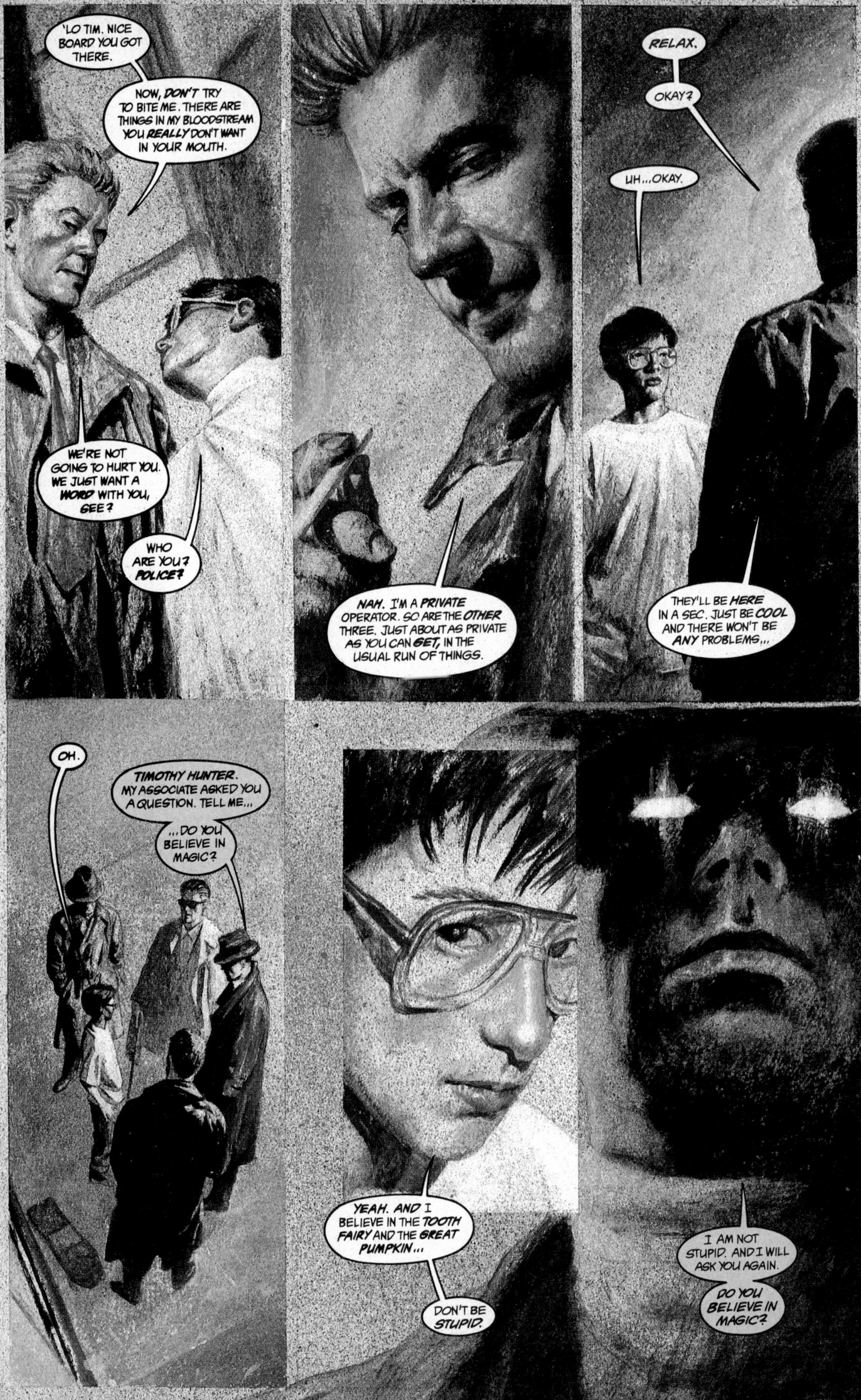
'LO TIM. NICE BOARD YOU GOT THERE.
NOW, DON'T TRY TO BITE ME. THERE ARE THINGS IN MY BLOODSTREAM YOU REALLY DON'T WANT IN YOUR MOUTH.
WE'RE NOT GOING TO HURT YOU. WE JUST WANT A WORD WITH YOU, SEE?
WHO ARE YOU? POLICE?
NAH. I'M A PRIVATE OPERATOR. SO ARE THE OTHER THREE. JUST ABOUT AS PRIVATE AS YOU CAN GET, IN THE USUAL RUN OF THINGS.
RELAX.
OKAY?
UH...OKAY.
THEY'LL BE HERE IN A SEC. JUST BE COOL AND THERE WON'T BE ANY PROBLEMS...
OH.
TIMOTHY HUNTER. MY ASSOCIATE ASKED YOU A QUESTION. TELL ME...
...DO YOU BELIEVE IN MAGIC?
YEAH. AND I BELIEVE IN THE TOOTH FAIRY AND THE GREAT PUMPKIN...
DON'T BE STUPID.
I AM NOT STUPID. AND I WILL ASK YOU AGAIN.
DO YOU BELIEVE IN MAGIC?

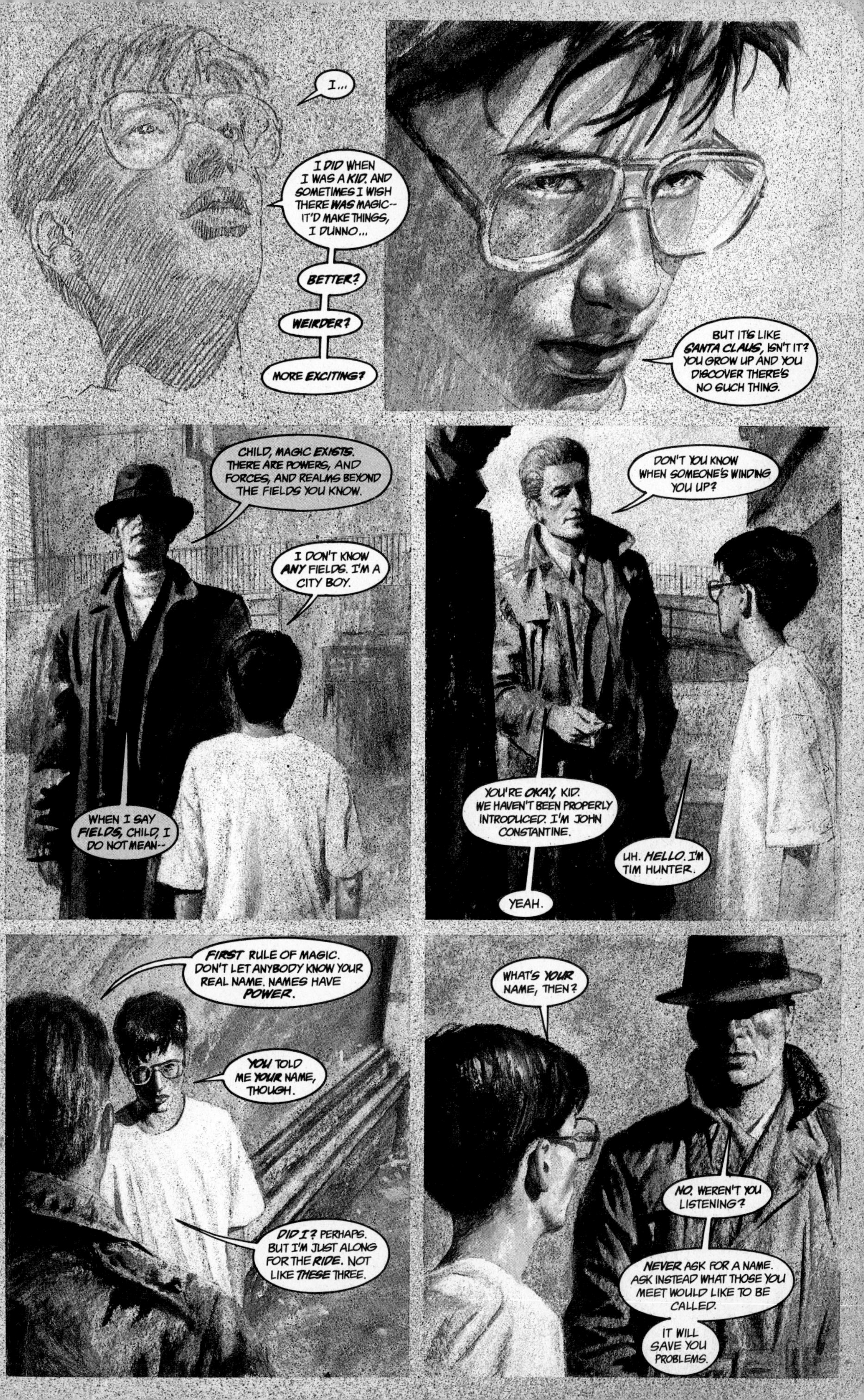

I...
I DID WHEN I WAS A KID. AND SOMETIMES I WISH THERE WAS MAGIC-- IT'D MAKE THINGS, I DUNNO...
BETTER?
WEIRDER?
MORE EXCITING?
BUT IT'S LIKE SANTA CLAUS, ISN'T IT? YOU GROW UP AND YOU DISCOVER THERE'S NO SUCH THING.
CHILD, MAGIC EXISTS. THERE ARE POWERS, AND FORCES, AND REALMS BEYOND THE FIELDS YOU KNOW.
I DON'T KNOW ANY FIELDS. I'M A CITY BOY.
WHEN I SAY FIELDS, CHILD, I DO NOT MEAN--
DON'T YOU KNOW WHEN SOMEONE'S WINDING YOU UP?
YOU'RE OKAY, KID. WE HAVEN'T BEEN PROPERLY INTRODUCED. I'M JOHN CONSTANTINE.
UH. HELLO. I'M TIM HUNTER.
YEAH.
FIRST RULE OF MAGIC. DON'T LET ANYBODY KNOW YOUR REAL NAME. NAMES HAVE POWER.
YOU TOLD ME YOUR NAME, THOUGH.
DID I? PERHAPS. BUT I'M JUST ALONG FOR THE RIDE. NOT LIKE THESE THREE.
WHAT'S YOUR NAME, THEN?
NO. WEREN'T YOU LISTENING?
NEVER ASK FOR A NAME. ASK INSTEAD WHAT THOSE YOU MEET WOULD LIKE TO BE CALLED.
IT WILL SAVE YOU PROBLEMS.

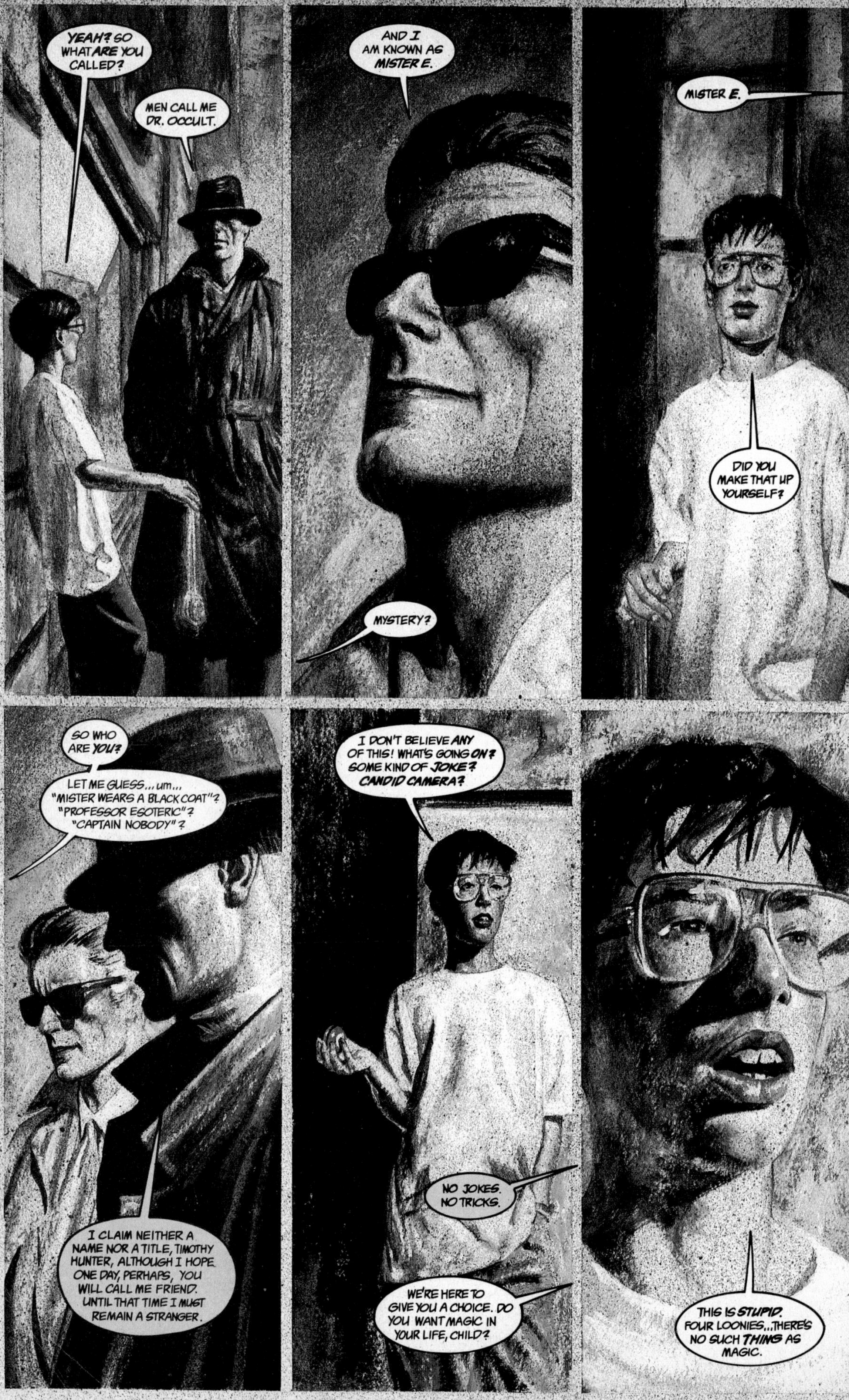
YEAH? SO WHAT ARE YOU CALLED?
MEN CALL ME DR. OCCULT.
AND I AM KNOWN AS MISTER E.
MYSTERY?
MISTER E.
DID YOU MAKE THAT UP YOURSELF?
SO WHO ARE YOU?
LET ME GUESS... UM... "MISTER WEARS A BLACK COAT"? "PROFESSOR ESOTERIC"? "CAPTAIN NOBODY"?
I CLAIM NEITHER A NAME NOR A TITLE, TIMOTHY HUNTER, ALTHOUGH I HOPE ONE DAY, PERHAPS, YOU WILL CALL ME FRIEND. UNTIL THAT TIME I MUST REMAIN A STRANGER.
I DON'T BELIEVE ANY OF THIS! WHAT'S GOING ON? SOME KIND OF JOKE? CANDID CAMERA?
NO JOKES. NO TRICKS.
WE'RE HERE TO GIVE YOU A CHOICE. DO YOU WANT MAGIC IN YOUR LIFE, CHILD?
THIS IS STUPID. FOUR LOONIES... THERE'S NO SUCH THING AS MAGIC.

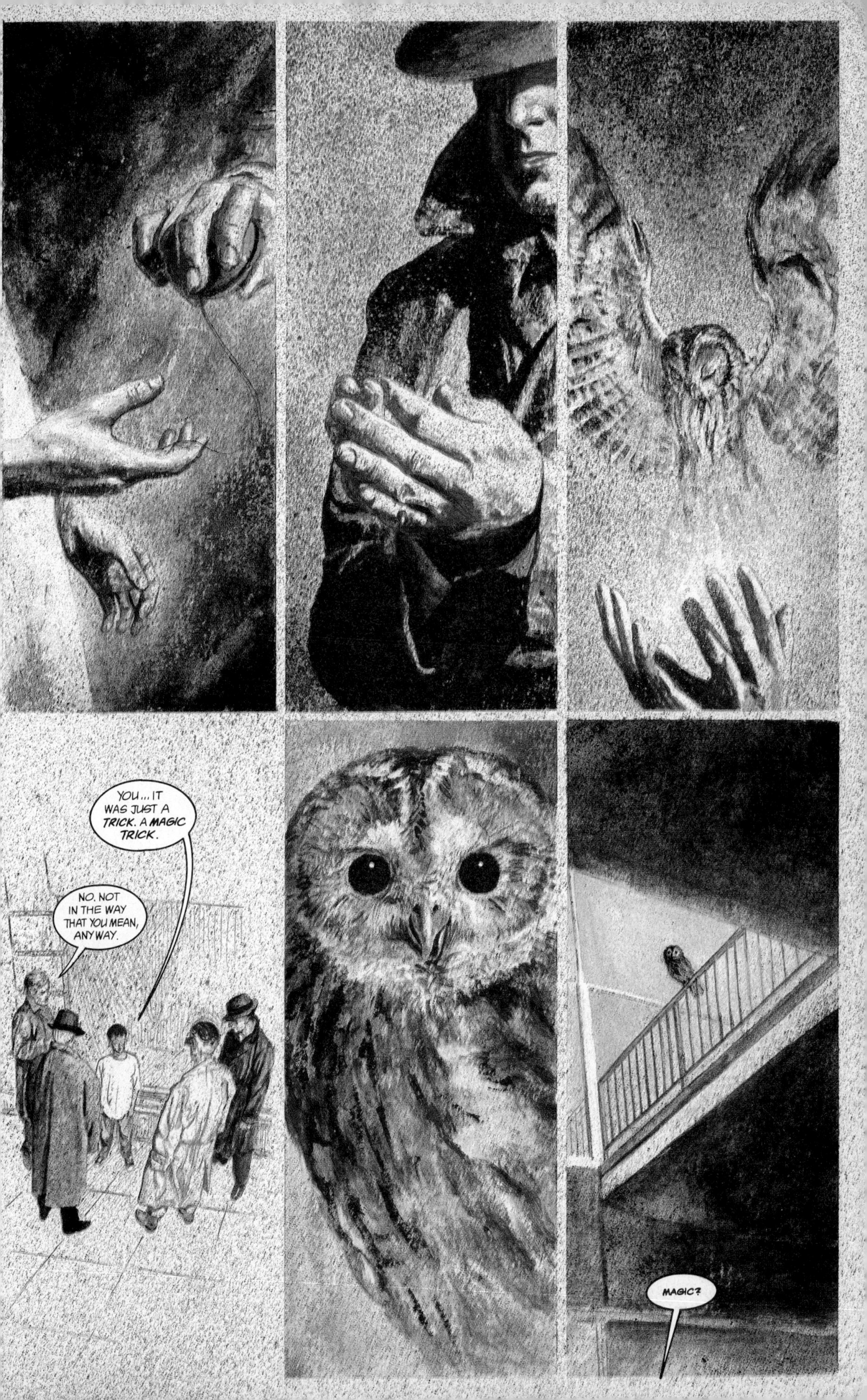
YOU... IT WAS JUST A TRICK. A MAGIC TRICK.
NO. NOT IN THE WAY THAT YOU MEAN, ANYWAY.
MAGIC?

MAGIC.

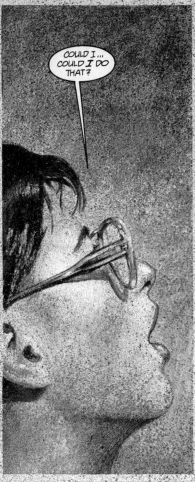

COULD I... COULD I DO THAT?

IF THAT IS THE ROUTE YOU WISH TO WALK, TIMOTHY. THAT IS WHY WE ARE HERE.

OUR ROLE IS TO EDUCATE, TIMOTHY. TO SHOW YOU THE PATH OF ENCHANTMENT, OF THE ART, OF GRAMARYE AND GLAMOUR-- WHETHER YOU CHOOSE TO WALK IT AFTER THAT WILL BE YOUR OWN AFFAIR.

WILL YOU COME WITH ME, TIMOTHY HUNTER?

IF I COULD DO THAT STUFF THEY'D HAVE TO TREAT ME DIFFERENT. THAT'S FOR CERTAIN.

I WOULDN'T HAVE TO TAKE ANY CRAP FROM ANYBODY. NOT EVER.

NOT EVER AGAIN.

I'LL COME WITH YOU. WHERE ARE WE GOING?

THROUGH THE DOOR.

DO YOU GET PAID FOR SPEAKING IN RIDDLES OR SOMETHING?

THE PAST IS ALWAYS KNOCKING AT THE DOOR, TRY- ING TO BREAK THROUGH, INTO TODAY.

WE WILL SEE THE PAST, BUT WE CANNOT INFLUENCE IT.

WALK WITH ME, THROUGH THE DOOR.

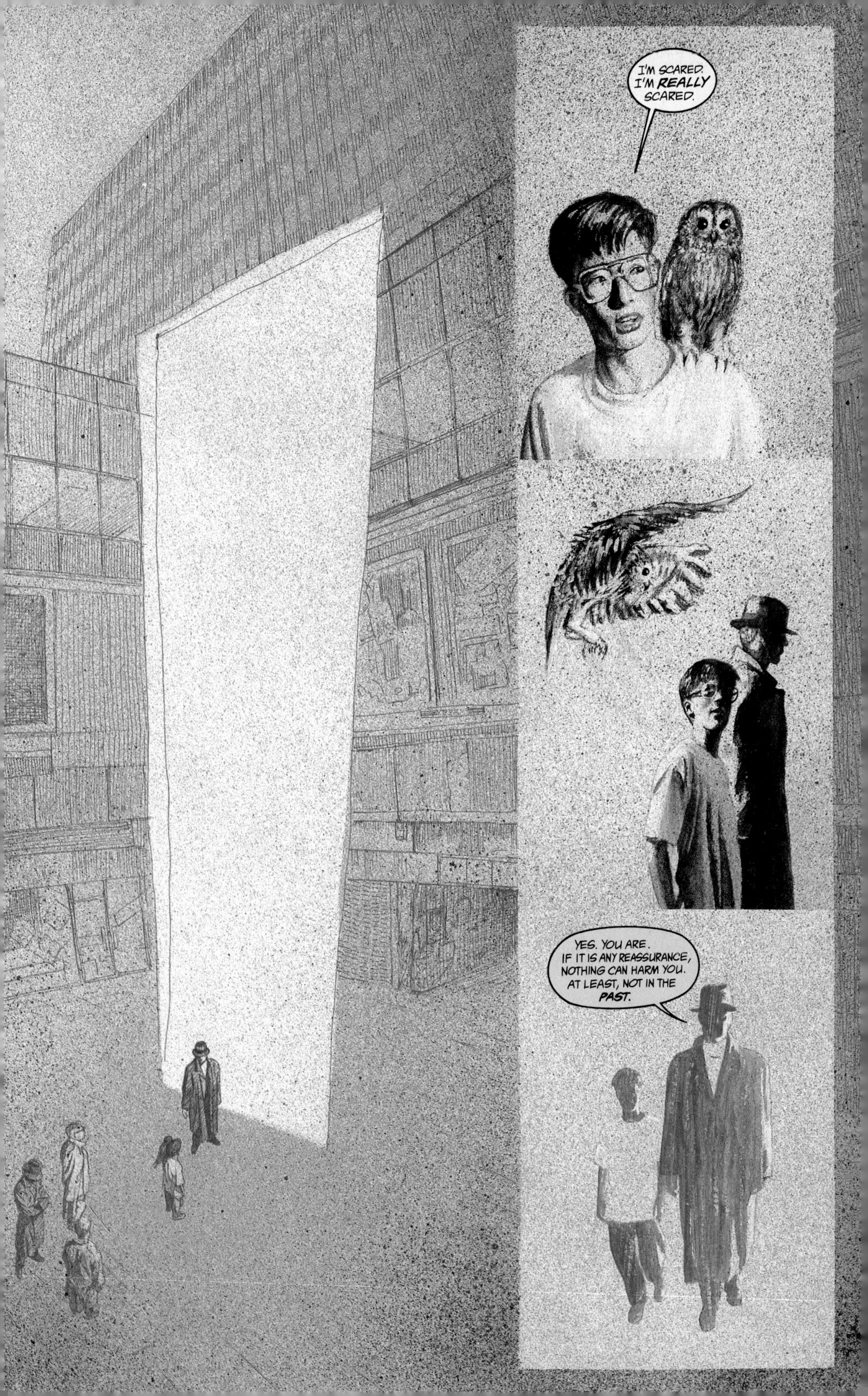
I'M SCARED. I'M REALLY SCARED.
YES. YOU ARE. IF IT IS ANY REASSURANCE, NOTHING CAN HARM YOU. AT LEAST, NOT IN THE PAST.

"WHERE ARE WE?"
THIS IS NO PLACE, CHILD. THIS IS THE VOID, THE SPACE BEFORE THERE WAS ANY WHERE TO TRAVEL TO, THE TIME BEFORE THERE WAS CHANGE.
THERE IS A SILENCE THAT IS MORE THAN SILENCE, IN THE COLD DAWN OF TIME. THEN:
...THAT NOISE. IT SOUNDS LIKE SOMEBODY... SOMEBODY HUGE... SCREAMING.
WHAT-- WHAT IS IT?

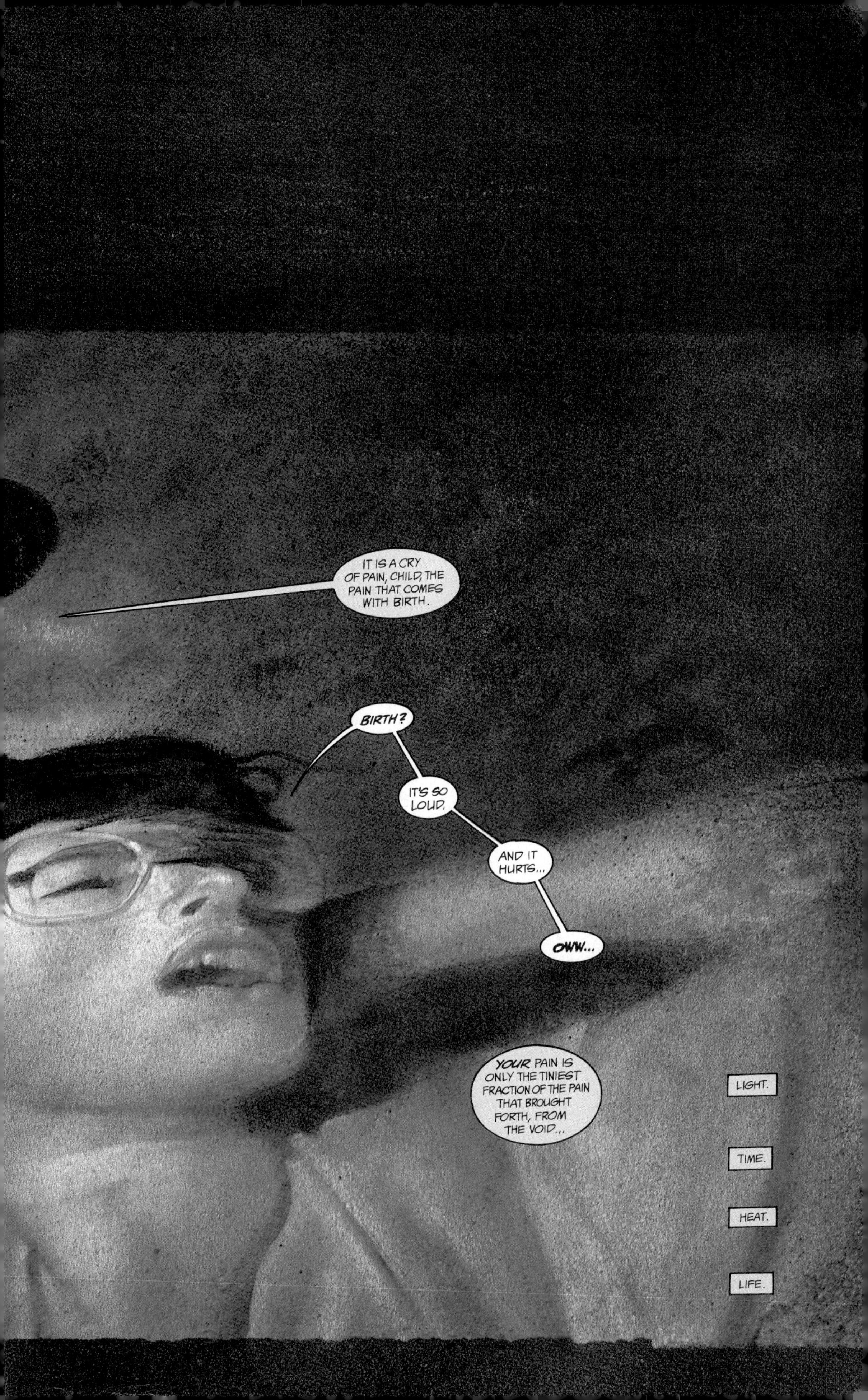
IT IS A CRY OF PAIN, CHILD, THE PAIN THAT COMES WITH BIRTH.
BIRTH?
IT'S SO LOUD.
AND IT HURTS...
OWW...
YOUR PAIN IS ONLY THE TINIEST FRACTION OF THE PAIN THAT BROUGHT FORTH, FROM THE VOID...
LIGHT.
TIME.
HEAT.
LIFE.

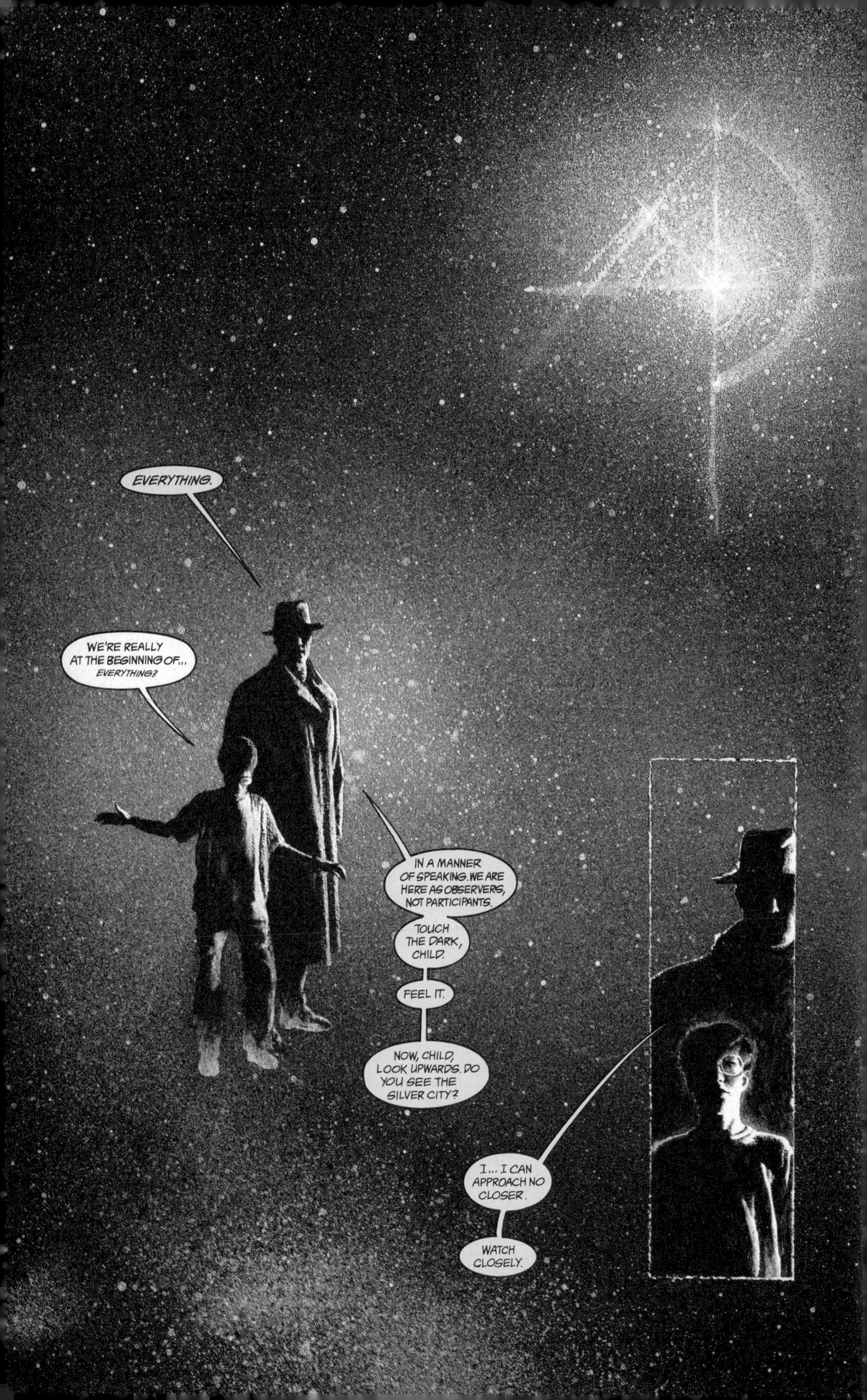
EVERYTHING.
WE'RE REALLY AT THE BEGINNING OF... EVERYTHING?
IN A MANNER OF SPEAKING. WE ARE HERE AS OBSERVERS, NOT PARTICIPANTS.
TOUCH THE DARK, CHILD.
FEEL IT.
NOW, CHILD, LOOK UPWARDS. DO YOU SEE THE SILVER CITY?
I... I CAN APPROACH NO CLOSER.
WATCH CLOSELY.

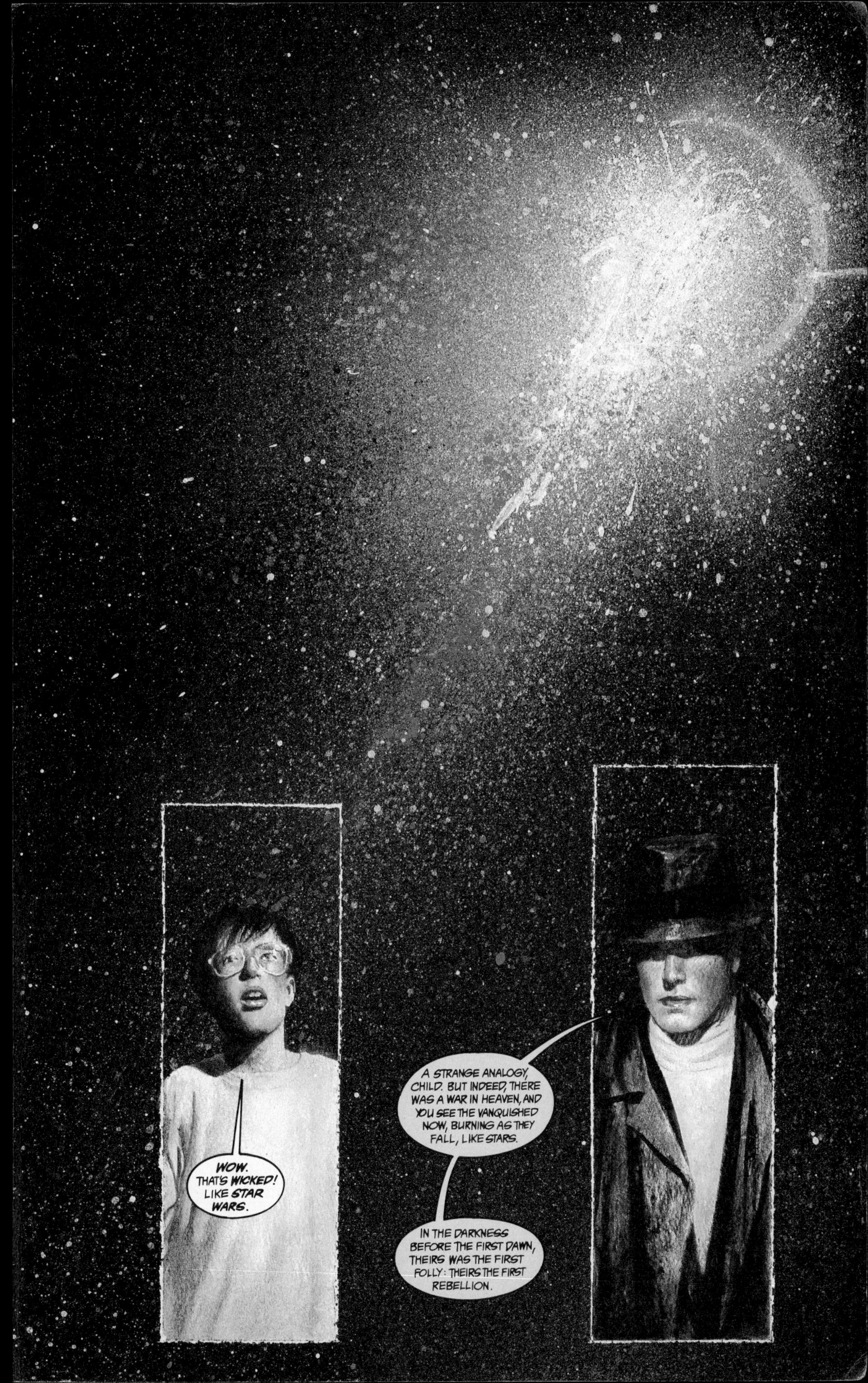
WOW. THAT'S WICKED! LIKE STAR WARS.
A STRANGE ANALOGY, CHILD. BUT INDEED, THERE WAS A WAR IN HEAVEN, AND YOU SEE THE VANQUISHED NOW, BURNING AS THEY FALL, LIKE STARS.
IN THE DARKNESS BEFORE THE FIRST DAWN, THEIRS WAS THE FIRST FOLLY: THEIRS THE FIRST REBELLION.

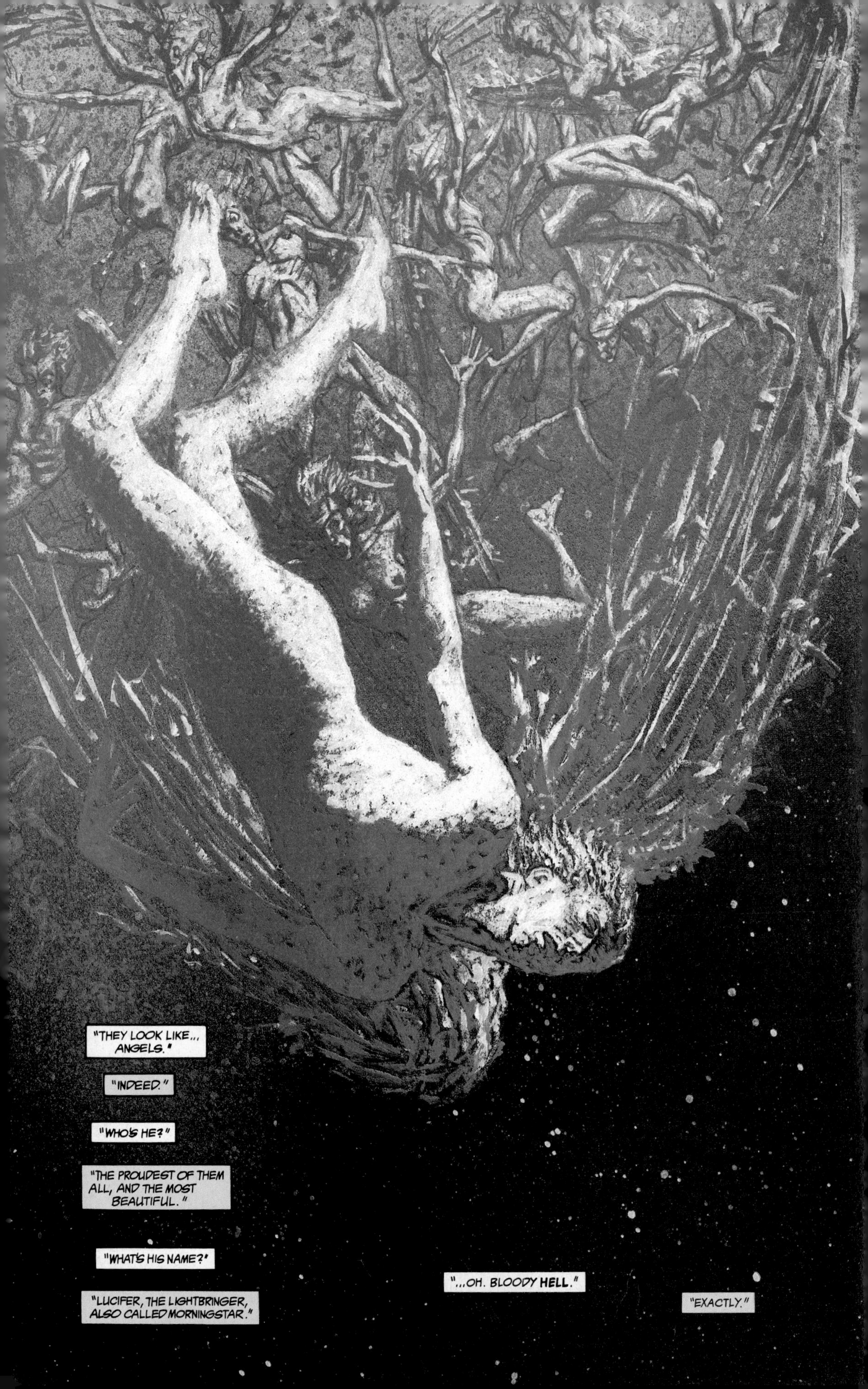
"THEY LOOK LIKE... ANGELS."
"INDEED."
"WHO'S HE?"
"THE PROUDEST OF THEM ALL, AND THE MOST BEAUTIFUL."
"WHAT'S HIS NAME?"
"LUCIFER, THE LIGHTBRINGER, ALSO CALLED MORNINGSTAR."
"...OH. BLOODY HELL."
"EXACTLY."

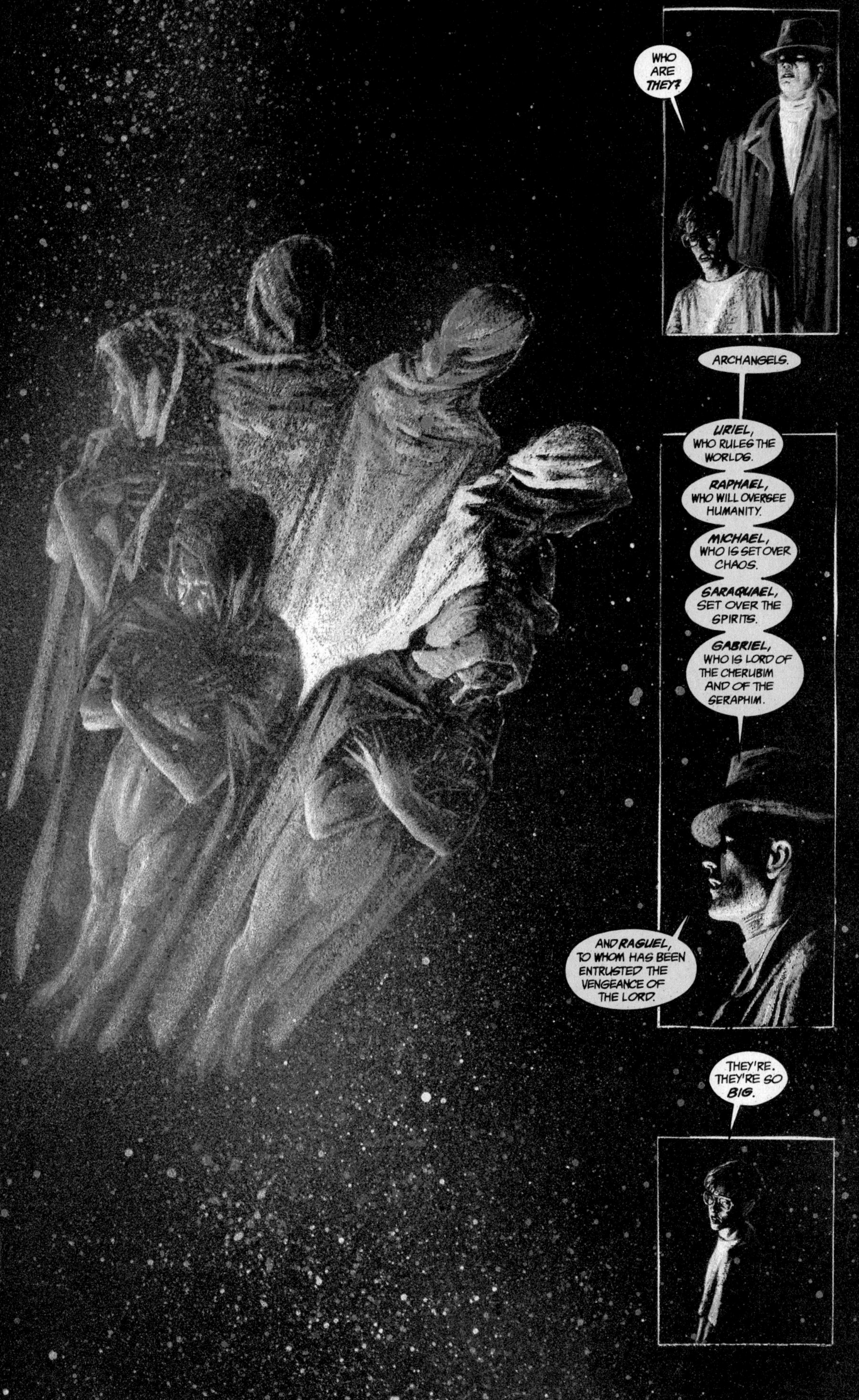
WHO ARE THEY?
ARCHANGELS.
URIEL, WHO RULES THE WORLDS.
RAPHAEL, WHO WILL OVERSEE HUMANITY.
MICHAEL, WHO IS SET OVER CHAOS.
SARAQUAEL, SET OVER THE SPIRITS.
GABRIEL, WHO IS LORD OF THE CHERUBIM AND OF THE SERAPHIM.
AND RAGUEL, TO WHOM HAS BEEN ENTRUSTED THE VENGEANCE OF THE LORD.
THEY'RE. THEY'RE SO BIG.

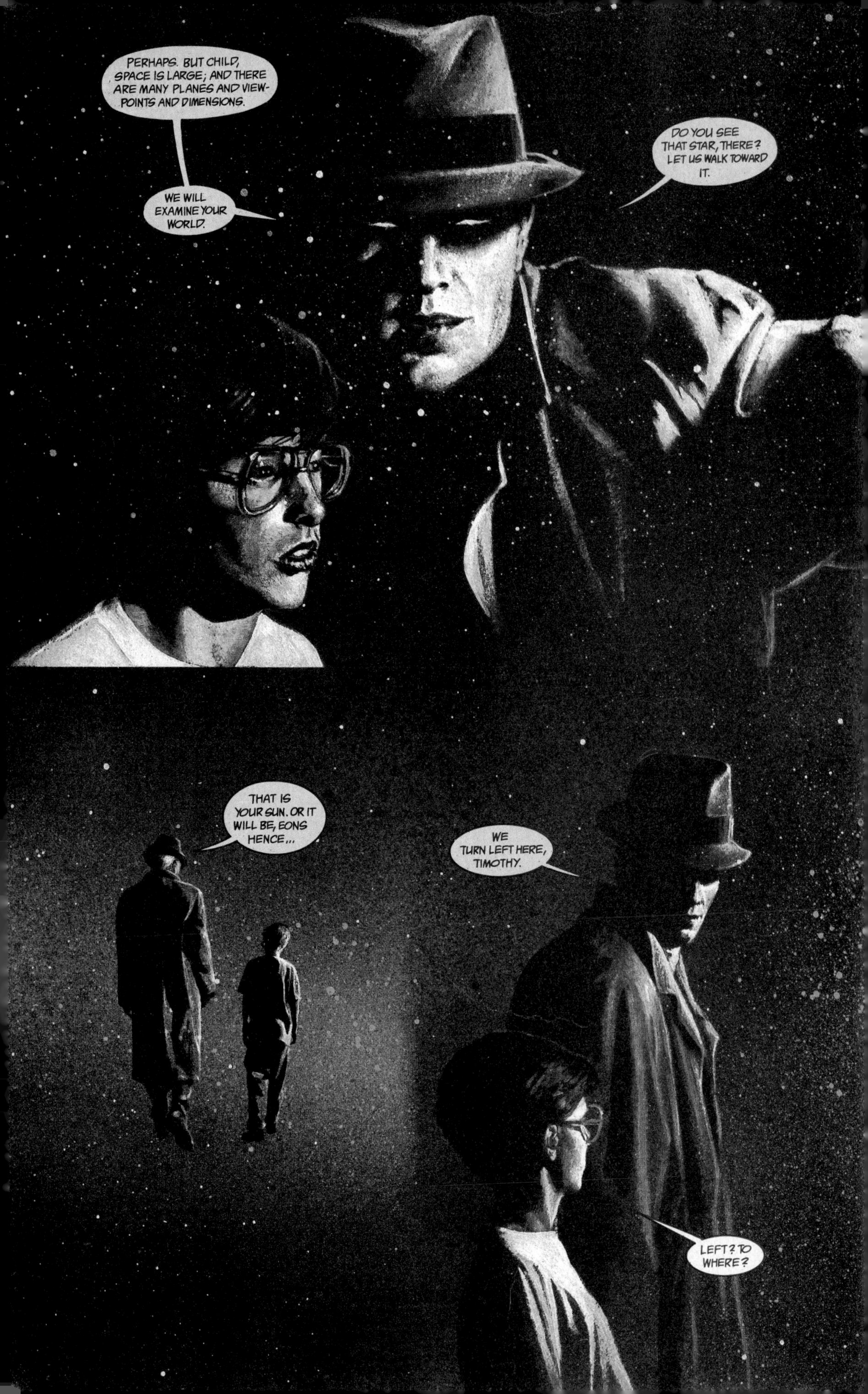
PERHAPS. BUT CHILD, SPACE IS LARGE; AND THERE ARE MANY PLANES AND VIEW-POINTS AND DIMENSIONS.
WE WILL EXAMINE YOUR WORLD.
DO YOU SEE THAT STAR, THERE? LET US WALK TOWARD IT.
THAT IS YOUR SUN. OR IT WILL BE, EONS HENCE...
WE TURN LEFT HERE, TIMOTHY.
LEFT? TO WHERE?

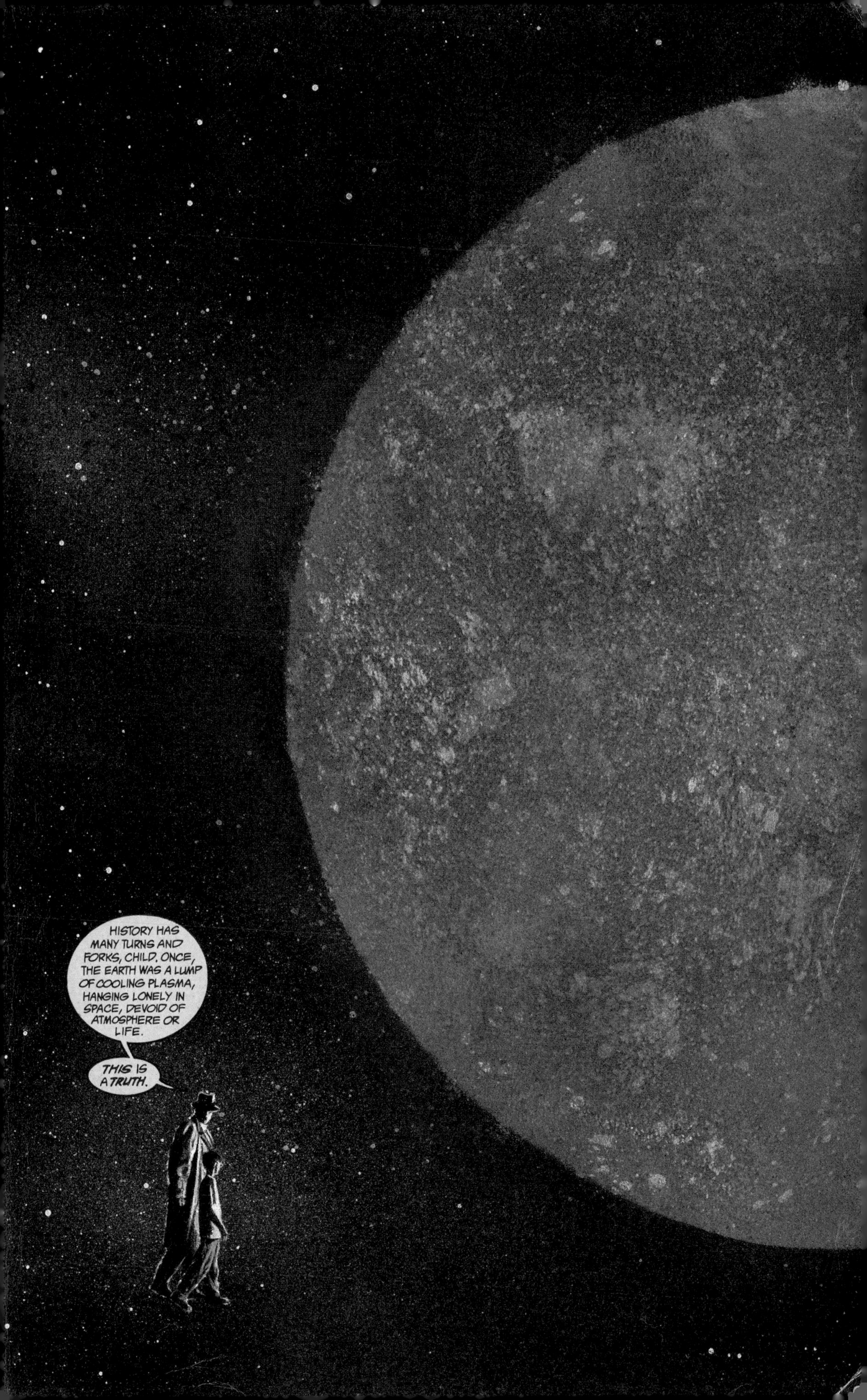
HISTORY HAS MANY TURNS AND FORKS, CHILD. ONCE, THE EARTH WAS A LUMP OF COOLING PLASMA, HANGING LONELY IN SPACE, DEVOID OF ATMOSPHERE OR LIFE.
THIS IS A TRUTH.

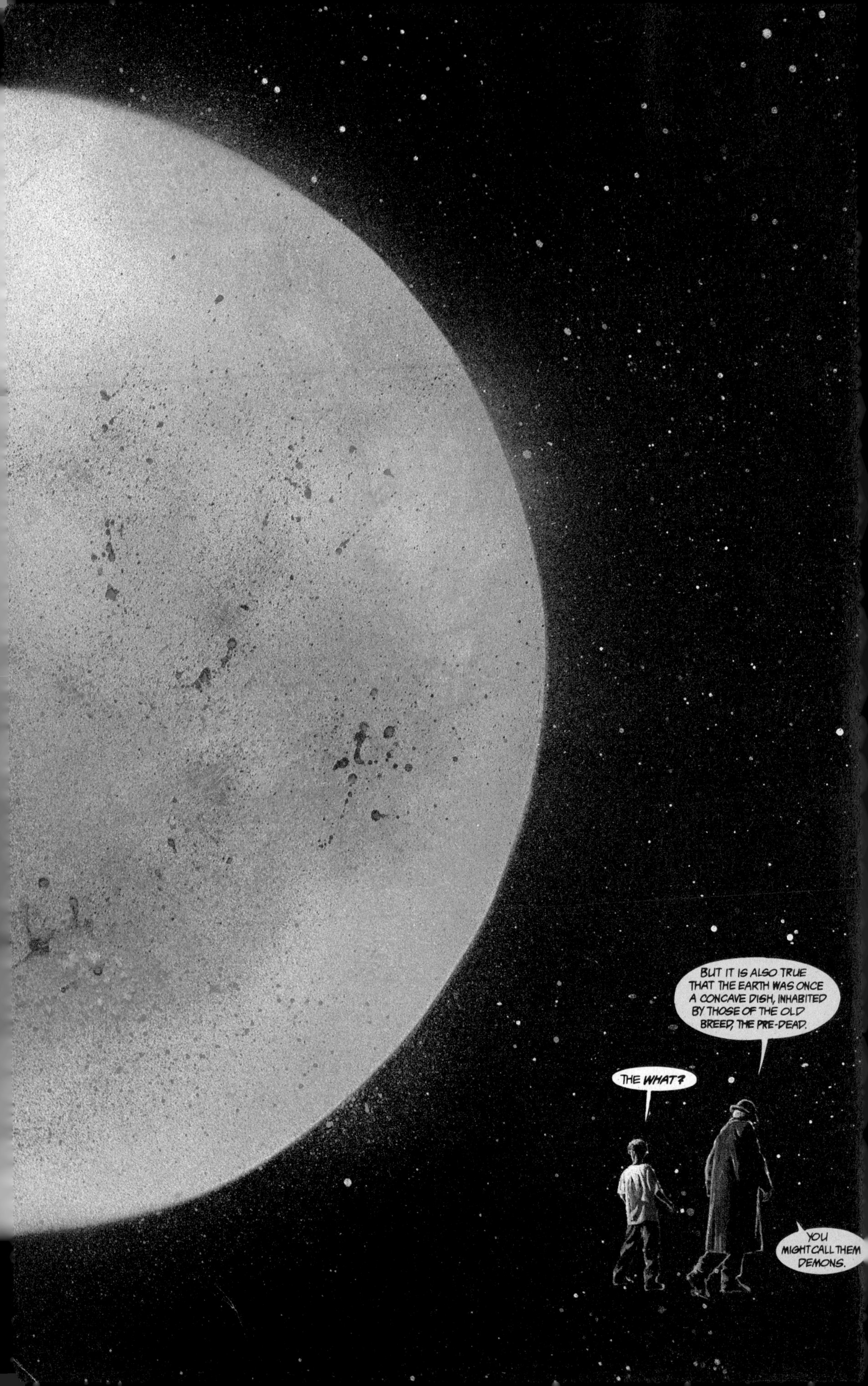
BUT IT IS ALSO TRUE THAT THE EARTH WAS ONCE A CONCAVE DISH, INHABITED BY THOSE OF THE OLD BREED, THE PRE-DEAD.
THE *WHAT?*
YOU MIGHT CALL THEM DEMONS.

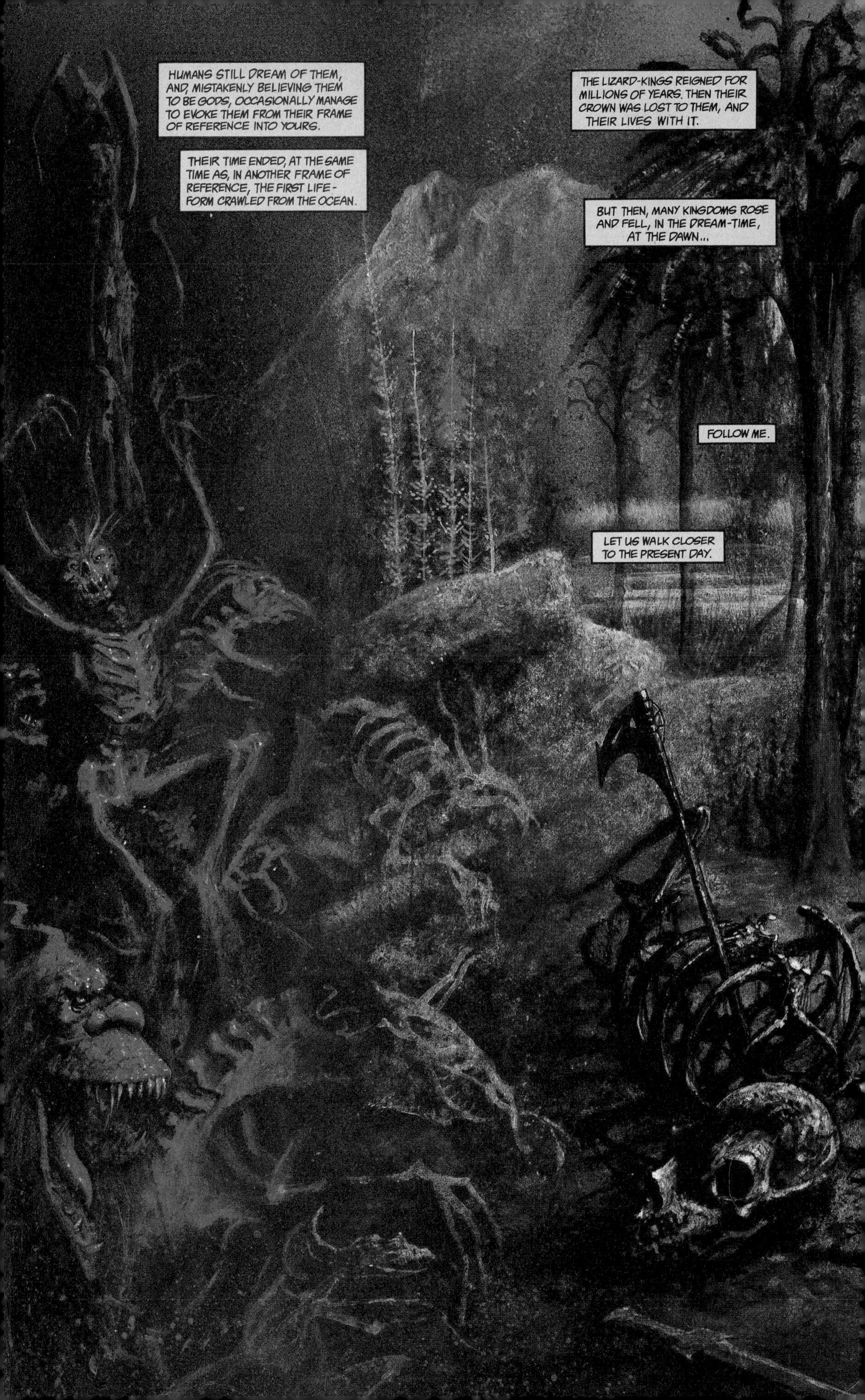
HUMANS STILL DREAM OF THEM, AND, MISTAKENLY BELIEVING THEM TO BE GODS, OCCASIONALLY MANAGE TO EVOKE THEM FROM THEIR FRAME OF REFERENCE INTO YOURS.
THEIR TIME ENDED, AT THE SAME TIME AS, IN ANOTHER FRAME OF REFERENCE, THE FIRST LIFE-FORM CRAWLED FROM THE OCEAN.
THE LIZARD-KINGS REIGNED FOR MILLIONS OF YEARS. THEN THEIR CROWN WAS LOST TO THEM, AND THEIR LIVES WITH IT.
BUT THEN, MANY KINGDOMS ROSE AND FELL, IN THE DREAM-TIME, AT THE DAWN...
FOLLOW ME.
LET US WALK CLOSER TO THE PRESENT DAY.

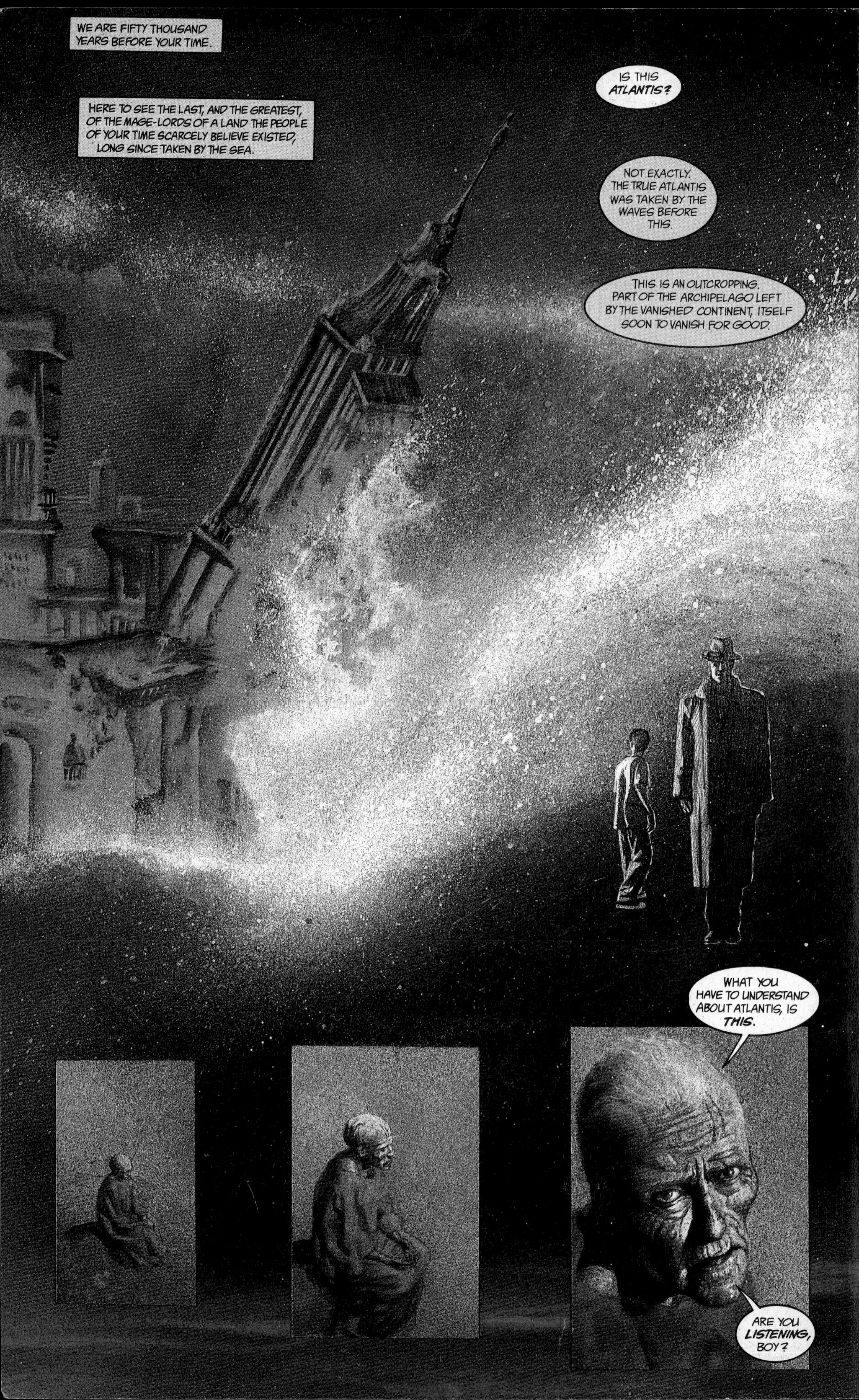
WE ARE FIFTY THOUSAND YEARS BEFORE YOUR TIME.
HERE TO SEE THE LAST, AND THE GREATEST, OF THE MAGE-LORDS OF A LAND THE PEOPLE OF YOUR TIME SCARCELY BELIEVE EXISTED, LONG SINCE TAKEN BY THE SEA.
IS THIS ATLANTIS?
NOT EXACTLY. THE TRUE ATLANTIS WAS TAKEN BY THE WAVES BEFORE THIS.
THIS IS AN OUTCROPPING. PART OF THE ARCHIPELAGO LEFT BY THE VANISHED CONTINENT, ITSELF SOON TO VANISH FOR GOOD.
WHAT YOU HAVE TO UNDERSTAND ABOUT ATLANTIS, IS THIS.
ARE YOU LISTENING, BOY?

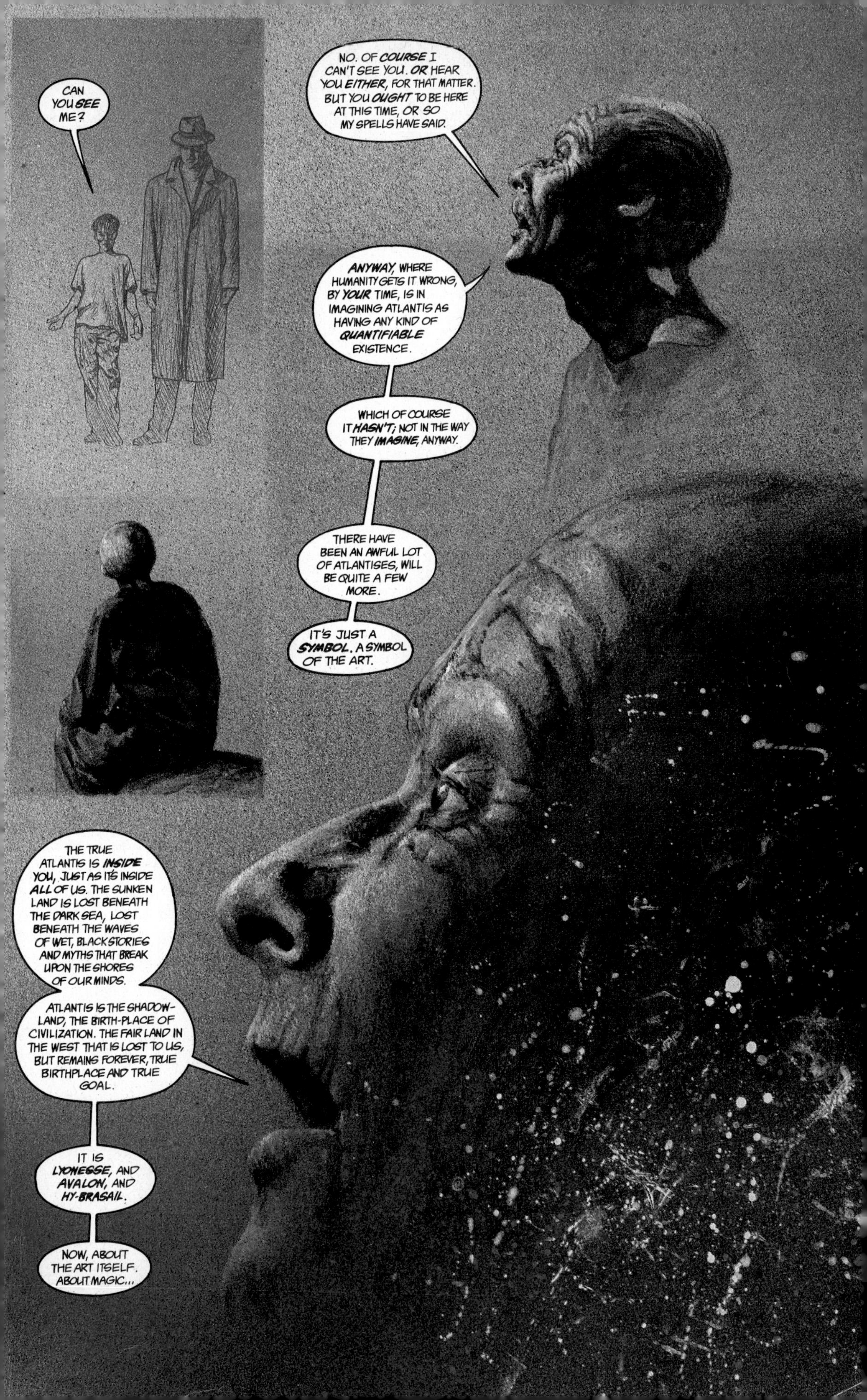
CAN YOU SEE ME?
NO. OF COURSE I CAN'T SEE YOU. OR HEAR YOU EITHER, FOR THAT MATTER. BUT YOU OUGHT TO BE HERE AT THIS TIME, OR SO MY SPELLS HAVE SAID.
ANYWAY, WHERE HUMANITY GETS IT WRONG, BY YOUR TIME, IS IN IMAGINING ATLANTIS AS HAVING ANY KIND OF QUANTIFIABLE EXISTENCE.
WHICH OF COURSE IT HASN'T; NOT IN THE WAY THEY IMAGINE, ANYWAY.
THERE HAVE BEEN AN AWFUL LOT OF ATLANTISES, WILL BE QUITE A FEW MORE.
IT'S JUST A SYMBOL. A SYMBOL OF THE ART.
THE TRUE ATLANTIS IS INSIDE YOU, JUST AS IT'S INSIDE ALL OF US. THE SUNKEN LAND IS LOST BENEATH THE DARK SEA, LOST BENEATH THE WAVES OF WET, BLACK STORIES AND MYTHS THAT BREAK UPON THE SHORES OF OUR MINDS.
ATLANTIS IS THE SHADOW-LAND, THE BIRTH-PLACE OF CIVILIZATION. THE FAIR LAND IN THE WEST THAT IS LOST TO US, BUT REMAINS FOREVER, TRUE BIRTHPLACE AND TRUE GOAL.
IT IS LYONESSE, AND AVALON, AND HY-BRASAIL.
NOW, ABOUT THE ART ITSELF. ABOUT MAGIC...

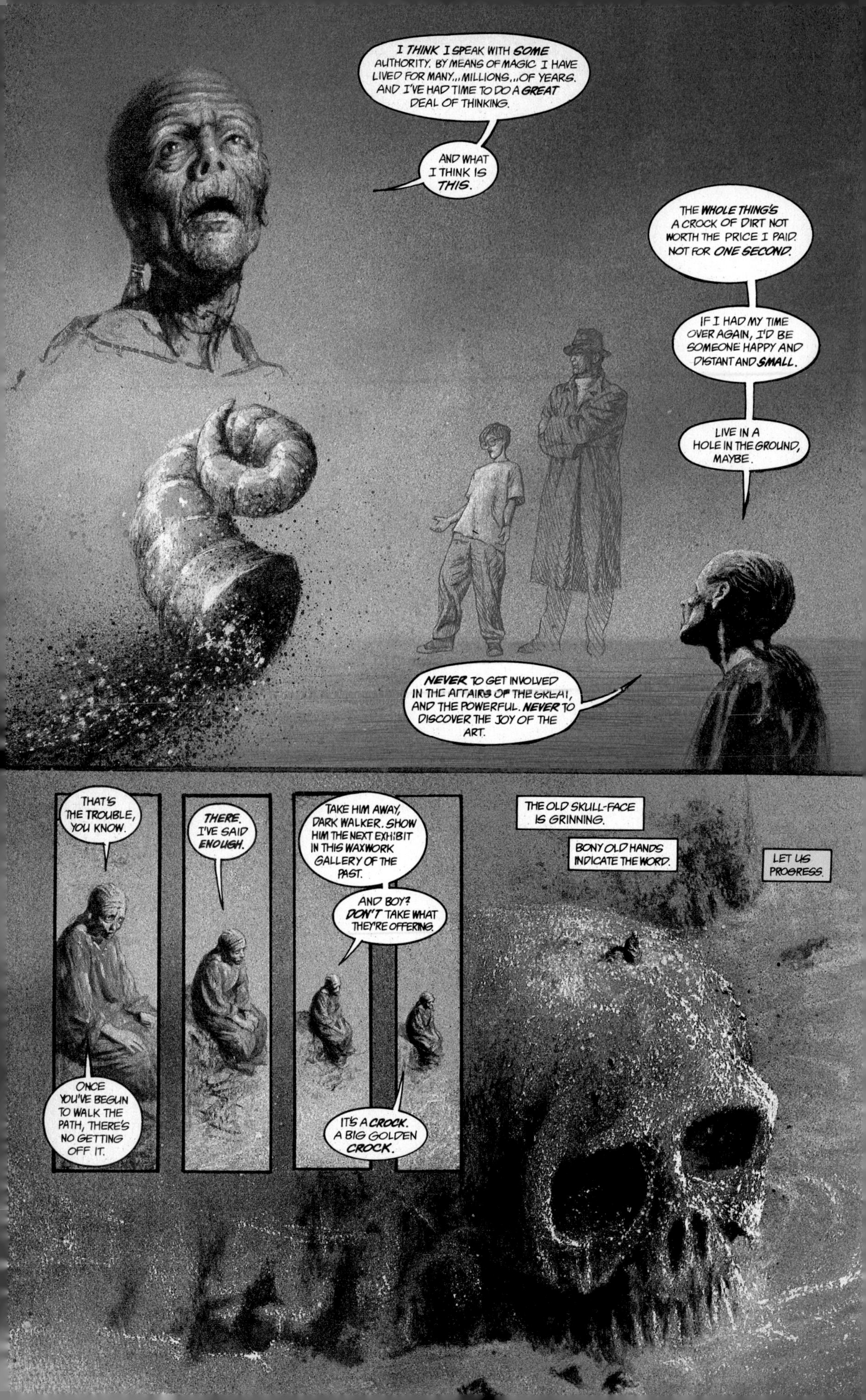
I THINK I SPEAK WITH SOME AUTHORITY. BY MEANS OF MAGIC I HAVE LIVED FOR MANY... MILLIONS... OF YEARS. AND I'VE HAD TIME TO DO A GREAT DEAL OF THINKING.
AND WHAT I THINK IS THIS.
THE WHOLE THING'S A CROCK OF DIRT NOT WORTH THE PRICE I PAID. NOT FOR ONE SECOND.
IF I HAD MY TIME OVER AGAIN, I'D BE SOMEONE HAPPY AND DISTANT AND SMALL.
LIVE IN A HOLE IN THE GROUND, MAYBE.
NEVER TO GET INVOLVED IN THE AFFAIRS OF THE GREAT, AND THE POWERFUL. NEVER TO DISCOVER THE JOY OF THE ART.
THAT'S THE TROUBLE, YOU KNOW.
ONCE YOU'VE BEGUN TO WALK THE PATH, THERE'S NO GETTING OFF IT.
THERE. I'VE SAID ENOUGH.
TAKE HIM AWAY, DARK WALKER. SHOW HIM THE NEXT EXHIBIT IN THIS WAXWORK GALLERY OF THE PAST.
AND BOY? DON'T TAKE WHAT THEY'RE OFFERING.
IT'S A CROCK. A BIG GOLDEN CROCK.
THE OLD SKULL-FACE IS GRINNING.
BONY OLD HANDS INDICATE THE WORD.
LET US PROGRESS.

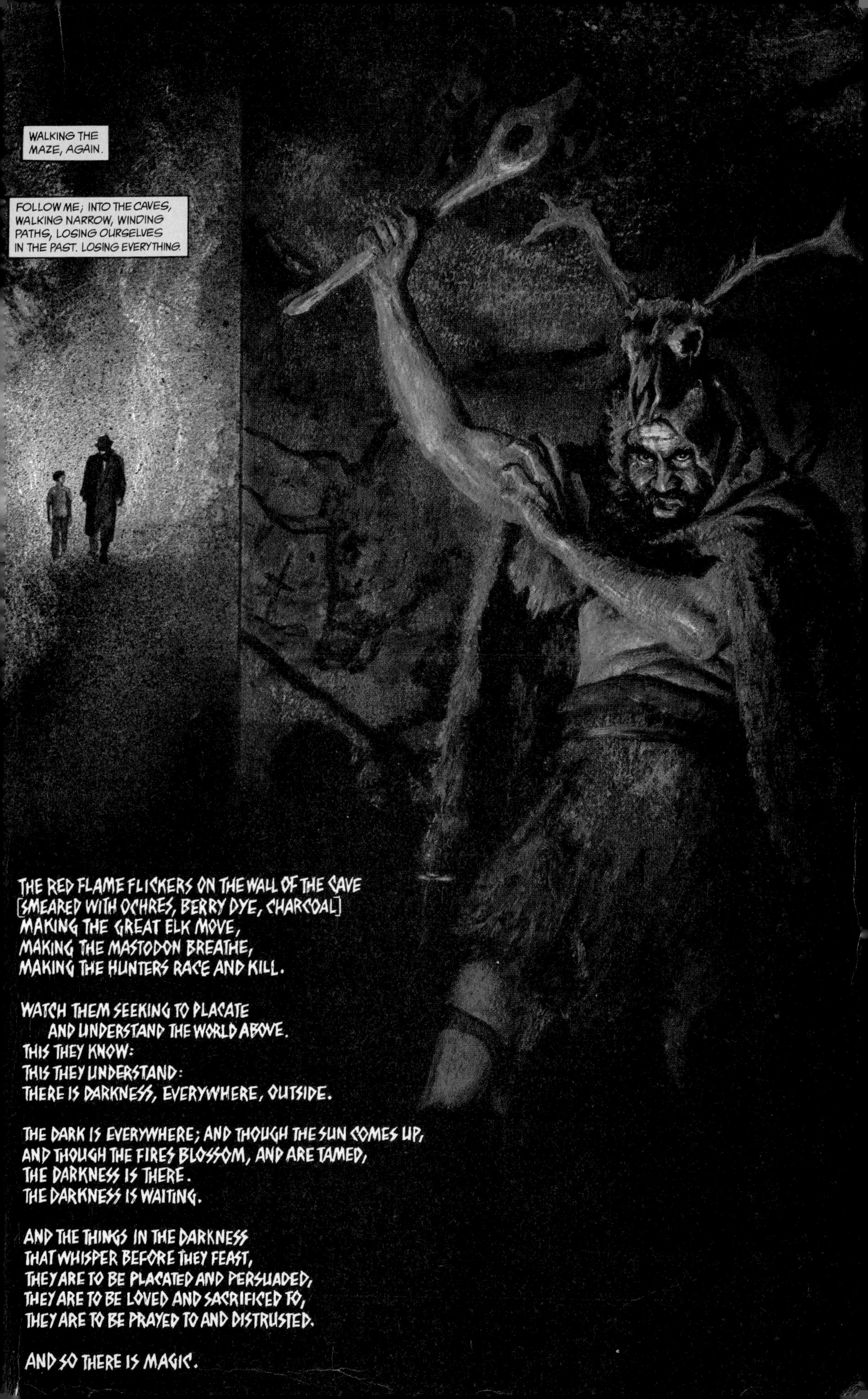
WALKING THE MAZE, AGAIN.
FOLLOW ME; INTO THE CAVES, WALKING NARROW, WINDING PATHS, LOSING OURSELVES IN THE PAST. LOSING EVERYTHING.
THE RED FLAME FLICKERS ON THE WALL OF THE CAVE
[SMEARED WITH OCHRES, BERRY DYE, CHARCOAL]
MAKING THE GREAT ELK MOVE,
MAKING THE MASTODON BREATHE,
MAKING THE HUNTERS RACE AND KILL.
WATCH THEM SEEKING TO PLACATE
AND UNDERSTAND THE WORLD ABOVE.
THIS THEY KNOW:
THIS THEY UNDERSTAND:
THERE IS DARKNESS, EVERYWHERE, OUTSIDE.
THE DARK IS EVERYWHERE; AND THOUGH THE SUN COMES UP,
AND THOUGH THE FIRES BLOSSOM, AND ARE TAMED,
THE DARKNESS IS THERE.
THE DARKNESS IS WAITING.
AND THE THINGS IN THE DARKNESS
THAT WHISPER BEFORE THEY FEAST,
THEY ARE TO BE PLACATED AND PERSUADED,
THEY ARE TO BE LOVED AND SACRIFICED TO,
THEY ARE TO BE PRAYED TO AND DISTRUSTED.
AND SO THERE IS MAGIC.

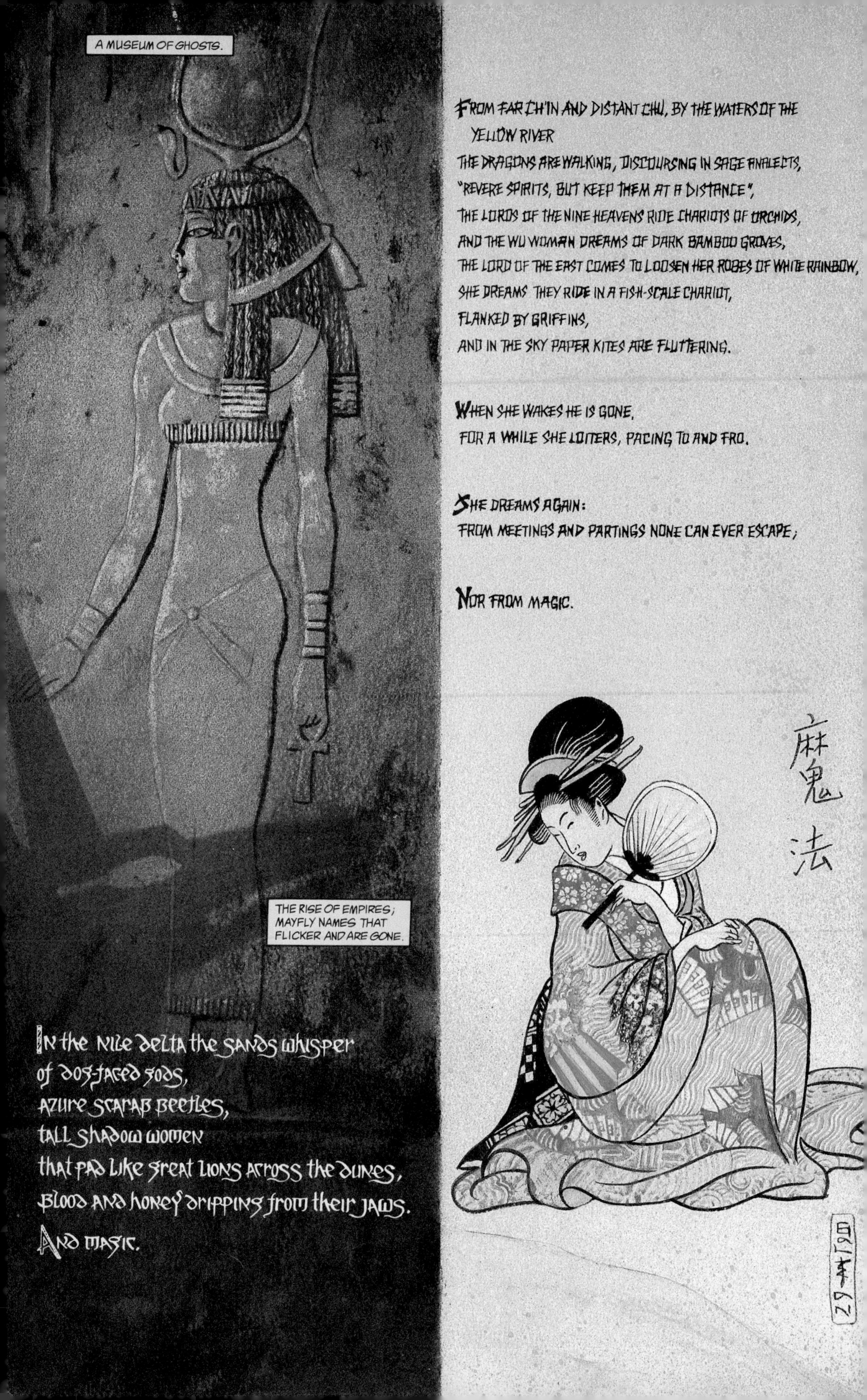
A MUSEUM OF GHOSTS.
THE RISE OF EMPIRES; MAYFLY NAMES THAT FLICKER AND ARE GONE.
In the Nile delta the sands whisper
of dog-faced gods,
azure scarab beetles,
tall shadow women
that pad like great lions across the dunes,
blood and honey dripping from their jaws.
And magic.
FROM FAR CH'IN AND DISTANT CHU, BY THE WATERS OF THE
YELLOW RIVER
THE DRAGONS ARE WALKING, DISCOURSING IN SAGE ANALECTS,
"REVERE SPIRITS, BUT KEEP THEM AT A DISTANCE",
THE LORDS OF THE NINE HEAVENS RIDE CHARIOTS OF ORCHIDS,
AND THE WU WOMAN DREAMS OF DARK BAMBOO GROVES,
THE LORD OF THE EAST COMES TO LOOSEN HER ROBES OF WHITE RAINBOW,
SHE DREAMS THEY RIDE IN A FISH-SCALE CHARIOT,
FLANKED BY GRIFFINS,
AND IN THE SKY PAPER KITES ARE FLUTTERING.
WHEN SHE WAKES HE IS GONE.
FOR A WHILE SHE LOITERS, PACING TO AND FRO.
SHE DREAMS AGAIN:
FROM MEETINGS AND PARTINGS NONE CAN EVER ESCAPE;
NOR FROM MAGIC.
魔法

IN THE LANDS OF OLIVE AND LAUREL,
WHERE THE GODS WALK,
WE WATCH A SOLDIER PISS AROUND HIS CLOTHES,
LOPE AWAY A WOLF.

--AT THE HEART OF EVERY MYSTERY,
WHISPERS THE TWICE-BORN BOY, WHO ROSE FROM THE DEAD,
--IS THE GRAIN OF MY CORN, AND THE WINE OF MY BLOOD.
DRAMA, VINES AND GOAT-FEET FOLLOW HIM INTO THE WORLD.

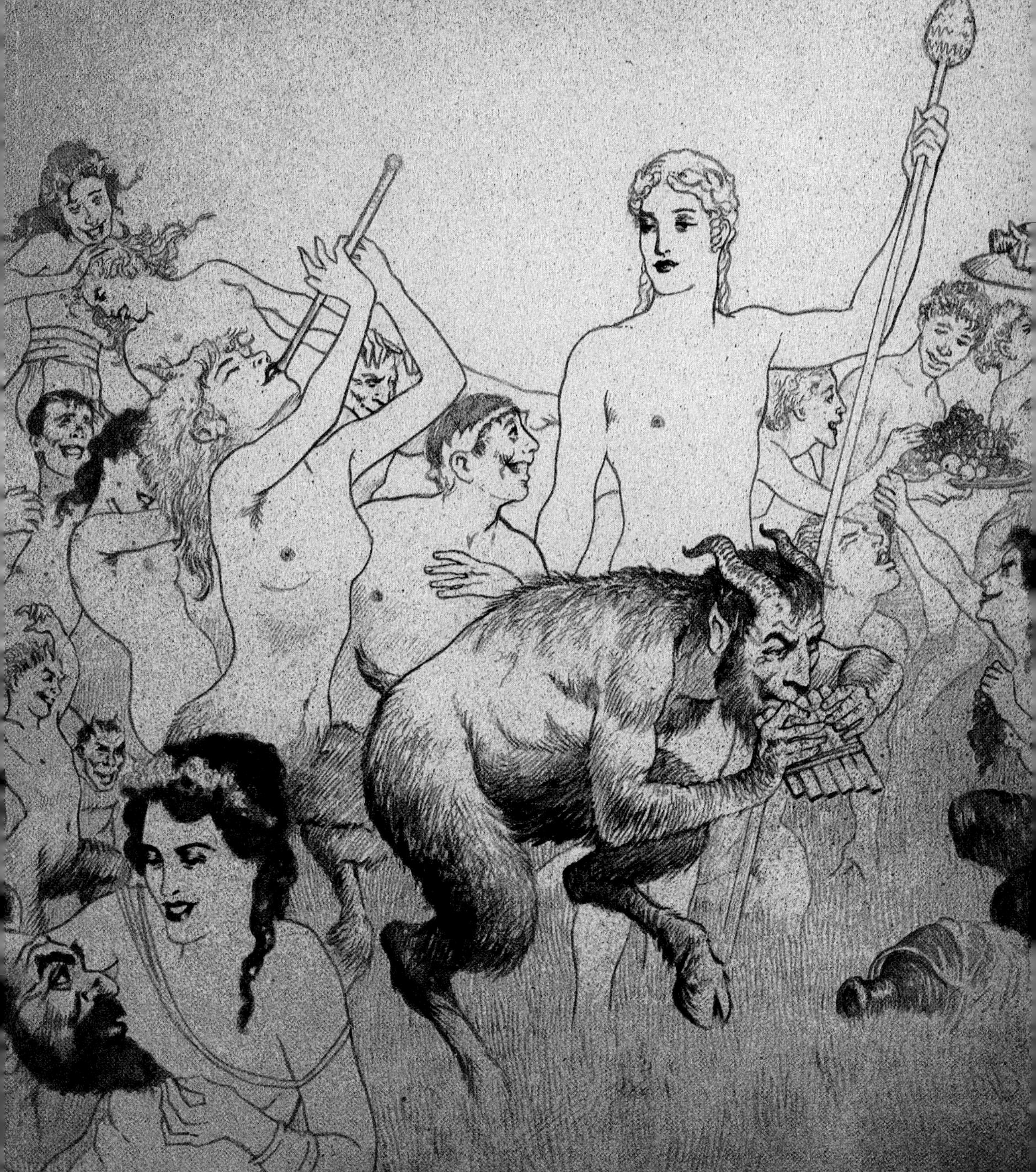

THE WITCH-QUEEN ALWAYS HAS THREE FACES; WHO WAITS AT THE CROSSROADS,
FOR YOUR SACRIFICE;
WAITS IN THE UNDERWORLD,
IN THE SACRED GROVES,
IN THE MOON.
SHE SITS BENEATH A DEAD KING, HANGING FROM A TREE BRANCH,
AND WILL SHOW YOU ALL MANNER OF ELEGANT CHARMS.

ABRACADABRA.
ABRAXAS...

MAGIC.

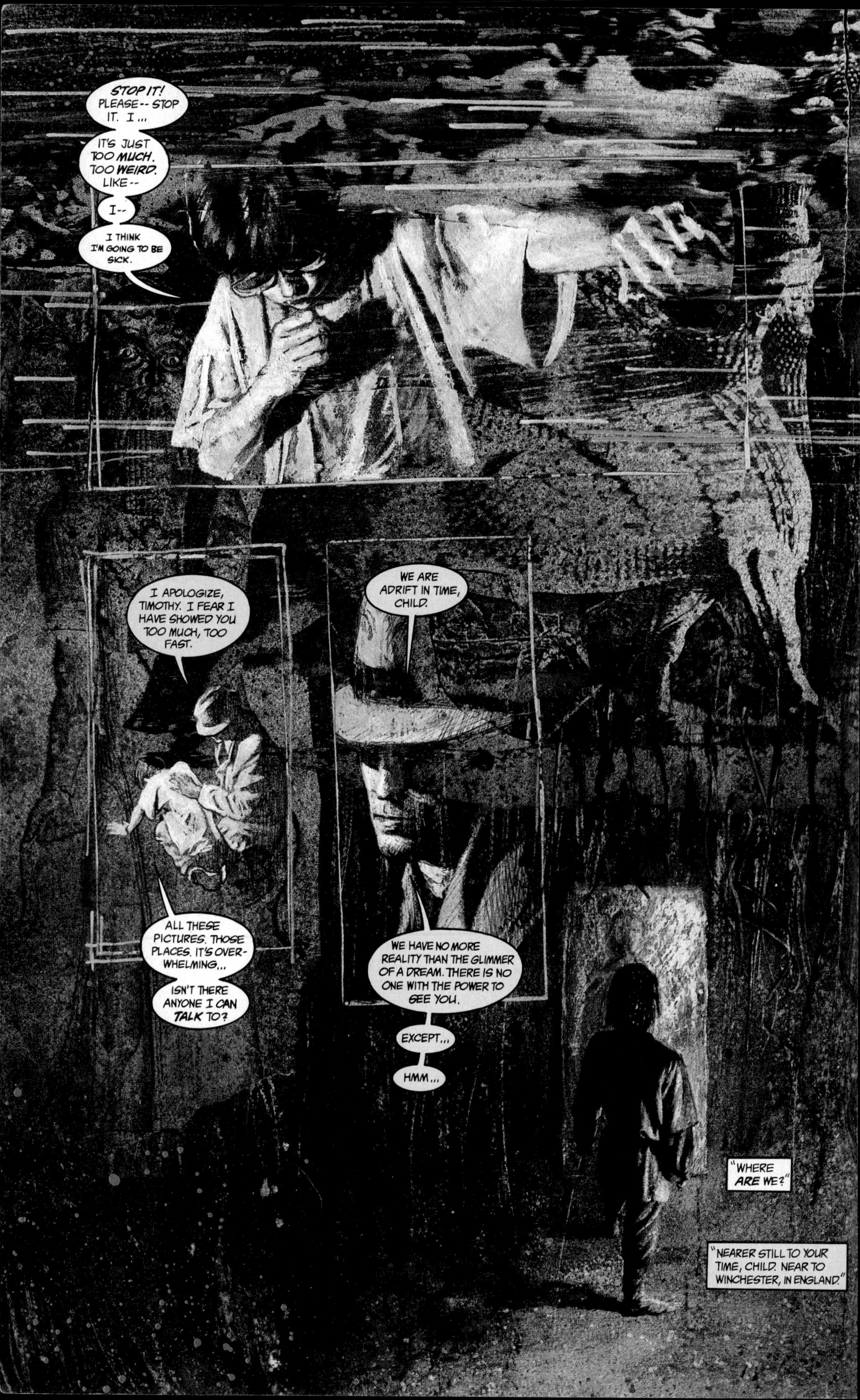

STOP IT! PLEASE-- STOP IT. I...
IT'S JUST TOO MUCH. TOO WEIRD. LIKE--
I--
I THINK I'M GOING TO BE SICK.
I APOLOGIZE, TIMOTHY. I FEAR I HAVE SHOWED YOU TOO MUCH, TOO FAST.
WE ARE ADRIFT IN TIME, CHILD.
ALL THESE PICTURES. THOSE PLACES. IT'S OVER-WHELMING...
ISN'T THERE ANYONE I CAN TALK TO?
WE HAVE NO MORE REALITY THAN THE GLIMMER OF A DREAM. THERE IS NO ONE WITH THE POWER TO SEE YOU.
EXCEPT...
HMM...
"WHERE ARE WE?"
"NEARER STILL TO YOUR TIME, CHILD. NEAR TO WINCHESTER, IN ENGLAND."

WHAT SPIRITS COME AROUND ME? SPEAK! SPEAK! SPEAK!
UM... HULLO?
WHAT MANNER OF CREATURE ARE YOU?
I'M A KID. A BOY. AND THIS IS, UM...
I RECOGNIZE YOU, BROTHERLESS ONE. WHAT WOULD YOU WITH ME?
AS YOUR MASTER BLAISE TO YOU, SO I TO THIS CHILD.
AH. HE TUTORS YOU. GIVES YOU YOUR DEVOIRS. I DO NOT ENVY YOU.
PLEASE. WHAT ARE YOU CALLED?

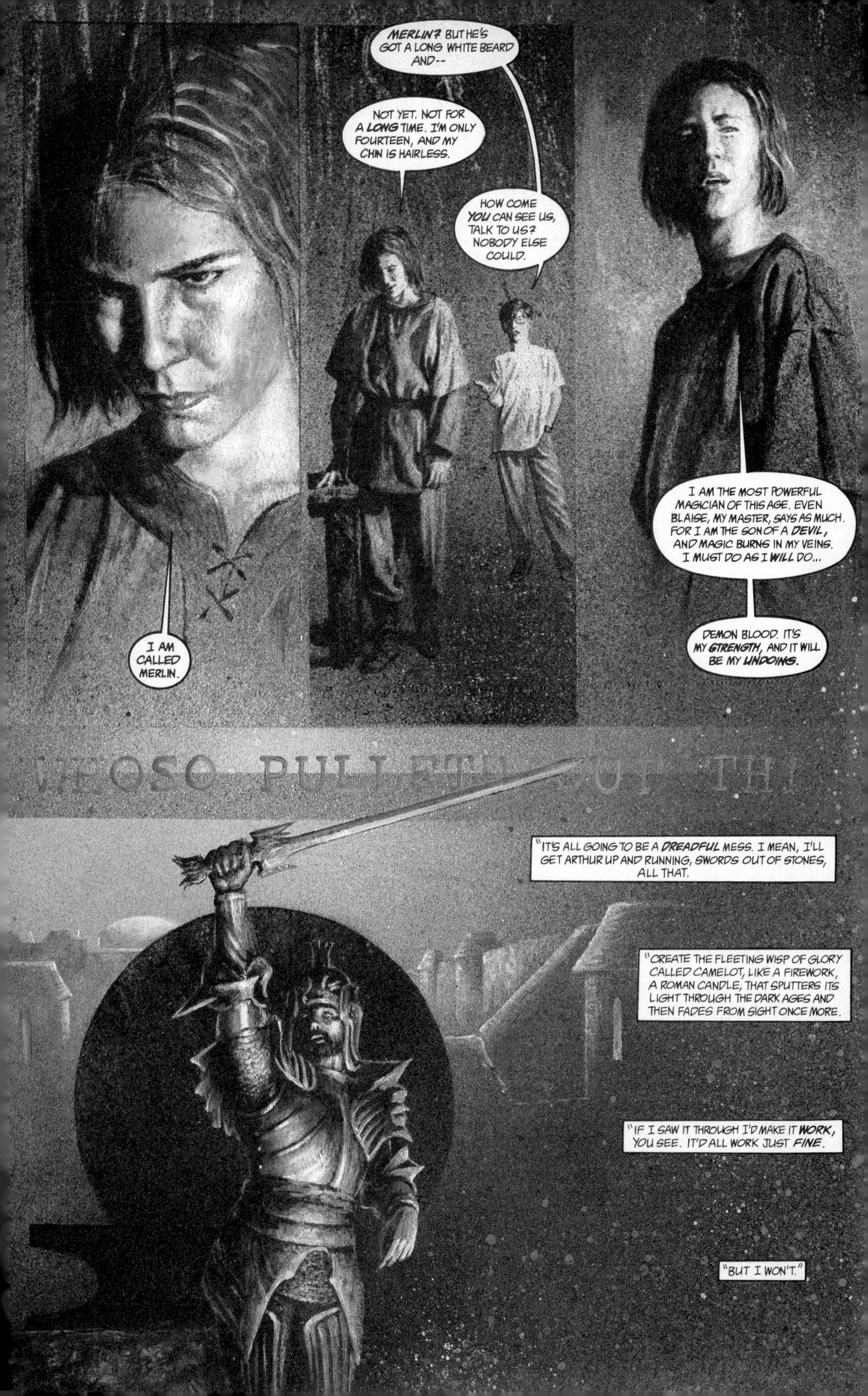
I AM CALLED MERLIN.
MERLIN? BUT HE'S GOT A LONG WHITE BEARD AND--
NOT YET. NOT FOR A LONG TIME. I'M ONLY FOURTEEN, AND MY CHIN IS HAIRLESS.
HOW COME YOU CAN SEE US, TALK TO US? NOBODY ELSE COULD.
I AM THE MOST POWERFUL MAGICIAN OF THIS AGE. EVEN BLAISE, MY MASTER, SAYS AS MUCH. FOR I AM THE SON OF A DEVIL, AND MAGIC BURNS IN MY VEINS. I MUST DO AS I WILL DO...
DEMON BLOOD. IT'S MY STRENGTH, AND IT WILL BE MY UNDOING.
WHOSO PULLETH OUT THI
"IT'S ALL GOING TO BE A DREADFUL MESS. I MEAN, I'LL GET ARTHUR UP AND RUNNING, SWORDS OUT OF STONES, ALL THAT.
"CREATE THE FLEETING WISP OF GLORY CALLED CAMELOT, LIKE A FIREWORK, A ROMAN CANDLE, THAT SPUTTERS ITS LIGHT THROUGH THE DARK AGES AND THEN FADES FROM SIGHT ONCE MORE.
"IF I SAW IT THROUGH I'D MAKE IT WORK, YOU SEE. IT'D ALL WORK JUST FINE.
"BUT I WON'T."

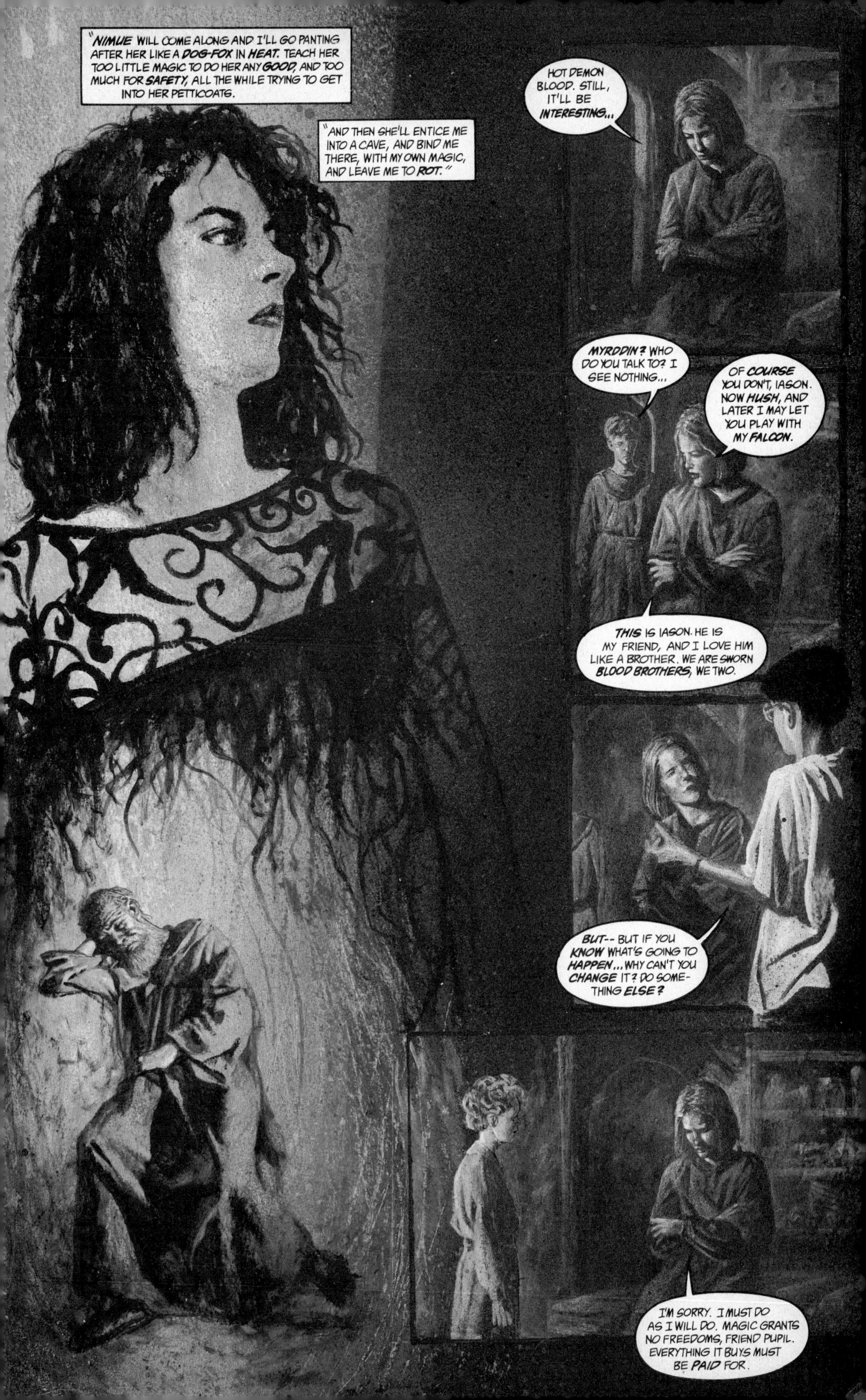
"NIMUE WILL COME ALONG AND I'LL GO PANTING AFTER HER LIKE A DOG-FOX IN HEAT. TEACH HER TOO LITTLE MAGIC TO DO HER ANY GOOD, AND TOO MUCH FOR SAFETY, ALL THE WHILE TRYING TO GET INTO HER PETTICOATS.
"AND THEN SHE'LL ENTICE ME INTO A CAVE, AND BIND ME THERE, WITH MY OWN MAGIC, AND LEAVE ME TO ROT."
HOT DEMON BLOOD. STILL, IT'LL BE INTERESTING...
MYRDDIN? WHO DO YOU TALK TO? I SEE NOTHING...
OF COURSE YOU DON'T, IASON. NOW HUSH, AND LATER I MAY LET YOU PLAY WITH MY FALCON.
THIS IS IASON. HE IS MY FRIEND, AND I LOVE HIM LIKE A BROTHER. WE ARE SWORN BLOOD BROTHERS, WE TWO.
BUT-- BUT IF YOU KNOW WHAT'S GOING TO HAPPEN... WHY CAN'T YOU CHANGE IT? DO SOME-THING ELSE?
I'M SORRY. I MUST DO AS I WILL DO. MAGIC GRANTS NO FREEDOMS, FRIEND PUPIL. EVERYTHING IT BUYS MUST BE PAID FOR.

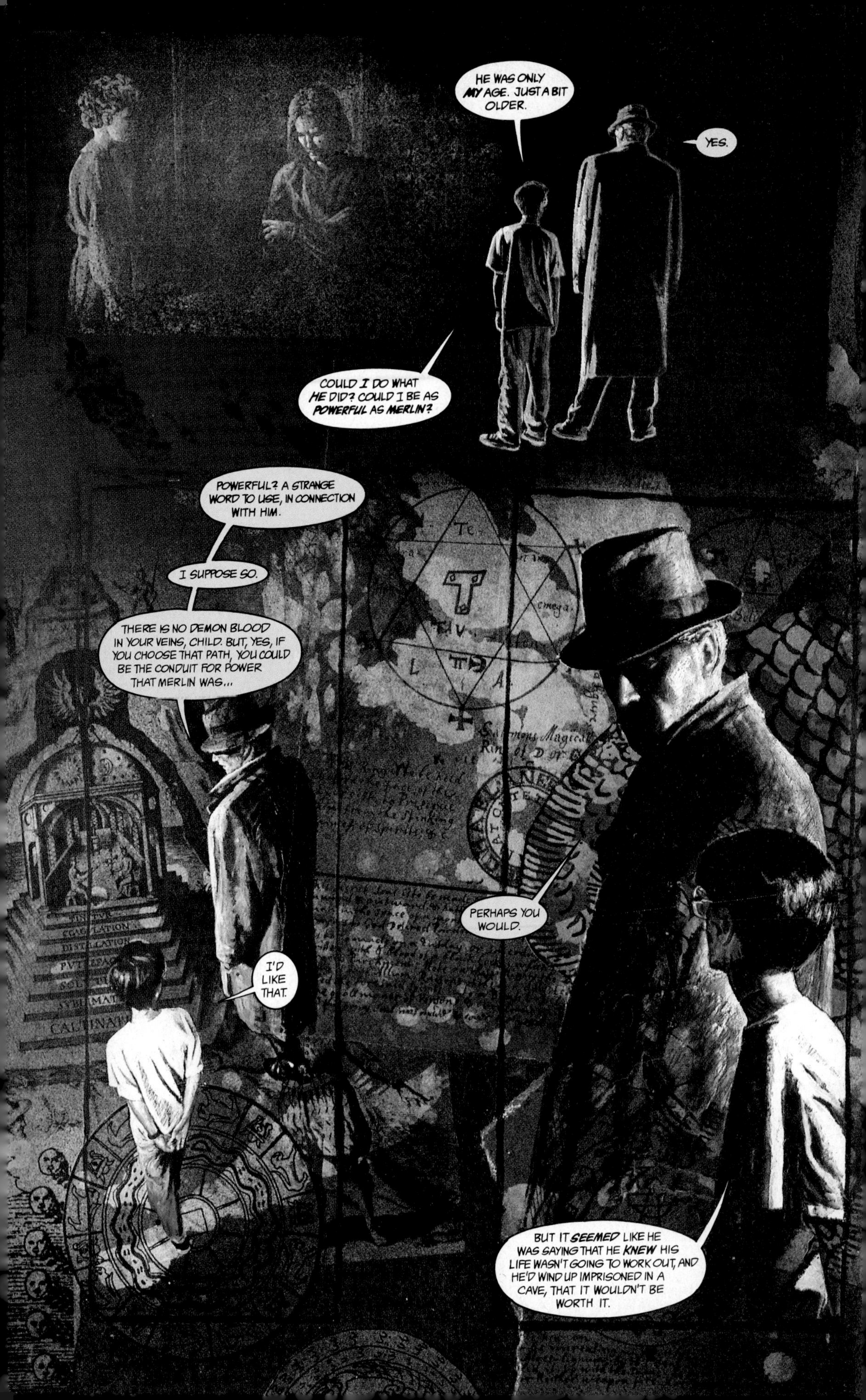
HE WAS ONLY MY AGE. JUST A BIT OLDER.
YES.
COULD I DO WHAT HE DID? COULD I BE AS POWERFUL AS MERLIN?
POWERFUL? A STRANGE WORD TO USE, IN CONNECTION WITH HIM.
I SUPPOSE SO.
THERE IS NO DEMON BLOOD IN YOUR VEINS, CHILD. BUT, YES, IF YOU CHOOSE THAT PATH, YOU COULD BE THE CONDUIT FOR POWER THAT MERLIN WAS...
I'D LIKE THAT.
PERHAPS YOU WOULD.
BUT IT SEEMED LIKE HE WAS SAYING THAT HE KNEW HIS LIFE WASN'T GOING TO WORK OUT, AND HE'D WIND UP IMPRISONED IN A CAVE, THAT IT WOULDN'T BE WORTH IT.

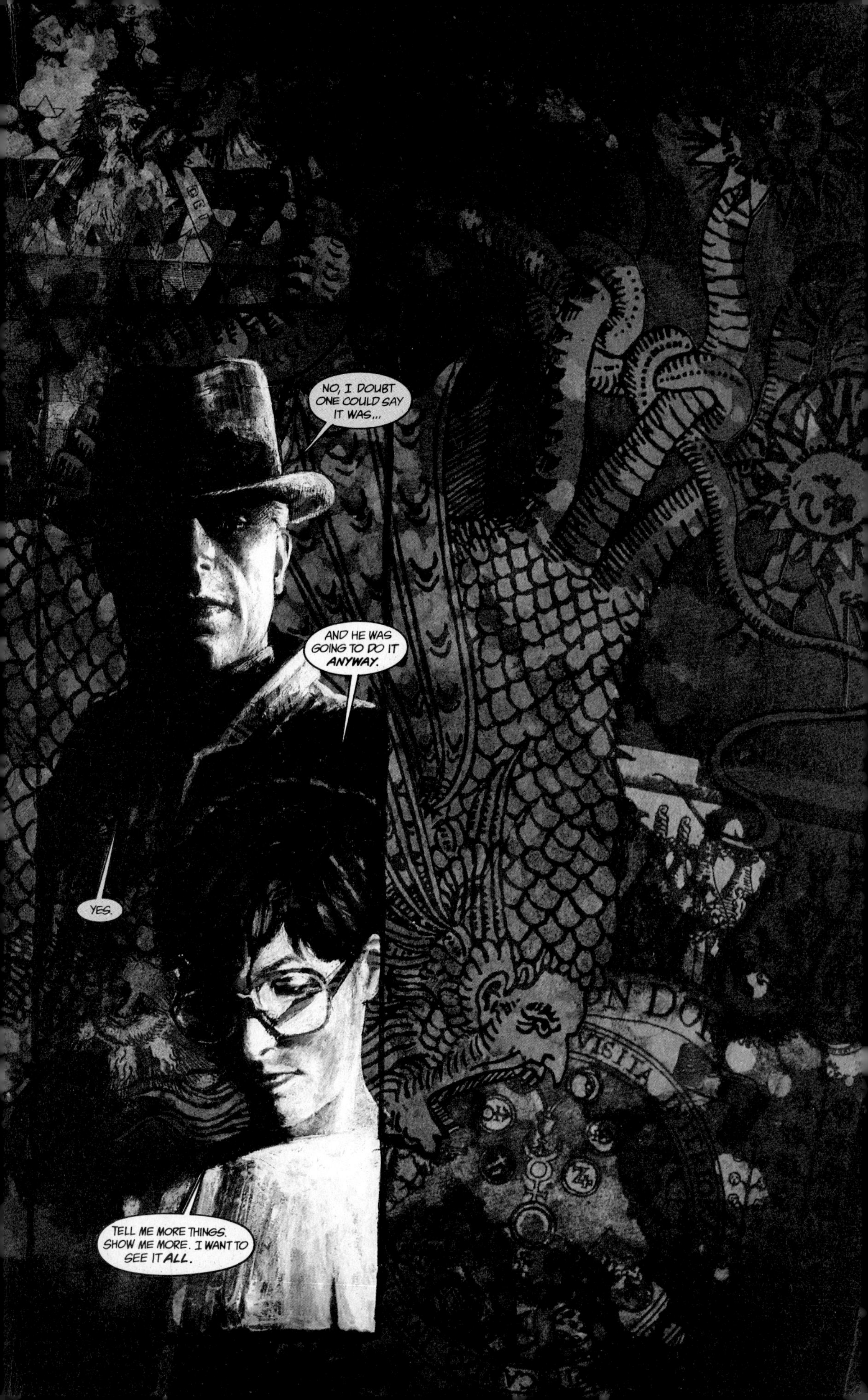
NO, I DOUBT ONE COULD SAY IT WAS...
AND HE WAS GOING TO DO IT ANYWAY.
YES.
TELL ME MORE THINGS. SHOW ME MORE. I WANT TO SEE IT ALL.

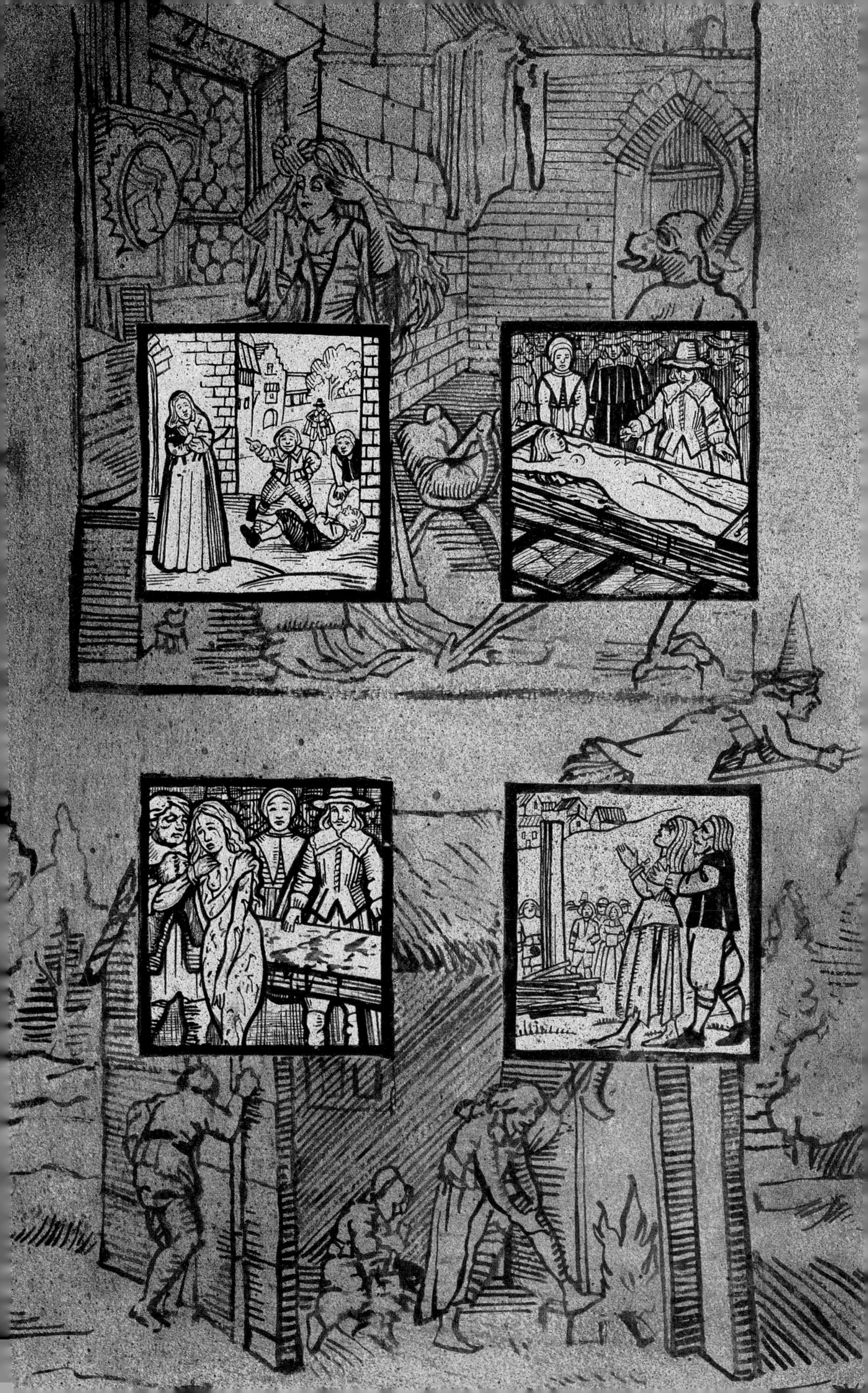

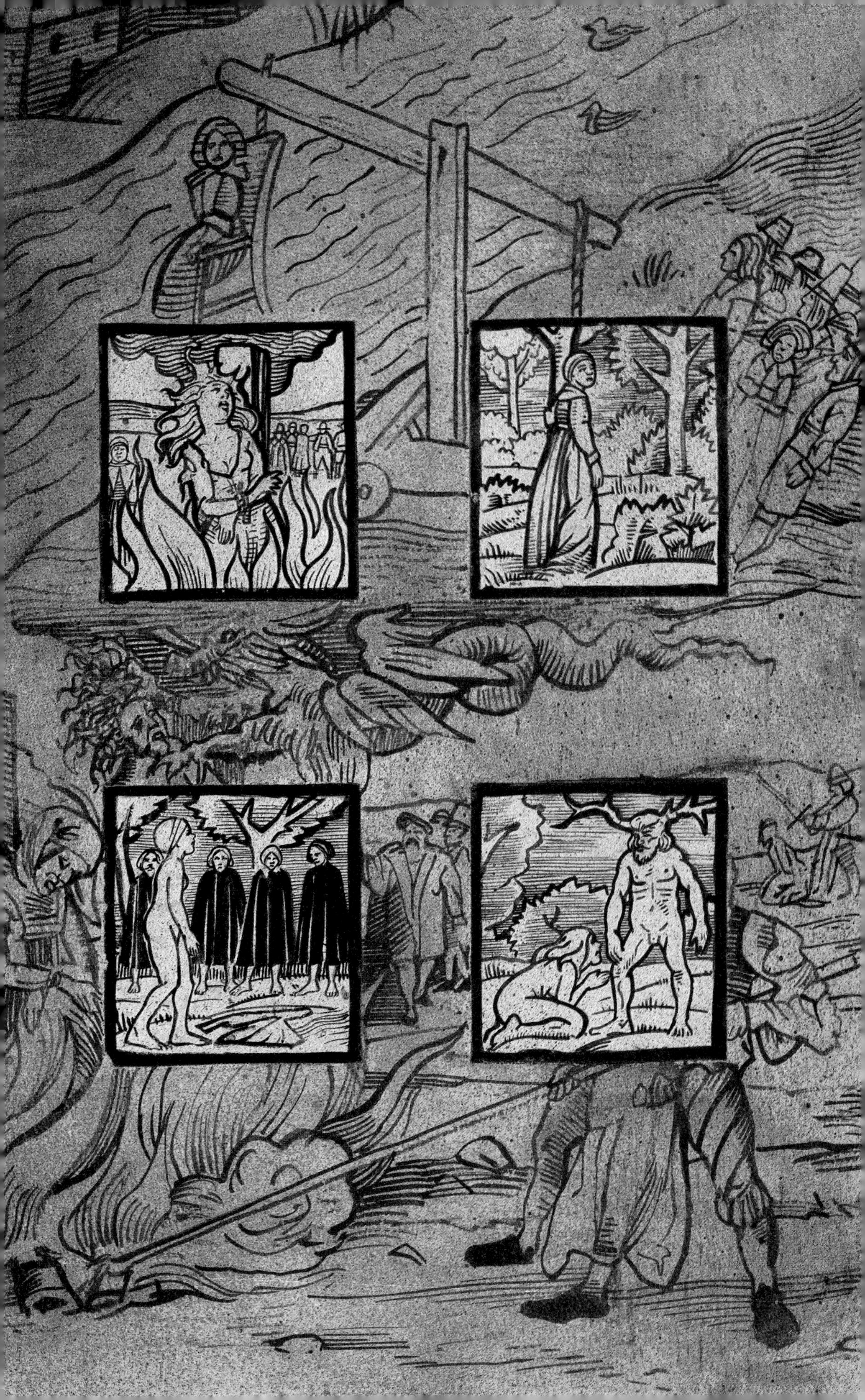

I...I'M NOT SURE I UNDERSTOOD ALL THAT.
PEOPLE KILL WHAT THEY FEAR, TIMOTHY.
THEY BURNED, AND DROWNED, AND HANGED THOSE THEY SAW AS WITCHES, THE DEVIL'S SERVANTS: THE WISE WOMEN AND THE CUNNING MEN, THE UNFORTUNATE, THE LOST AND THE STRANGE.
WHILE IN THE FORESTS AND THE HIGH PLACES AND BESIDE THE GREAT STONES, THE OLD RELIGIONS ENDURED.
IT DOESN'T SEEM LIKE THERE'S ANY REAL MAGIC ANYMORE. NOT LIKE IT **WAS.** WHERE DID ALL THE MAGIC **GO?**
MUCH MAGIC WAS LOST WHEN THE LAST VESTIGES OF ATLANTIS SANK-- ALTHOUGH **MISPLACED** WOULD, PERHAPS, BE A MORE PRECISE TERM.
BETWEEN THE DARK AGES AND THE MIDDLE AGES MANY OF THE POWERS OF FAERIE AND GRAMARYE LEFT THIS PLANE FOR GOOD. SOME FOR ONE PLACE, SOME FOR ANOTHER.
AND AS SCIENCE AROSE IT LEFT LITTLE ROOM FOR MAGIC.
WHY?

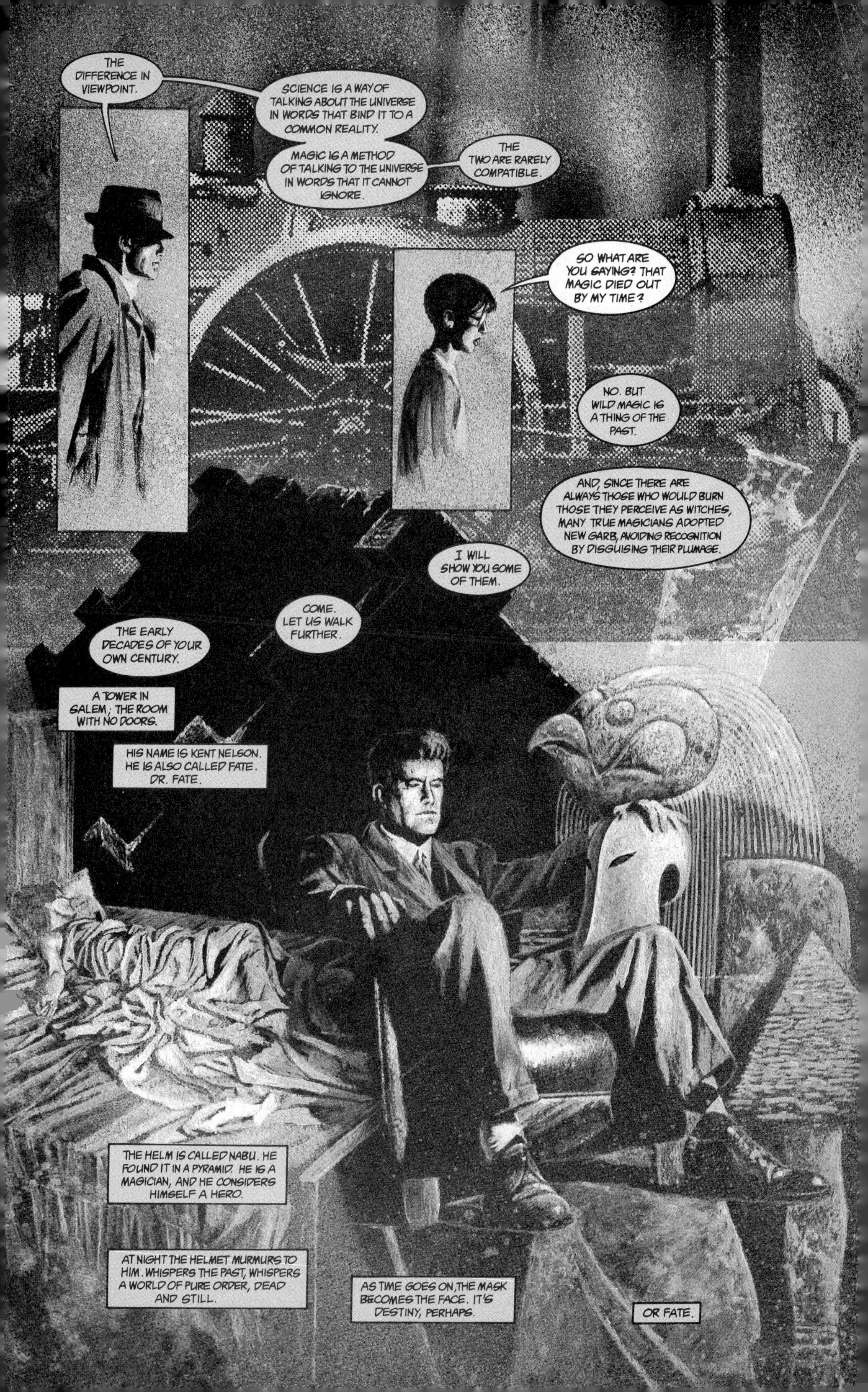
THE DIFFERENCE IN VIEWPOINT.
SCIENCE IS A WAY OF TALKING ABOUT THE UNIVERSE IN WORDS THAT BIND IT TO A COMMON REALITY.
MAGIC IS A METHOD OF TALKING TO THE UNIVERSE IN WORDS THAT IT CANNOT IGNORE.
THE TWO ARE RARELY COMPATIBLE.
SO WHAT ARE YOU SAYING? THAT MAGIC DIED OUT BY MY TIME?
NO. BUT WILD MAGIC IS A THING OF THE PAST.
AND, SINCE THERE ARE ALWAYS THOSE WHO WOULD BURN THOSE THEY PERCEIVE AS WITCHES, MANY TRUE MAGICIANS ADOPTED NEW GARB, AVOIDING RECOGNITION BY DISGUISING THEIR PLUMAGE.
I WILL SHOW YOU SOME OF THEM.
COME. LET US WALK FURTHER.
THE EARLY DECADES OF YOUR OWN CENTURY.
A TOWER IN SALEM; THE ROOM WITH NO DOORS.
HIS NAME IS KENT NELSON. HE IS ALSO CALLED FATE. DR. FATE.
THE HELM IS CALLED NABU. HE FOUND IT IN A PYRAMID. HE IS A MAGICIAN, AND HE CONSIDERS HIMSELF A HERO.
AT NIGHT THE HELMET MURMURS TO HIM. WHISPERS THE PAST, WHISPERS A WORLD OF PURE ORDER, DEAD AND STILL.
AS TIME GOES ON, THE MASK BECOMES THE FACE. IT'S DESTINY, PERHAPS.
OR FATE.

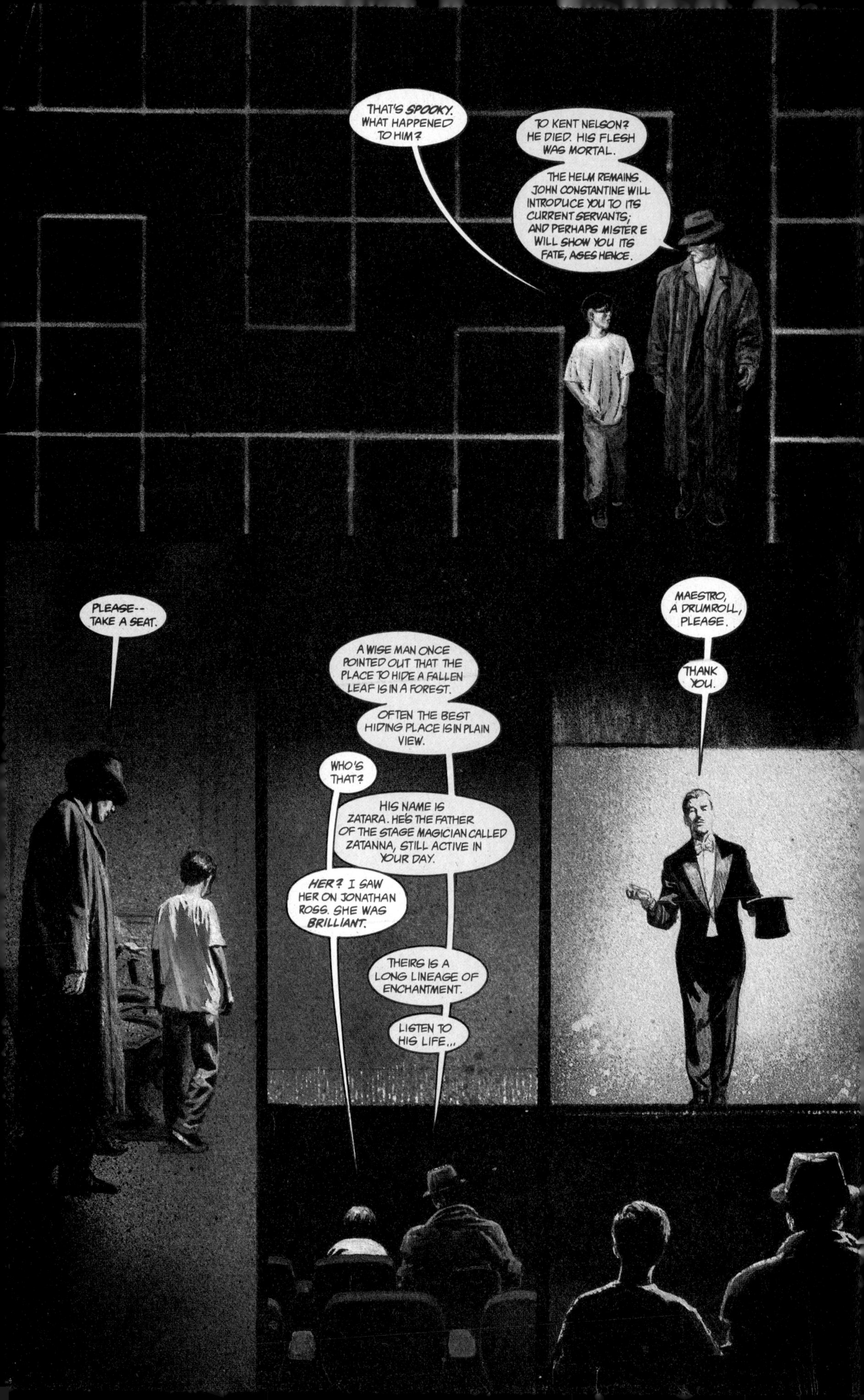

THAT'S SPOOKY. WHAT HAPPENED TO HIM?
TO KENT NELSON? HE DIED. HIS FLESH WAS MORTAL.
THE HELM REMAINS. JOHN CONSTANTINE WILL INTRODUCE YOU TO ITS CURRENT SERVANTS; AND PERHAPS MISTER E WILL SHOW YOU ITS FATE, AGES HENCE.
PLEASE-- TAKE A SEAT.
A WISE MAN ONCE POINTED OUT THAT THE PLACE TO HIDE A FALLEN LEAF IS IN A FOREST.
OFTEN THE BEST HIDING PLACE IS IN PLAIN VIEW.
WHO'S THAT?
HIS NAME IS ZATARA. HE'S THE FATHER OF THE STAGE MAGICIAN CALLED ZATANNA, STILL ACTIVE IN YOUR DAY.
HER? I SAW HER ON JONATHAN ROSS. SHE WAS BRILLIANT.
THEIRS IS A LONG LINEAGE OF ENCHANTMENT.
LISTEN TO HIS LIFE...
MAESTRO, A DRUMROLL, PLEASE.
THANK YOU.

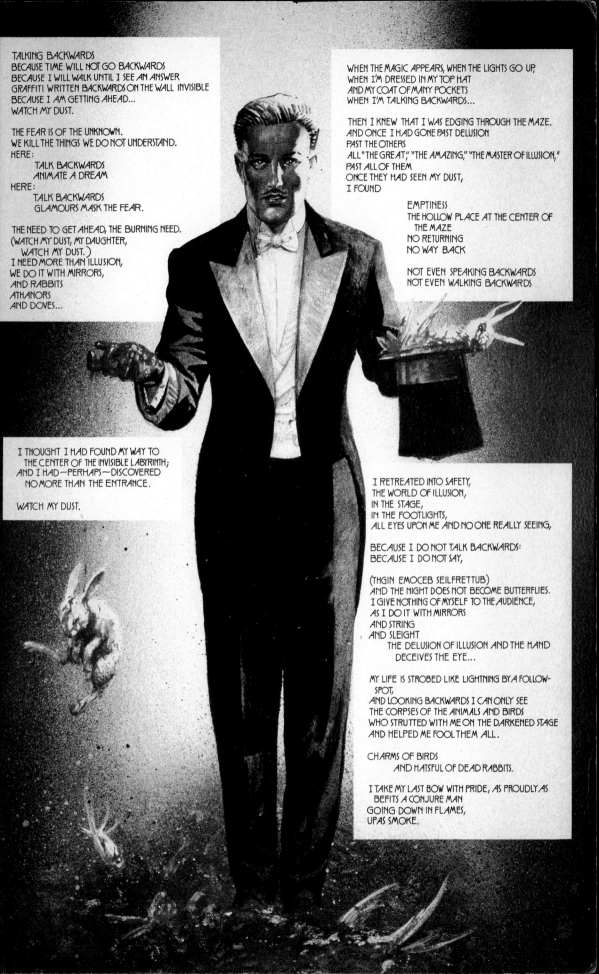

TALKING BACKWARDS
BECAUSE TIME WILL NOT GO BACKWARDS
BECAUSE I WILL WALK UNTIL I SEE AN ANSWER
GRAFFITI WRITTEN BACKWARDS ON THE WALL INVISIBLE
BECAUSE I AM GETTING AHEAD...
WATCH MY DUST.

THE FEAR IS OF THE UNKNOWN.
WE KILL THE THINGS WE DO NOT UNDERSTAND.
HERE:
     TALK BACKWARDS
     ANIMATE A DREAM
HERE:
     TALK BACKWARDS
     GLAMOURS MASK THE FEAR.

THE NEED TO GET AHEAD, THE BURNING NEED.
(WATCH MY DUST, MY DAUGHTER,
  WATCH MY DUST.)
I NEED MORE THAN ILLUSION,
WE DO IT WITH MIRRORS,
AND RABBITS
ATHANORS
AND DOVES...

WHEN THE MAGIC APPEARS, WHEN THE LIGHTS GO UP,
WHEN I'M DRESSED IN MY TOP HAT
AND MY COAT OF MANY POCKETS
WHEN I'M TALKING BACKWARDS...

THEN I KNEW THAT I WAS EDGING THROUGH THE MAZE.
AND ONCE I HAD GONE PAST DELUSION
PAST THE OTHERS
ALL "THE GREAT," "THE AMAZING," "THE MASTER OF ILLUSION,"
PAST ALL OF THEM
ONCE THEY HAD SEEN MY DUST,
I FOUND

    EMPTINESS
    THE HOLLOW PLACE AT THE CENTER OF
      THE MAZE
    NO RETURNING
    NO WAY BACK

    NOT EVEN SPEAKING BACKWARDS
    NOT EVEN WALKING BACKWARDS

I THOUGHT I HAD FOUND MY WAY TO
  THE CENTER OF THE INVISIBLE LABYRINTH;
  AND I HAD—PERHAPS—DISCOVERED
  NO MORE THAN THE ENTRANCE.

WATCH MY DUST.

I RETREATED INTO SAFETY,
  THE WORLD OF ILLUSION,
  IN THE STAGE,
  IN THE FOOTLIGHTS,
  ALL EYES UPON ME AND NO ONE REALLY SEEING,

BECAUSE I DO NOT TALK BACKWARDS:
BECAUSE I DO NOT SAY,

(THGIN EMOCEB SEILFRETTUB)
AND THE NIGHT DOES NOT BECOME BUTTERFLIES.
I GIVE NOTHING OF MYSELF TO THE AUDIENCE,
AS I DO IT WITH MIRRORS
AND STRING
AND SLEIGHT
    THE DELUSION OF ILLUSION AND THE HAND
      DECEIVES THE EYE...

MY LIFE IS STROBED LIKE LIGHTNING BY A FOLLOW-
    SPOT,
AND LOOKING BACKWARDS I CAN ONLY SEE
THE CORPSES OF THE ANIMALS AND BIRDS
WHO STRUTTED WITH ME ON THE DARKENED STAGE
AND HELPED ME FOOL THEM ALL.

CHARMS OF BIRDS
    AND HATSFUL OF DEAD RABBITS.

I TAKE MY LAST BOW WITH PRIDE, AS PROUDLY AS
  BEFITS A CONJURE MAN
GOING DOWN IN FLAMES,
UPAS SMOKE.

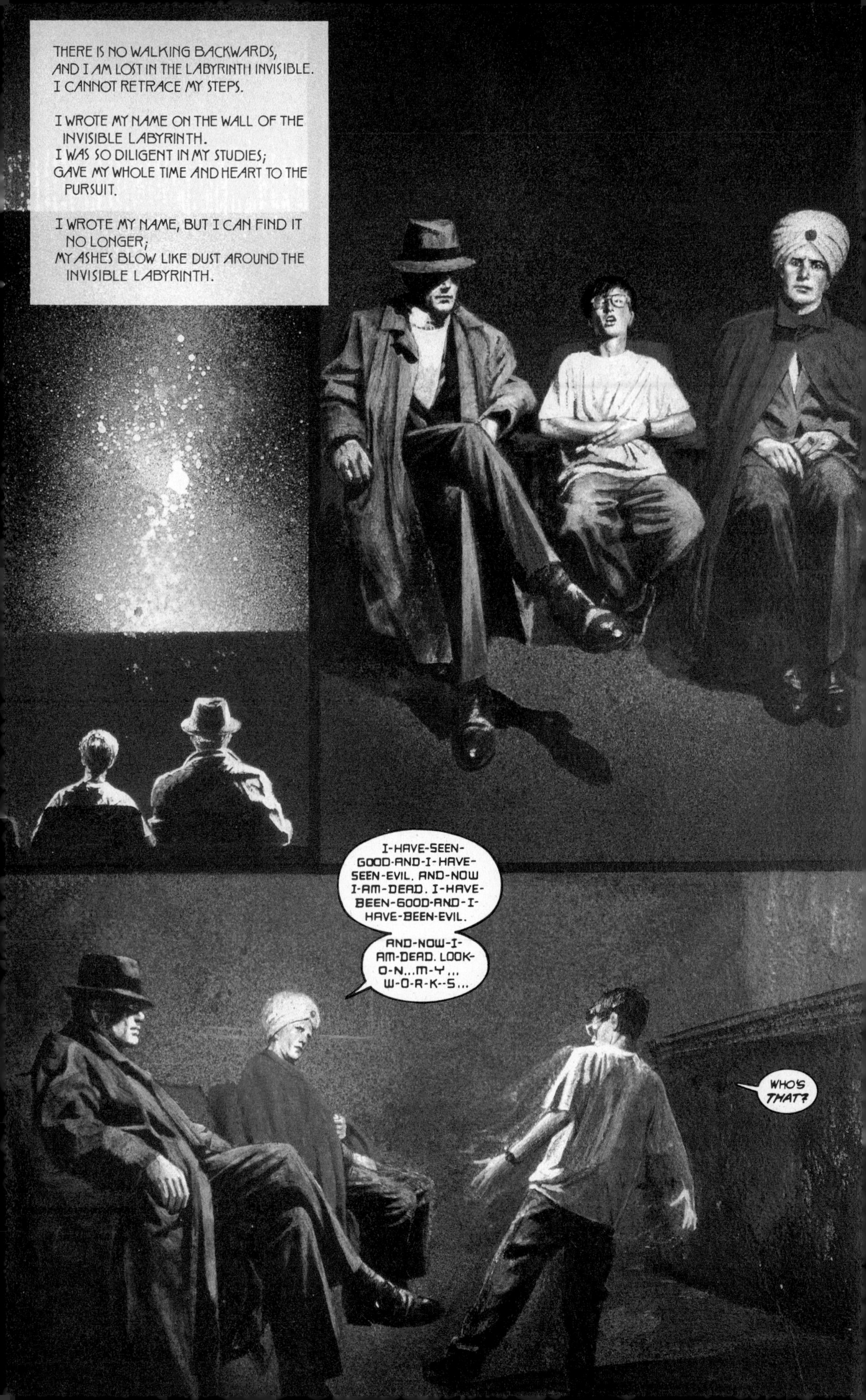
THERE IS NO WALKING BACKWARDS, AND I AM LOST IN THE LABYRINTH INVISIBLE. I CANNOT RETRACE MY STEPS.
I WROTE MY NAME ON THE WALL OF THE INVISIBLE LABYRINTH. I WAS SO DILIGENT IN MY STUDIES; GAVE MY WHOLE TIME AND HEART TO THE PURSUIT.
I WROTE MY NAME, BUT I CAN FIND IT NO LONGER; MY ASHES BLOW LIKE DUST AROUND THE INVISIBLE LABYRINTH.
I-HAVE-SEEN-GOOD-AND-I-HAVE-SEEN-EVIL. AND-NOW I-AM-DEAD. I-HAVE-BEEN-GOOD-AND-I-HAVE-BEEN-EVIL.
AND-NOW-I-AM-DEAD. LOOK-O-N...M-Y... W-O-R-K--S...
WHO'S THAT?

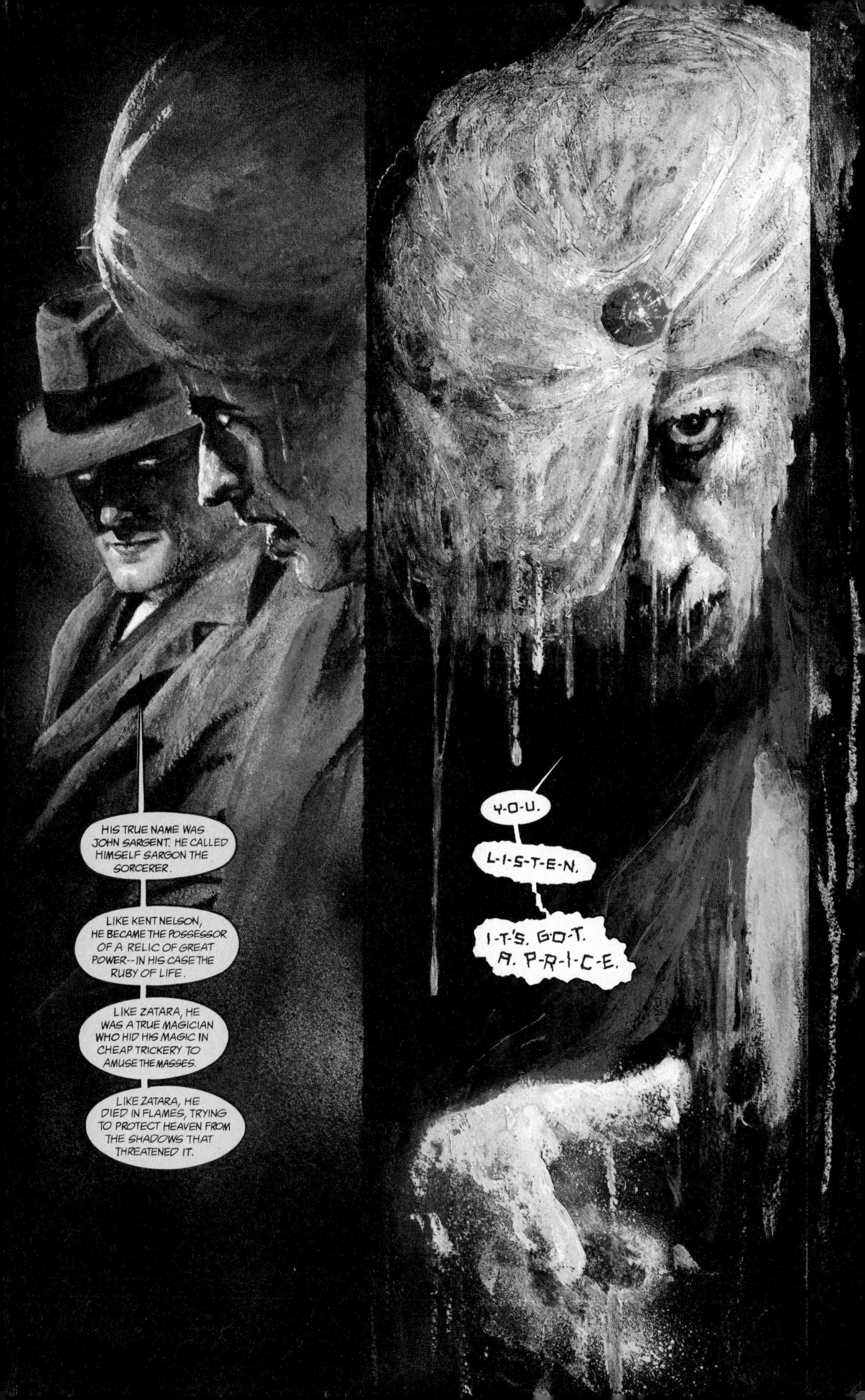
HIS TRUE NAME WAS JOHN SARGENT. HE CALLED HIMSELF SARGON THE SORCERER.
LIKE KENT NELSON, HE BECAME THE POSSESSOR OF A RELIC OF GREAT POWER--IN HIS CASE THE RUBY OF LIFE.
LIKE ZATARA, HE WAS A TRUE MAGICIAN WHO HID HIS MAGIC IN CHEAP TRICKERY TO AMUSE THE MASSES.
LIKE ZATARA, HE DIED IN FLAMES, TRYING TO PROTECT HEAVEN FROM THE SHADOWS THAT THREATENED IT.
Y-O-U.
L-I-S-T-E-N.
I-T-'S. G-O-T. A. P-R-I-C-E.

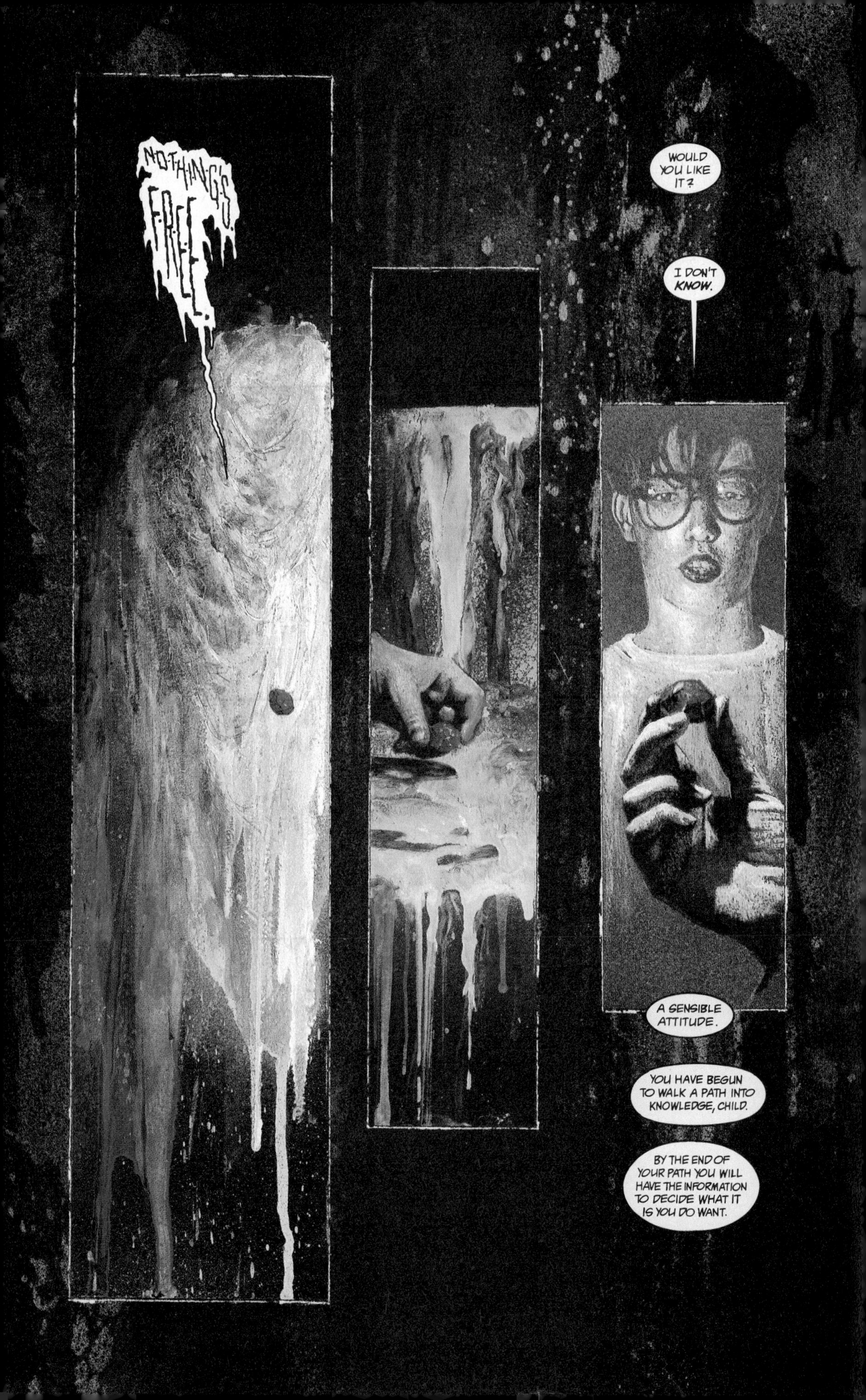
NOTHING'S FREE.
WOULD YOU LIKE IT?
I DON'T KNOW.
A SENSIBLE ATTITUDE.
YOU HAVE BEGUN TO WALK A PATH INTO KNOWLEDGE, CHILD.
BY THE END OF YOUR PATH YOU WILL HAVE THE INFORMATION TO DECIDE WHAT IT IS YOU DO WANT.

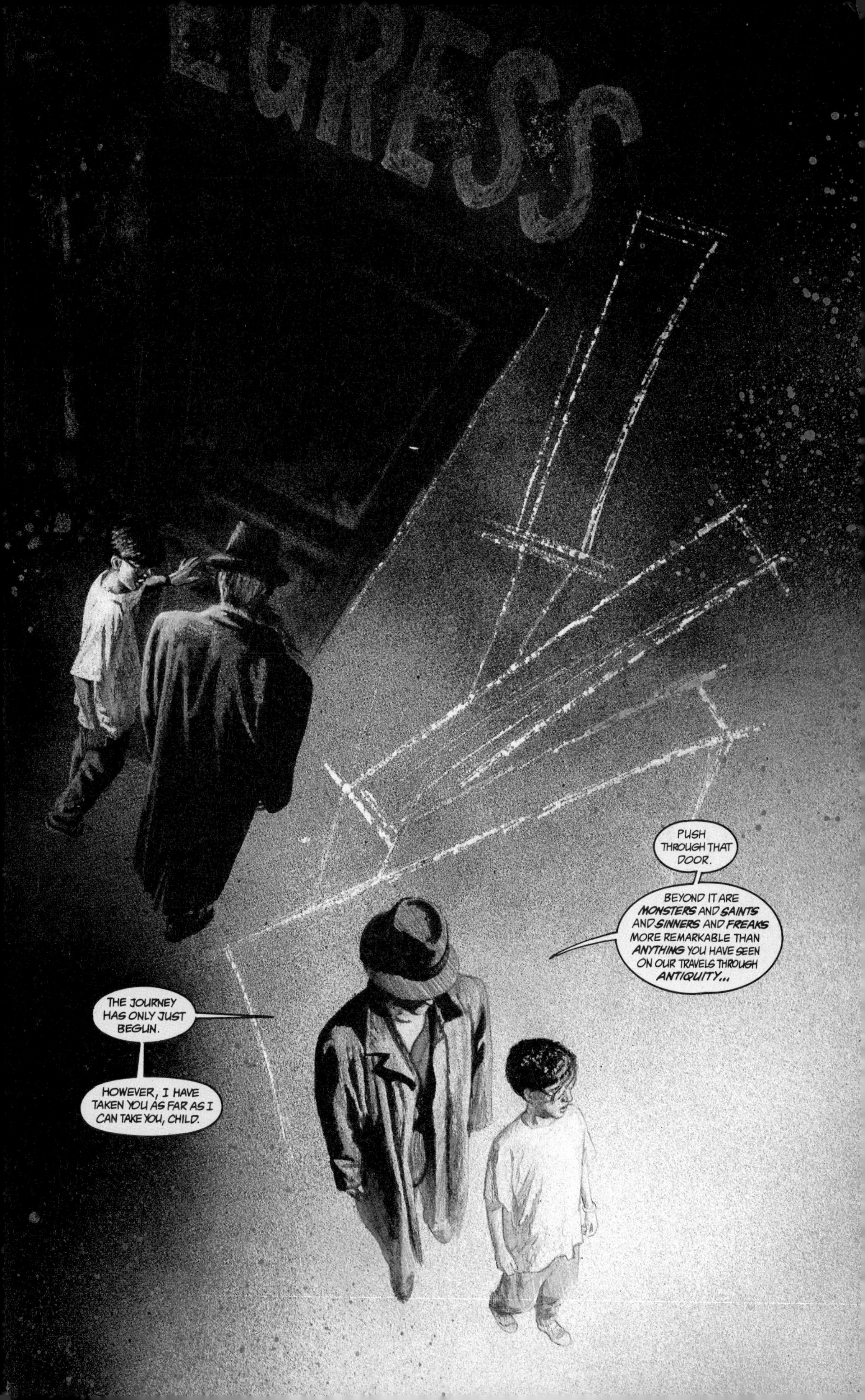
EGRESS
PUSH THROUGH THAT DOOR.
BEYOND IT ARE MONSTERS AND SAINTS AND SINNERS AND FREAKS MORE REMARKABLE THAN ANYTHING YOU HAVE SEEN ON OUR TRAVELS THROUGH ANTIQUITY...
THE JOURNEY HAS ONLY JUST BEGUN.
HOWEVER, I HAVE TAKEN YOU AS FAR AS I CAN TAKE YOU, CHILD.

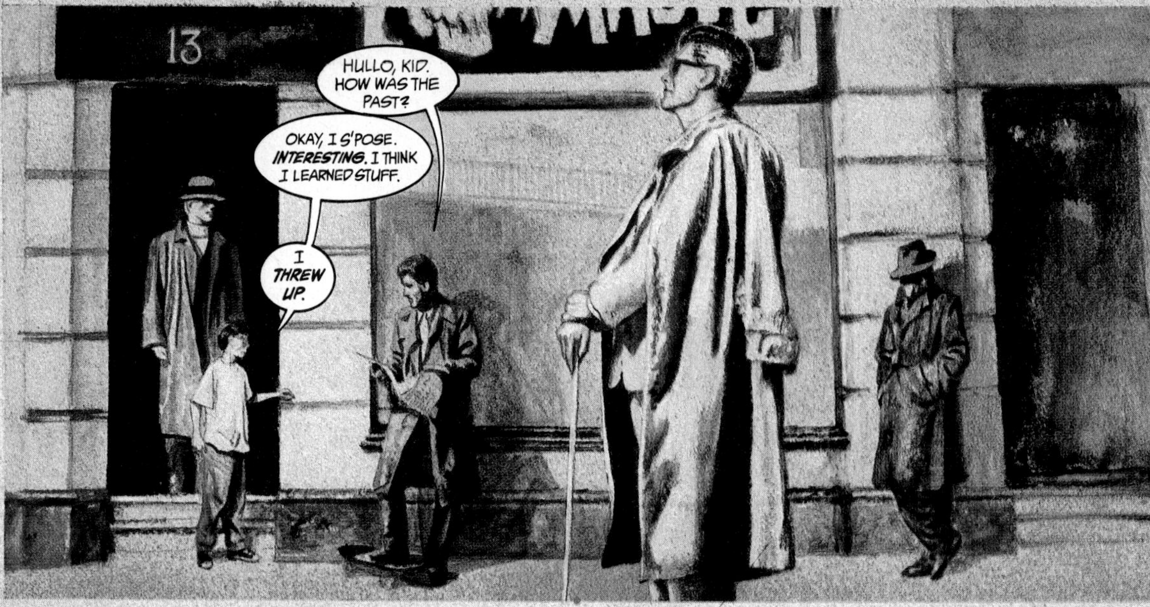
13
HULLO, KID. HOW WAS THE PAST?
OKAY, I S'POSE. INTERESTING. I THINK I LEARNED STUFF.
I THREW UP.

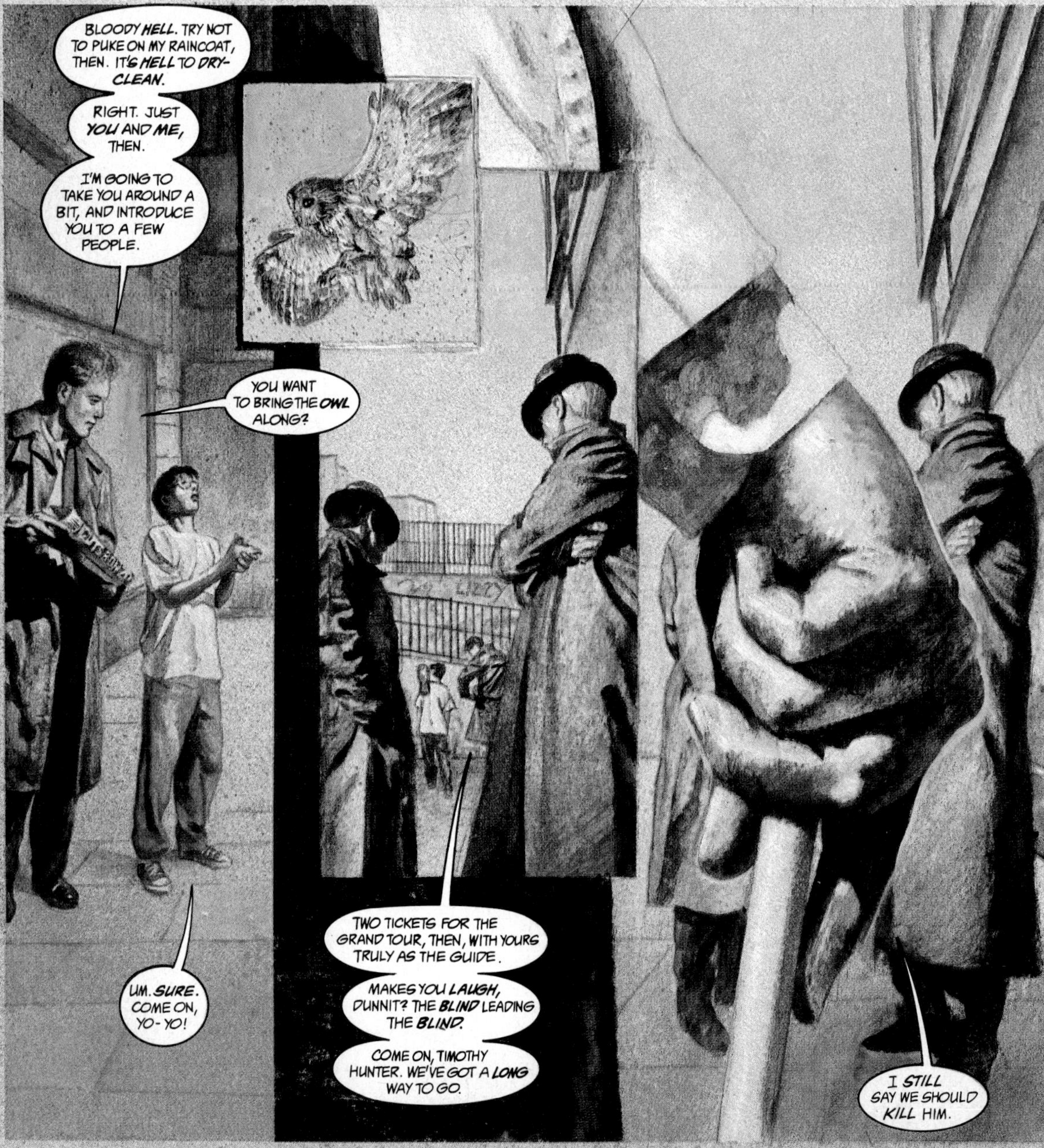
BLOODY HELL. TRY NOT TO PUKE ON MY RAINCOAT, THEN. IT'S HELL TO DRY-CLEAN.
RIGHT. JUST YOU AND ME, THEN.
I'M GOING TO TAKE YOU AROUND A BIT, AND INTRODUCE YOU TO A FEW PEOPLE.
YOU WANT TO BRING THE OWL ALONG?
UM. SURE. COME ON, YO-YO!
TWO TICKETS FOR THE GRAND TOUR, THEN, WITH YOURS TRULY AS THE GUIDE.
MAKES YOU LAUGH, DUNNIT? THE BLIND LEADING THE BLIND.
COME ON, TIMOTHY HUNTER. WE'VE GOT A LONG WAY TO GO.
I STILL SAY WE SHOULD KILL HIM.

II

The Shadow World

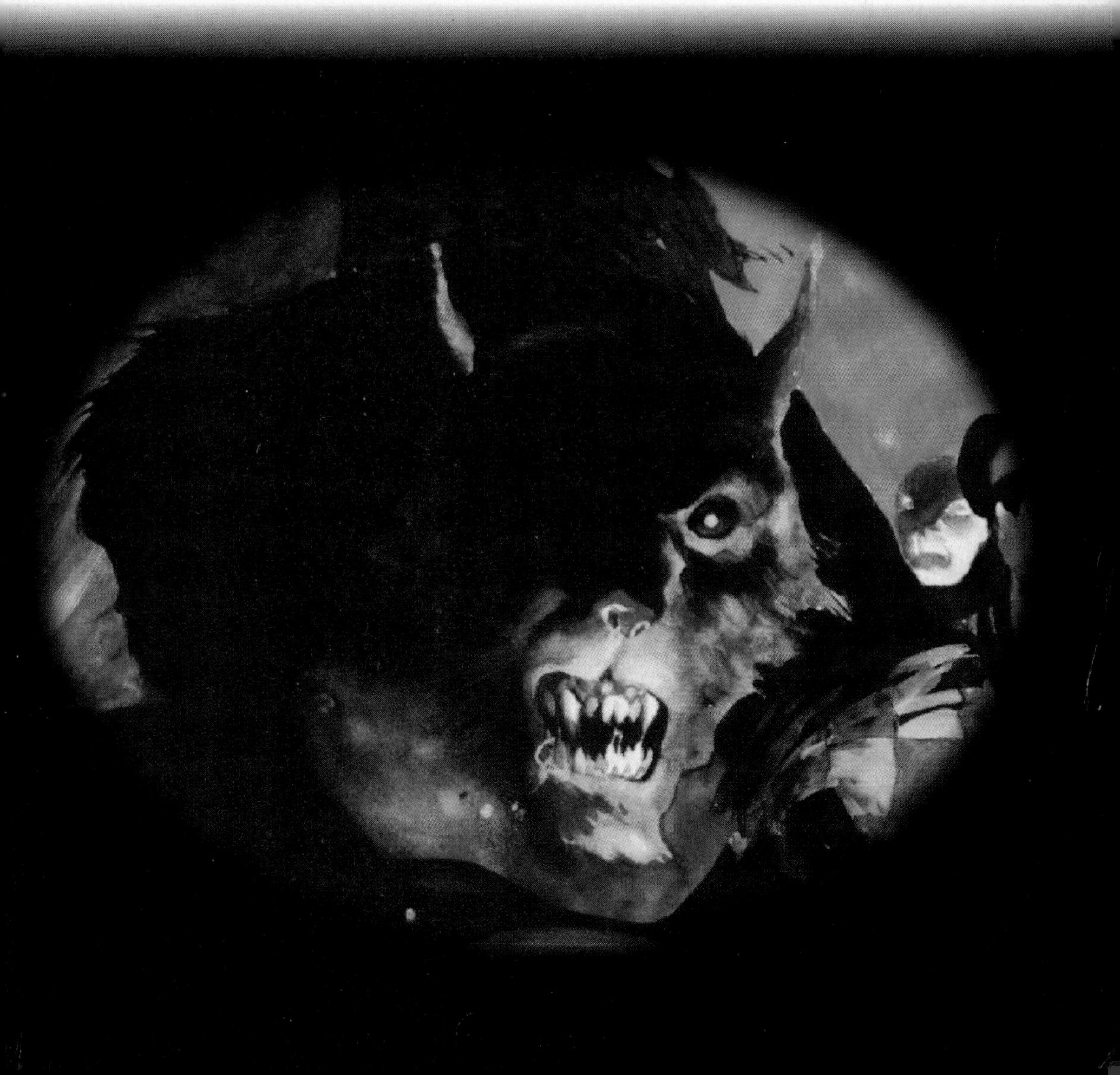

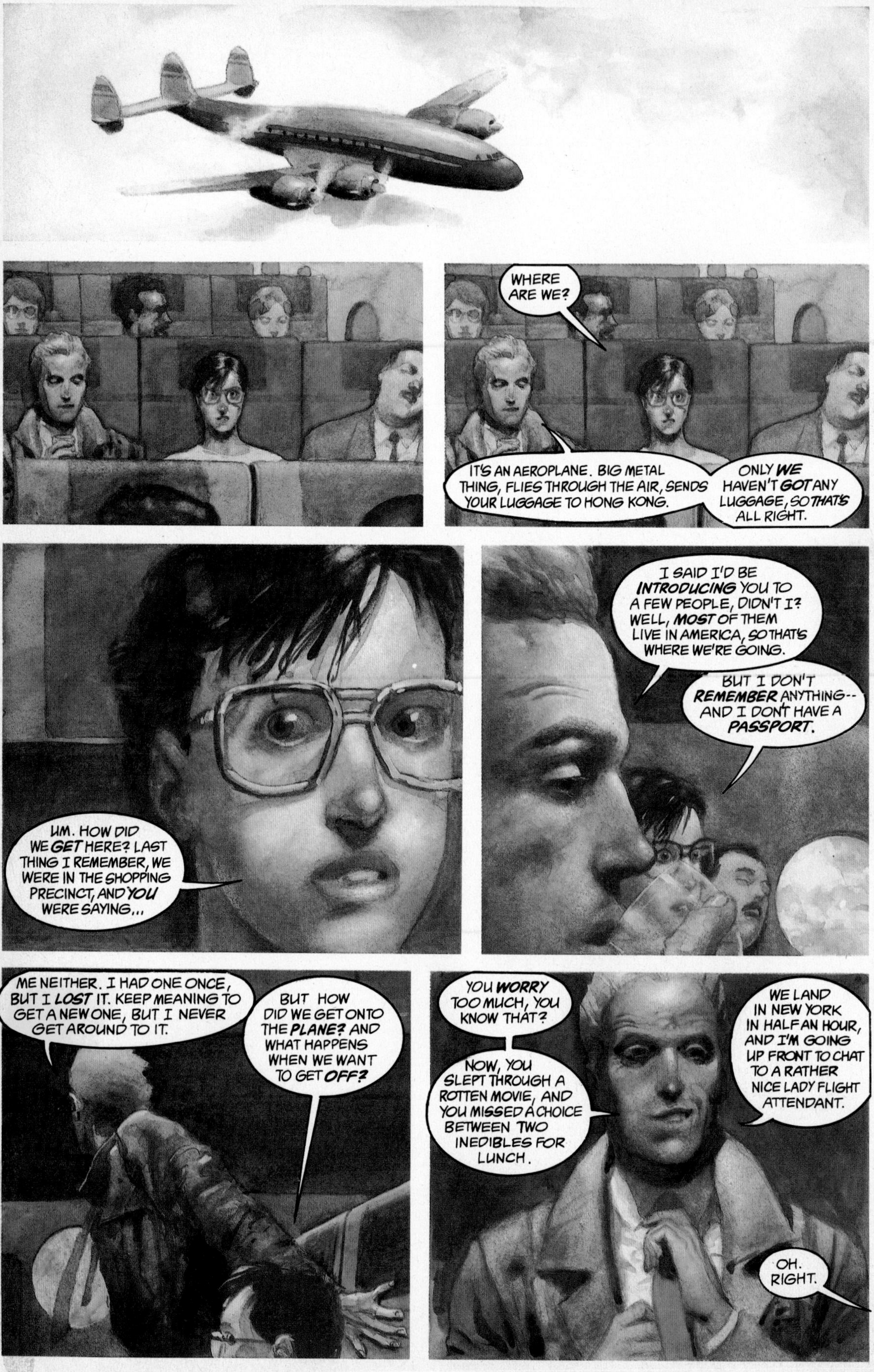
WHERE ARE WE?
IT'S AN AEROPLANE. BIG METAL THING, FLIES THROUGH THE AIR, SENDS YOUR LUGGAGE TO HONG KONG.
ONLY WE HAVEN'T GOT ANY LUGGAGE, SO THAT'S ALL RIGHT.
UM. HOW DID WE GET HERE? LAST THING I REMEMBER, WE WERE IN THE SHOPPING PRECINCT, AND YOU WERE SAYING...
I SAID I'D BE INTRODUCING YOU TO A FEW PEOPLE, DIDN'T I? WELL, MOST OF THEM LIVE IN AMERICA, SO THAT'S WHERE WE'RE GOING.
BUT I DON'T REMEMBER ANYTHING-- AND I DON'T HAVE A PASSPORT.
ME NEITHER. I HAD ONE ONCE, BUT I LOST IT. KEEP MEANING TO GET A NEW ONE, BUT I NEVER GET AROUND TO IT.
BUT HOW DID WE GET ONTO THE PLANE? AND WHAT HAPPENS WHEN WE WANT TO GET OFF?
YOU WORRY TOO MUCH, YOU KNOW THAT?
NOW, YOU SLEPT THROUGH A ROTTEN MOVIE, AND YOU MISSED A CHOICE BETWEEN TWO INEDIBLES FOR LUNCH.
WE LAND IN NEW YORK IN HALF AN HOUR, AND I'M GOING UP FRONT TO CHAT TO A RATHER NICE LADY FLIGHT ATTENDANT.
OH. RIGHT.

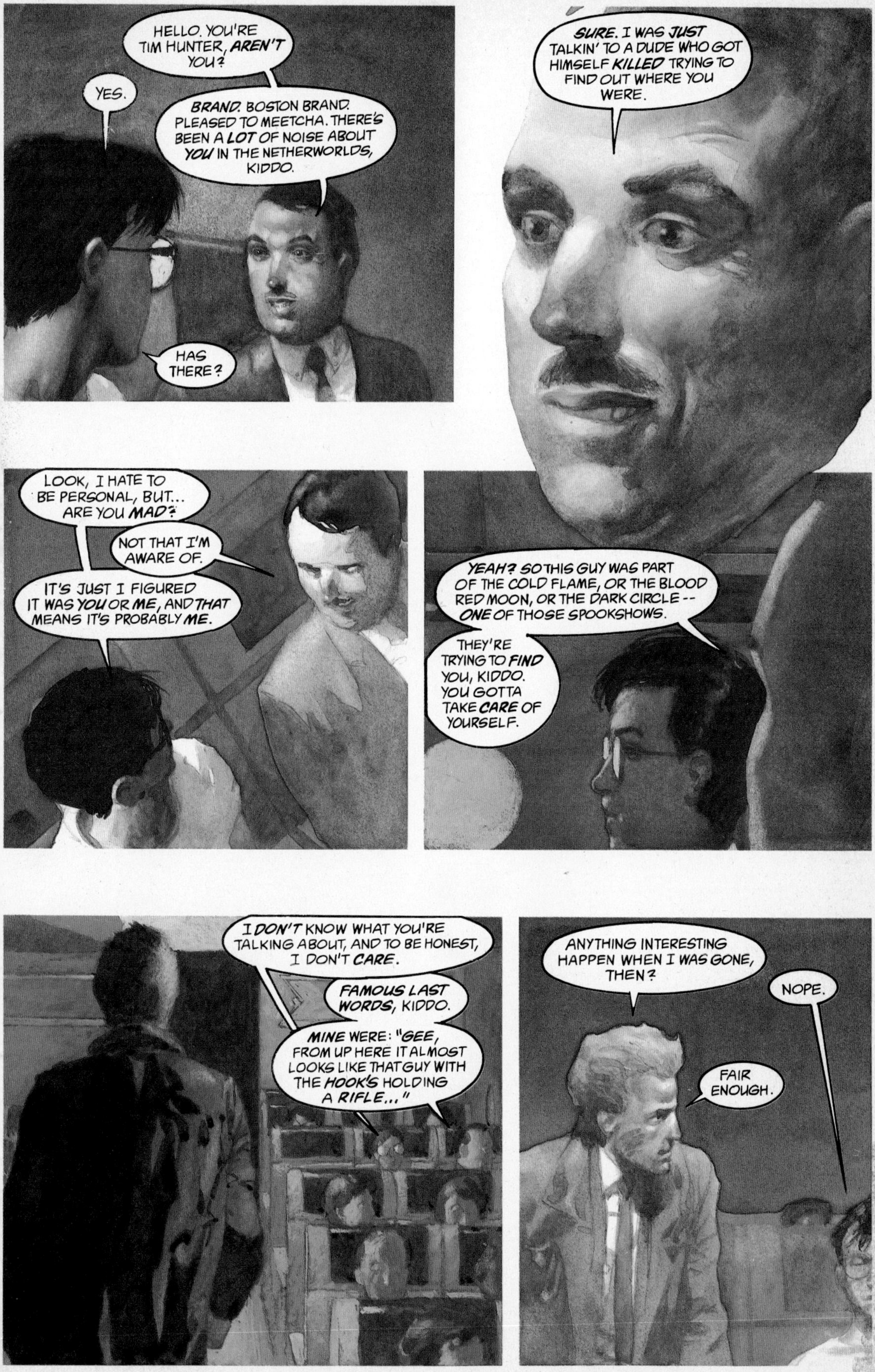
HELLO. YOU'RE TIM HUNTER, AREN'T YOU?
YES.
BRAND. BOSTON BRAND. PLEASED TO MEETCHA. THERE'S BEEN A LOT OF NOISE ABOUT YOU IN THE NETHERWORLDS, KIDDO.
HAS THERE?
SURE. I WAS JUST TALKIN' TO A DUDE WHO GOT HIMSELF KILLED TRYING TO FIND OUT WHERE YOU WERE.
LOOK, I HATE TO BE PERSONAL, BUT... ARE YOU MAD?
NOT THAT I'M AWARE OF.
IT'S JUST I FIGURED IT WAS YOU OR ME, AND THAT MEANS IT'S PROBABLY ME.
YEAH? SO THIS GUY WAS PART OF THE COLD FLAME, OR THE BLOOD RED MOON, OR THE DARK CIRCLE -- ONE OF THOSE SPOOKSHOWS.
THEY'RE TRYING TO FIND YOU, KIDDO. YOU GOTTA TAKE CARE OF YOURSELF.
I DON'T KNOW WHAT YOU'RE TALKING ABOUT, AND TO BE HONEST, I DON'T CARE.
FAMOUS LAST WORDS, KIDDO.
MINE WERE: "GEE, FROM UP HERE IT ALMOST LOOKS LIKE THAT GUY WITH THE HOOK'S HOLDING A RIFLE..."
ANYTHING INTERESTING HAPPEN WHEN I WAS GONE, THEN?
NOPE.
FAIR ENOUGH.

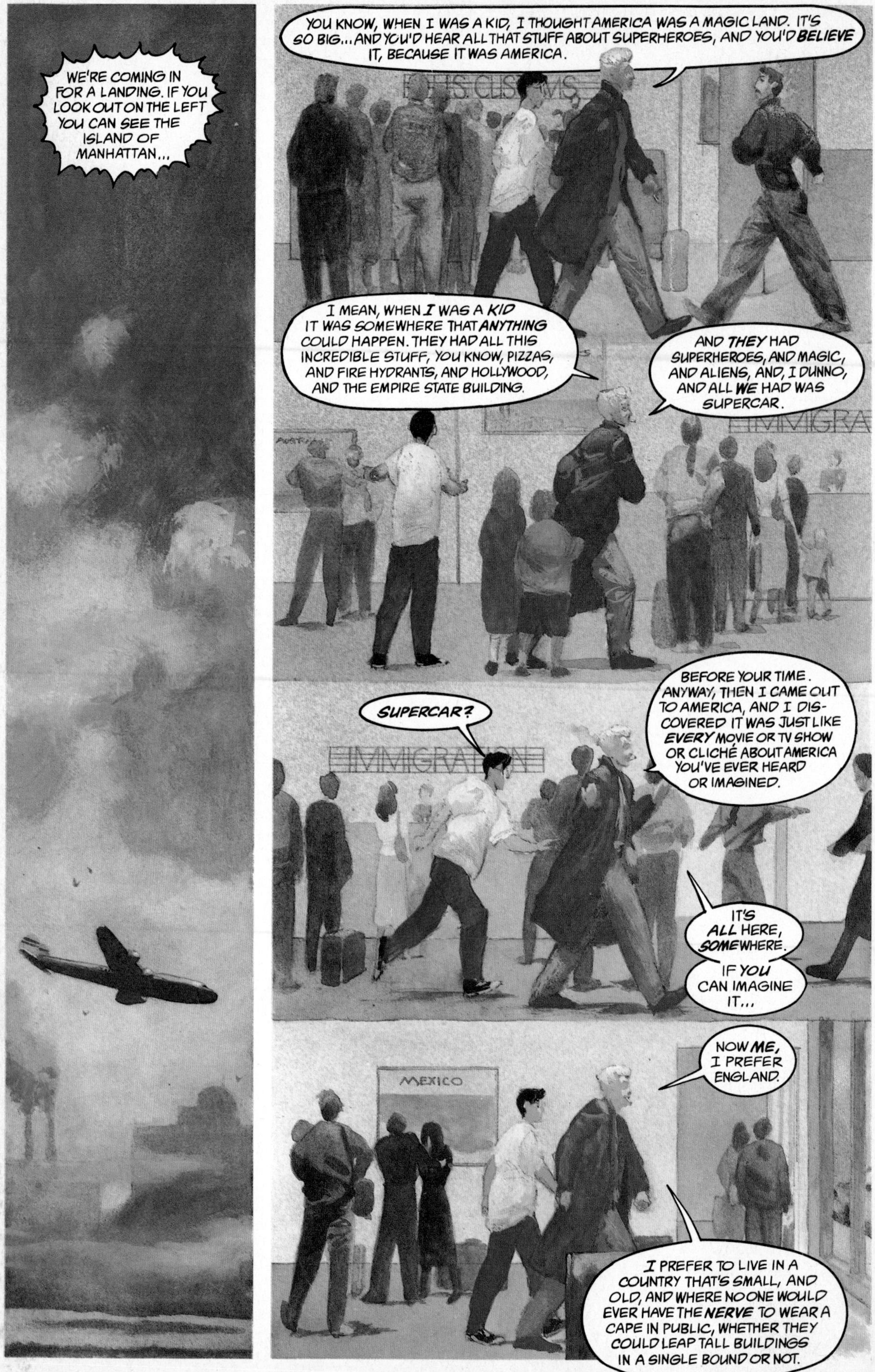
WE'RE COMING IN FOR A LANDING. IF YOU LOOK OUT ON THE LEFT YOU CAN SEE THE ISLAND OF MANHATTAN...
YOU KNOW, WHEN I WAS A KID, I THOUGHT AMERICA WAS A MAGIC LAND. IT'S SO BIG... AND YOU'D HEAR ALL THAT STUFF ABOUT SUPERHEROES, AND YOU'D BELIEVE IT, BECAUSE IT WAS AMERICA.
I MEAN, WHEN I WAS A KID IT WAS SOMEWHERE THAT ANYTHING COULD HAPPEN. THEY HAD ALL THIS INCREDIBLE STUFF, YOU KNOW, PIZZAS, AND FIRE HYDRANTS, AND HOLLYWOOD, AND THE EMPIRE STATE BUILDING.
AND THEY HAD SUPERHEROES, AND MAGIC, AND ALIENS, AND, I DUNNO, AND ALL WE HAD WAS SUPERCAR.
IMMIGRA
SUPERCAR?
BEFORE YOUR TIME. ANYWAY, THEN I CAME OUT TO AMERICA, AND I DISCOVERED IT WAS JUST LIKE EVERY MOVIE OR TV SHOW OR CLICHÉ ABOUT AMERICA YOU'VE EVER HEARD OR IMAGINED.
IT'S ALL HERE, SOMEWHERE.
IF YOU CAN IMAGINE IT...
MEXICO
NOW ME, I PREFER ENGLAND.
I PREFER TO LIVE IN A COUNTRY THAT'S SMALL, AND OLD, AND WHERE NO ONE WOULD EVER HAVE THE NERVE TO WEAR A CAPE IN PUBLIC, WHETHER THEY COULD LEAP TALL BUILDINGS IN A SINGLE BOUND OR NOT.

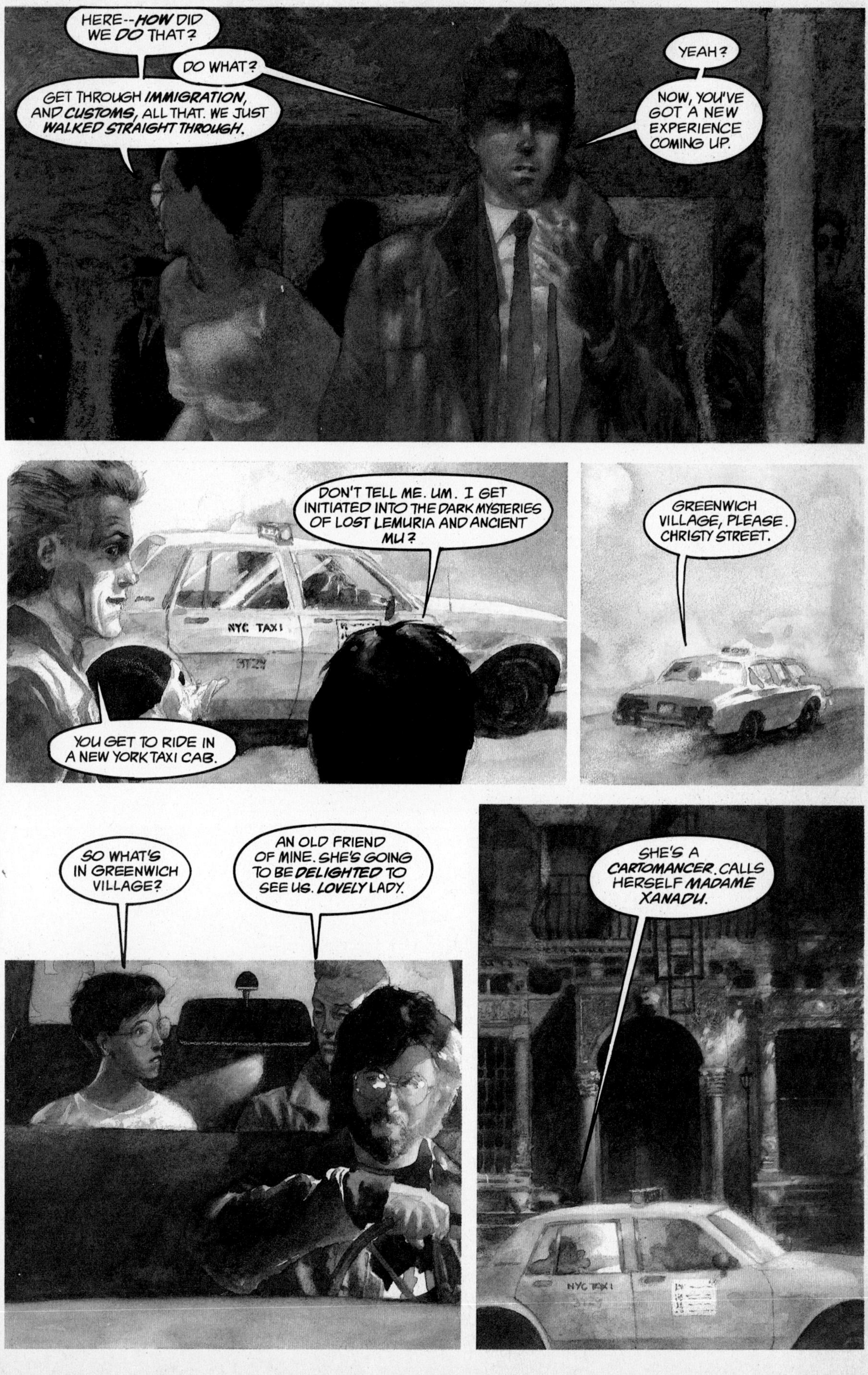
HERE--HOW DID WE DO THAT?
DO WHAT?
GET THROUGH IMMIGRATION, AND CUSTOMS, ALL THAT. WE JUST WALKED STRAIGHT THROUGH.
YEAH?
NOW, YOU'VE GOT A NEW EXPERIENCE COMING UP.
DON'T TELL ME. UM. I GET INITIATED INTO THE DARK MYSTERIES OF LOST LEMURIA AND ANCIENT MU?
YOU GET TO RIDE IN A NEW YORK TAXI CAB.
NYC TAXI
GREENWICH VILLAGE, PLEASE. CHRISTY STREET.
SO WHAT'S IN GREENWICH VILLAGE?
AN OLD FRIEND OF MINE. SHE'S GOING TO BE DELIGHTED TO SEE US. LOVELY LADY.
SHE'S A CARTOMANCER. CALLS HERSELF MADAME XANADU.
NYC TAXI

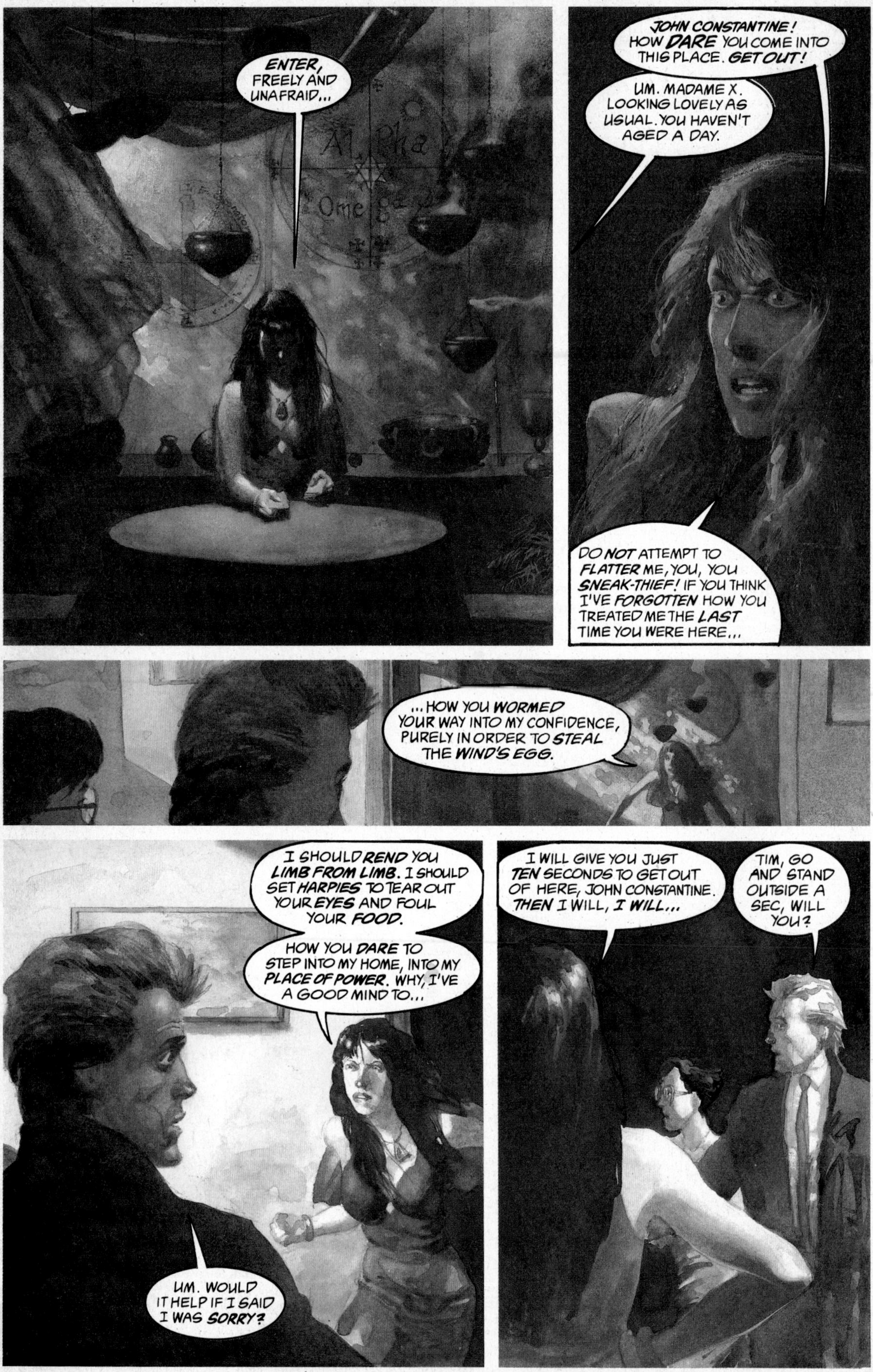
ENTER, FREELY AND UNAFRAID...
JOHN CONSTANTINE! HOW DARE YOU COME INTO THIS PLACE. GET OUT!
UM. MADAME X. LOOKING LOVELY AS USUAL. YOU HAVEN'T AGED A DAY.
DO NOT ATTEMPT TO FLATTER ME, YOU, YOU SNEAK-THIEF! IF YOU THINK I'VE FORGOTTEN HOW YOU TREATED ME THE LAST TIME YOU WERE HERE...
...HOW YOU WORMED YOUR WAY INTO MY CONFIDENCE, PURELY IN ORDER TO STEAL THE WIND'S EGG.
I SHOULD REND YOU LIMB FROM LIMB. I SHOULD SET HARPIES TO TEAR OUT YOUR EYES AND FOUL YOUR FOOD.
HOW YOU DARE TO STEP INTO MY HOME, INTO MY PLACE OF POWER. WHY, I'VE A GOOD MIND TO...
UM. WOULD IT HELP IF I SAID I WAS SORRY?
I WILL GIVE YOU JUST TEN SECONDS TO GET OUT OF HERE, JOHN CONSTANTINE. THEN I WILL, I WILL...
TIM, GO AND STAND OUTSIDE A SEC, WILL YOU?

YEAH. I'M *SURE* IT'S THE BOY.

NO PROBLEM. I CAN TAKE CARE OF HIM.

COME ON IN, TIM. LET ME INTRODUCE YOU PROPERLY.

TIM, THIS LADY'S CALLED *MADAME XANADU.* MADAME X, THIS IS TIM HUNTER.

I AM PLEASED TO MEET YOU, CHILD. THE CONSTANTINE HAS TOLD ME A LITTLE ABOUT YOU. SIT *DOWN.*

I WILL READ YOUR CARDS.

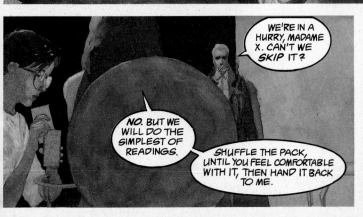

WE'RE IN A HURRY, MADAME X. CAN'T WE *SKIP* IT?

NO. BUT WE WILL DO THE SIMPLEST OF READINGS.

SHUFFLE THE PACK, UNTIL YOU FEEL COMFORTABLE WITH IT, THEN HAND IT BACK TO ME.

FOUR CARDS: EVERYTHING IS HERE, CHILD. *ELEMENTS, HUMORS,* AND THE *CORNERS* OF THE *WORLD.* HMM. ALL MAJOR ARCANA, ALTHOUGH I'D'VE BEEN *SURPRISED* HAD THEY BEEN ANYTHING ELSE. SO...

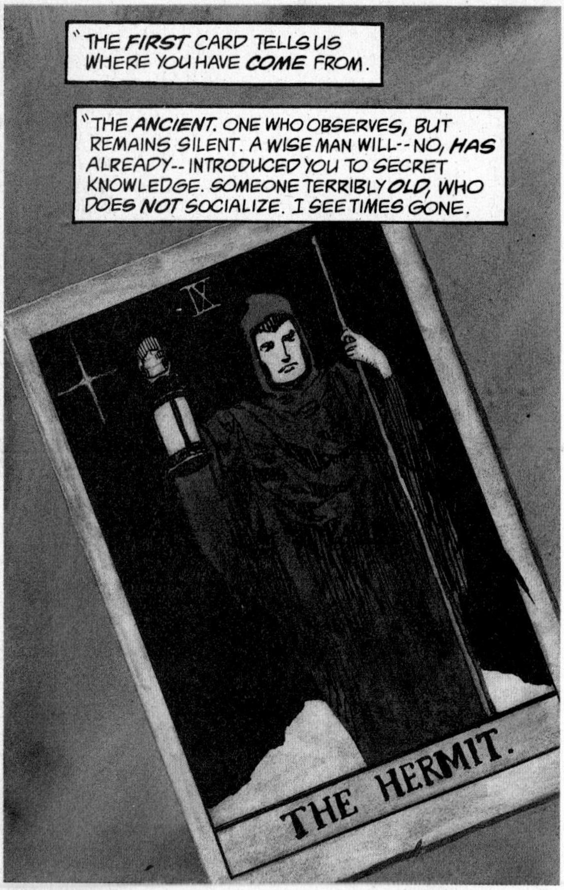
"THE FIRST CARD TELLS US WHERE YOU HAVE COME FROM.
"THE ANCIENT. ONE WHO OBSERVES, BUT REMAINS SILENT. A WISE MAN WILL--NO, HAS ALREADY-- INTRODUCED YOU TO SECRET KNOWLEDGE. SOMEONE TERRIBLY OLD, WHO DOES NOT SOCIALIZE. I SEE TIMES GONE.
IX
THE HERMIT.

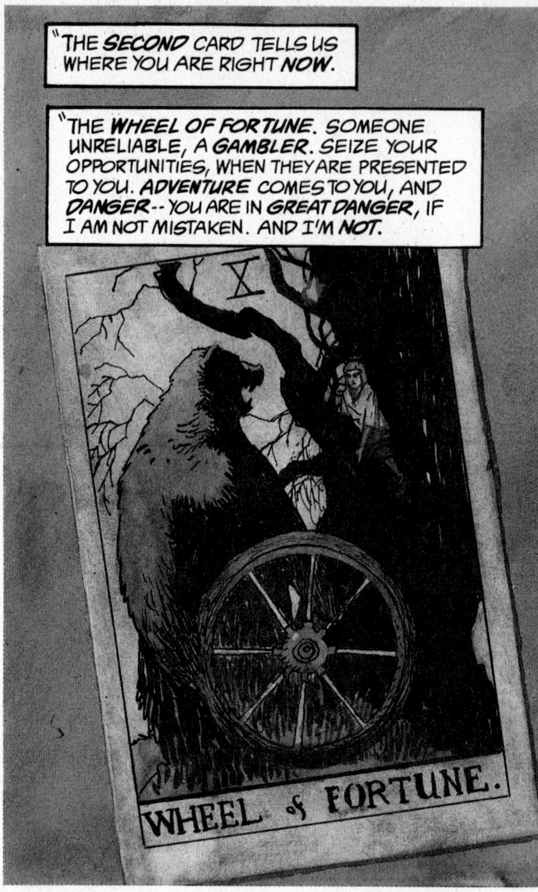
"THE SECOND CARD TELLS US WHERE YOU ARE RIGHT NOW.
"THE WHEEL OF FORTUNE. SOMEONE UNRELIABLE, A GAMBLER. SEIZE YOUR OPPORTUNITIES, WHEN THEY ARE PRESENTED TO YOU. ADVENTURE COMES TO YOU, AND DANGER--YOU ARE IN GREAT DANGER, IF I AM NOT MISTAKEN. AND I'M NOT.
X
WHEEL of FORTUNE.

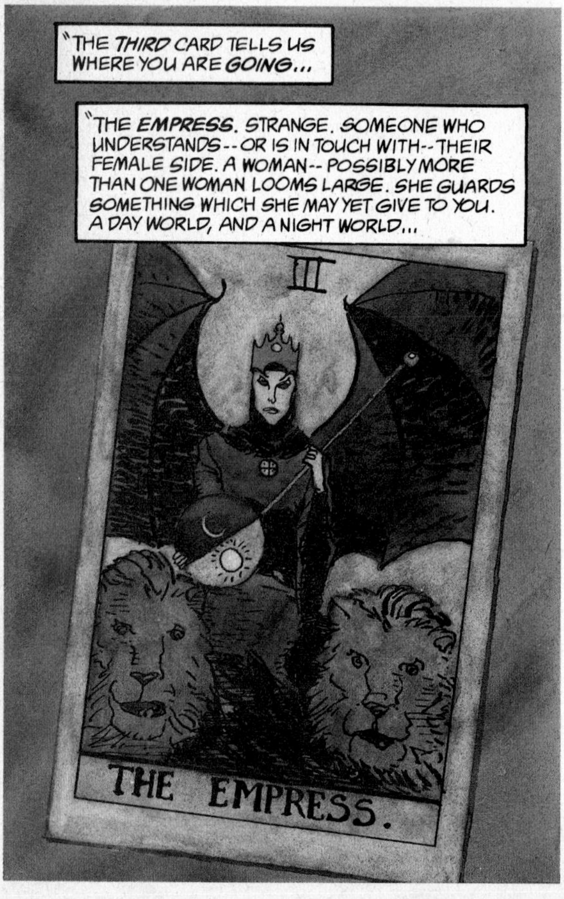
"THE THIRD CARD TELLS US WHERE YOU ARE GOING...
"THE EMPRESS. STRANGE. SOMEONE WHO UNDERSTANDS--OR IS IN TOUCH WITH--THEIR FEMALE SIDE. A WOMAN--POSSIBLY MORE THAN ONE WOMAN LOOMS LARGE. SHE GUARDS SOMETHING WHICH SHE MAY YET GIVE TO YOU. A DAY WORLD, AND A NIGHT WORLD...
III
THE EMPRESS.

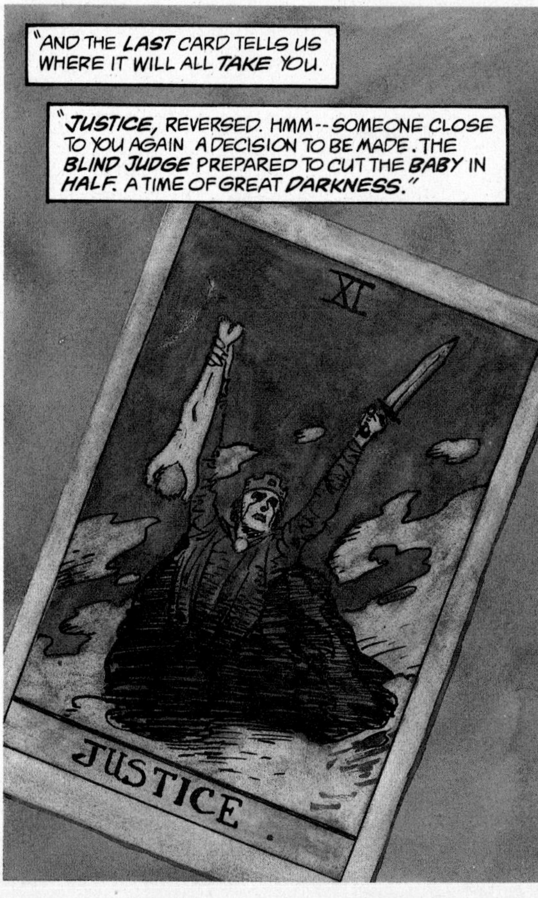
"AND THE LAST CARD TELLS US WHERE IT WILL ALL TAKE YOU.
"JUSTICE, REVERSED. HMM--SOMEONE CLOSE TO YOU AGAIN. A DECISION TO BE MADE. THE BLIND JUDGE PREPARED TO CUT THE BABY IN HALF. A TIME OF GREAT DARKNESS."
XI
JUSTICE.

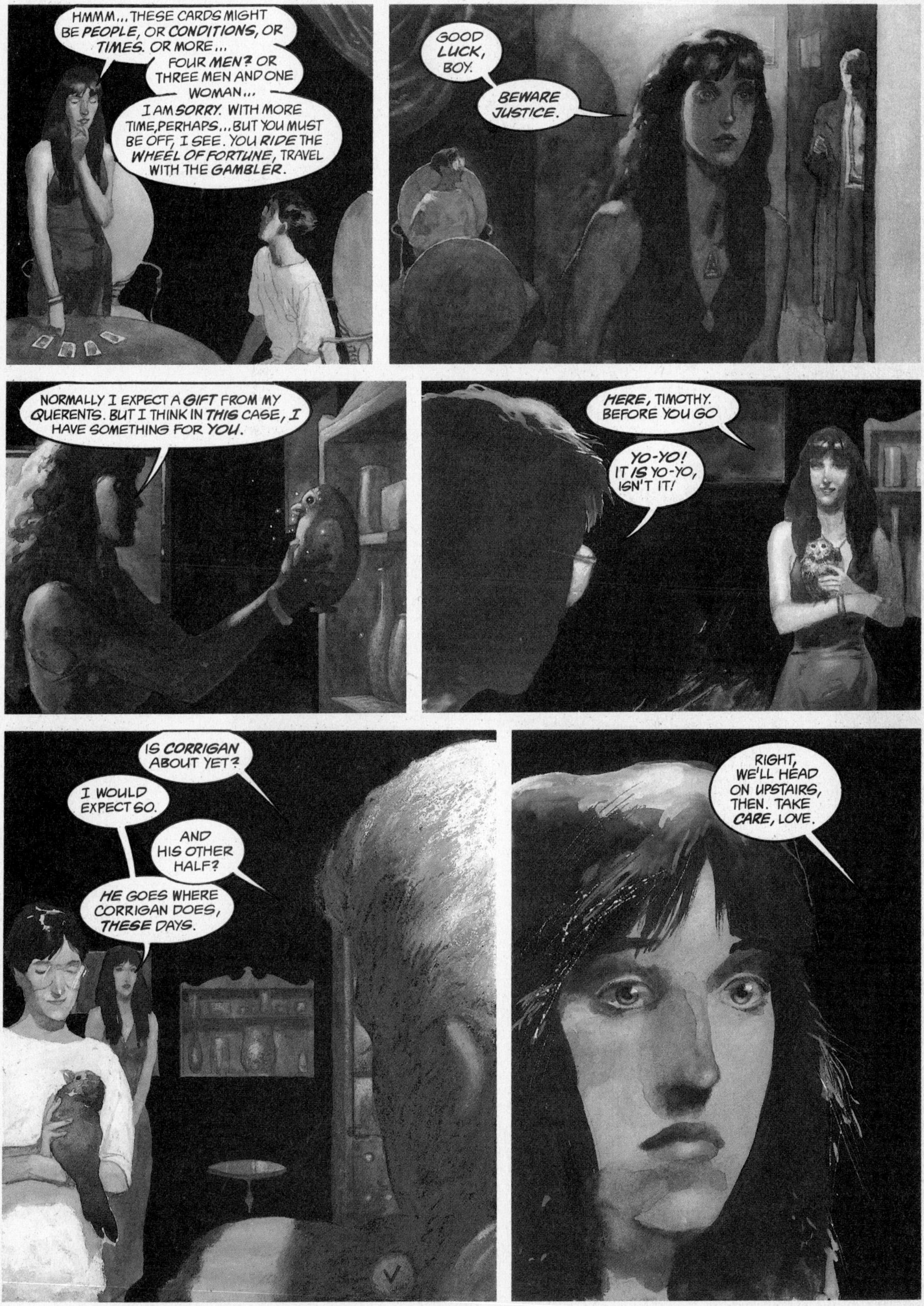
HMMM... THESE CARDS MIGHT BE PEOPLE, OR CONDITIONS, OR TIMES. OR MORE...
FOUR MEN? OR THREE MEN AND ONE WOMAN...
I AM SORRY. WITH MORE TIME, PERHAPS... BUT YOU MUST BE OFF, I SEE. YOU RIDE THE WHEEL OF FORTUNE, TRAVEL WITH THE GAMBLER.
GOOD LUCK, BOY.
BEWARE JUSTICE.
NORMALLY I EXPECT A GIFT FROM MY QUERENTS. BUT I THINK IN THIS CASE, I HAVE SOMETHING FOR YOU.
HERE, TIMOTHY. BEFORE YOU GO
YO-YO! IT IS YO-YO, ISN'T IT!
IS CORRIGAN ABOUT YET?
I WOULD EXPECT SO.
AND HIS OTHER HALF?
HE GOES WHERE CORRIGAN DOES, THESE DAYS.
RIGHT, WE'LL HEAD ON UPSTAIRS, THEN. TAKE CARE, LOVE.

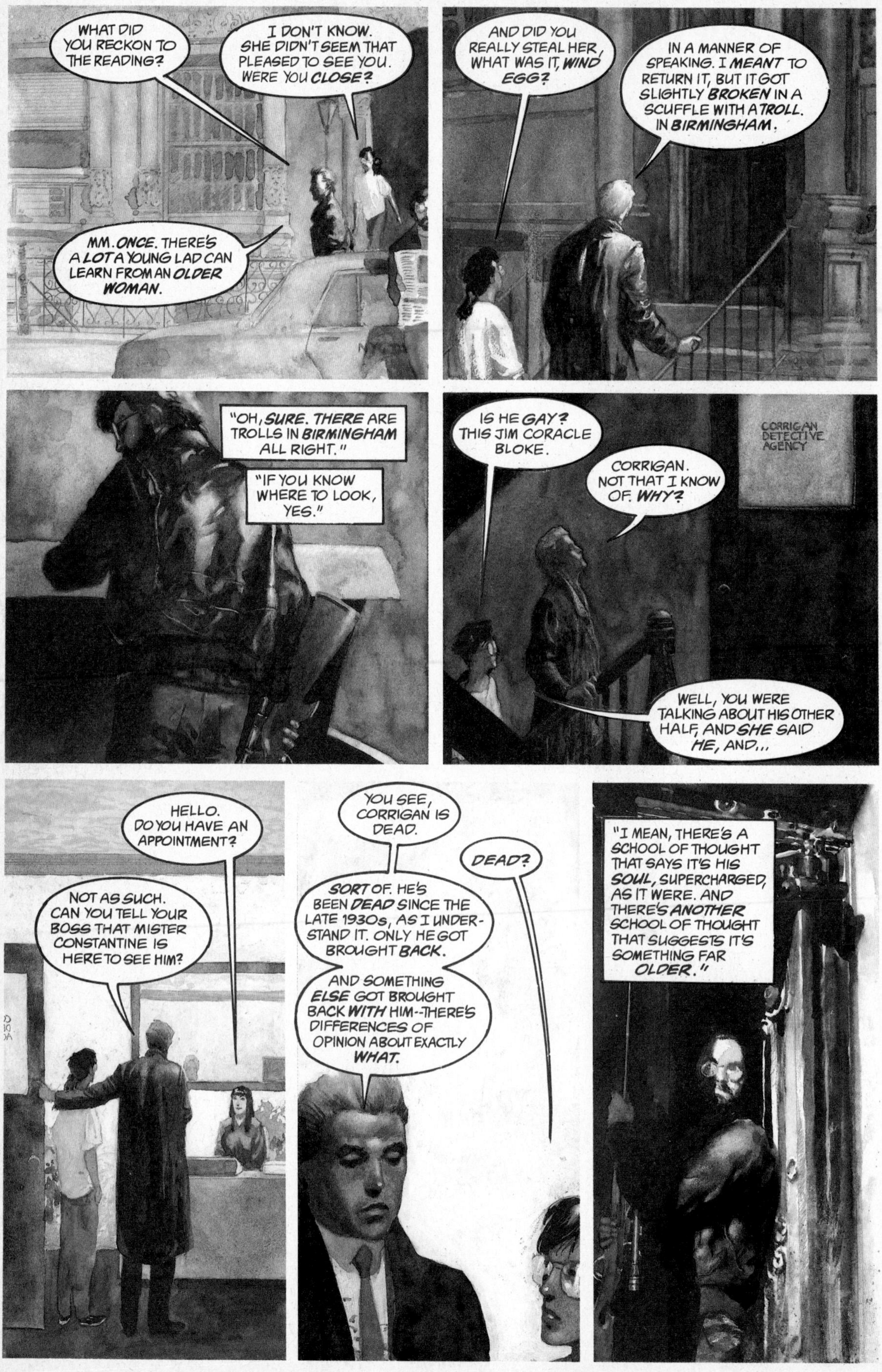
WHAT DID YOU RECKON TO THE READING?
I DON'T KNOW. SHE DIDN'T SEEM THAT PLEASED TO SEE YOU. WERE YOU CLOSE?
MM. ONCE. THERE'S A LOT A YOUNG LAD CAN LEARN FROM AN OLDER WOMAN.
AND DID YOU REALLY STEAL HER, WHAT WAS IT, WIND EGG?
IN A MANNER OF SPEAKING. I MEANT TO RETURN IT, BUT IT GOT SLIGHTLY BROKEN IN A SCUFFLE WITH A TROLL. IN BIRMINGHAM.
"OH, SURE. THERE ARE TROLLS IN BIRMINGHAM ALL RIGHT."
"IF YOU KNOW WHERE TO LOOK, YES."
CORRIGAN DETECTIVE AGENCY
IS HE GAY? THIS JIM CORACLE BLOKE.
CORRIGAN. NOT THAT I KNOW OF. WHY?
WELL, YOU WERE TALKING ABOUT HIS OTHER HALF, AND SHE SAID HE, AND...
HELLO. DO YOU HAVE AN APPOINTMENT?
NOT AS SUCH. CAN YOU TELL YOUR BOSS THAT MISTER CONSTANTINE IS HERE TO SEE HIM?
YOU SEE, CORRIGAN IS DEAD.
DEAD?
SORT OF. HE'S BEEN DEAD SINCE THE LATE 1930s, AS I UNDERSTAND IT. ONLY HE GOT BROUGHT BACK.
AND SOMETHING ELSE GOT BROUGHT BACK WITH HIM--THERE'S DIFFERENCES OF OPINION ABOUT EXACTLY WHAT.
"I MEAN, THERE'S A SCHOOL OF THOUGHT THAT SAYS IT'S HIS SOUL, SUPERCHARGED, AS IT WERE. AND THERE'S ANOTHER SCHOOL OF THOUGHT THAT SUGGESTS IT'S SOMETHING FAR OLDER."

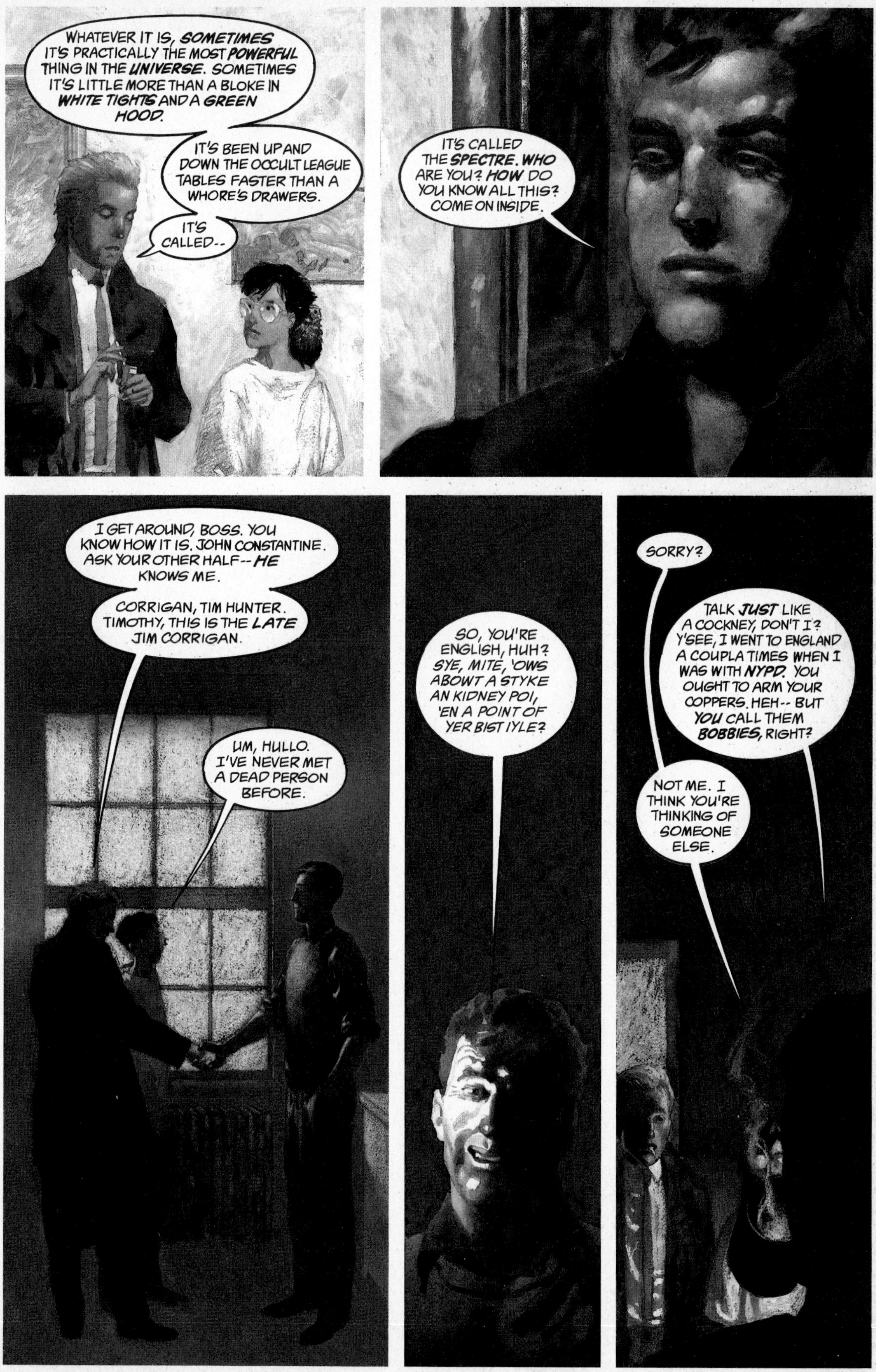
WHATEVER IT IS, SOMETIMES IT'S PRACTICALLY THE MOST POWERFUL THING IN THE UNIVERSE. SOMETIMES IT'S LITTLE MORE THAN A BLOKE IN WHITE TIGHTS AND A GREEN HOOD.
IT'S BEEN UP AND DOWN THE OCCULT LEAGUE TABLES FASTER THAN A WHORE'S DRAWERS.
IT'S CALLED--
IT'S CALLED THE SPECTRE. WHO ARE YOU? HOW DO YOU KNOW ALL THIS? COME ON INSIDE.
I GET AROUND, BOSS. YOU KNOW HOW IT IS. JOHN CONSTANTINE. ASK YOUR OTHER HALF--HE KNOWS ME.
CORRIGAN, TIM HUNTER. TIMOTHY, THIS IS THE LATE JIM CORRIGAN.
UM, HULLO. I'VE NEVER MET A DEAD PERSON BEFORE.
SO, YOU'RE ENGLISH, HUH? SYE, MITE, 'OWS ABOWT A STYKE AN KIDNEY POI, 'EN A POINT OF YER BIST IYLE?
SORRY?
TALK JUST LIKE A COCKNEY, DON'T I? Y'SEE, I WENT TO ENGLAND A COUPLA TIMES WHEN I WAS WITH NYPD. YOU OUGHT TO ARM YOUR COPPERS. HEH-- BUT YOU CALL THEM BOBBIES, RIGHT?
NOT ME. I THINK YOU'RE THINKING OF SOMEONE ELSE.

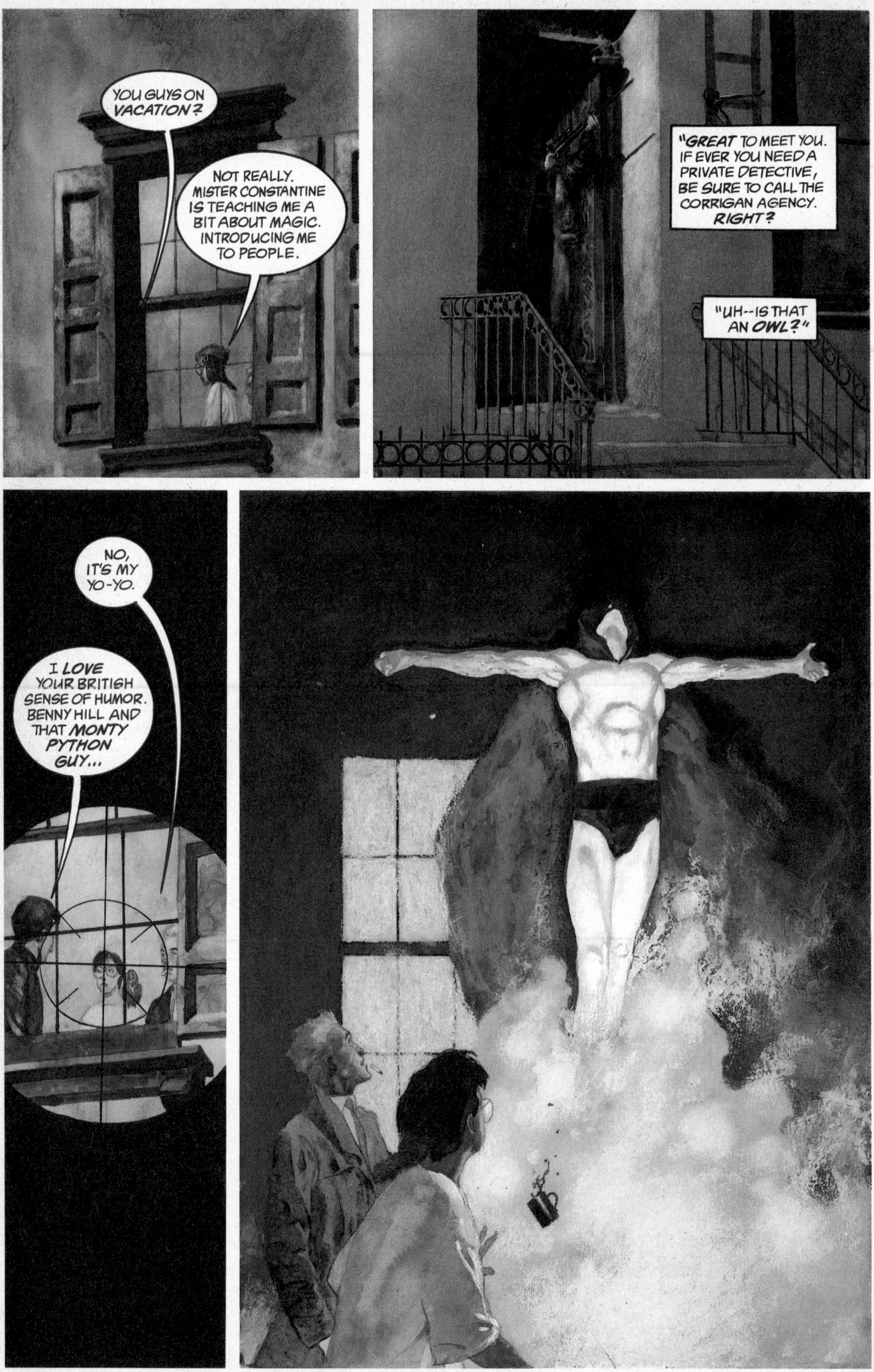

YOU GUYS ON VACATION?
NOT REALLY. MISTER CONSTANTINE IS TEACHING ME A BIT ABOUT MAGIC. INTRODUCING ME TO PEOPLE.
"GREAT TO MEET YOU. IF EVER YOU NEED A PRIVATE DETECTIVE, BE SURE TO CALL THE CORRIGAN AGENCY. RIGHT?
"UH--IS THAT AN OWL?"
NO, IT'S MY YO-YO.
I LOVE YOUR BRITISH SENSE OF HUMOR. BENNY HILL AND THAT MONTY PYTHON GUY...

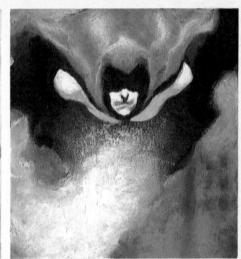

YOU ARE TIMOTHY HUNTER. YOU ARE JOHN CONSTANTINE.

WHAT WAS *THAT* ABOUT?

SOMEONE TRIED TO KILL YOU.

OH.

THE FORCES OF DARKNESS ARE ALWAYS AMONG US, CHILD. AND THE LIGHT CRIES OUT EVER FOR VENGEANCE.

THERE IS LIGHT AND THERE IS DARKNESS: AND I CANNOT REST UNTIL THE DARKNESS IS DESTROYED AND THE LIGHT SHINES INTO THE HEARTS OF ALL.

OH.

I FELL FROM GRACE. NOW I AM CONDEMNED TO WALK THE SHADOW WORLD. ONCE, IT WAS I WHO CAST THE SHADOW...

THEY WILL TRY TO KILL YOU, AND THEY WILL TRY TO SEDUCE YOU. STAY PURE, CHILD, STAY PURE.

UM. THANKS.

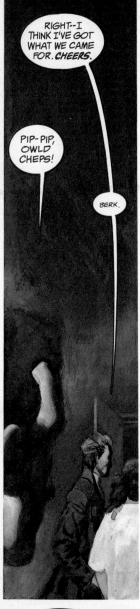

RIGHT--I THINK I'VE GOT WHAT WE CAME FOR. *CHEERS.*

PIP-PIP, OWLD CHEPS!

BERK.

UM ... JOHN? WASN'T HE OUR TAXI DRIVER?

WAS BEING THE OPERATIVE WORD. YEAH.

CHRIST--I FIGURED WE'D HAVE A GOOD *WEEK* BEFORE THEY GOT ON TO US.

BUGGER.

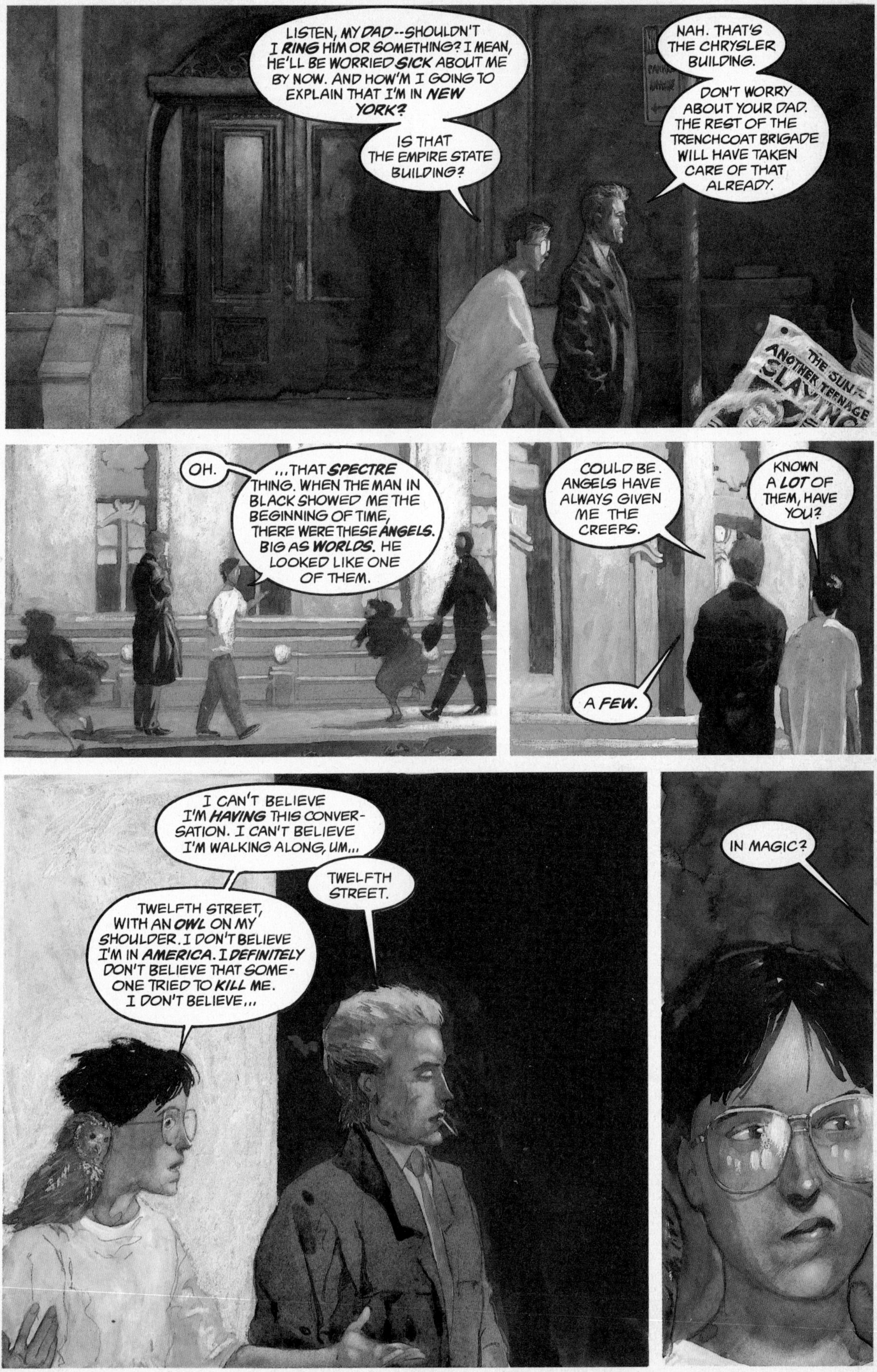
LISTEN, MY DAD--SHOULDN'T I RING HIM OR SOMETHING? I MEAN, HE'LL BE WORRIED SICK ABOUT ME BY NOW. AND HOW'M I GOING TO EXPLAIN THAT I'M IN NEW YORK?
IS THAT THE EMPIRE STATE BUILDING?
NAH. THAT'S THE CHRYSLER BUILDING.
DON'T WORRY ABOUT YOUR DAD. THE REST OF THE TRENCHCOAT BRIGADE WILL HAVE TAKEN CARE OF THAT ALREADY.
THE SUN
ANOTHER TEENAGE
SLAYING
OH.
...THAT SPECTRE THING. WHEN THE MAN IN BLACK SHOWED ME THE BEGINNING OF TIME, THERE WERE THESE ANGELS. BIG AS WORLDS. HE LOOKED LIKE ONE OF THEM.
COULD BE. ANGELS HAVE ALWAYS GIVEN ME THE CREEPS.
KNOWN A LOT OF THEM, HAVE YOU?
A FEW.
I CAN'T BELIEVE I'M HAVING THIS CONVERSATION. I CAN'T BELIEVE I'M WALKING ALONG, UM...
TWELFTH STREET.
TWELFTH STREET, WITH AN OWL ON MY SHOULDER. I DON'T BELIEVE I'M IN AMERICA. I DEFINITELY DON'T BELIEVE THAT SOMEONE TRIED TO KILL ME. I DON'T BELIEVE...
IN MAGIC?

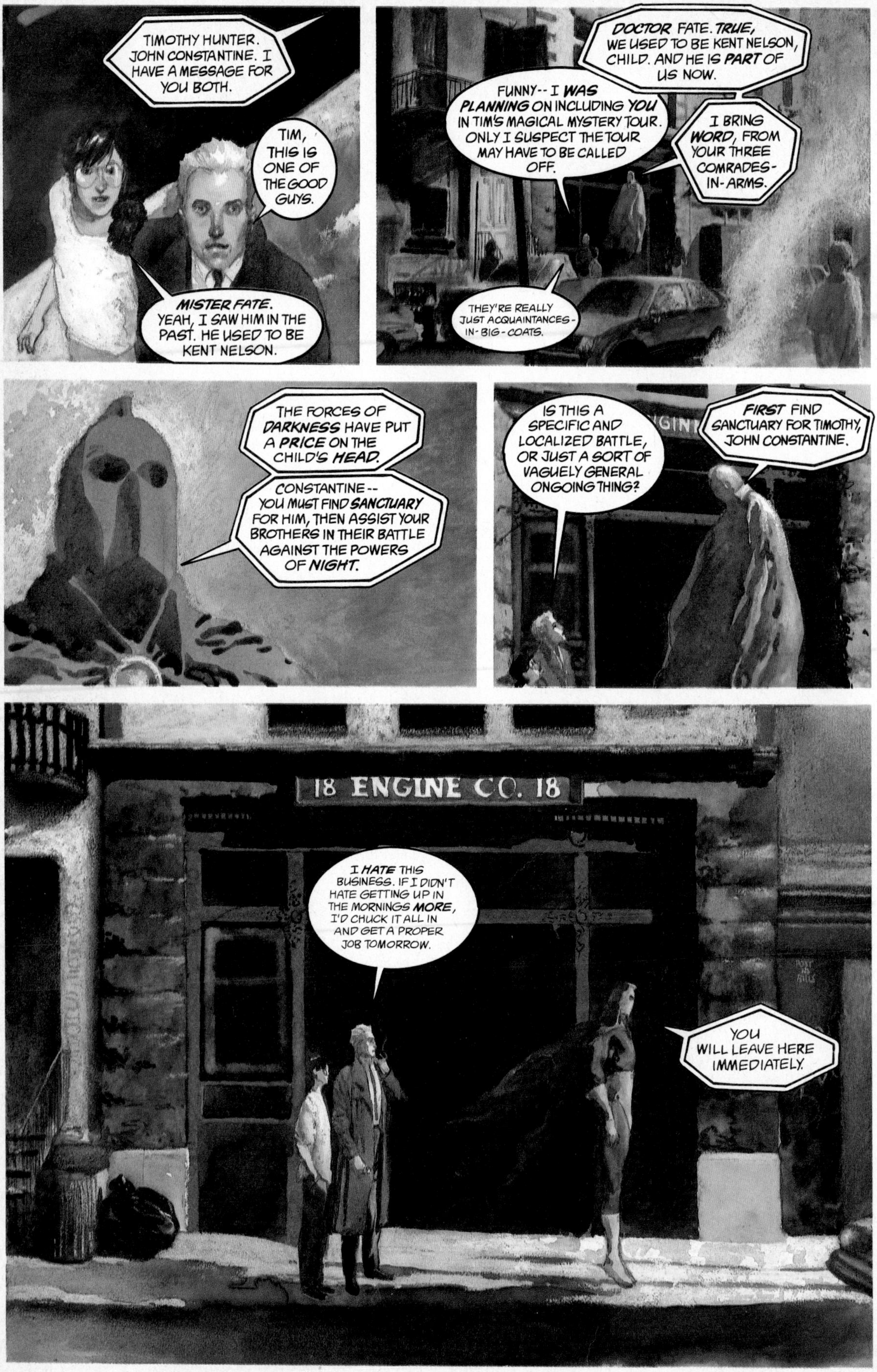

TIMOTHY HUNTER. JOHN CONSTANTINE. I HAVE A MESSAGE FOR YOU BOTH.
TIM, THIS IS ONE OF THE GOOD GUYS.
MISTER FATE. YEAH, I SAW HIM IN THE PAST. HE USED TO BE KENT NELSON.
DOCTOR FATE. TRUE, WE USED TO BE KENT NELSON, CHILD. AND HE IS PART OF US NOW.
FUNNY-- I WAS PLANNING ON INCLUDING YOU IN TIM'S MAGICAL MYSTERY TOUR. ONLY I SUSPECT THE TOUR MAY HAVE TO BE CALLED OFF.
I BRING WORD, FROM YOUR THREE COMRADES-IN-ARMS.
THEY'RE REALLY JUST ACQUAINTANCES-IN-BIG-COATS.
THE FORCES OF DARKNESS HAVE PUT A PRICE ON THE CHILD'S HEAD.
CONSTANTINE -- YOU MUST FIND SANCTUARY FOR HIM, THEN ASSIST YOUR BROTHERS IN THEIR BATTLE AGAINST THE POWERS OF NIGHT.
IS THIS A SPECIFIC AND LOCALIZED BATTLE, OR JUST A SORT OF VAGUELY GENERAL ONGOING THING?
FIRST FIND SANCTUARY FOR TIMOTHY, JOHN CONSTANTINE.
18 ENGINE CO. 18
I HATE THIS BUSINESS. IF I DIDN'T HATE GETTING UP IN THE MORNINGS MORE, I'D CHUCK IT ALL IN AND GET A PROPER JOB TOMORROW.
YOU WILL LEAVE HERE IMMEDIATELY.

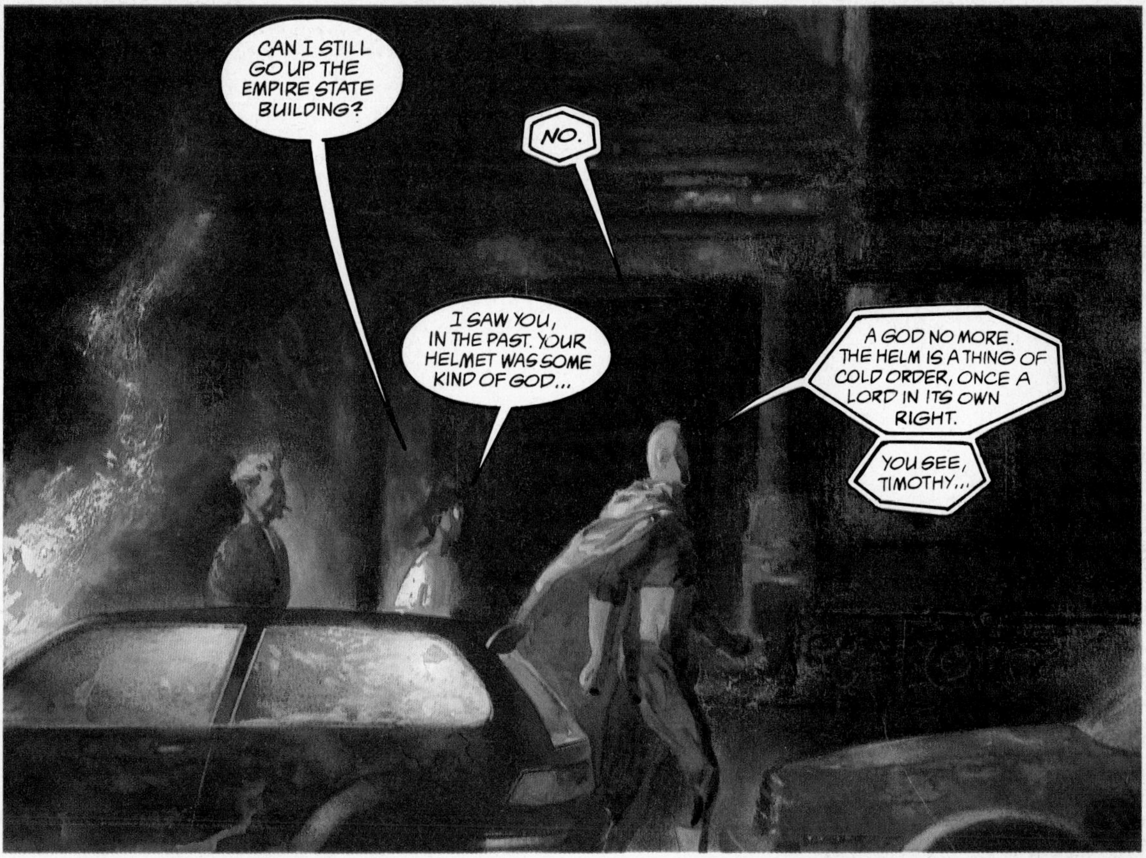
CAN I STILL GO UP THE EMPIRE STATE BUILDING?
NO.
I SAW YOU, IN THE PAST. YOUR HELMET WAS SOME KIND OF GOD...
A GOD NO MORE. THE HELM IS A THING OF COLD ORDER, ONCE A LORD IN ITS OWN RIGHT.
YOU SEE, TIMOTHY...

ALL THINGS ARE DIVIDED INTO THE TWIN FORCES OF ***ORDER*** AND ***CHAOS,*** FOREVER CONTENDING FOR DOMINANCE.

LIFE IS SOMETHING THAT OCCURS IN THE ***INTERFACE; NOT*** IN THE WRITHING DISCORD OF UTTER CHAOS, ***NOR*** IN THE FLATLINE PERFECTION OF PURE ORDER, BUT SOMEWHERE BETWEEN.

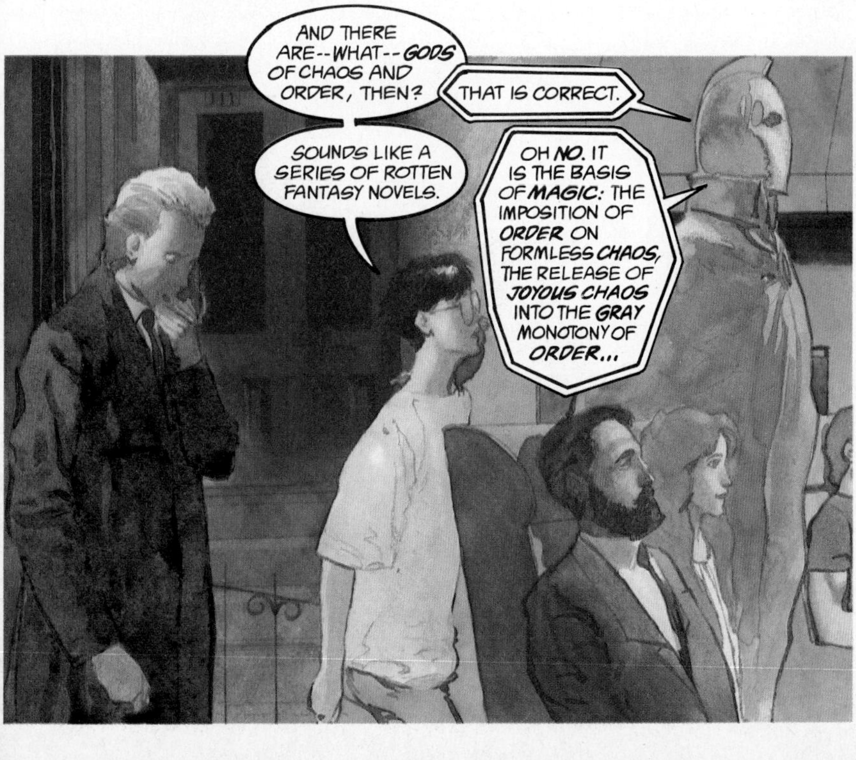
AND THERE ARE--WHAT--GODS OF CHAOS AND ORDER, THEN?
THAT IS CORRECT.
SOUNDS LIKE A SERIES OF ROTTEN FANTASY NOVELS.
OH NO. IT IS THE BASIS OF MAGIC: THE IMPOSITION OF ORDER ON FORMLESS CHAOS, THE RELEASE OF JOYOUS CHAOS INTO THE GRAY MONOTONY OF ORDER...

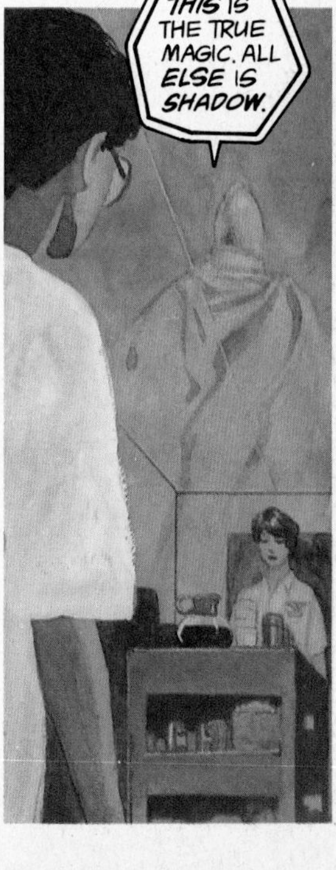
THIS IS THE TRUE MAGIC. ALL ELSE IS SHADOW.

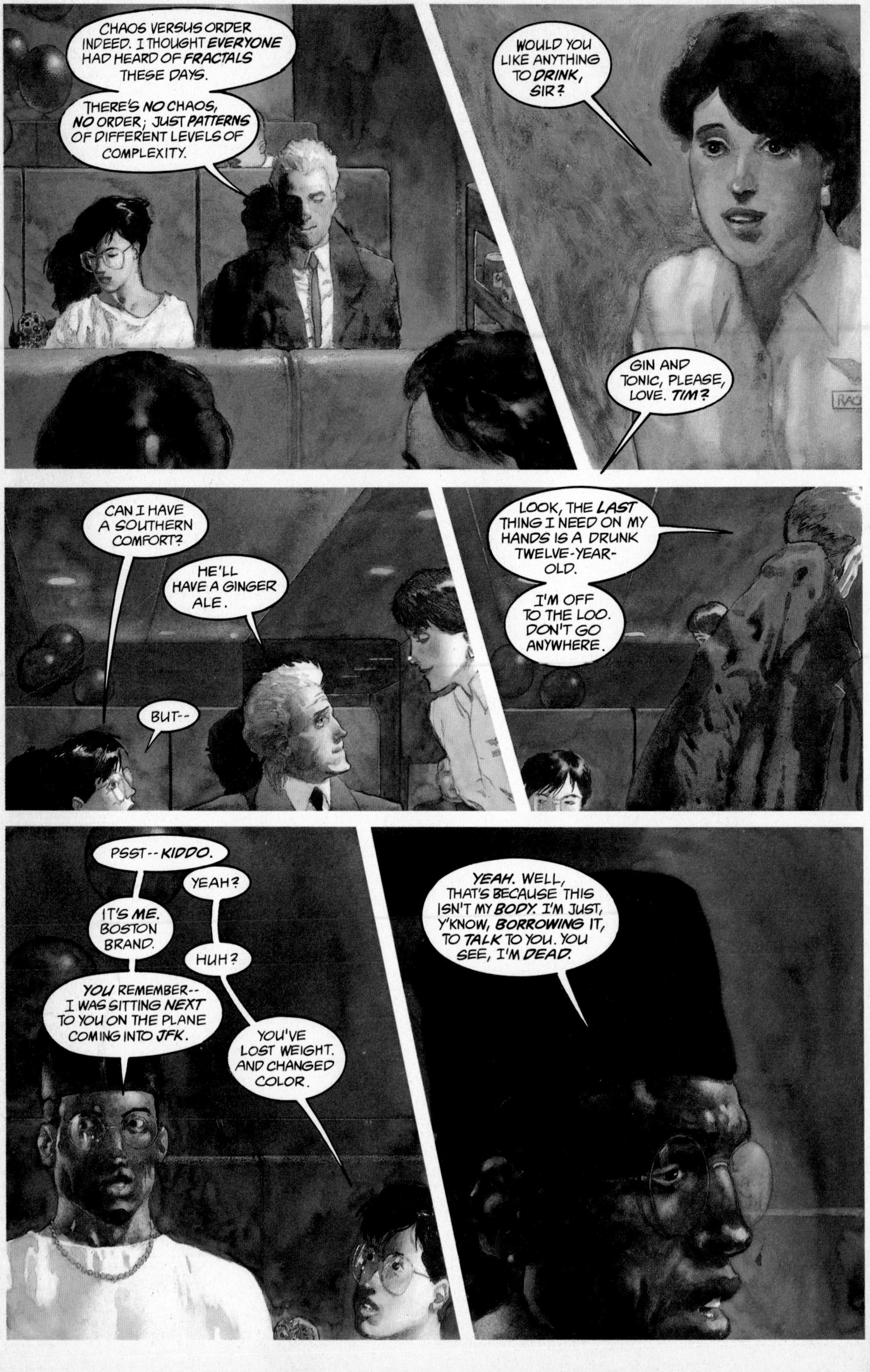
CHAOS VERSUS ORDER INDEED. I THOUGHT EVERYONE HAD HEARD OF FRACTALS THESE DAYS.
THERE'S NO CHAOS, NO ORDER; JUST PATTERNS OF DIFFERENT LEVELS OF COMPLEXITY.
WOULD YOU LIKE ANYTHING TO DRINK, SIR?
GIN AND TONIC, PLEASE, LOVE. TIM?
CAN I HAVE A SOUTHERN COMFORT?
HE'LL HAVE A GINGER ALE.
BUT--
LOOK, THE LAST THING I NEED ON MY HANDS IS A DRUNK TWELVE-YEAR-OLD.
I'M OFF TO THE LOO. DON'T GO ANYWHERE.
PSST--KIDDO.
YEAH?
IT'S ME. BOSTON BRAND.
HUH?
YOU REMEMBER-- I WAS SITTING NEXT TO YOU ON THE PLANE COMING INTO JFK.
YOU'VE LOST WEIGHT. AND CHANGED COLOR.
YEAH. WELL, THAT'S BECAUSE THIS ISN'T MY BODY. I'M JUST, Y'KNOW, BORROWING IT, TO TALK TO YOU. YOU SEE, I'M DEAD.

WHAT'S SO FUNNY?

WELL, EARLIER TODAY I WAS SAYING THAT I'D NEVER *MET* A DEAD PERSON BEFORE, AND NOW I'VE MET *TWO* IN A DAY.

THREE, IF YOU COUNT THE TAXI DRIVER, ONLY *HE* STOPPED *TALKING* WHEN HE DIED.

THEY SAY THE THIRD TIME'S THE CHARM.

SO WHAT DO YOU MAKE OF *CONSTANTINE?*

HE'S ALL RIGHT, I SPOSE -- EASIER TO TALK TO THAN THE OTHER THREE. ONLY THING I CAN'T FIGURE OUT IS HOW WE GET FROM *PLACE TO PLACE...*

THAT ONE'S EASY, *KIDDO.* HE'S RIDING THE *SYNCHRONICITY FREEWAY,* AND SO EVERYTHING JUST FALLS INTO PLACE; *TIME, MOVEMENT,* EVEN *DISTANCE* JUST SIT UP AND BEG FOR HIM.

YOU'RE HAVING AN *ADVENTURE, KIDDO.* IF YOU SURVIVE IT, IT'LL BE *FUN.*

I'LL DO WHAT *I* CAN.

ANYWAY, I'VE BEEN TRYING TO TELL YOU SOMETHING *IMPORTANT.* LISTEN --

MORNING STAR

BOY NUMBER 8'S BODY FOUND IN SEWER

WHO'S YOUR FRIEND?

UM, THIS IS BOSTON BRAND.

BRAND? NAH. MY NAME'S *MATTHESON.* WHOA -- I FEEL SORTA *DIZZY...*

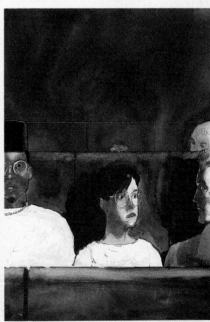

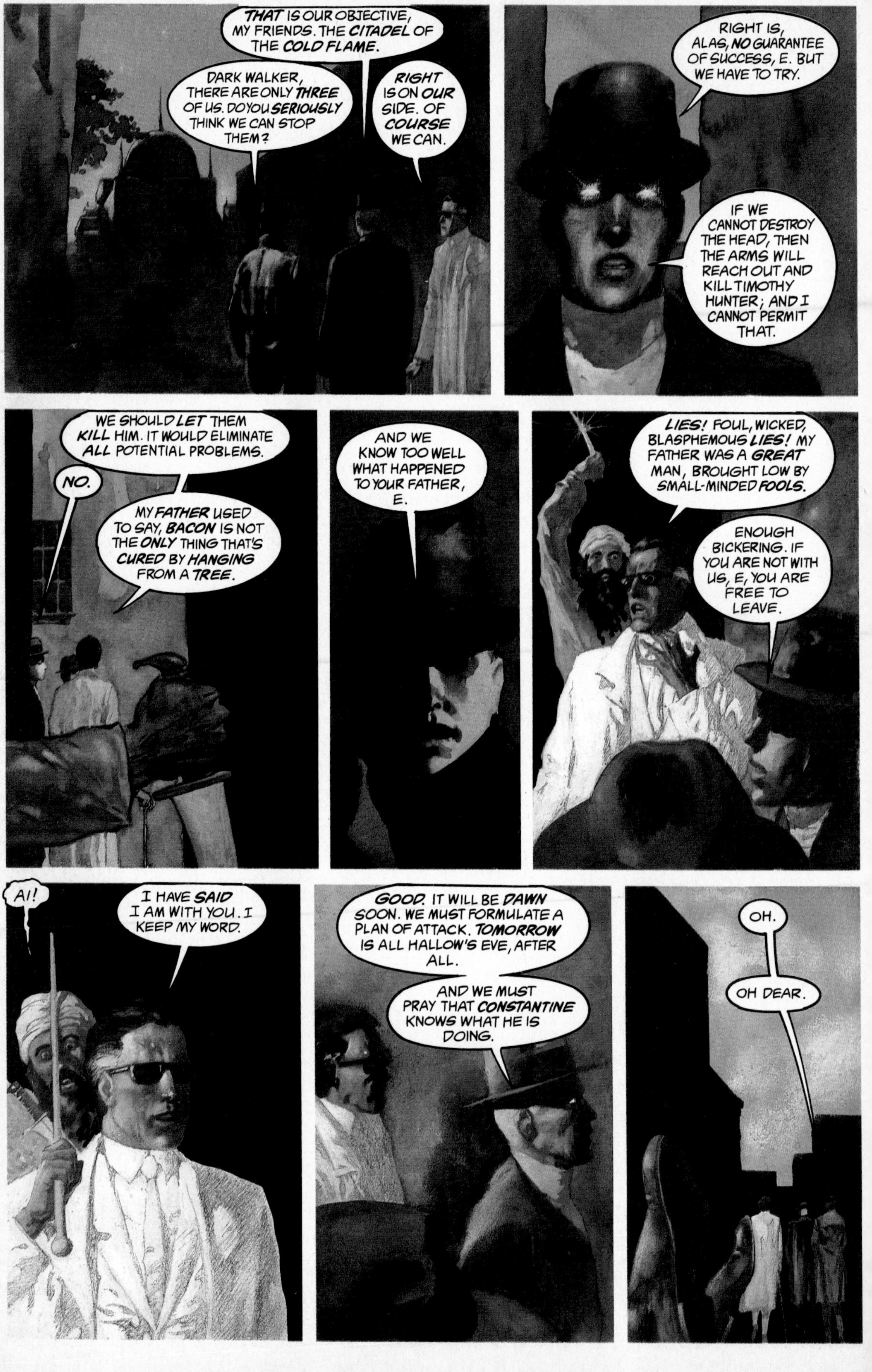
THAT IS OUR OBJECTIVE, MY FRIENDS. THE CITADEL OF THE COLD FLAME.
DARK WALKER, THERE ARE ONLY THREE OF US. DO YOU SERIOUSLY THINK WE CAN STOP THEM?
RIGHT IS ON OUR SIDE. OF COURSE WE CAN.
RIGHT IS, ALAS, NO GUARANTEE OF SUCCESS, E. BUT WE HAVE TO TRY.
IF WE CANNOT DESTROY THE HEAD, THEN THE ARMS WILL REACH OUT AND KILL TIMOTHY HUNTER; AND I CANNOT PERMIT THAT.
WE SHOULD LET THEM KILL HIM. IT WOULD ELIMINATE ALL POTENTIAL PROBLEMS.
NO.
MY FATHER USED TO SAY, BACON IS NOT THE ONLY THING THAT'S CURED BY HANGING FROM A TREE.
AND WE KNOW TOO WELL WHAT HAPPENED TO YOUR FATHER, E.
LIES! FOUL, WICKED, BLASPHEMOUS LIES! MY FATHER WAS A GREAT MAN, BROUGHT LOW BY SMALL-MINDED FOOLS.
ENOUGH BICKERING. IF YOU ARE NOT WITH US, E, YOU ARE FREE TO LEAVE.
AI!
I HAVE SAID I AM WITH YOU. I KEEP MY WORD.
GOOD. IT WILL BE DAWN SOON. WE MUST FORMULATE A PLAN OF ATTACK. TOMORROW IS ALL HALLOW'S EVE, AFTER ALL.
AND WE MUST PRAY THAT CONSTANTINE KNOWS WHAT HE IS DOING.
OH.
OH DEAR.

YOU'D NEVER BELIEVE *THIS* WAS THE POWER HUB OF AMERICA.

POSH AREA.

YOU SAID IT. FAT CATS AND POWER BROKERS.

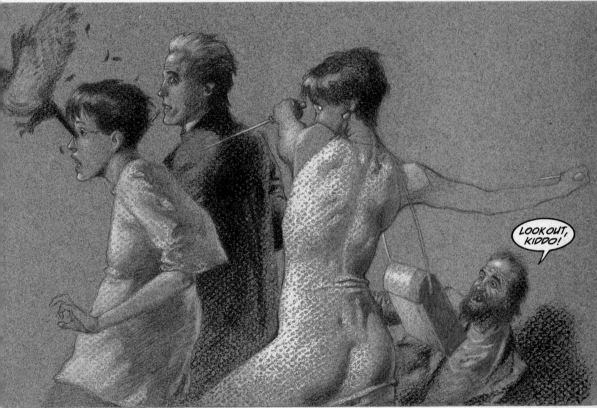

LOOK OUT, KIDDO!

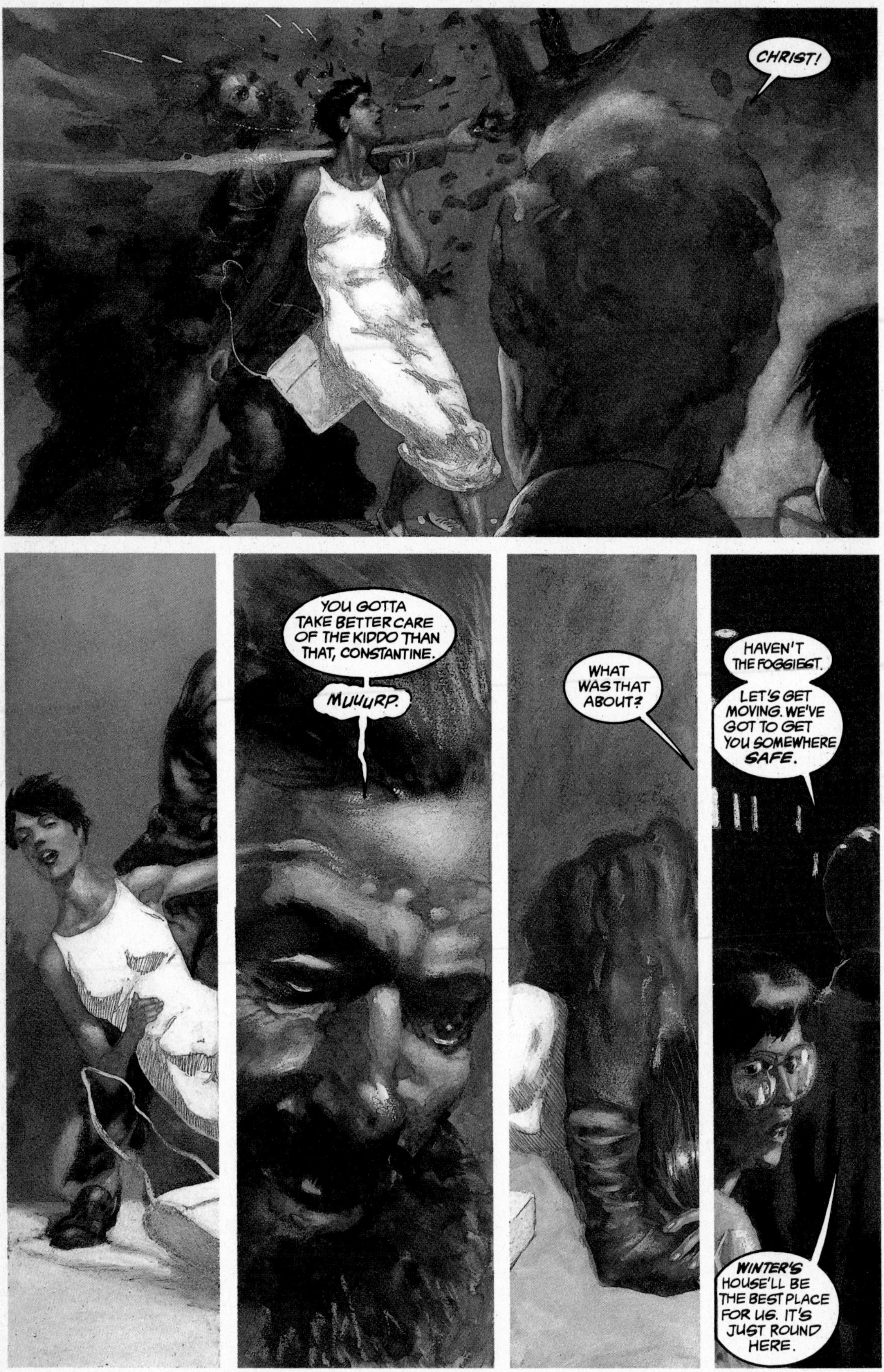
CHRIST!
YOU GOTTA TAKE BETTER CARE OF THE KIDDO THAN THAT, CONSTANTINE.
MUUURP.
WHAT WAS THAT ABOUT?
HAVEN'T THE FOGGIEST.
LET'S GET MOVING. WE'VE GOT TO GET YOU SOMEWHERE SAFE.
WINTER'S HOUSE'LL BE THE BEST PLACE FOR US. IT'S JUST ROUND HERE.

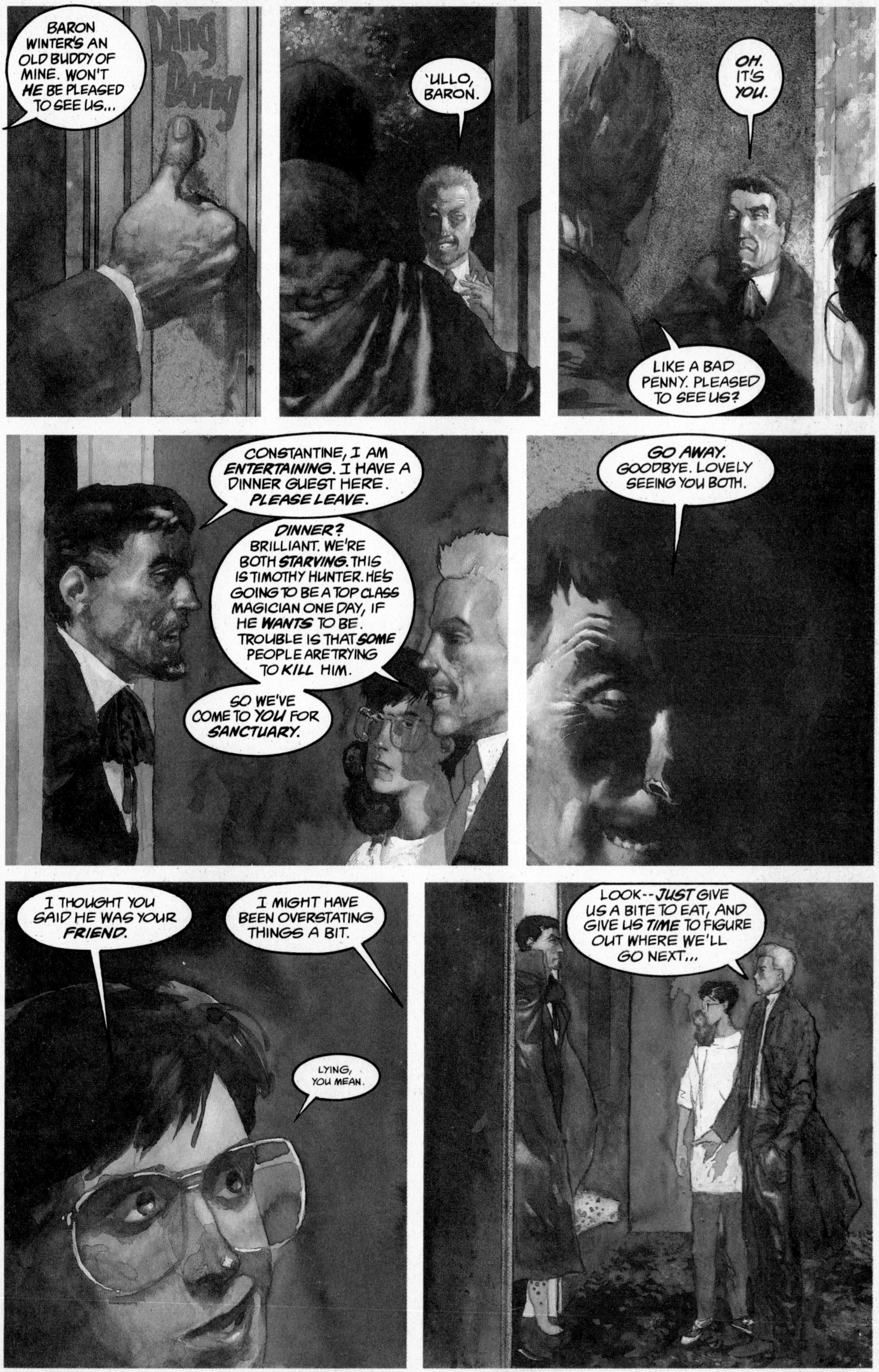
Ding Dong
BARON WINTER'S AN OLD BUDDY OF MINE. WON'T HE BE PLEASED TO SEE US...
'ULLO, BARON.
OH. IT'S YOU.
LIKE A BAD PENNY. PLEASED TO SEE US?
CONSTANTINE, I AM ENTERTAINING. I HAVE A DINNER GUEST HERE. PLEASE LEAVE.
DINNER? BRILLIANT. WE'RE BOTH STARVING. THIS IS TIMOTHY HUNTER. HE'S GOING TO BE A TOP CLASS MAGICIAN ONE DAY, IF HE WANTS TO BE. TROUBLE IS THAT SOME PEOPLE ARE TRYING TO KILL HIM.
SO WE'VE COME TO YOU FOR SANCTUARY.
GO AWAY. GOODBYE. LOVELY SEEING YOU BOTH.
I THOUGHT YOU SAID HE WAS YOUR FRIEND.
I MIGHT HAVE BEEN OVERSTATING THINGS A BIT.
LYING, YOU MEAN.
LOOK--JUST GIVE US A BITE TO EAT, AND GIVE US TIME TO FIGURE OUT WHERE WE'LL GO NEXT...

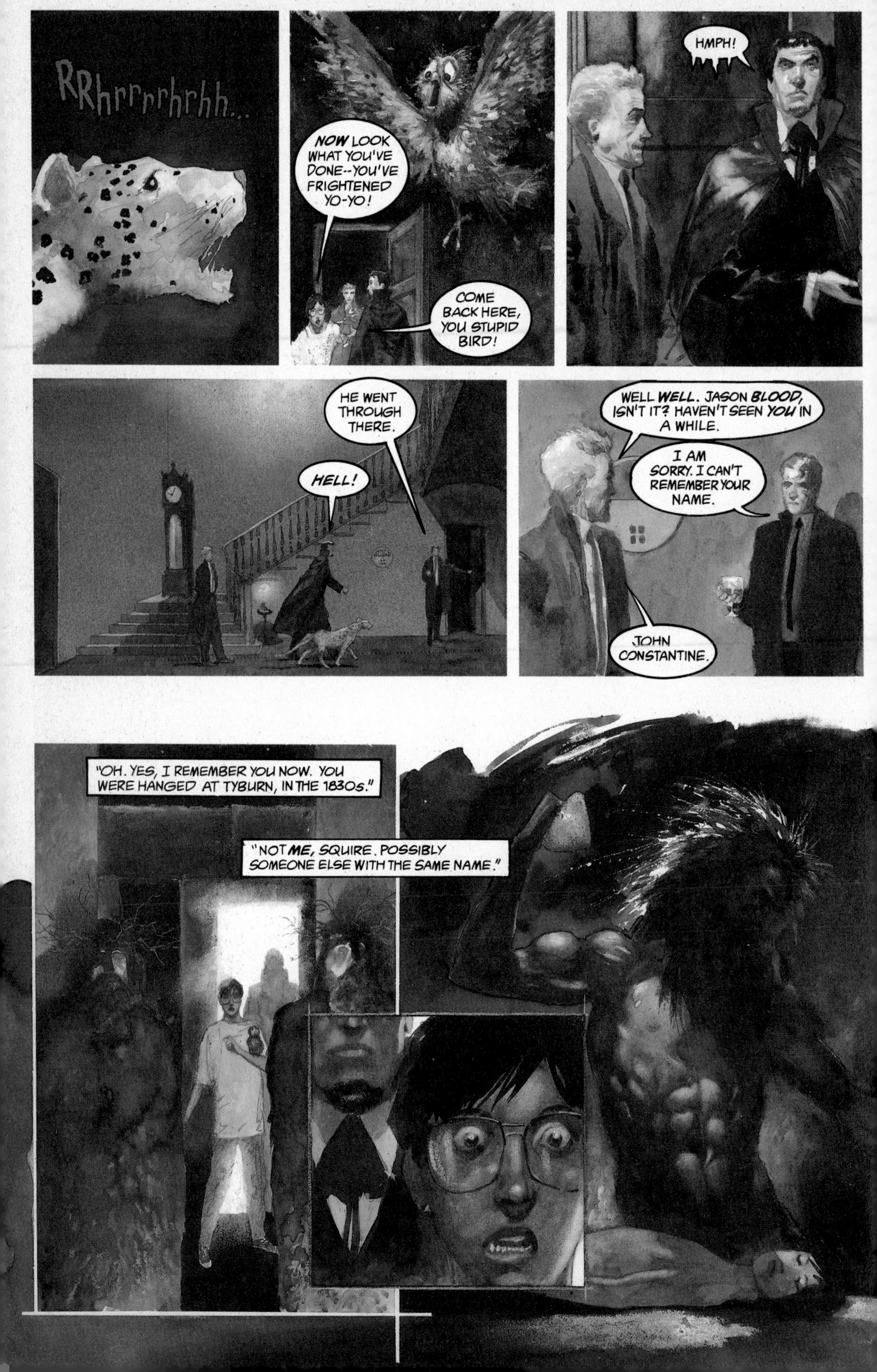
RRhrrrrhrhh...
NOW LOOK WHAT YOU'VE DONE--YOU'VE FRIGHTENED YO-YO!
COME BACK HERE, YOU STUPID BIRD!
HMPH!
HE WENT THROUGH THERE.
HELL!
WELL WELL. JASON BLOOD, ISN'T IT? HAVEN'T SEEN YOU IN A WHILE.
I AM SORRY. I CAN'T REMEMBER YOUR NAME.
JOHN CONSTANTINE.
"OH. YES, I REMEMBER YOU NOW. YOU WERE HANGED AT TYBURN, IN THE 1830s."
"NOT ME, SQUIRE. POSSIBLY SOMEONE ELSE WITH THE SAME NAME."

VERY LIKELY.

WE MET WHEN YOU WERE WORKING AS AN OCCULTIST IN GOTHAM, ABOUT TEN YEARS BACK. REMEMBER? I SAW YOU ABOUT THAT LUPUS BUSINESS.

NO.

SUIT YOURSELF.

...BUT IT WAS NIGHTTIME ALREADY! AND -- I MEAN THOSE PEOPLE...

I HAVE NO IDEA WHAT YOU'RE TALKING ABOUT!

ANOTHER CREATURE OF THE NIGHT, EH? WELL, WE ARE WELL-MATCHED. MY NAME IS JASON BLOOD.

HANG ON. JASON... "JASON"? YOU WERE WITH MERLIN. YOU'VE GOT THE SAME STREAKY HAIRSTYLE.

WE'VE MET BEFORE?

NOT REALLY.

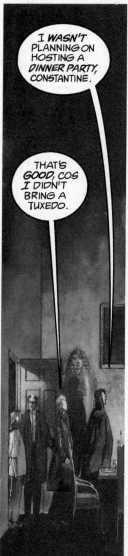

I WASN'T PLANNING ON HOSTING A DINNER PARTY, CONSTANTINE.

THAT'S GOOD, COS I DIDN'T BRING A TUXEDO.

ARE YOU A REAL BARON?

SOMETIMES.

AH.

YOU WILL EAT AND LEAVE, DO YOU UNDERSTAND ME? YOU ARE NOT WELCOME HERE, CONSTANTINE.

TELL ME, BARON. ARE YOU GETTING OUT MUCH? STILL PART OF THE WASHINGTON SOCIAL WHIRL?

HMPH. YOUR ATTEMPTS AT HUMOR ARE AS PITIFUL AS EVER.

YOU SEE, TIM, THE BARON DOESN'T GO OUT. NOT OUT THE FRONT DOOR, AT ANY RATE. NOT INTO THE HERE AND NOW.

OH.

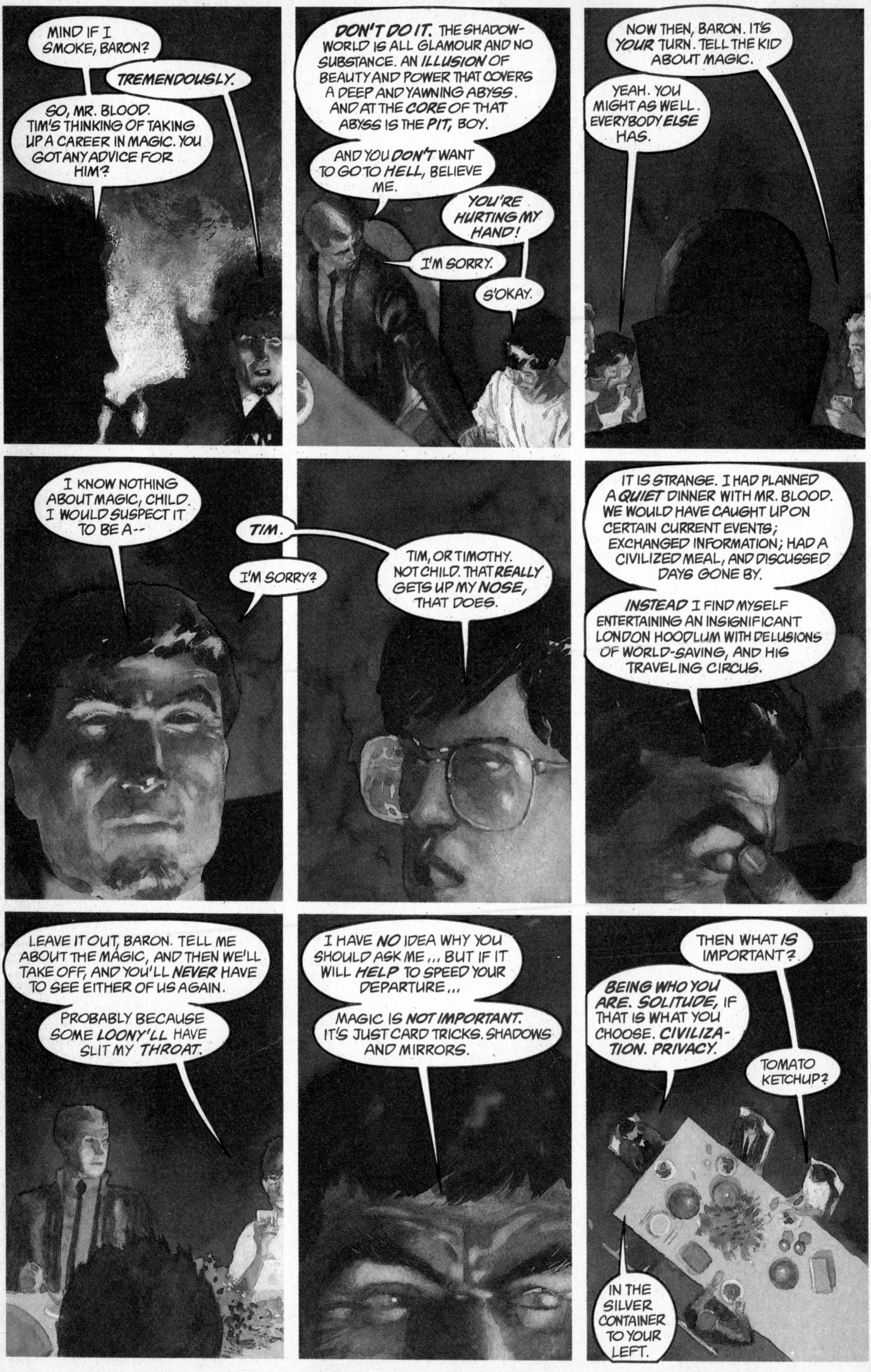
MIND IF I SMOKE, BARON?
TREMENDOUSLY.
SO, MR. BLOOD. TIM'S THINKING OF TAKING UP A CAREER IN MAGIC. YOU GOT ANY ADVICE FOR HIM?
DON'T DO IT. THE SHADOW-WORLD IS ALL GLAMOUR AND NO SUBSTANCE. AN ILLUSION OF BEAUTY AND POWER THAT COVERS A DEEP AND YAWNING ABYSS. AND AT THE CORE OF THAT ABYSS IS THE PIT, BOY.
AND YOU DON'T WANT TO GO TO HELL, BELIEVE ME.
YOU'RE HURTING MY HAND!
I'M SORRY.
S'OKAY.
NOW THEN, BARON. IT'S YOUR TURN. TELL THE KID ABOUT MAGIC.
YEAH. YOU MIGHT AS WELL. EVERYBODY ELSE HAS.
I KNOW NOTHING ABOUT MAGIC, CHILD. I WOULD SUSPECT IT TO BE A--
TIM.
I'M SORRY?
TIM, OR TIMOTHY. NOT CHILD. THAT REALLY GETS UP MY NOSE, THAT DOES.
IT IS STRANGE. I HAD PLANNED A QUIET DINNER WITH MR. BLOOD. WE WOULD HAVE CAUGHT UP ON CERTAIN CURRENT EVENTS; EXCHANGED INFORMATION; HAD A CIVILIZED MEAL, AND DISCUSSED DAYS GONE BY.
INSTEAD I FIND MYSELF ENTERTAINING AN INSIGNIFICANT LONDON HOODLUM WITH DELUSIONS OF WORLD-SAVING, AND HIS TRAVELING CIRCUS.
LEAVE IT OUT, BARON. TELL ME ABOUT THE MAGIC, AND THEN WE'LL TAKE OFF, AND YOU'LL NEVER HAVE TO SEE EITHER OF US AGAIN.
PROBABLY BECAUSE SOME LOONY'LL HAVE SLIT MY THROAT.
I HAVE NO IDEA WHY YOU SHOULD ASK ME... BUT IF IT WILL HELP TO SPEED YOUR DEPARTURE...
MAGIC IS NOT IMPORTANT. IT'S JUST CARD TRICKS. SHADOWS AND MIRRORS.
THEN WHAT IS IMPORTANT?
BEING WHO YOU ARE. SOLITUDE, IF THAT IS WHAT YOU CHOOSE. CIVILIZATION. PRIVACY.
TOMATO KETCHUP?
IN THE SILVER CONTAINER TO YOUR LEFT.

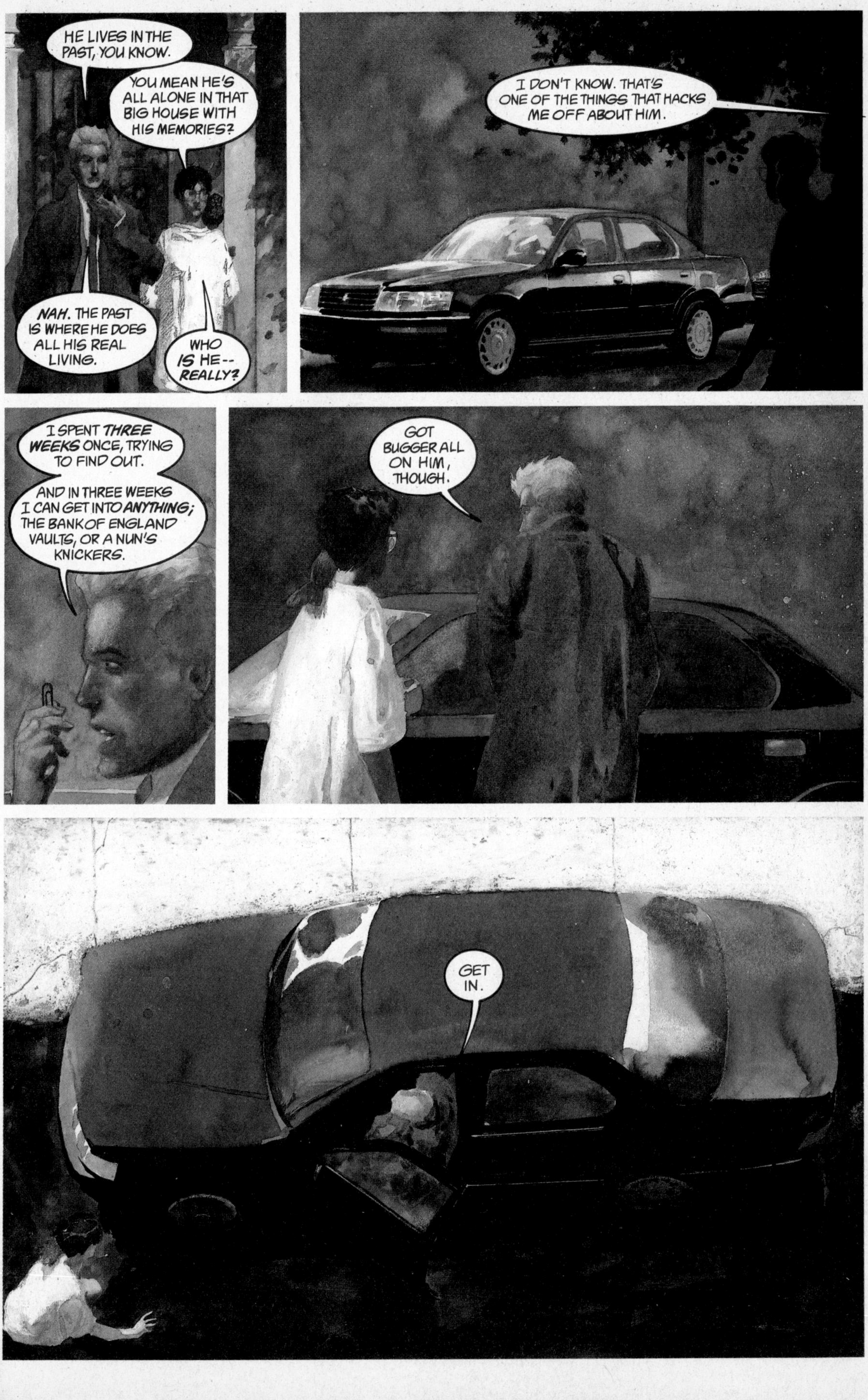

HE LIVES IN THE PAST, YOU KNOW.
YOU MEAN HE'S ALL ALONE IN THAT BIG HOUSE WITH HIS MEMORIES?
NAH. THE PAST IS WHERE HE DOES ALL HIS REAL LIVING.
WHO IS HE-- REALLY?
I DON'T KNOW. THAT'S ONE OF THE THINGS THAT HACKS ME OFF ABOUT HIM.
I SPENT THREE WEEKS ONCE, TRYING TO FIND OUT.
AND IN THREE WEEKS I CAN GET INTO ANYTHING; THE BANK OF ENGLAND VAULTS, OR A NUN'S KNICKERS.
GOT BUGGER ALL ON HIM, THOUGH.
GET IN.

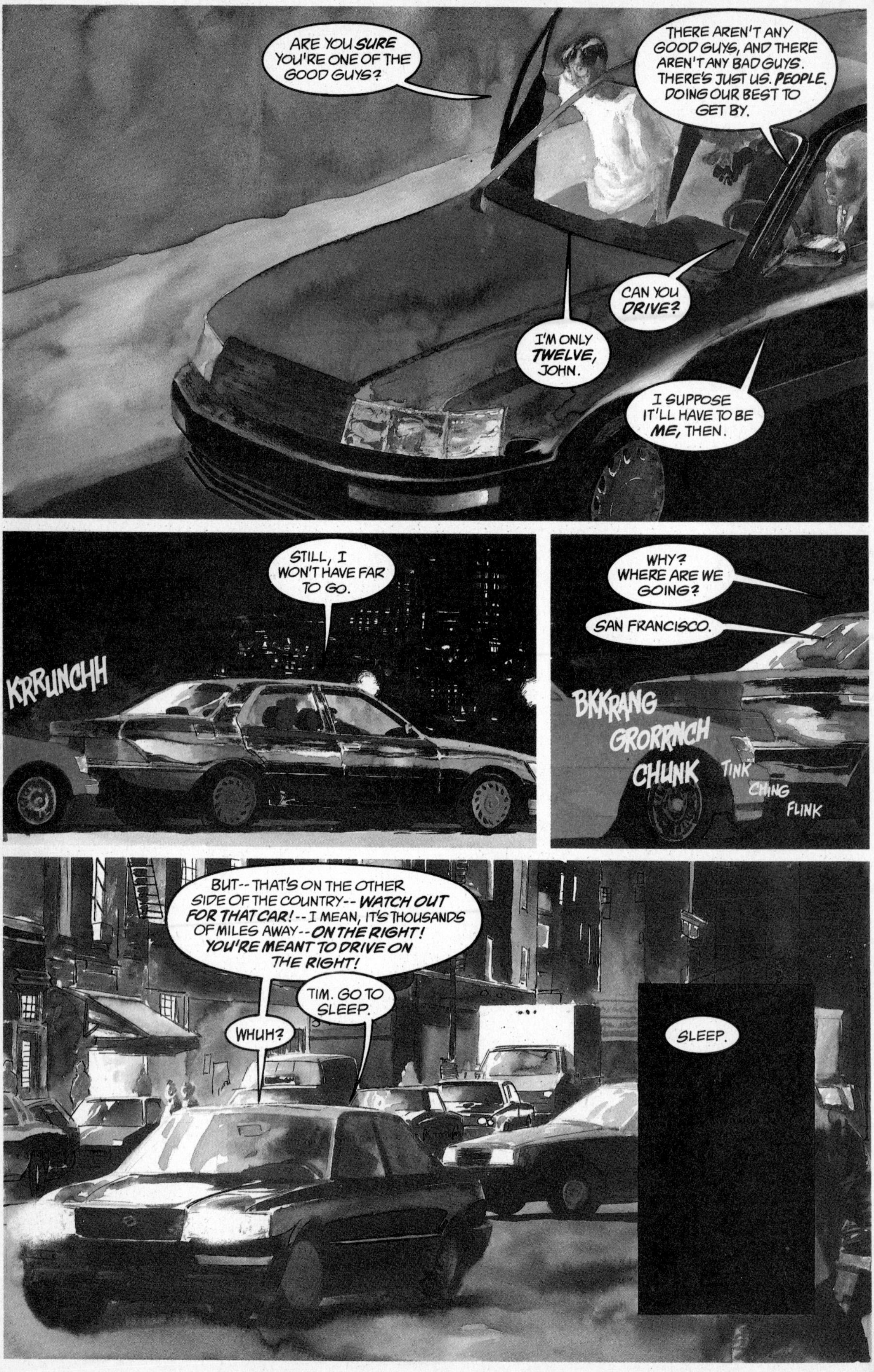
ARE YOU SURE YOU'RE ONE OF THE GOOD GUYS?
THERE AREN'T ANY GOOD GUYS, AND THERE AREN'T ANY BAD GUYS. THERE'S JUST US. PEOPLE. DOING OUR BEST TO GET BY.
CAN YOU DRIVE?
I'M ONLY TWELVE, JOHN.
I SUPPOSE IT'LL HAVE TO BE ME, THEN.
STILL, I WON'T HAVE FAR TO GO.
KRRUNCHH
WHY? WHERE ARE WE GOING?
SAN FRANCISCO.
BKKRANG
GRORRNCH
CHUNK
TINK
CHING
FLINK
BUT-- THAT'S ON THE OTHER SIDE OF THE COUNTRY-- WATCH OUT FOR THAT CAR! -- I MEAN, IT'S THOUSANDS OF MILES AWAY-- ON THE RIGHT! YOU'RE MEANT TO DRIVE ON THE RIGHT!
WHUH?
TIM. GO TO SLEEP.
SLEEP.

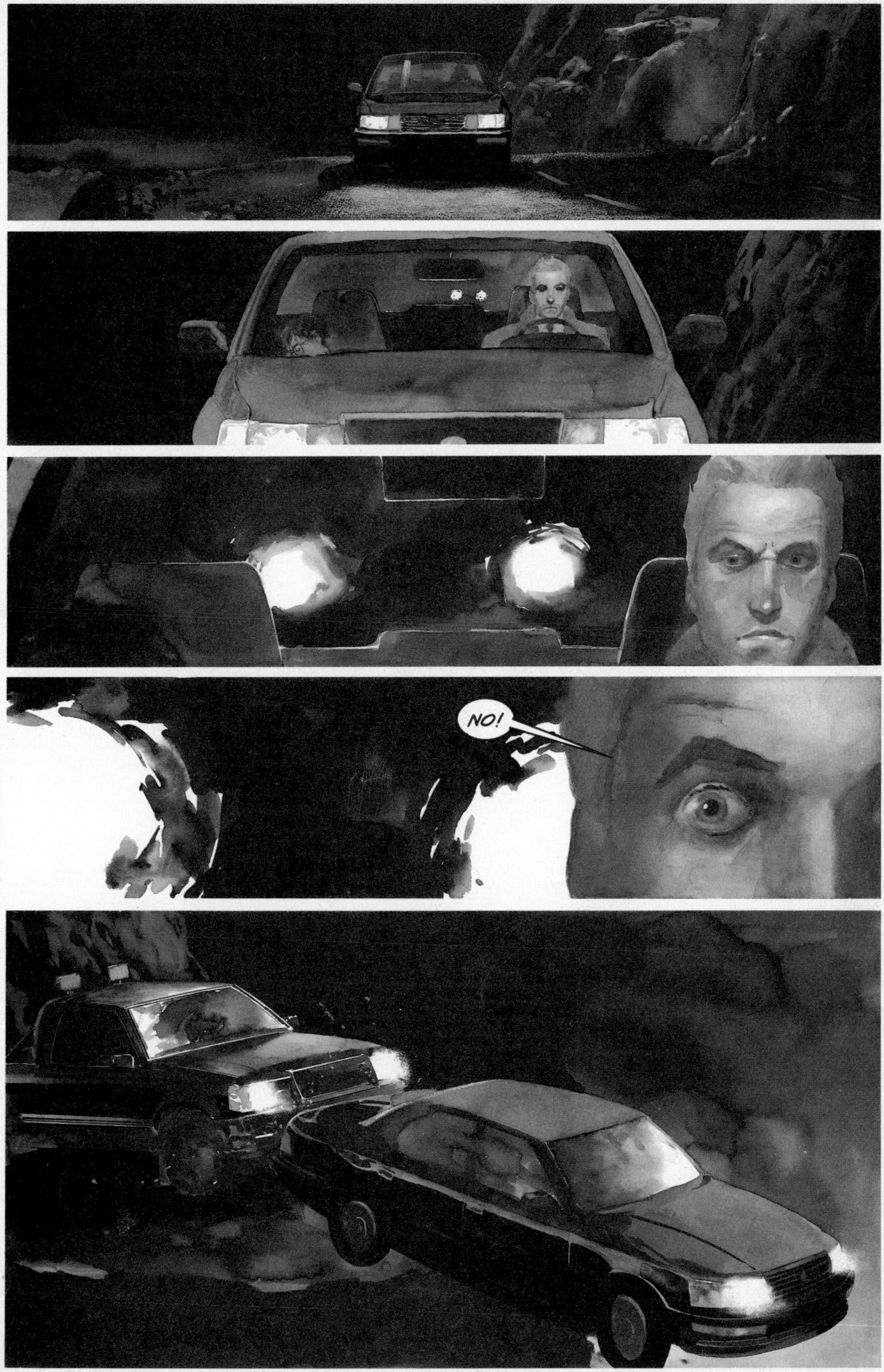
NO!

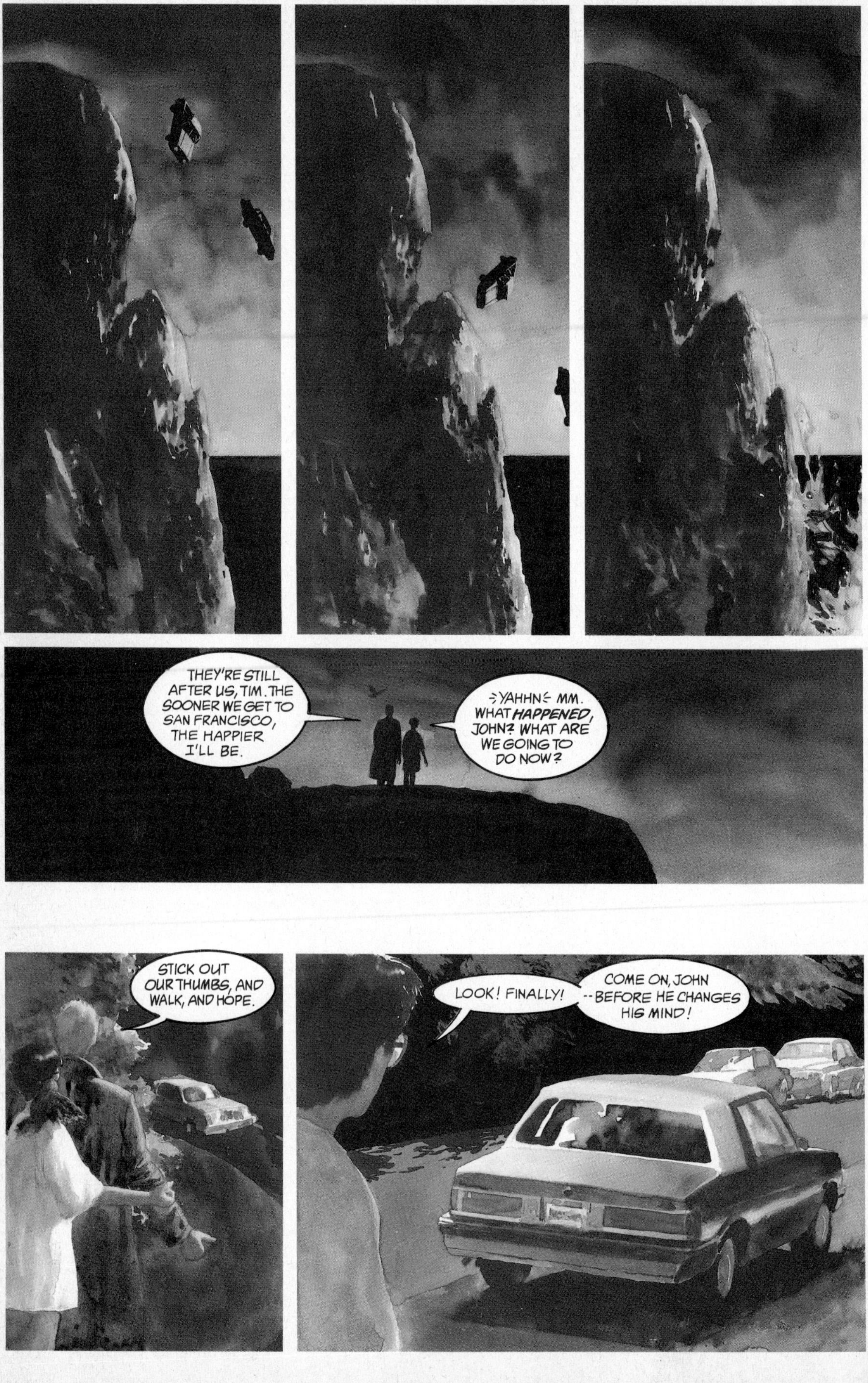
THEY'RE STILL AFTER US, TIM. THE SOONER WE GET TO SAN FRANCISCO, THE HAPPIER I'LL BE.
=YAHHN= MM. WHAT HAPPENED, JOHN? WHAT ARE WE GOING TO DO NOW?
STICK OUT OUR THUMBS, AND WALK, AND HOPE.
LOOK! FINALLY!
COME ON, JOHN --BEFORE HE CHANGES HIS MIND!

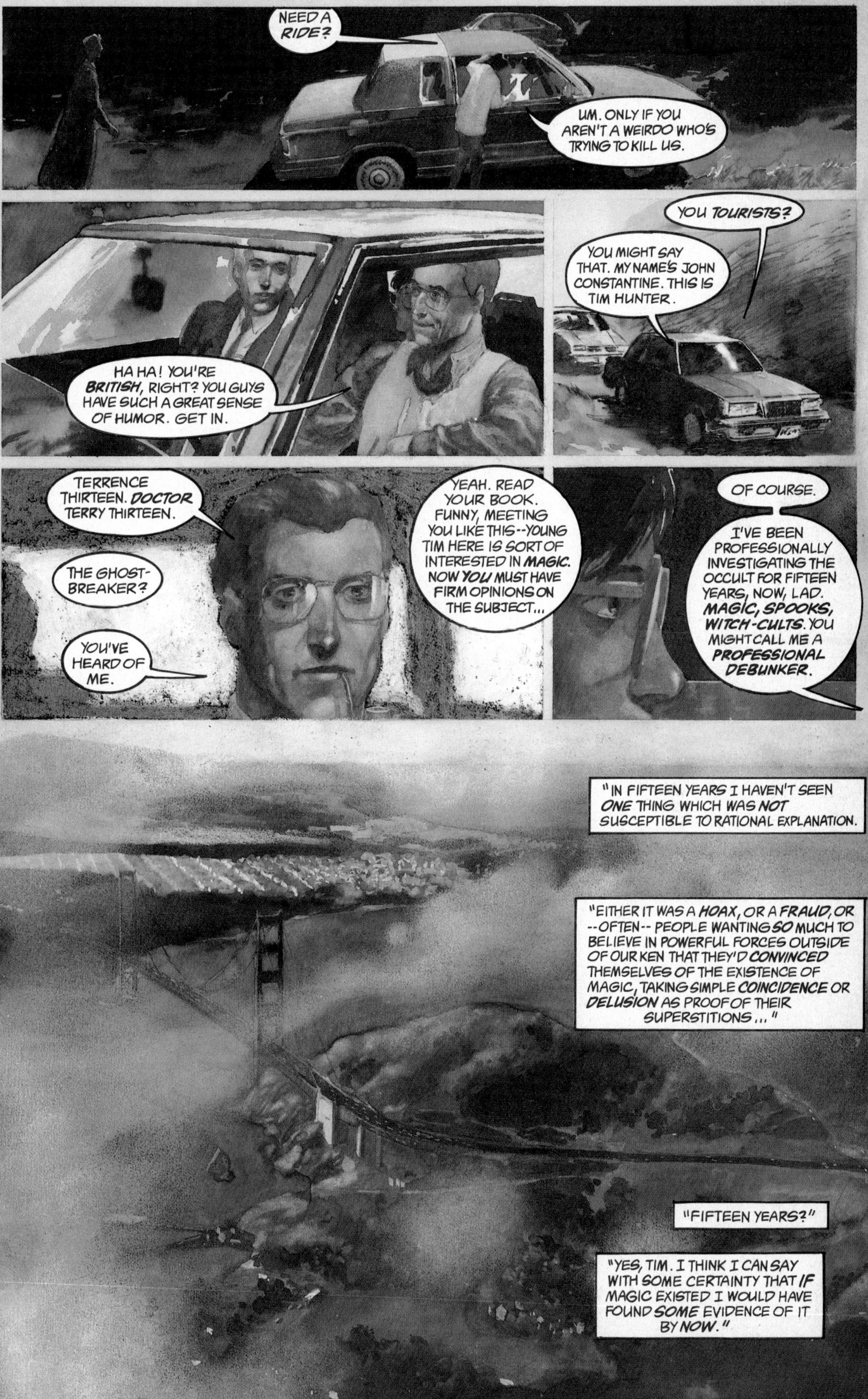
NEED A RIDE?
UM. ONLY IF YOU AREN'T A WEIRDO WHO'S TRYING TO KILL US.
HA HA! YOU'RE BRITISH, RIGHT? YOU GUYS HAVE SUCH A GREAT SENSE OF HUMOR. GET IN.
YOU TOURISTS?
YOU MIGHT SAY THAT. MY NAME'S JOHN CONSTANTINE. THIS IS TIM HUNTER.
TERRENCE THIRTEEN. DOCTOR TERRY THIRTEEN.
THE GHOST-BREAKER?
YOU'VE HEARD OF ME.
YEAH. READ YOUR BOOK. FUNNY, MEETING YOU LIKE THIS--YOUNG TIM HERE IS SORT OF INTERESTED IN MAGIC. NOW YOU MUST HAVE FIRM OPINIONS ON THE SUBJECT...
OF COURSE.
I'VE BEEN PROFESSIONALLY INVESTIGATING THE OCCULT FOR FIFTEEN YEARS, NOW, LAD. MAGIC, SPOOKS, WITCH-CULTS. YOU MIGHT CALL ME A PROFESSIONAL DEBUNKER.
"IN FIFTEEN YEARS I HAVEN'T SEEN ONE THING WHICH WAS NOT SUSCEPTIBLE TO RATIONAL EXPLANATION.
"EITHER IT WAS A HOAX, OR A FRAUD, OR --OFTEN-- PEOPLE WANTING SO MUCH TO BELIEVE IN POWERFUL FORCES OUTSIDE OF OUR KEN THAT THEY'D CONVINCED THEMSELVES OF THE EXISTENCE OF MAGIC, TAKING SIMPLE COINCIDENCE OR DELUSION AS PROOF OF THEIR SUPERSTITIONS..."
"FIFTEEN YEARS?"
"YES, TIM. I THINK I CAN SAY WITH SOME CERTAINTY THAT IF MAGIC EXISTED I WOULD HAVE FOUND SOME EVIDENCE OF IT BY NOW."

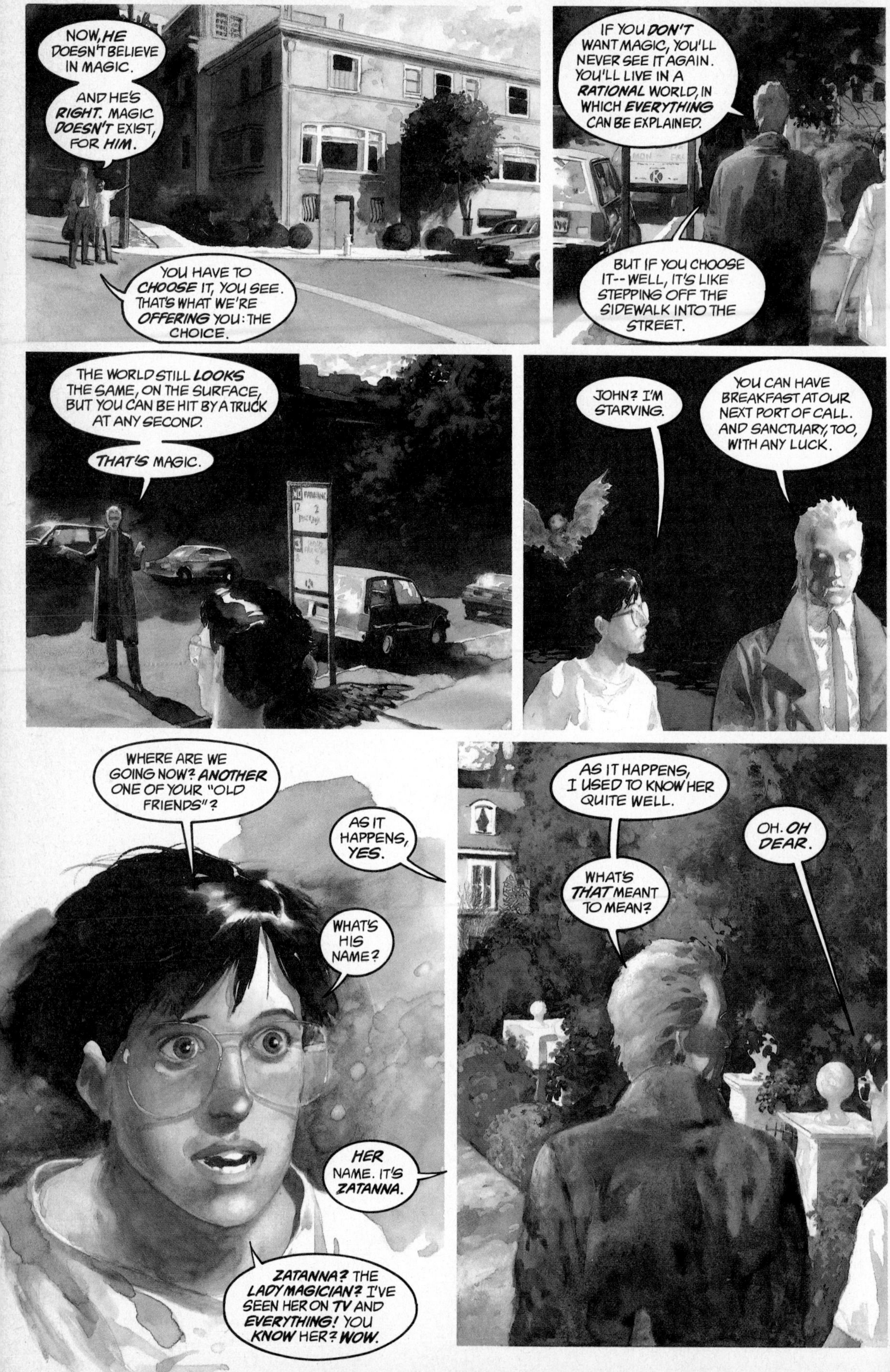
NOW, HE DOESN'T BELIEVE IN MAGIC.
AND HE'S RIGHT. MAGIC DOESN'T EXIST, FOR HIM.
YOU HAVE TO CHOOSE IT, YOU SEE. THAT'S WHAT WE'RE OFFERING YOU: THE CHOICE.
IF YOU DON'T WANT MAGIC, YOU'LL NEVER SEE IT AGAIN. YOU'LL LIVE IN A RATIONAL WORLD, IN WHICH EVERYTHING CAN BE EXPLAINED.
BUT IF YOU CHOOSE IT-- WELL, IT'S LIKE STEPPING OFF THE SIDEWALK INTO THE STREET.
THE WORLD STILL LOOKS THE SAME, ON THE SURFACE, BUT YOU CAN BE HIT BY A TRUCK AT ANY SECOND.
THAT'S MAGIC.
JOHN? I'M STARVING.
YOU CAN HAVE BREAKFAST AT OUR NEXT PORT OF CALL. AND SANCTUARY, TOO, WITH ANY LUCK.
WHERE ARE WE GOING NOW? ANOTHER ONE OF YOUR "OLD FRIENDS"?
AS IT HAPPENS, YES.
WHAT'S HIS NAME?
HER NAME. IT'S ZATANNA.
ZATANNA? THE LADY MAGICIAN? I'VE SEEN HER ON TV AND EVERYTHING! YOU KNOW HER? WOW.
AS IT HAPPENS, I USED TO KNOW HER QUITE WELL.
WHAT'S THAT MEANT TO MEAN?
OH. OH DEAR.

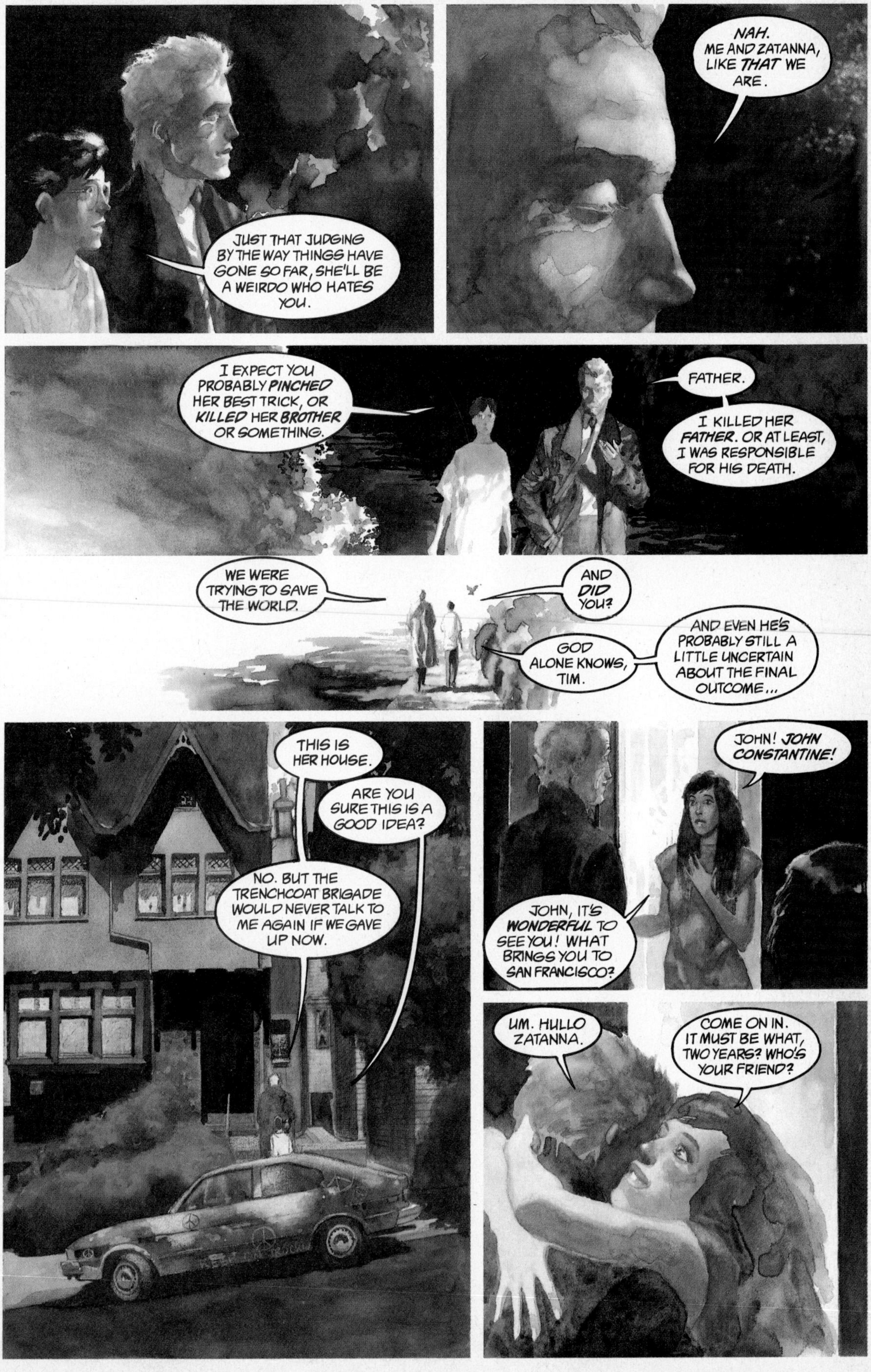
JUST THAT JUDGING BY THE WAY THINGS HAVE GONE SO FAR, SHE'LL BE A WEIRDO WHO HATES YOU.
NAH. ME AND ZATANNA, LIKE *THAT* WE ARE.
I EXPECT YOU PROBABLY *PINCHED* HER BEST TRICK, OR *KILLED* HER *BROTHER* OR SOMETHING.
FATHER.
I KILLED HER *FATHER*. OR AT LEAST, I WAS RESPONSIBLE FOR HIS DEATH.
WE WERE TRYING TO SAVE THE WORLD.
AND *DID* YOU?
GOD ALONE KNOWS, TIM.
AND EVEN HE'S PROBABLY STILL A LITTLE UNCERTAIN ABOUT THE FINAL OUTCOME...
THIS IS HER HOUSE.
ARE YOU SURE THIS IS A GOOD IDEA?
NO. BUT THE TRENCHCOAT BRIGADE WOULD NEVER TALK TO ME AGAIN IF WE GAVE UP NOW.
JOHN! *JOHN CONSTANTINE!*
JOHN, IT'S *WONDERFUL* TO SEE YOU! WHAT BRINGS YOU TO SAN FRANCISCO?
UM. HULLO ZATANNA.
COME ON IN. IT MUST BE WHAT, TWO YEARS? WHO'S YOUR FRIEND?

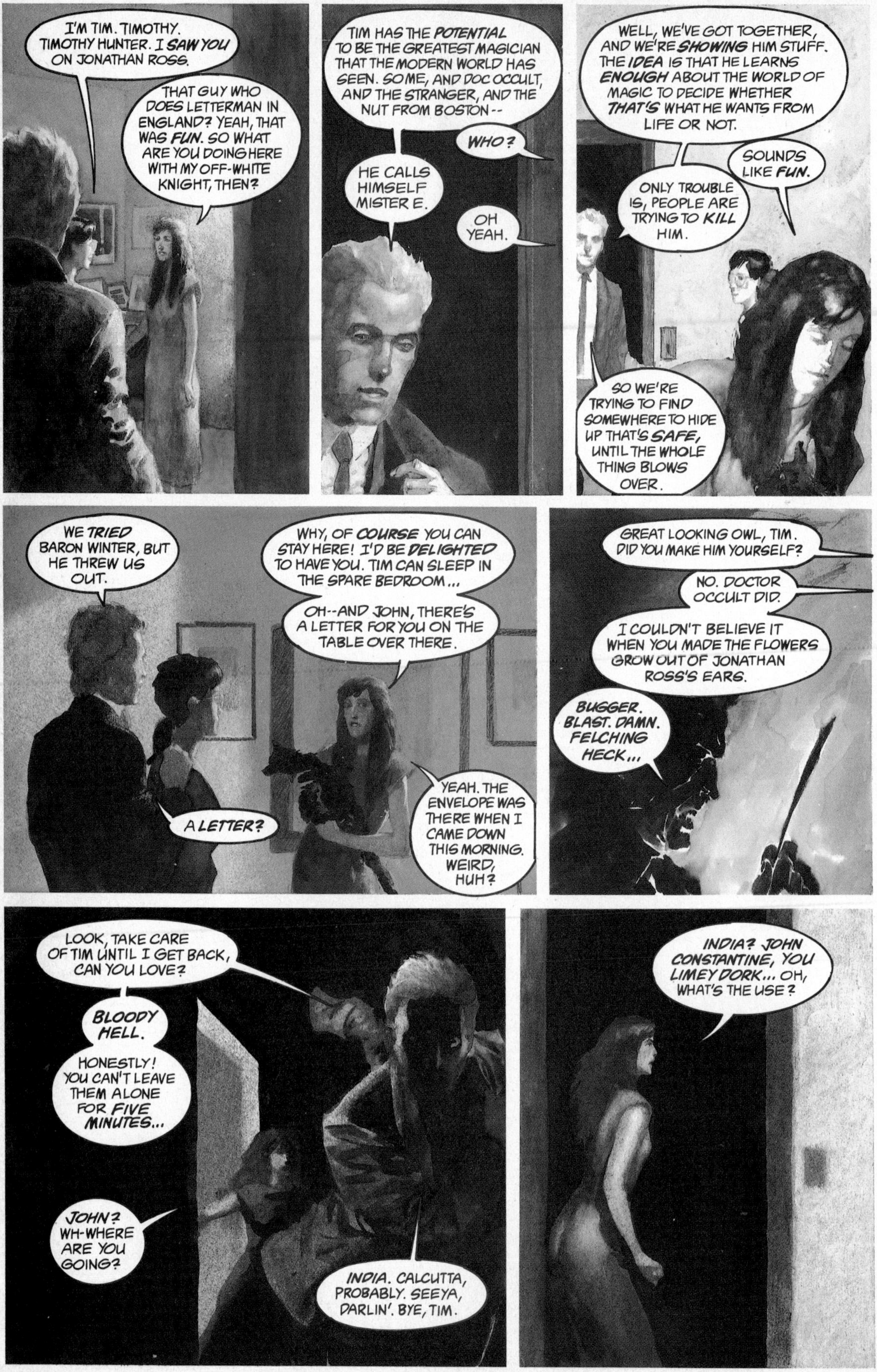
I'M TIM. TIMOTHY. TIMOTHY HUNTER. I SAW YOU ON JONATHAN ROSS.
THAT GUY WHO DOES LETTERMAN IN ENGLAND? YEAH, THAT WAS FUN. SO WHAT ARE YOU DOING HERE WITH MY OFF-WHITE KNIGHT, THEN?
TIM HAS THE POTENTIAL TO BE THE GREATEST MAGICIAN THAT THE MODERN WORLD HAS SEEN. SOME, AND DOC OCCULT, AND THE STRANGER, AND THE NUT FROM BOSTON --
WHO?
HE CALLS HIMSELF MISTER E.
OH YEAH.
WELL, WE'VE GOT TOGETHER, AND WE'RE SHOWING HIM STUFF. THE IDEA IS THAT HE LEARNS ENOUGH ABOUT THE WORLD OF MAGIC TO DECIDE WHETHER THAT'S WHAT HE WANTS FROM LIFE OR NOT.
SOUNDS LIKE FUN.
ONLY TROUBLE IS, PEOPLE ARE TRYING TO KILL HIM.
SO WE'RE TRYING TO FIND SOMEWHERE TO HIDE UP THAT'S SAFE, UNTIL THE WHOLE THING BLOWS OVER.
WE TRIED BARON WINTER, BUT HE THREW US OUT.
WHY, OF COURSE YOU CAN STAY HERE! I'D BE DELIGHTED TO HAVE YOU. TIM CAN SLEEP IN THE SPARE BEDROOM...
OH--AND JOHN, THERE'S A LETTER FOR YOU ON THE TABLE OVER THERE.
A LETTER?
YEAH. THE ENVELOPE WAS THERE WHEN I CAME DOWN THIS MORNING. WEIRD, HUH?
GREAT LOOKING OWL, TIM. DID YOU MAKE HIM YOURSELF?
NO. DOCTOR OCCULT DID.
I COULDN'T BELIEVE IT WHEN YOU MADE THE FLOWERS GROW OUT OF JONATHAN ROSS'S EARS.
BUGGER. BLAST. DAMN. FELCHING HECK...
LOOK, TAKE CARE OF TIM UNTIL I GET BACK, CAN YOU LOVE?
BLOODY HELL.
HONESTLY! YOU CAN'T LEAVE THEM ALONE FOR FIVE MINUTES...
JOHN? WH-WHERE ARE YOU GOING?
INDIA. CALCUTTA, PROBABLY. SEEYA, DARLIN'. BYE, TIM.
INDIA? JOHN CONSTANTINE, YOU LIMEY DORK... OH, WHAT'S THE USE?

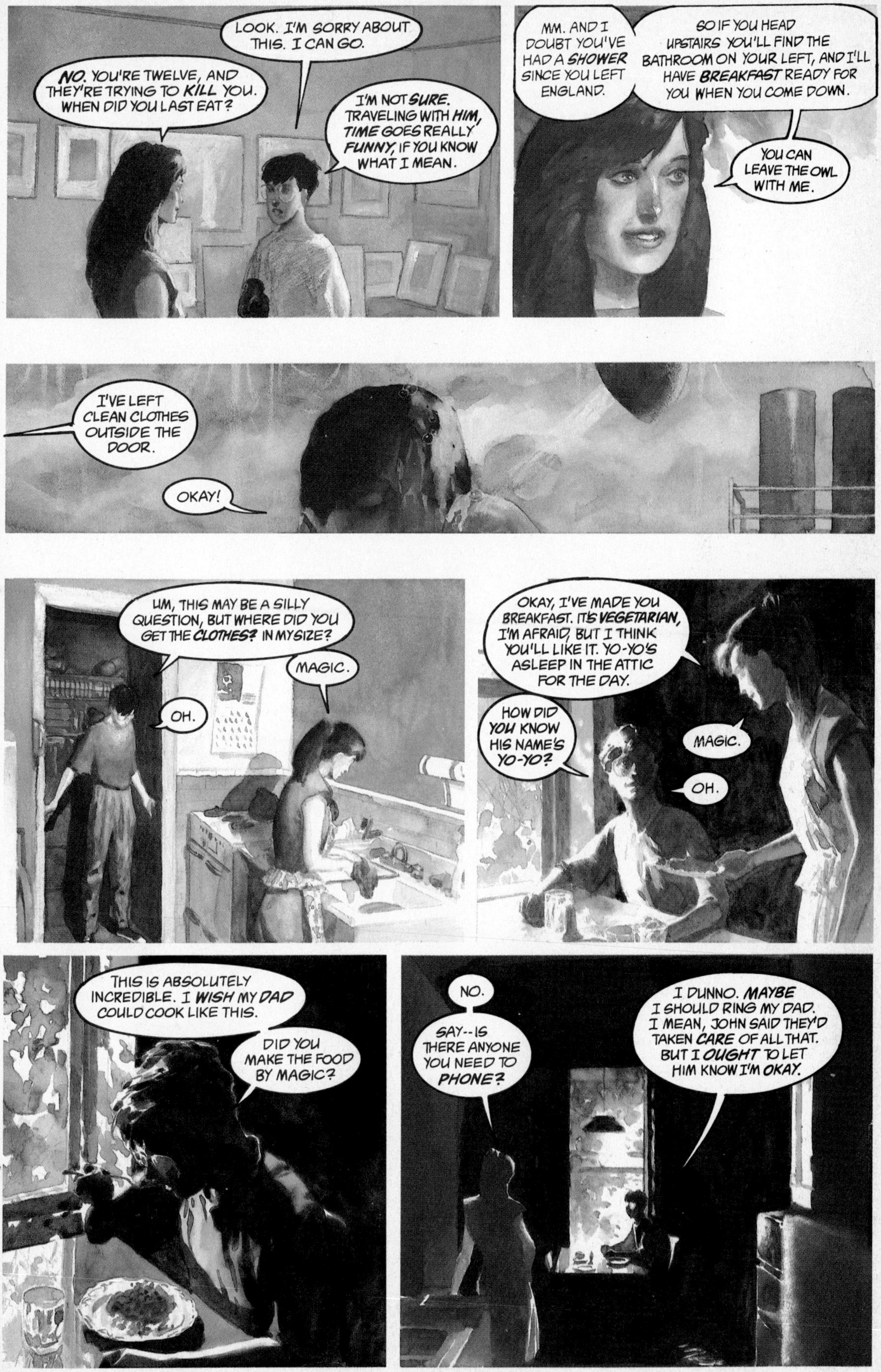
LOOK. I'M SORRY ABOUT THIS. I CAN GO.
NO. YOU'RE TWELVE, AND THEY'RE TRYING TO KILL YOU. WHEN DID YOU LAST EAT?
I'M NOT SURE. TRAVELING WITH HIM, TIME GOES REALLY FUNNY, IF YOU KNOW WHAT I MEAN.
MM. AND I DOUBT YOU'VE HAD A SHOWER SINCE YOU LEFT ENGLAND.
SO IF YOU HEAD UPSTAIRS YOU'LL FIND THE BATHROOM ON YOUR LEFT, AND I'LL HAVE BREAKFAST READY FOR YOU WHEN YOU COME DOWN.
YOU CAN LEAVE THE OWL WITH ME.
I'VE LEFT CLEAN CLOTHES OUTSIDE THE DOOR.
OKAY!
UM, THIS MAY BE A SILLY QUESTION, BUT WHERE DID YOU GET THE CLOTHES? IN MY SIZE?
MAGIC.
OH.
OKAY, I'VE MADE YOU BREAKFAST. IT'S VEGETARIAN, I'M AFRAID, BUT I THINK YOU'LL LIKE IT. YO-YO'S ASLEEP IN THE ATTIC FOR THE DAY.
HOW DID YOU KNOW HIS NAME'S YO-YO?
MAGIC.
OH.
THIS IS ABSOLUTELY INCREDIBLE. I WISH MY DAD COULD COOK LIKE THIS.
DID YOU MAKE THE FOOD BY MAGIC?
NO.
SAY--IS THERE ANYONE YOU NEED TO PHONE?
I DUNNO. MAYBE I SHOULD RING MY DAD. I MEAN, JOHN SAID THEY'D TAKEN CARE OF ALL THAT. BUT I OUGHT TO LET HIM KNOW I'M OKAY.

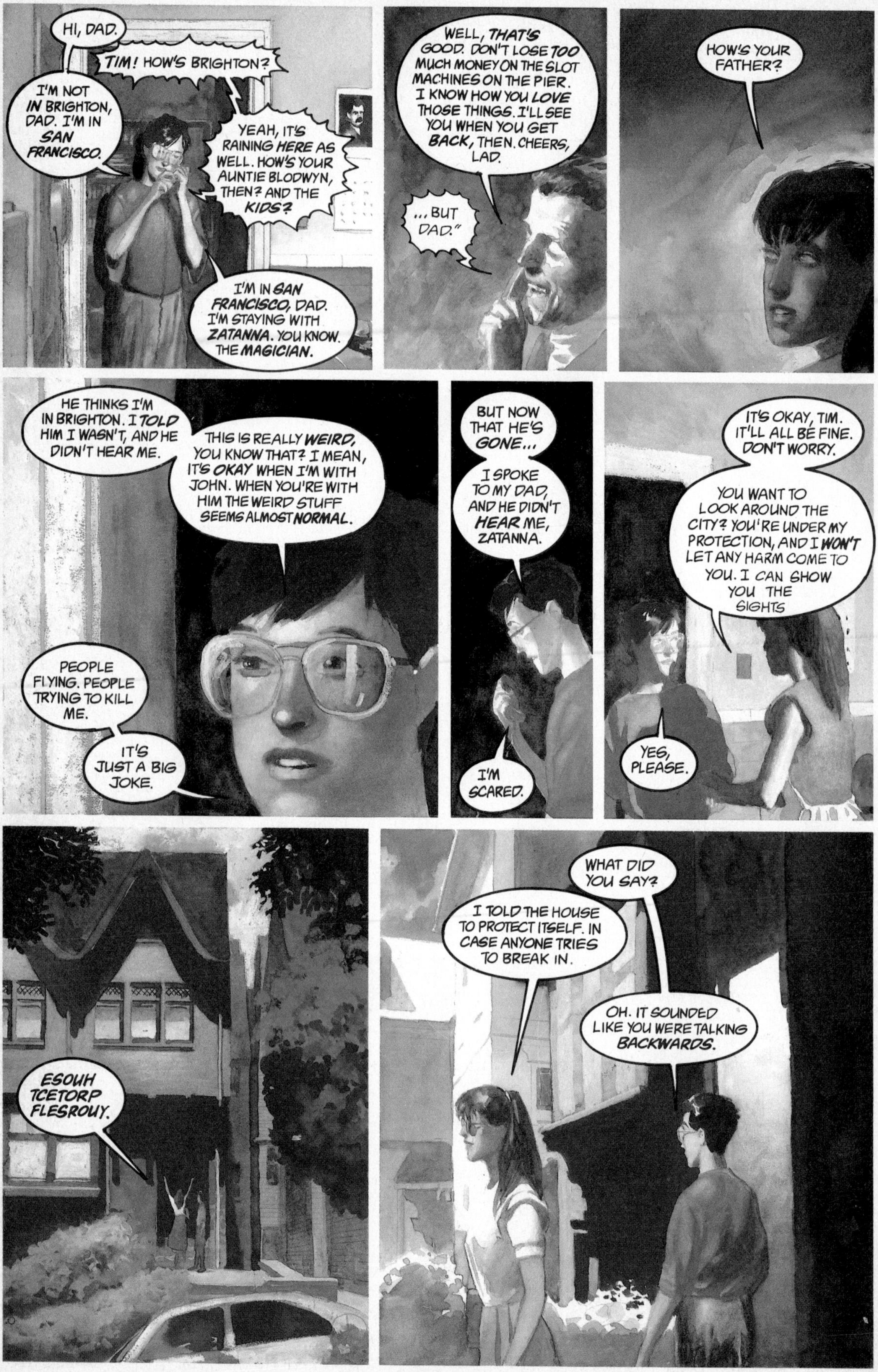
HI, DAD.
TIM! HOW'S BRIGHTON?
I'M NOT IN BRIGHTON, DAD. I'M IN SAN FRANCISCO.
YEAH, IT'S RAINING HERE AS WELL. HOW'S YOUR AUNTIE BLODWYN, THEN? AND THE KIDS?
I'M IN SAN FRANCISCO, DAD. I'M STAYING WITH ZATANNA. YOU KNOW. THE MAGICIAN.
WELL, THAT'S GOOD. DON'T LOSE TOO MUCH MONEY ON THE SLOT MACHINES ON THE PIER. I KNOW HOW YOU LOVE THOSE THINGS. I'LL SEE YOU WHEN YOU GET BACK, THEN. CHEERS, LAD.
...BUT DAD."
HOW'S YOUR FATHER?
HE THINKS I'M IN BRIGHTON. I TOLD HIM I WASN'T, AND HE DIDN'T HEAR ME.
THIS IS REALLY WEIRD, YOU KNOW THAT? I MEAN, IT'S OKAY WHEN I'M WITH JOHN. WHEN YOU'RE WITH HIM THE WEIRD STUFF SEEMS ALMOST NORMAL.
PEOPLE FLYING. PEOPLE TRYING TO KILL ME.
IT'S JUST A BIG JOKE.
BUT NOW THAT HE'S GONE...
I SPOKE TO MY DAD, AND HE DIDN'T HEAR ME, ZATANNA.
I'M SCARED.
IT'S OKAY, TIM. IT'LL ALL BE FINE. DON'T WORRY.
YOU WANT TO LOOK AROUND THE CITY? YOU'RE UNDER MY PROTECTION, AND I WON'T LET ANY HARM COME TO YOU. I CAN SHOW YOU THE SIGHTS
YES, PLEASE.
ESOUH TCETORP FLESROUY.
WHAT DID YOU SAY?
I TOLD THE HOUSE TO PROTECT ITSELF. IN CASE ANYONE TRIES TO BREAK IN.
OH. IT SOUNDED LIKE YOU WERE TALKING BACKWARDS.

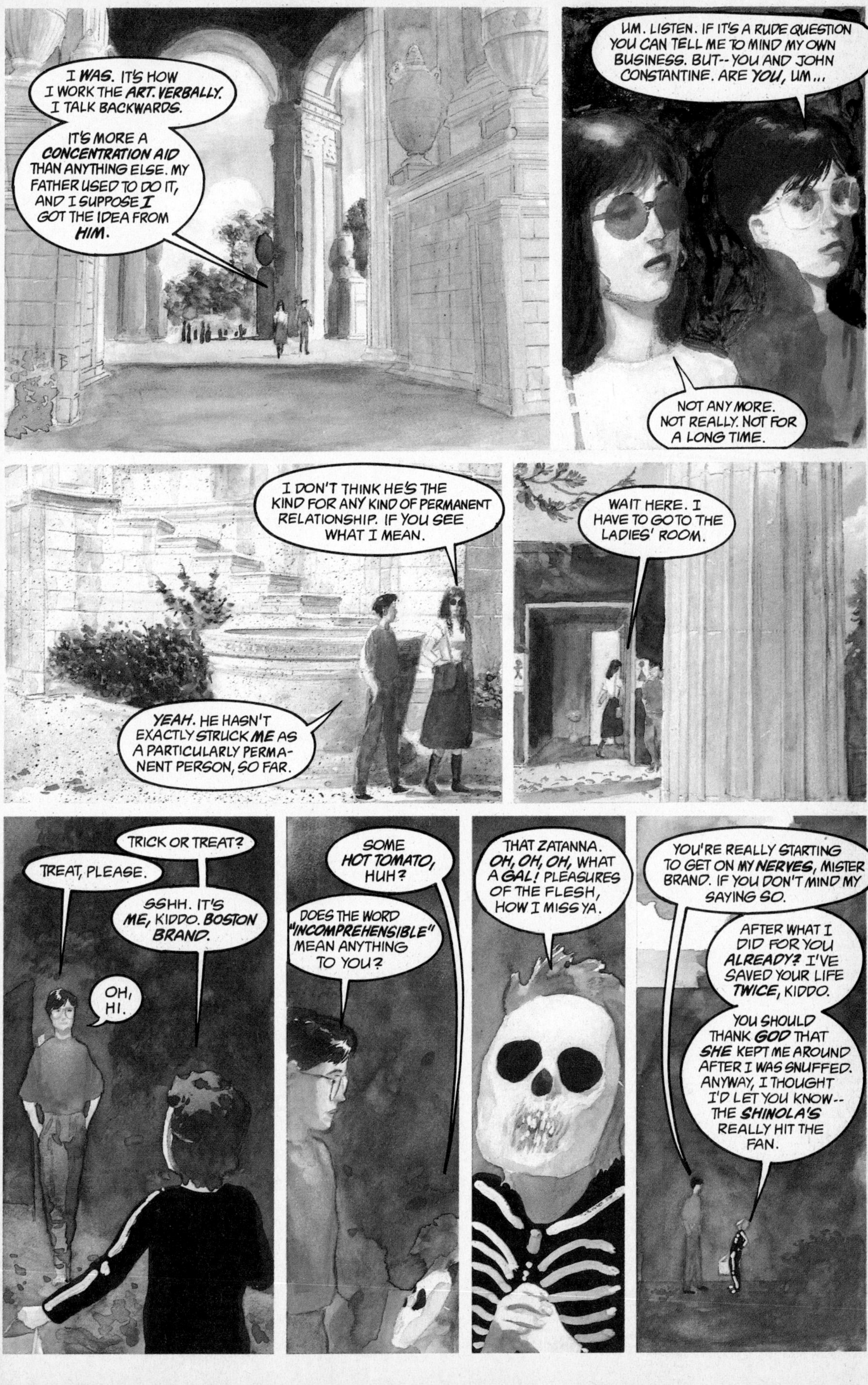
I WAS. IT'S HOW I WORK THE ART. VERBALLY. I TALK BACKWARDS.
IT'S MORE A CONCENTRATION AID THAN ANYTHING ELSE. MY FATHER USED TO DO IT, AND I SUPPOSE I GOT THE IDEA FROM HIM.
UM. LISTEN. IF IT'S A RUDE QUESTION YOU CAN TELL ME TO MIND MY OWN BUSINESS. BUT--YOU AND JOHN CONSTANTINE. ARE YOU, UM...
NOT ANY MORE. NOT REALLY. NOT FOR A LONG TIME.
I DON'T THINK HE'S THE KIND FOR ANY KIND OF PERMANENT RELATIONSHIP. IF YOU SEE WHAT I MEAN.
YEAH. HE HASN'T EXACTLY STRUCK ME AS A PARTICULARLY PERMA-NENT PERSON, SO FAR.
WAIT HERE. I HAVE TO GO TO THE LADIES' ROOM.
TRICK OR TREAT?
TREAT, PLEASE.
SSHH. IT'S ME, KIDDO. BOSTON BRAND.
OH, HI.
SOME HOT TOMATO, HUH?
DOES THE WORD "INCOMPREHENSIBLE" MEAN ANYTHING TO YOU?
THAT ZATANNA. OH, OH, OH, WHAT A GAL! PLEASURES OF THE FLESH, HOW I MISS YA.
YOU'RE REALLY STARTING TO GET ON MY NERVES, MISTER BRAND. IF YOU DON'T MIND MY SAYING SO.
AFTER WHAT I DID FOR YOU ALREADY? I'VE SAVED YOUR LIFE TWICE, KIDDO.
YOU SHOULD THANK GOD THAT SHE KEPT ME AROUND AFTER I WAS SNUFFED. ANYWAY, I THOUGHT I'D LET YOU KNOW-- THE SHINOLA'S REALLY HIT THE FAN.

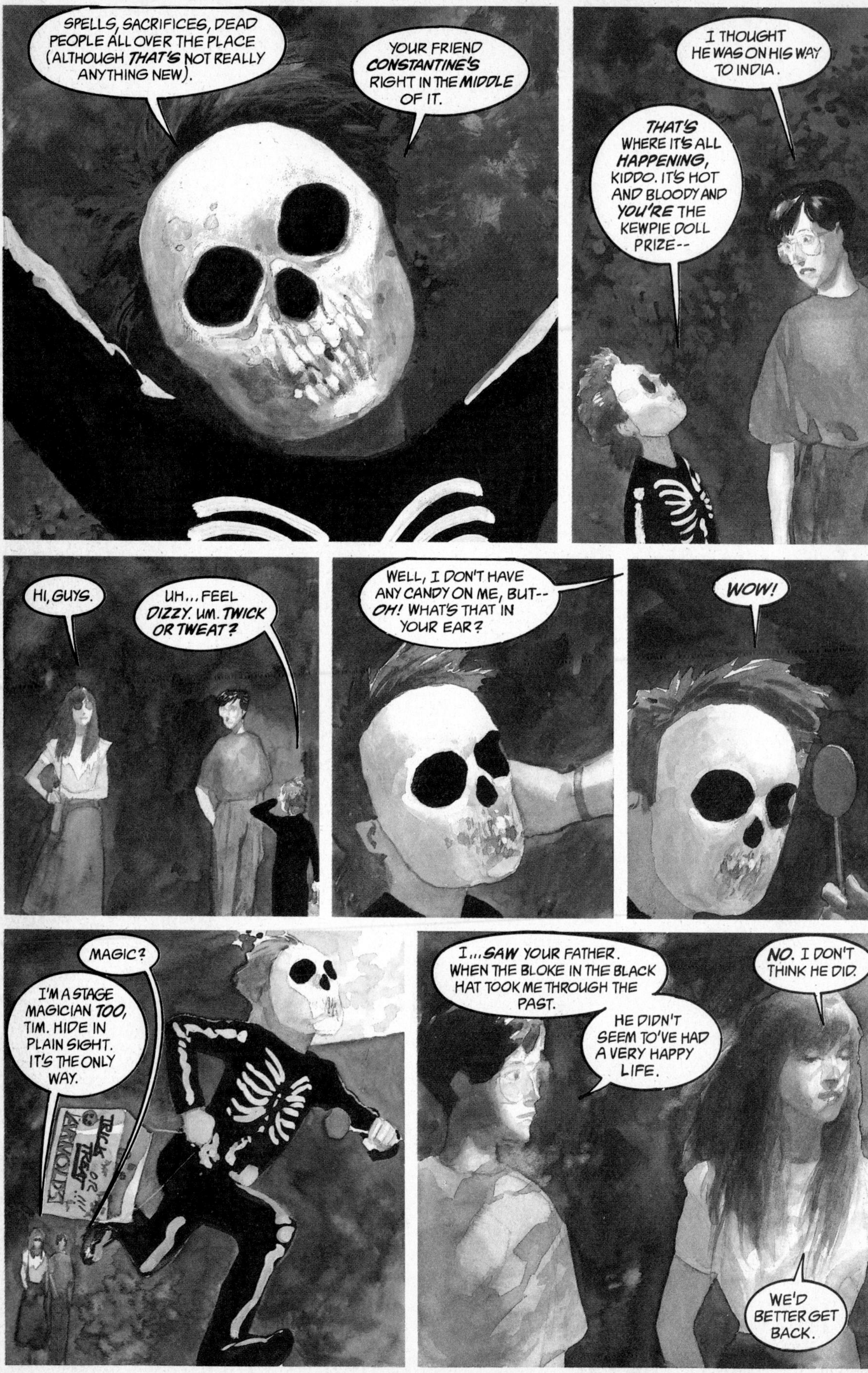
SPELLS, SACRIFICES, DEAD PEOPLE ALL OVER THE PLACE (ALTHOUGH *THAT'S* NOT REALLY ANYTHING NEW).
YOUR FRIEND *CONSTANTINE'S* RIGHT IN THE *MIDDLE* OF IT.
I THOUGHT HE WAS ON HIS WAY TO INDIA.
THAT'S WHERE IT'S ALL *HAPPENING*, KIDDO. IT'S HOT AND BLOODY AND *YOU'RE* THE KEWPIE DOLL PRIZE--
HI, GUYS.
UH... FEEL *DIZZY*. UM. *TWICK OR TWEAT?*
WELL, I DON'T HAVE ANY CANDY ON ME, BUT-- *OH!* WHAT'S THAT IN YOUR EAR?
WOW!
MAGIC?
I'M A STAGE MAGICIAN *TOO*, TIM. HIDE IN PLAIN SIGHT. IT'S THE ONLY WAY.
I... *SAW* YOUR FATHER. WHEN THE BLOKE IN THE BLACK HAT TOOK ME THROUGH THE PAST.
HE DIDN'T SEEM TO'VE HAD A VERY HAPPY LIFE.
NO. I DON'T THINK HE DID.
WE'D BETTER GET BACK.

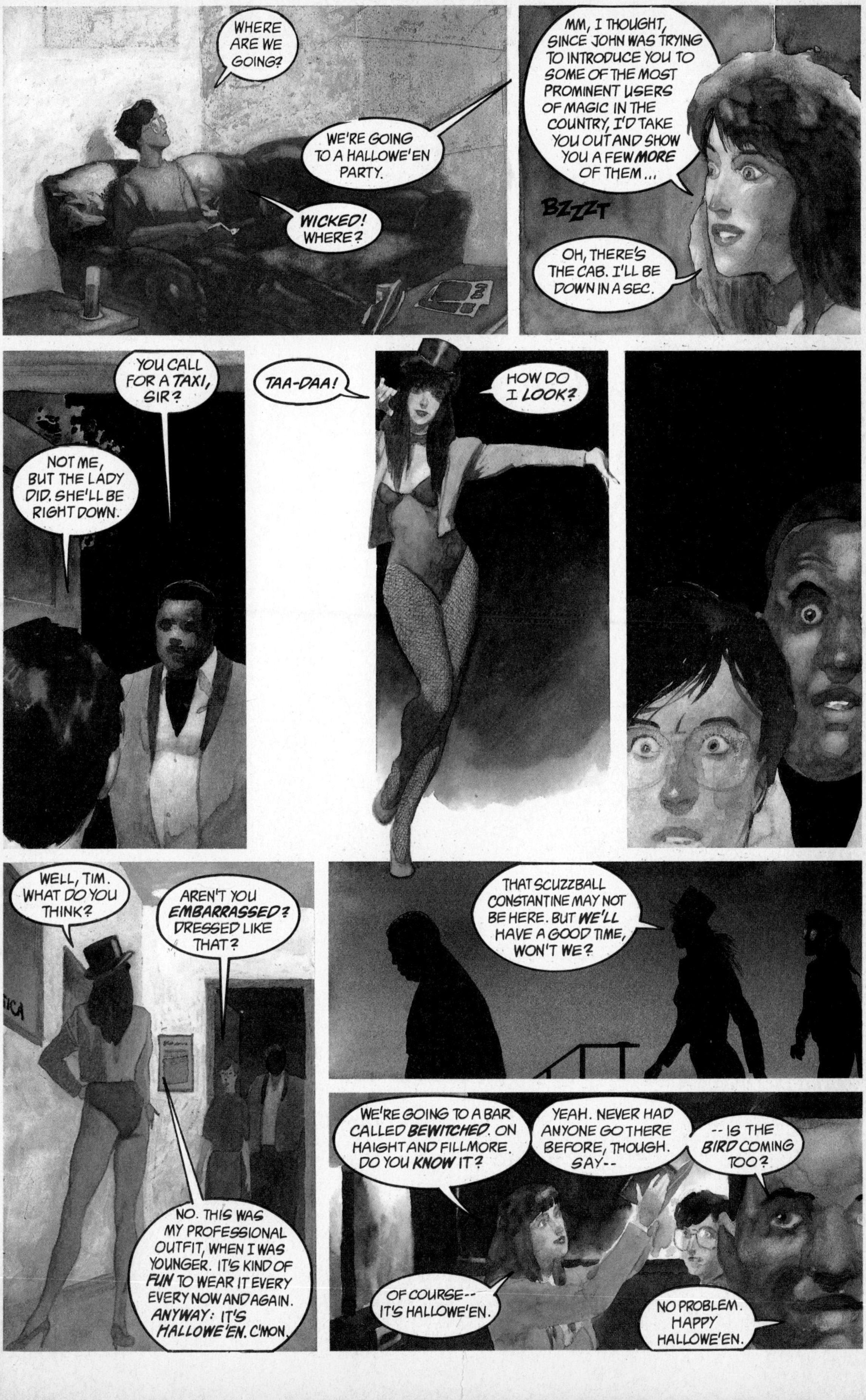
WHERE ARE WE GOING?
WE'RE GOING TO A HALLOWE'EN PARTY.
WICKED! WHERE?
MM, I THOUGHT, SINCE JOHN WAS TRYING TO INTRODUCE YOU TO SOME OF THE MOST PROMINENT USERS OF MAGIC IN THE COUNTRY, I'D TAKE YOU OUT AND SHOW YOU A FEW MORE OF THEM...
BZZZT
OH, THERE'S THE CAB. I'LL BE DOWN IN A SEC.
YOU CALL FOR A TAXI, SIR?
NOT ME, BUT THE LADY DID. SHE'LL BE RIGHT DOWN.
TAA-DAA!
HOW DO I LOOK?
WELL, TIM. WHAT DO YOU THINK?
AREN'T YOU EMBARRASSED? DRESSED LIKE THAT?
NO. THIS WAS MY PROFESSIONAL OUTFIT, WHEN I WAS YOUNGER. IT'S KIND OF FUN TO WEAR IT EVERY EVERY NOW AND AGAIN. ANYWAY: IT'S HALLOWE'EN. C'MON.
THAT SCUZZBALL CONSTANTINE MAY NOT BE HERE. BUT WE'LL HAVE A GOOD TIME, WON'T WE?
WE'RE GOING TO A BAR CALLED BEWITCHED. ON HAIGHT AND FILLMORE. DO YOU KNOW IT?
OF COURSE-- IT'S HALLOWE'EN.
YEAH. NEVER HAD ANYONE GO THERE BEFORE, THOUGH. SAY--
--IS THE BIRD COMING TOO?
NO PROBLEM. HAPPY HALLOWE'EN.

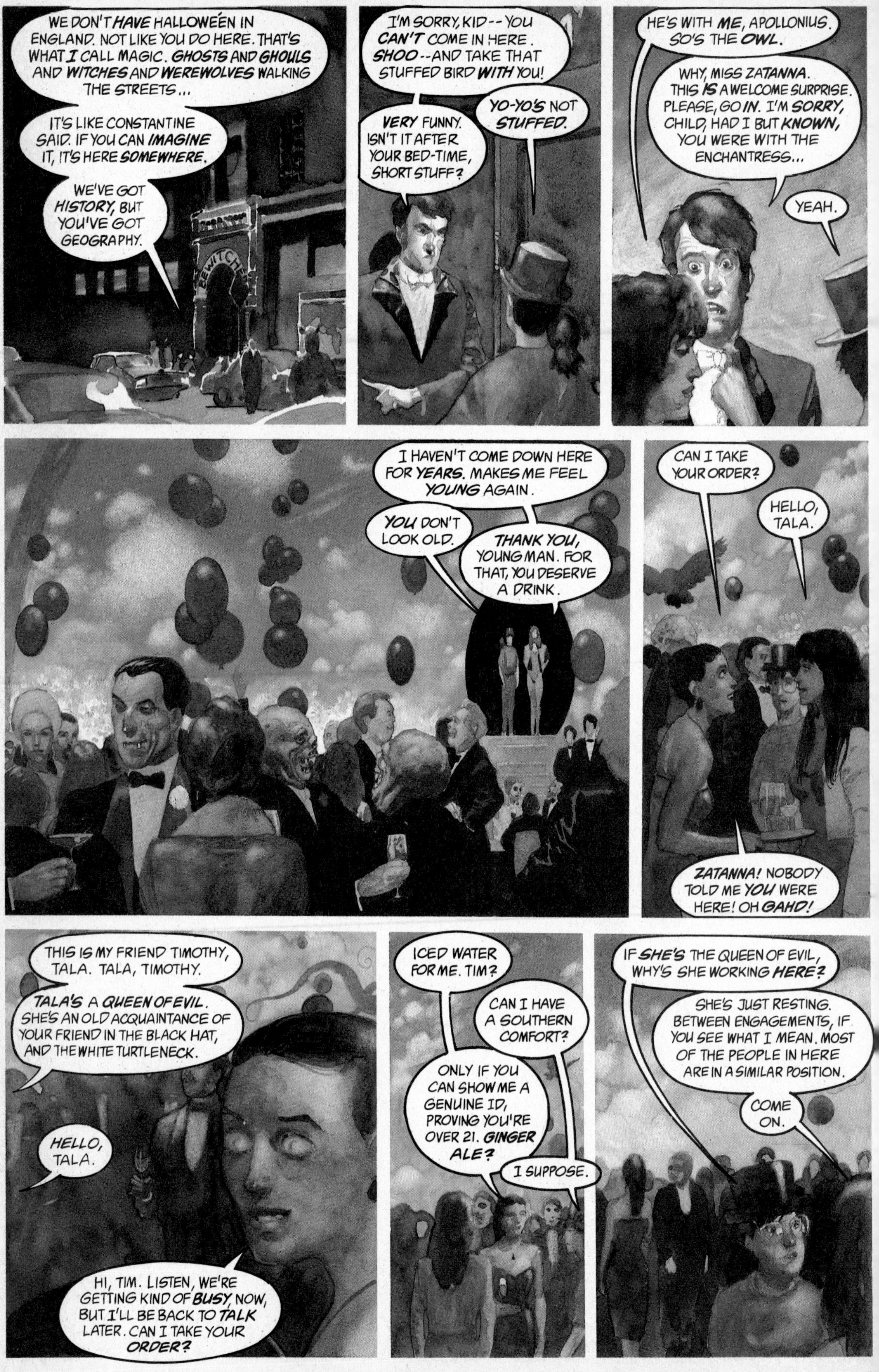
WE DON'T HAVE HALLOWEEN IN ENGLAND. NOT LIKE YOU DO HERE. THAT'S WHAT I CALL MAGIC. GHOSTS AND GHOULS AND WITCHES AND WEREWOLVES WALKING THE STREETS...
IT'S LIKE CONSTANTINE SAID. IF YOU CAN IMAGINE IT, IT'S HERE SOMEWHERE.
WE'VE GOT HISTORY, BUT YOU'VE GOT GEOGRAPHY.
I'M SORRY, KID-- YOU CAN'T COME IN HERE. SHOO--AND TAKE THAT STUFFED BIRD WITH YOU!
VERY FUNNY. ISN'T IT AFTER YOUR BED-TIME, SHORT STUFF?
YO-YO'S NOT STUFFED.
HE'S WITH ME, APOLLONIUS. SO'S THE OWL.
WHY, MISS ZATANNA. THIS IS A WELCOME SURPRISE. PLEASE, GO IN. I'M SORRY, CHILD, HAD I BUT KNOWN, YOU WERE WITH THE ENCHANTRESS...
YEAH.
I HAVEN'T COME DOWN HERE FOR YEARS. MAKES ME FEEL YOUNG AGAIN.
YOU DON'T LOOK OLD.
THANK YOU, YOUNG MAN. FOR THAT, YOU DESERVE A DRINK.
CAN I TAKE YOUR ORDER?
HELLO, TALA.
ZATANNA! NOBODY TOLD ME YOU WERE HERE! OH GAHD!
THIS IS MY FRIEND TIMOTHY, TALA. TALA, TIMOTHY.
TALA'S A QUEEN OF EVIL. SHE'S AN OLD ACQUAINTANCE OF YOUR FRIEND IN THE BLACK HAT, AND THE WHITE TURTLENECK.
HELLO, TALA.
HI, TIM. LISTEN, WE'RE GETTING KIND OF BUSY, NOW, BUT I'LL BE BACK TO TALK LATER. CAN I TAKE YOUR ORDER?
ICED WATER FOR ME. TIM?
CAN I HAVE A SOUTHERN COMFORT?
ONLY IF YOU CAN SHOW ME A GENUINE ID, PROVING YOU'RE OVER 21. GINGER ALE?
I SUPPOSE.
IF SHE'S THE QUEEN OF EVIL, WHY'S SHE WORKING HERE?
SHE'S JUST RESTING. BETWEEN ENGAGEMENTS, IF YOU SEE WHAT I MEAN. MOST OF THE PEOPLE IN HERE ARE IN A SIMILAR POSITION.
COME ON.

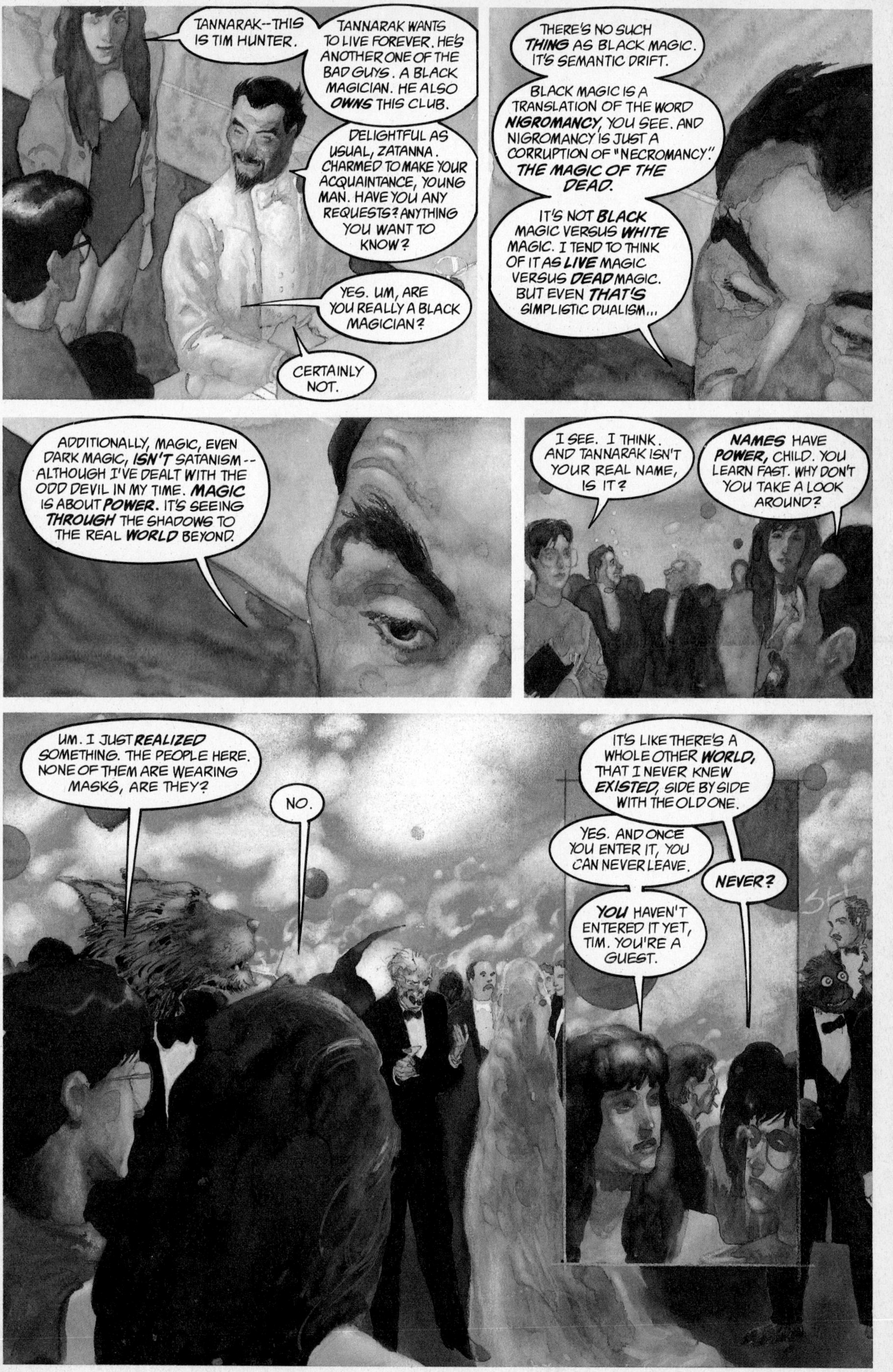
TANNARAK--THIS IS TIM HUNTER.
TANNARAK WANTS TO LIVE FOREVER. HE'S ANOTHER ONE OF THE BAD GUYS. A BLACK MAGICIAN. HE ALSO OWNS THIS CLUB.
DELIGHTFUL AS USUAL, ZATANNA. CHARMED TO MAKE YOUR ACQUAINTANCE, YOUNG MAN. HAVE YOU ANY REQUESTS? ANYTHING YOU WANT TO KNOW?
YES. UM, ARE YOU REALLY A BLACK MAGICIAN?
CERTAINLY NOT.
THERE'S NO SUCH THING AS BLACK MAGIC. IT'S SEMANTIC DRIFT.
BLACK MAGIC IS A TRANSLATION OF THE WORD NIGROMANCY, YOU SEE. AND NIGROMANCY IS JUST A CORRUPTION OF "NECROMANCY". THE MAGIC OF THE DEAD.
IT'S NOT BLACK MAGIC VERSUS WHITE MAGIC. I TEND TO THINK OF IT AS LIVE MAGIC VERSUS DEAD MAGIC. BUT EVEN THAT'S SIMPLISTIC DUALISM...
ADDITIONALLY, MAGIC, EVEN DARK MAGIC, ISN'T SATANISM--ALTHOUGH I'VE DEALT WITH THE ODD DEVIL IN MY TIME. MAGIC IS ABOUT POWER. IT'S SEEING THROUGH THE SHADOWS TO THE REAL WORLD BEYOND.
I SEE. I THINK. AND TANNARAK ISN'T YOUR REAL NAME, IS IT?
NAMES HAVE POWER, CHILD. YOU LEARN FAST. WHY DON'T YOU TAKE A LOOK AROUND?
UM. I JUST REALIZED SOMETHING. THE PEOPLE HERE. NONE OF THEM ARE WEARING MASKS, ARE THEY?
NO.
IT'S LIKE THERE'S A WHOLE OTHER WORLD, THAT I NEVER KNEW EXISTED, SIDE BY SIDE WITH THE OLD ONE.
YES. AND ONCE YOU ENTER IT, YOU CAN NEVER LEAVE.
NEVER?
YOU HAVEN'T ENTERED IT YET, TIM. YOU'RE A GUEST.

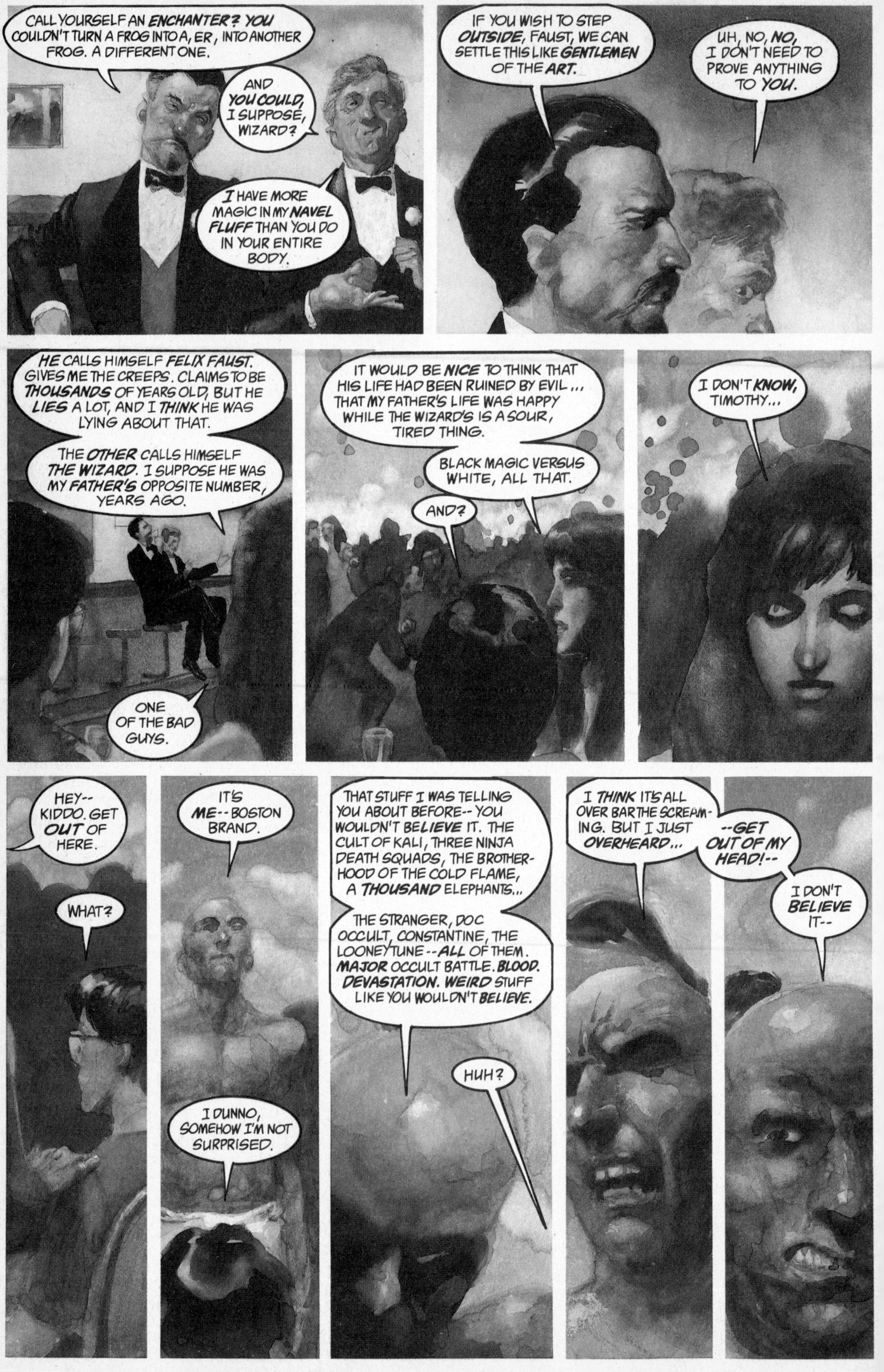
CALL YOURSELF AN ENCHANTER? YOU COULDN'T TURN A FROG INTO A, ER, INTO ANOTHER FROG. A DIFFERENT ONE.
AND YOU COULD, I SUPPOSE, WIZARD?
I HAVE MORE MAGIC IN MY NAVEL FLUFF THAN YOU DO IN YOUR ENTIRE BODY.
IF YOU WISH TO STEP OUTSIDE, FAUST, WE CAN SETTLE THIS LIKE GENTLEMEN OF THE ART.
UH, NO, NO, I DON'T NEED TO PROVE ANYTHING TO YOU.
HE CALLS HIMSELF FELIX FAUST. GIVES ME THE CREEPS. CLAIMS TO BE THOUSANDS OF YEARS OLD, BUT HE LIES A LOT, AND I THINK HE WAS LYING ABOUT THAT.
THE OTHER CALLS HIMSELF THE WIZARD. I SUPPOSE HE WAS MY FATHER'S OPPOSITE NUMBER, YEARS AGO.
ONE OF THE BAD GUYS.
IT WOULD BE NICE TO THINK THAT HIS LIFE HAD BEEN RUINED BY EVIL... THAT MY FATHER'S LIFE WAS HAPPY WHILE THE WIZARD'S IS A SOUR, TIRED THING.
BLACK MAGIC VERSUS WHITE, ALL THAT.
AND?
I DON'T KNOW, TIMOTHY...
HEY-- KIDDO. GET OUT OF HERE.
WHAT?
IT'S ME-- BOSTON BRAND.
I DUNNO, SOMEHOW I'M NOT SURPRISED.
THAT STUFF I WAS TELLING YOU ABOUT BEFORE-- YOU WOULDN'T BELIEVE IT. THE CULT OF KALI, THREE NINJA DEATH SQUADS, THE BROTHERHOOD OF THE COLD FLAME, A THOUSAND ELEPHANTS...
THE STRANGER, DOC OCCULT, CONSTANTINE, THE LOONEY TUNE --ALL OF THEM. MAJOR OCCULT BATTLE. BLOOD. DEVASTATION. WEIRD STUFF LIKE YOU WOULDN'T BELIEVE.
HUH?
I THINK IT'S ALL OVER BAR THE SCREAMING. BUT I JUST OVERHEARD...
--GET OUT OF MY HEAD!--
I DON'T BELIEVE IT--

-- LEAVE, I ABJURE THEE! NEASFYSHUE ORPGS N TSCASRPOI NU R'MELN, DMYLTCRIOS RE IHODSAYUR UN H'TGAH--

--YOW!--

PADPUIG-TOGASSO HRYFOTLO-SRVLIG AEI OKHIYAD-SIYA.

FRIGGIN' SPOOKS.

LADIES. GENTLEMEN. OTHER ENTITIES. I HAVE AN ANNOUNCEMENT.

IT SEEMS THERE'S A VERY SPECIAL YOUNG LAD IN OUR AUDIENCE TONIGHT.

SOME OF YOU MAY HAVE HEARD ABOUT HIM, ON THE GRAPEVINE. OTHERS OF YOU MIGHT HAVE HEARD ABOUT THE CURRENT FUN AND GAMES IN CALCUTTA.

OH, SHOOT. I'M SORRY, TIM-- I SHOULD NEVER HAVE BROUGHT YOU HERE.

AS YOU KNOW THERE IS A PRICE ON HIS HEAD--WHICH NEED NOT BE ATTACHED TO HIS BODY.

THIS BOY IS UNDER MY PROTEC-TION. ANYONE WHO WISHES TO HURT HIM MUST FIRST RECKON WITH ME.

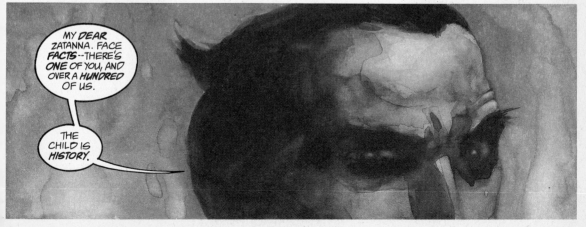

MY DEAR ZATANNA. FACE FACTS--THERE'S ONE OF YOU, AND OVER A HUNDRED OF US.

THE CHILD IS HISTORY.

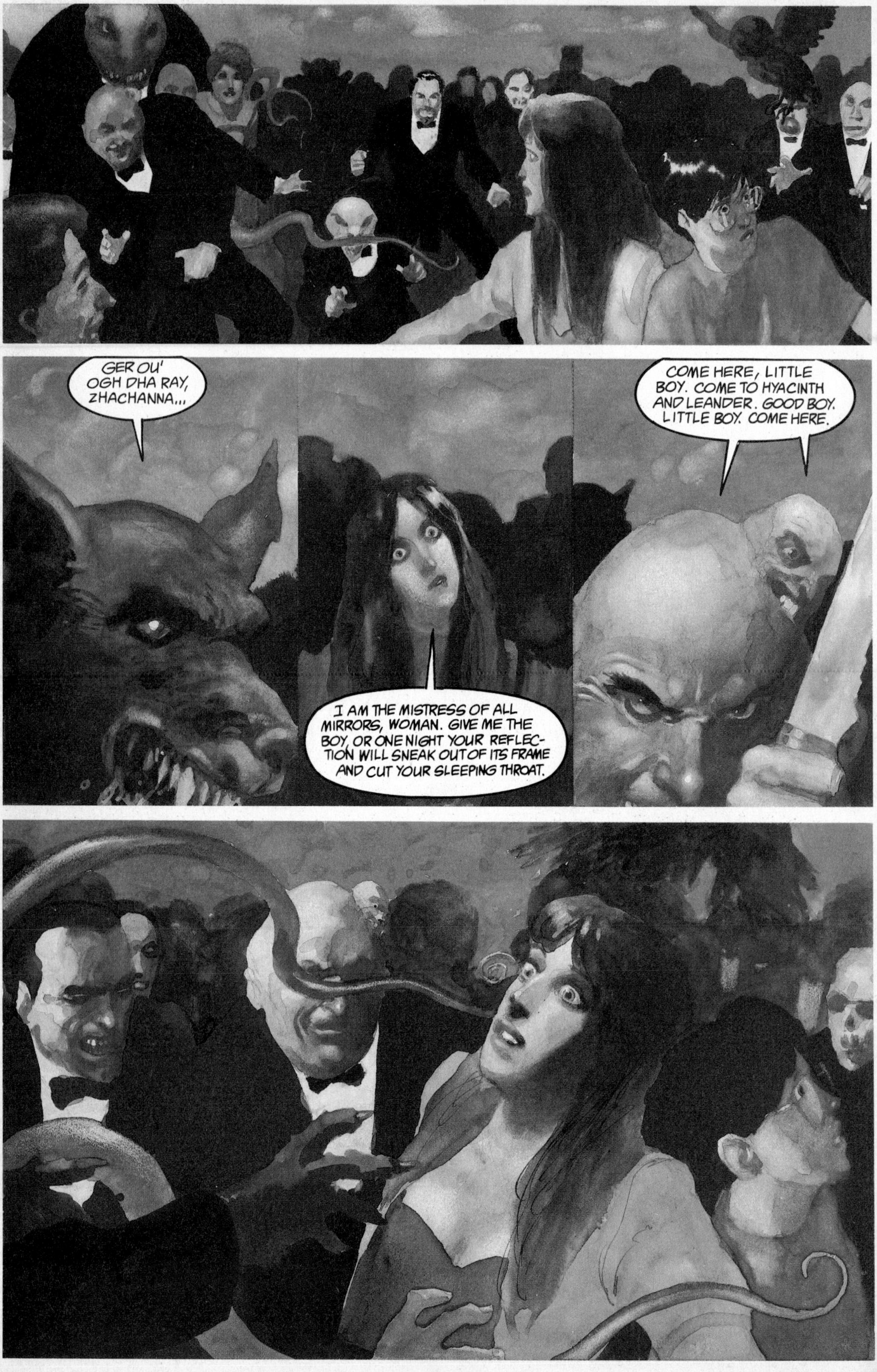
GER OU' OGH DHA RAY, ZHACHANNA...
I AM THE MISTRESS OF ALL MIRRORS, WOMAN. GIVE ME THE BOY, OR ONE NIGHT YOUR REFLECTION WILL SNEAK OUT OF ITS FRAME AND CUT YOUR SLEEPING THROAT.
COME HERE, LITTLE BOY. COME TO HYACINTH AND LEANDER. GOOD BOY. LITTLE BOY. COME HERE.

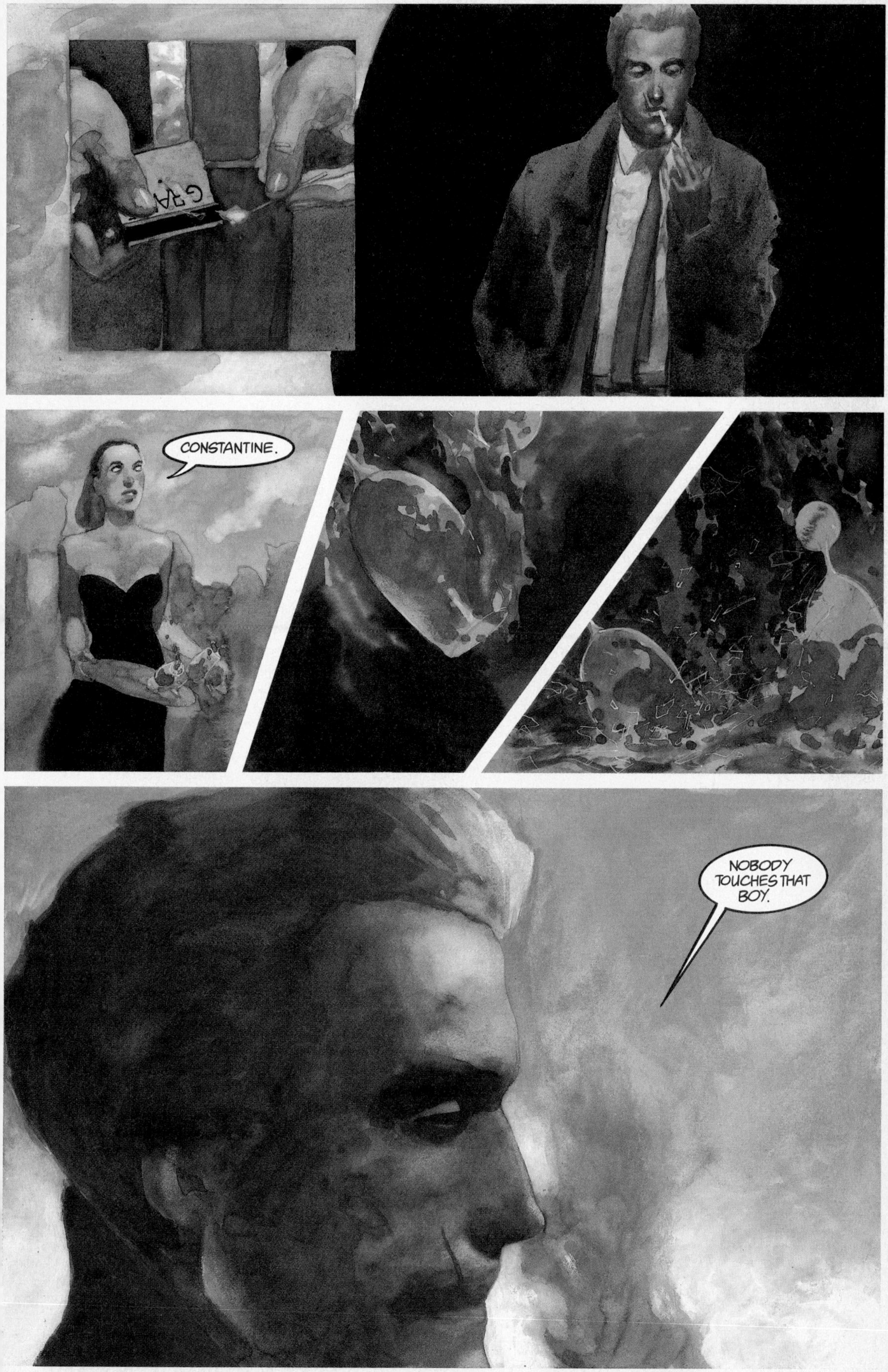
CONSTANTINE.
NOBODY TOUCHES THAT BOY.

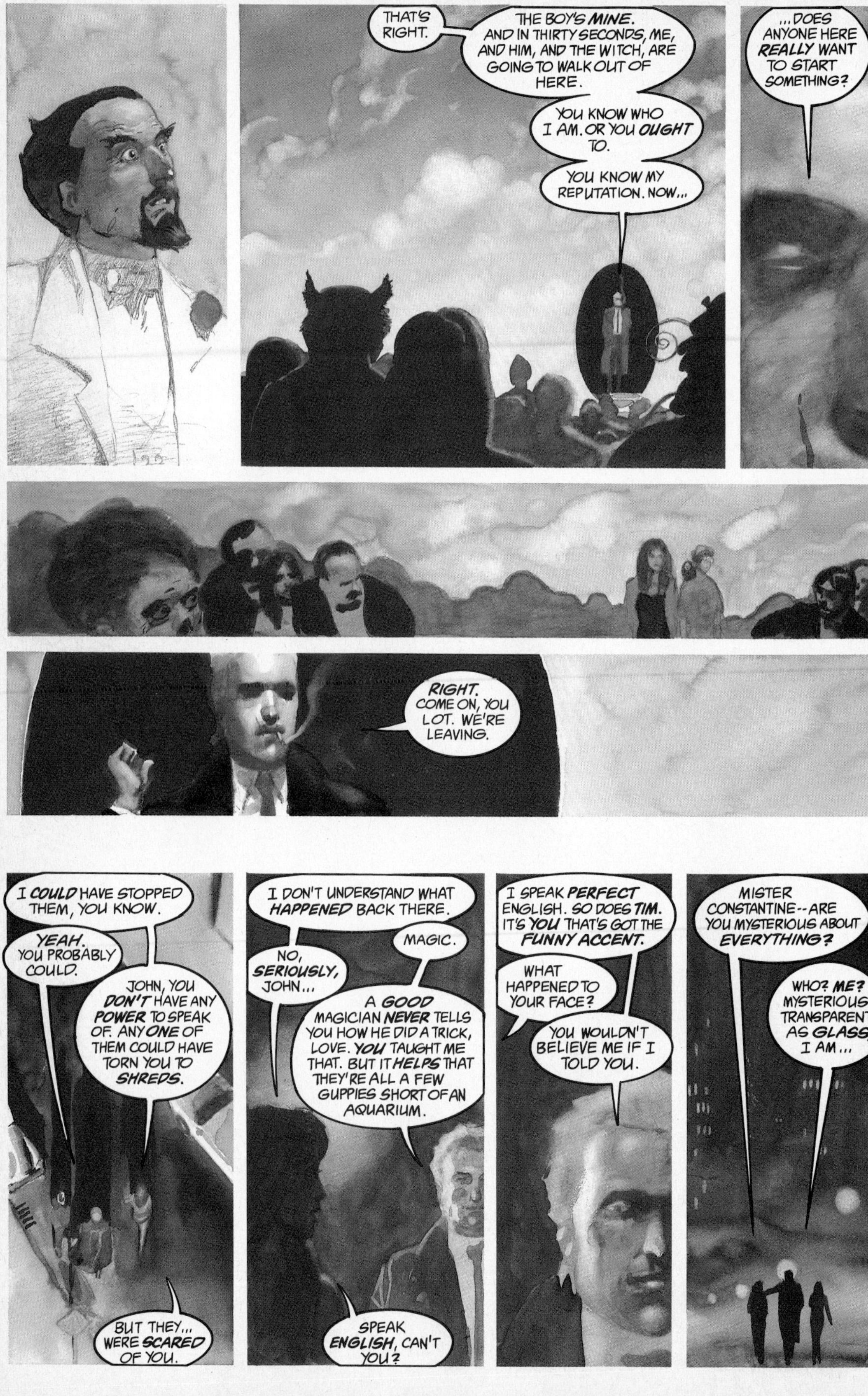
THAT'S RIGHT.
THE BOY'S MINE. AND IN THIRTY SECONDS, ME, AND HIM, AND THE WITCH, ARE GOING TO WALK OUT OF HERE.
YOU KNOW WHO I AM. OR YOU OUGHT TO.
YOU KNOW MY REPUTATION. NOW...
...DOES ANYONE HERE REALLY WANT TO START SOMETHING?
RIGHT. COME ON, YOU LOT. WE'RE LEAVING.
I COULD HAVE STOPPED THEM, YOU KNOW.
YEAH. YOU PROBABLY COULD.
JOHN, YOU DON'T HAVE ANY POWER TO SPEAK OF. ANY ONE OF THEM COULD HAVE TORN YOU TO SHREDS.
BUT THEY... WERE SCARED OF YOU.
I DON'T UNDERSTAND WHAT HAPPENED BACK THERE.
MAGIC.
NO, SERIOUSLY, JOHN...
A GOOD MAGICIAN NEVER TELLS YOU HOW HE DID A TRICK, LOVE. YOU TAUGHT ME THAT. BUT IT HELPS THAT THEY'RE ALL A FEW GUPPIES SHORT OF AN AQUARIUM.
SPEAK ENGLISH, CAN'T YOU?
I SPEAK PERFECT ENGLISH. SO DOES TIM. IT'S YOU THAT'S GOT THE FUNNY ACCENT.
WHAT HAPPENED TO YOUR FACE?
YOU WOULDN'T BELIEVE ME IF I TOLD YOU.
MISTER CONSTANTINE--ARE YOU MYSTERIOUS ABOUT EVERYTHING?
WHO? ME? MYSTERIOUS? TRANSPARENT AS GLASS, I AM...

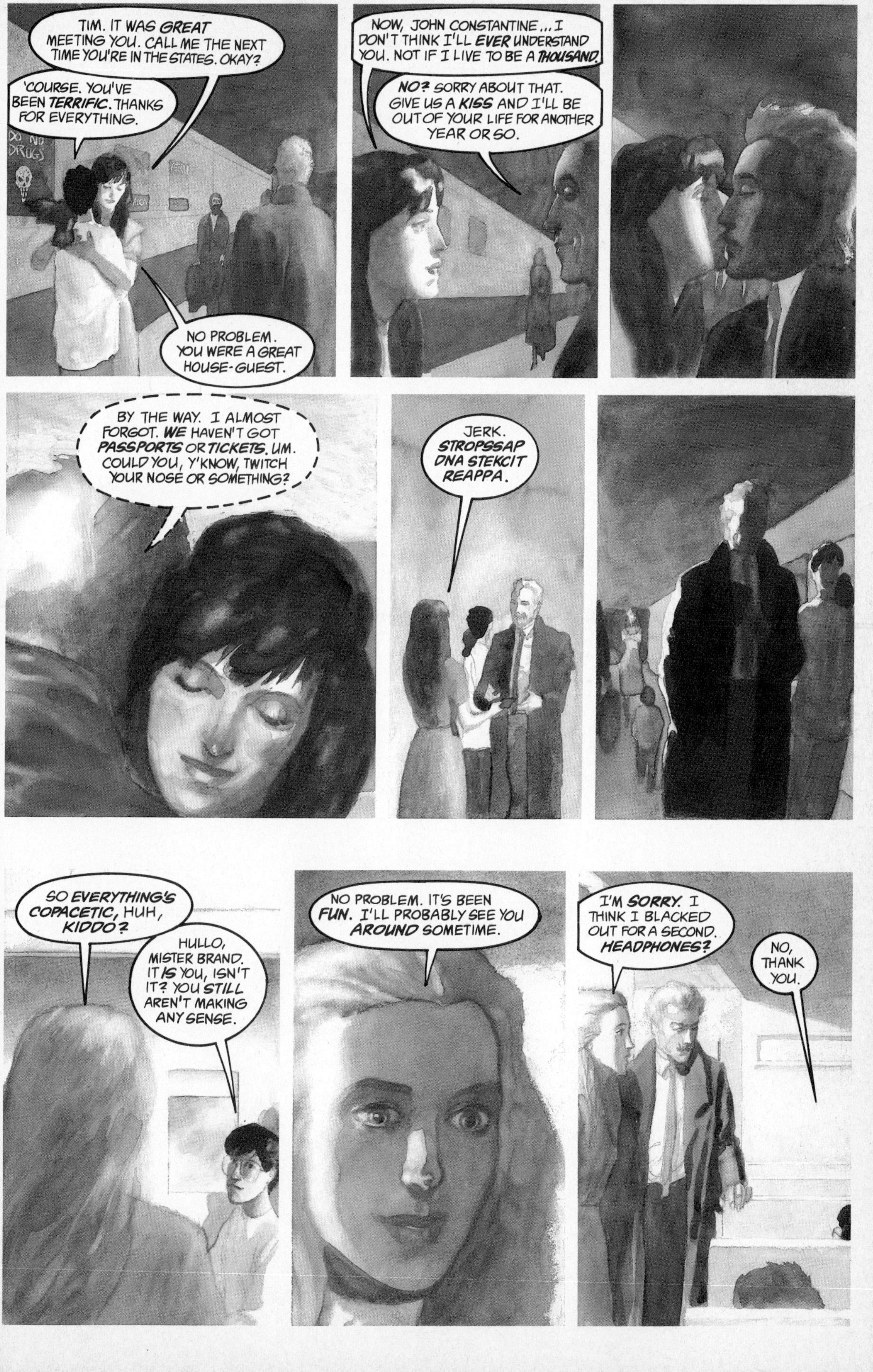

TIM. IT WAS GREAT MEETING YOU. CALL ME THE NEXT TIME YOU'RE IN THE STATES. OKAY?
'COURSE. YOU'VE BEEN TERRIFIC. THANKS FOR EVERYTHING.
NO PROBLEM. YOU WERE A GREAT HOUSE-GUEST.
NOW, JOHN CONSTANTINE... I DON'T THINK I'LL EVER UNDERSTAND YOU. NOT IF I LIVE TO BE A THOUSAND.
NO? SORRY ABOUT THAT. GIVE US A KISS AND I'LL BE OUT OF YOUR LIFE FOR ANOTHER YEAR OR SO.
BY THE WAY. I ALMOST FORGOT. WE HAVEN'T GOT PASSPORTS OR TICKETS. UM. COULD YOU, Y'KNOW, TWITCH YOUR NOSE OR SOMETHING?
JERK. STROPSSAP DNA STEKCIT REAPPA.
SO EVERYTHING'S COPACETIC, HUH, KIDDO?
HULLO, MISTER BRAND. IT IS YOU, ISN'T IT? YOU STILL AREN'T MAKING ANY SENSE.
NO PROBLEM. IT'S BEEN FUN. I'LL PROBABLY SEE YOU AROUND SOMETIME.
I'M SORRY. I THINK I BLACKED OUT FOR A SECOND. HEADPHONES?
NO, THANK YOU.

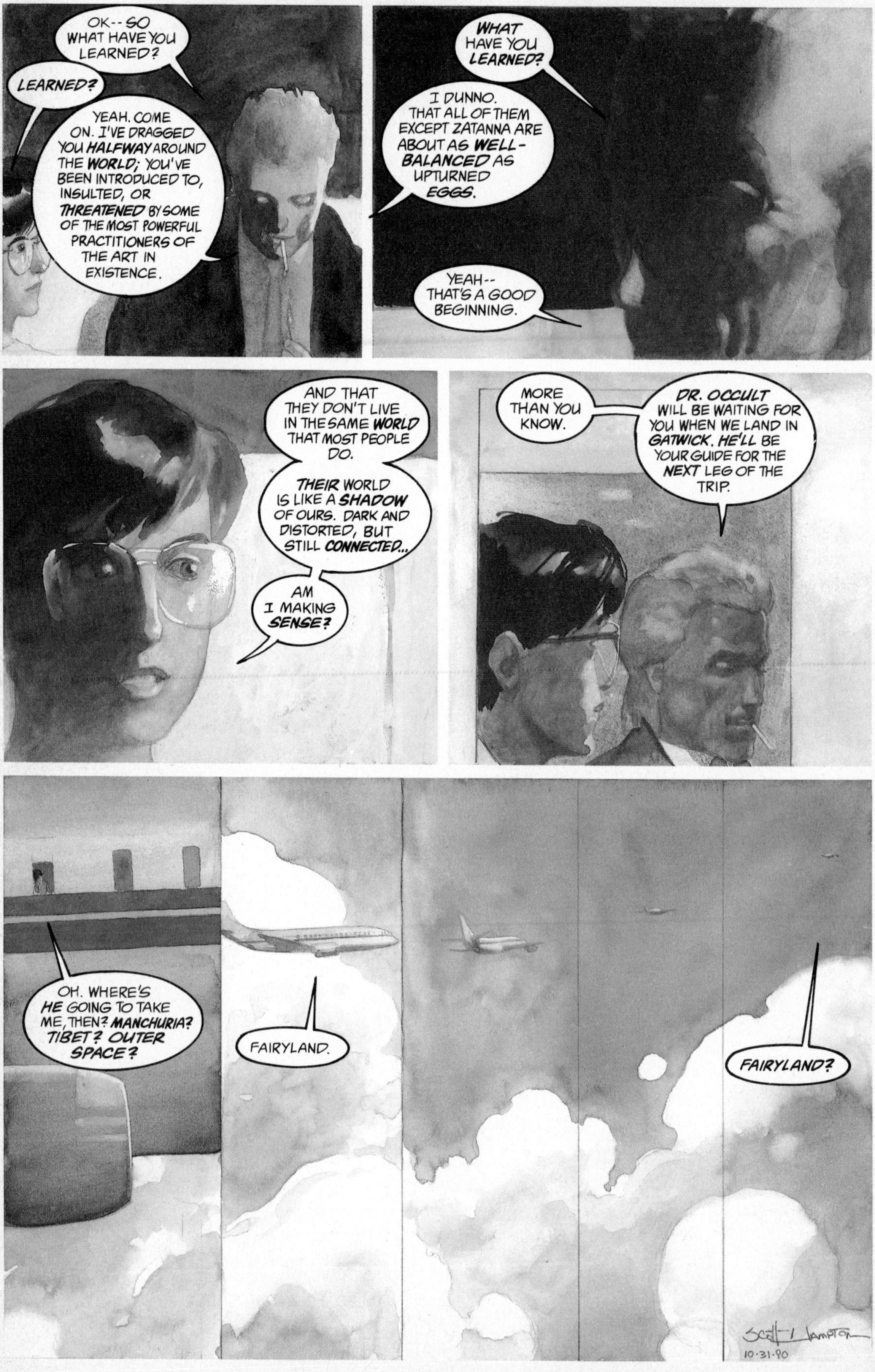
OK-- SO WHAT HAVE YOU LEARNED?
LEARNED?
YEAH. COME ON. I'VE DRAGGED YOU HALFWAY AROUND THE WORLD; YOU'VE BEEN INTRODUCED TO, INSULTED, OR THREATENED BY SOME OF THE MOST POWERFUL PRACTITIONERS OF THE ART IN EXISTENCE.
WHAT HAVE YOU LEARNED?
I DUNNO. THAT ALL OF THEM EXCEPT ZATANNA ARE ABOUT AS WELL-BALANCED AS UPTURNED EGGS.
YEAH-- THAT'S A GOOD BEGINNING.
AND THAT THEY DON'T LIVE IN THE SAME WORLD THAT MOST PEOPLE DO.
THEIR WORLD IS LIKE A SHADOW OF OURS. DARK AND DISTORTED, BUT STILL CONNECTED...
AM I MAKING SENSE?
MORE THAN YOU KNOW.
DR. OCCULT WILL BE WAITING FOR YOU WHEN WE LAND IN GATWICK. HE'LL BE YOUR GUIDE FOR THE NEXT LEG OF THE TRIP.
OH. WHERE'S HE GOING TO TAKE ME, THEN? MANCHURIA? TIBET? OUTER SPACE?
FAIRYLAND.
FAIRYLAND?
SCOTT HAMPTON
10·31·90

III

The Land of
Summer's Twilight

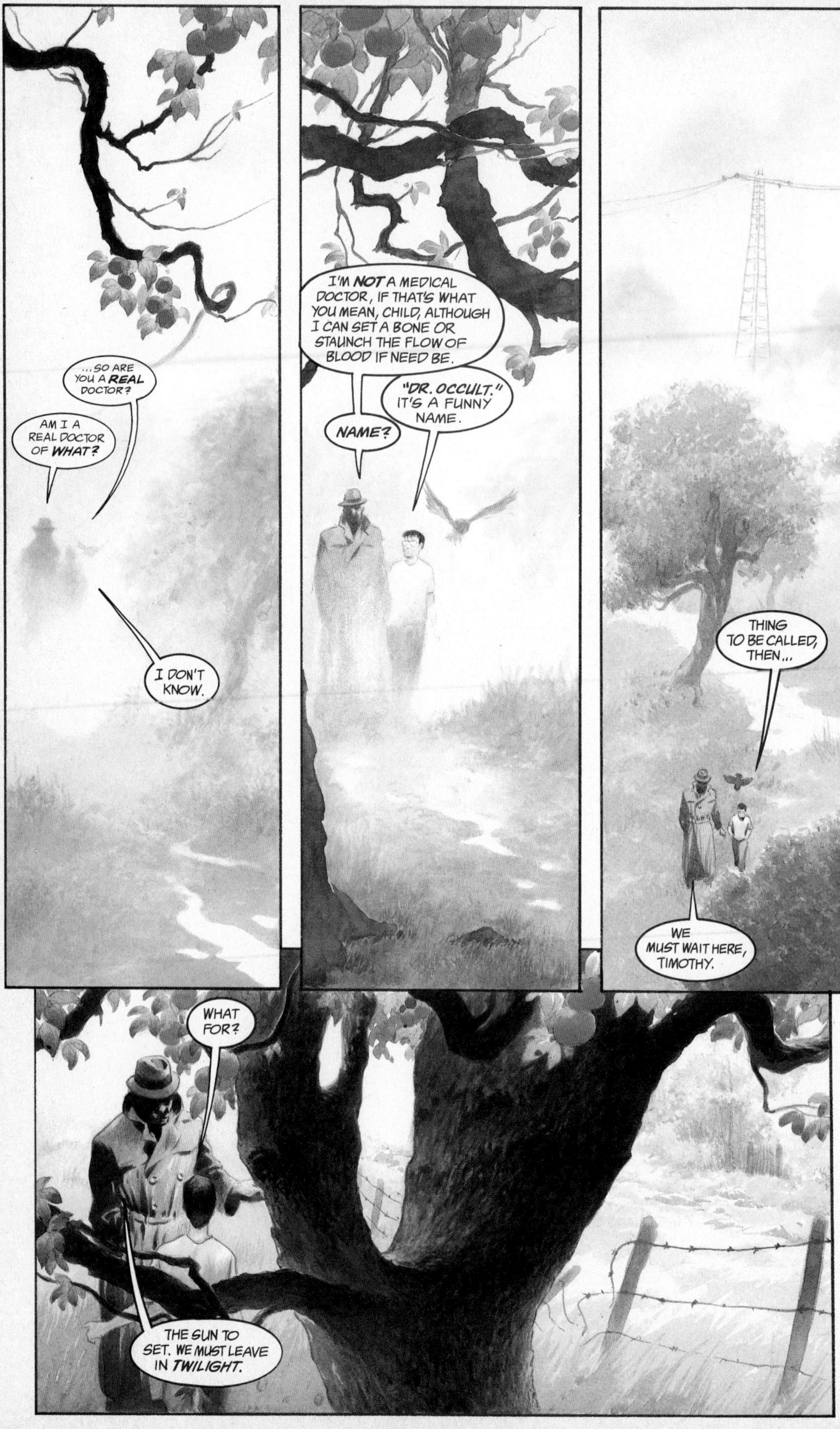
...SO ARE YOU A REAL DOCTOR?
AM I A REAL DOCTOR OF WHAT?
I DON'T KNOW.
I'M NOT A MEDICAL DOCTOR, IF THAT'S WHAT YOU MEAN, CHILD, ALTHOUGH I CAN SET A BONE OR STAUNCH THE FLOW OF BLOOD IF NEED BE.
"DR. OCCULT." IT'S A FUNNY NAME.
NAME?
THING TO BE CALLED, THEN...
WE MUST WAIT HERE, TIMOTHY.
WHAT FOR?
THE SUN TO SET. WE MUST LEAVE IN TWILIGHT.

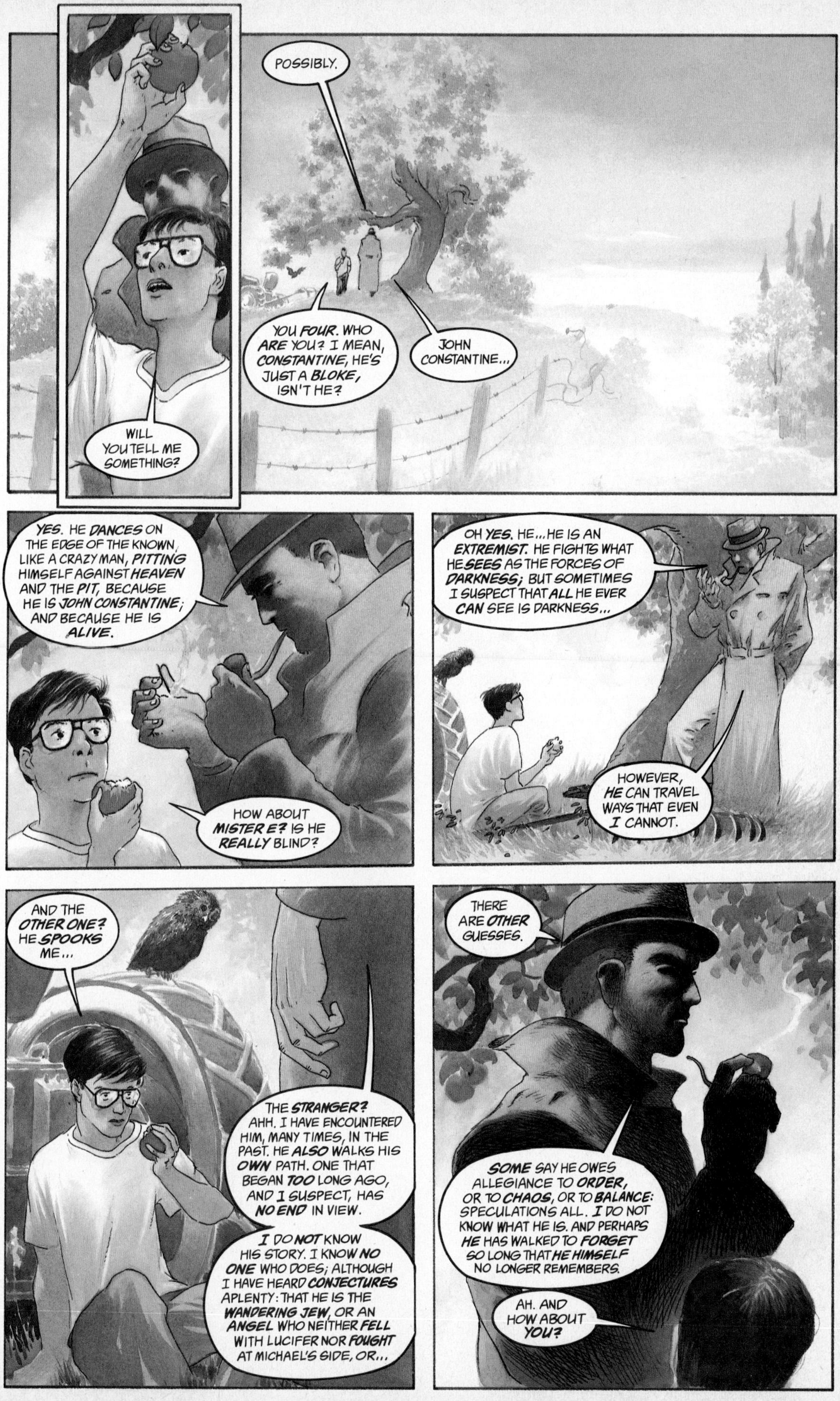
WILL YOU TELL ME SOMETHING?
POSSIBLY.
YOU FOUR. WHO ARE YOU? I MEAN, CONSTANTINE, HE'S JUST A BLOKE, ISN'T HE?
JOHN CONSTANTINE...
YES. HE DANCES ON THE EDGE OF THE KNOWN, LIKE A CRAZY MAN, PITTING HIMSELF AGAINST HEAVEN AND THE PIT, BECAUSE HE IS JOHN CONSTANTINE; AND BECAUSE HE IS ALIVE.
HOW ABOUT MISTER E? IS HE REALLY BLIND?
OH YES. HE...HE IS AN EXTREMIST. HE FIGHTS WHAT HE SEES AS THE FORCES OF DARKNESS; BUT SOMETIMES I SUSPECT THAT ALL HE EVER CAN SEE IS DARKNESS...
HOWEVER, HE CAN TRAVEL WAYS THAT EVEN I CANNOT.
AND THE OTHER ONE? HE SPOOKS ME...
THE STRANGER? AHH. I HAVE ENCOUNTERED HIM, MANY TIMES, IN THE PAST. HE ALSO WALKS HIS OWN PATH. ONE THAT BEGAN TOO LONG AGO, AND I SUSPECT, HAS NO END IN VIEW.
I DO NOT KNOW HIS STORY. I KNOW NO ONE WHO DOES; ALTHOUGH I HAVE HEARD CONJECTURES APLENTY: THAT HE IS THE WANDERING JEW, OR AN ANGEL WHO NEITHER FELL WITH LUCIFER NOR FOUGHT AT MICHAEL'S SIDE, OR...
THERE ARE OTHER GUESSES.
SOME SAY HE OWES ALLEGIANCE TO ORDER, OR TO CHAOS, OR TO BALANCE: SPECULATIONS ALL. I DO NOT KNOW WHAT HE IS. AND PERHAPS HE HAS WALKED TO FORGET SO LONG THAT HE HIMSELF NO LONGER REMEMBERS.
AH. AND HOW ABOUT YOU?

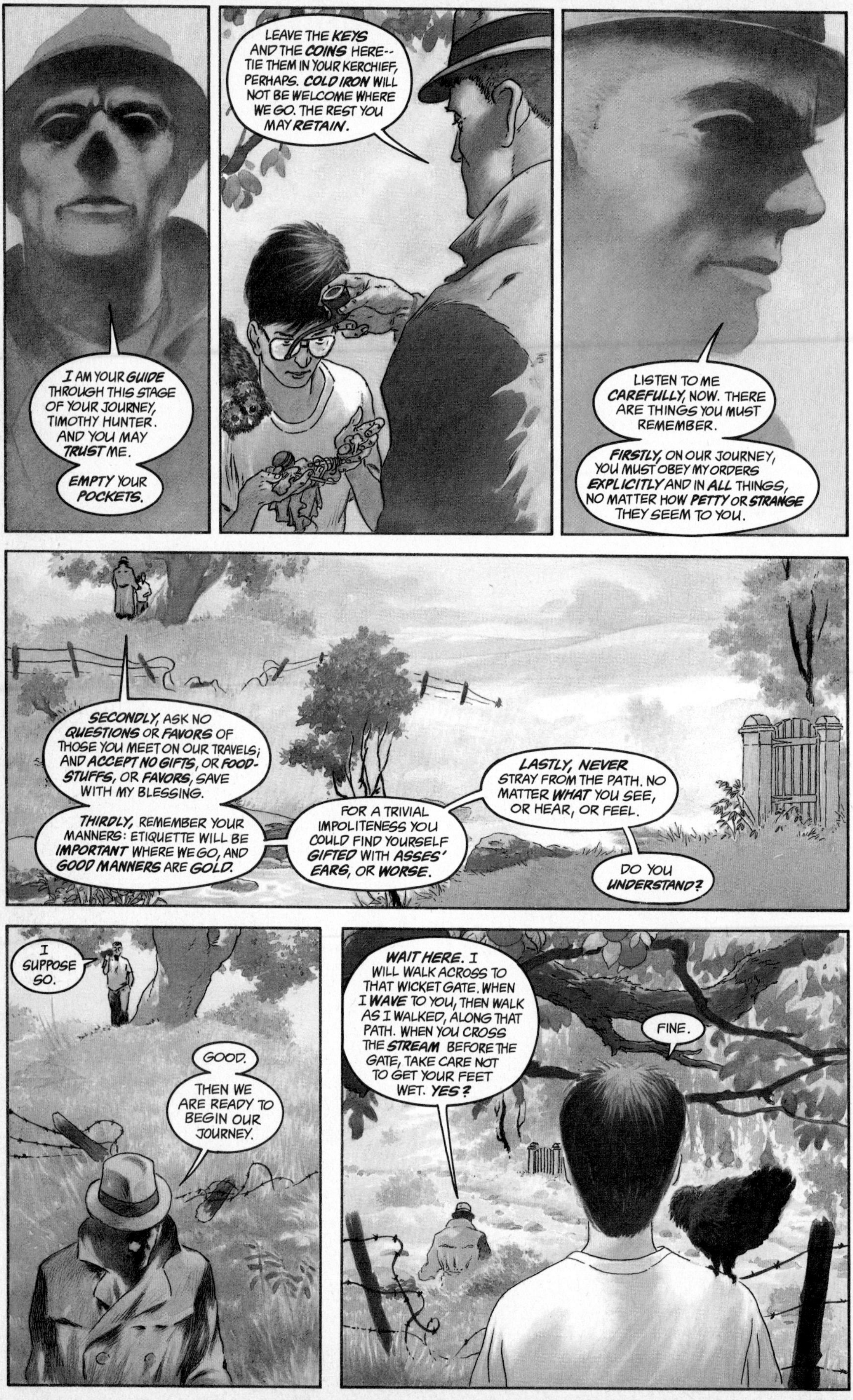
I AM YOUR GUIDE THROUGH THIS STAGE OF YOUR JOURNEY, TIMOTHY HUNTER. AND YOU MAY TRUST ME.
EMPTY YOUR POCKETS.
LEAVE THE KEYS AND THE COINS HERE-- TIE THEM IN YOUR KERCHIEF, PERHAPS. COLD IRON WILL NOT BE WELCOME WHERE WE GO. THE REST YOU MAY RETAIN.
LISTEN TO ME CAREFULLY, NOW. THERE ARE THINGS YOU MUST REMEMBER.
FIRSTLY, ON OUR JOURNEY, YOU MUST OBEY MY ORDERS EXPLICITLY AND IN ALL THINGS, NO MATTER HOW PETTY OR STRANGE THEY SEEM TO YOU.
SECONDLY, ASK NO QUESTIONS OR FAVORS OF THOSE YOU MEET ON OUR TRAVELS; AND ACCEPT NO GIFTS, OR FOOD-STUFFS, OR FAVORS, SAVE WITH MY BLESSING.
THIRDLY, REMEMBER YOUR MANNERS: ETIQUETTE WILL BE IMPORTANT WHERE WE GO, AND GOOD MANNERS ARE GOLD.
FOR A TRIVIAL IMPOLITENESS YOU COULD FIND YOURSELF GIFTED WITH ASSES' EARS, OR WORSE.
LASTLY, NEVER STRAY FROM THE PATH. NO MATTER WHAT YOU SEE, OR HEAR, OR FEEL.
DO YOU UNDERSTAND?
I SUPPOSE SO.
GOOD.
THEN WE ARE READY TO BEGIN OUR JOURNEY.
WAIT HERE. I WILL WALK ACROSS TO THAT WICKET GATE. WHEN I WAVE TO YOU, THEN WALK AS I WALKED, ALONG THAT PATH. WHEN YOU CROSS THE STREAM BEFORE THE GATE, TAKE CARE NOT TO GET YOUR FEET WET. YES?
FINE.

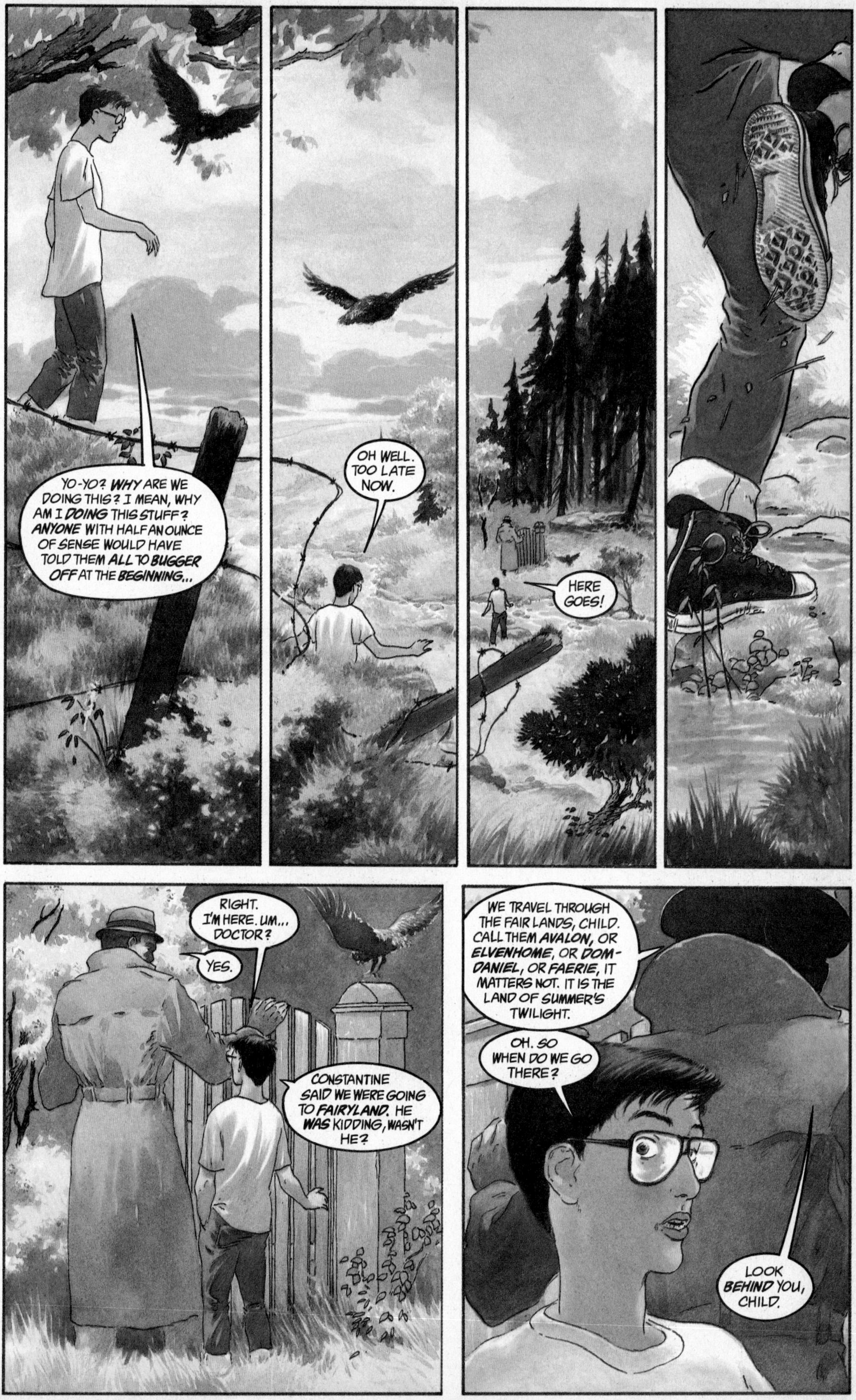
YO-YO? WHY ARE WE DOING THIS? I MEAN, WHY AM I DOING THIS STUFF? ANYONE WITH HALF AN OUNCE OF SENSE WOULD HAVE TOLD THEM ALL TO BUGGER OFF AT THE BEGINNING...
OH WELL. TOO LATE NOW.
HERE GOES!
RIGHT. I'M HERE. UM... DOCTOR?
YES.
CONSTANTINE SAID WE WERE GOING TO FAIRYLAND. HE WAS KIDDING, WASN'T HE?
WE TRAVEL THROUGH THE FAIR LANDS, CHILD. CALL THEM AVALON, OR ELVENHOME, OR DOM-DANIEL, OR FAERIE, IT MATTERS NOT. IT IS THE LAND OF SUMMER'S TWILIGHT.
OH. SO WHEN DO WE GO THERE?
LOOK BEHIND YOU, CHILD.

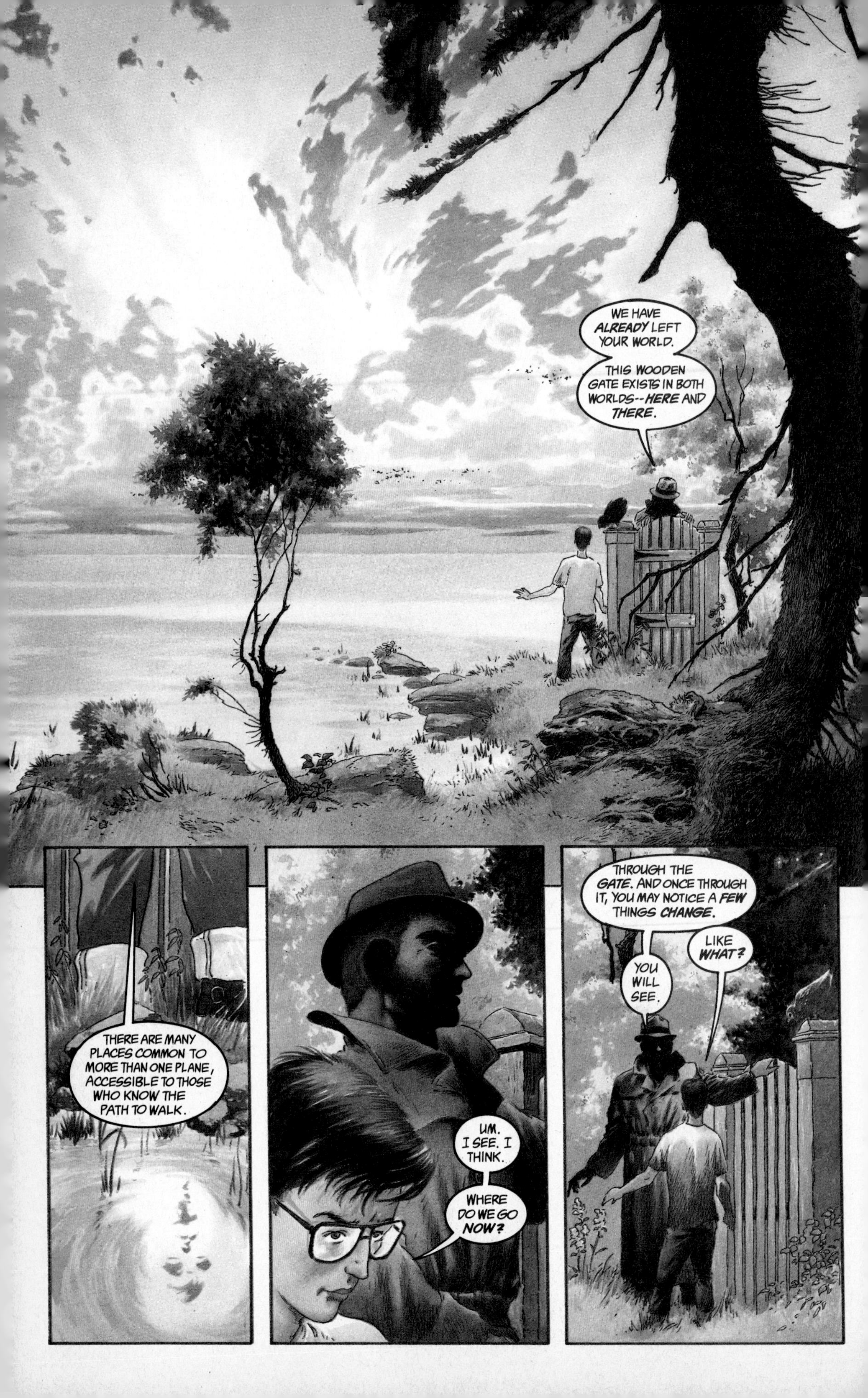
WE HAVE ALREADY LEFT YOUR WORLD.
THIS WOODEN GATE EXISTS IN BOTH WORLDS--HERE AND THERE.
THERE ARE MANY PLACES COMMON TO MORE THAN ONE PLANE, ACCESSIBLE TO THOSE WHO KNOW THE PATH TO WALK.
UM. I SEE. I THINK.
WHERE DO WE GO NOW?
THROUGH THE GATE. AND ONCE THROUGH IT, YOU MAY NOTICE A FEW THINGS CHANGE.
LIKE WHAT?
YOU WILL SEE.

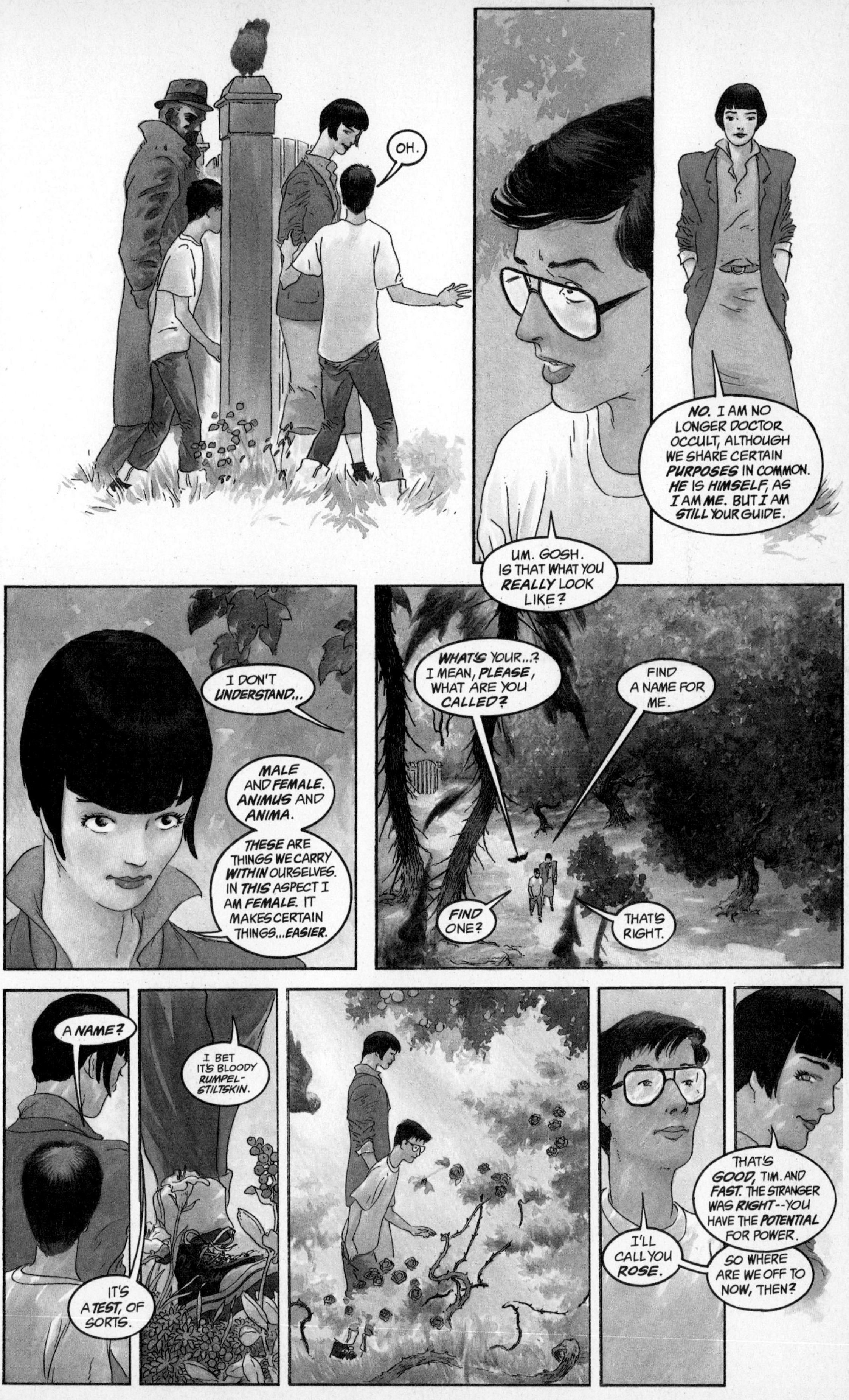

OH.
NO. I AM NO LONGER DOCTOR OCCULT, ALTHOUGH WE SHARE CERTAIN PURPOSES IN COMMON. HE IS HIMSELF, AS I AM ME. BUT I AM STILL YOUR GUIDE.
UM. GOSH. IS THAT WHAT YOU REALLY LOOK LIKE?
I DON'T UNDERSTAND...
MALE AND FEMALE. ANIMUS AND ANIMA.
THESE ARE THINGS WE CARRY WITHIN OURSELVES. IN THIS ASPECT I AM FEMALE. IT MAKES CERTAIN THINGS...EASIER.
WHAT'S YOUR...? I MEAN, PLEASE, WHAT ARE YOU CALLED?
FIND A NAME FOR ME.
FIND ONE?
THAT'S RIGHT.
A NAME?
IT'S A TEST, OF SORTS.
I BET IT'S BLOODY RUMPEL-STILTSKIN.
I'LL CALL YOU ROSE.
THAT'S GOOD, TIM. AND FAST. THE STRANGER WAS RIGHT--YOU HAVE THE POTENTIAL FOR POWER.
SO WHERE ARE WE OFF TO NOW, THEN?

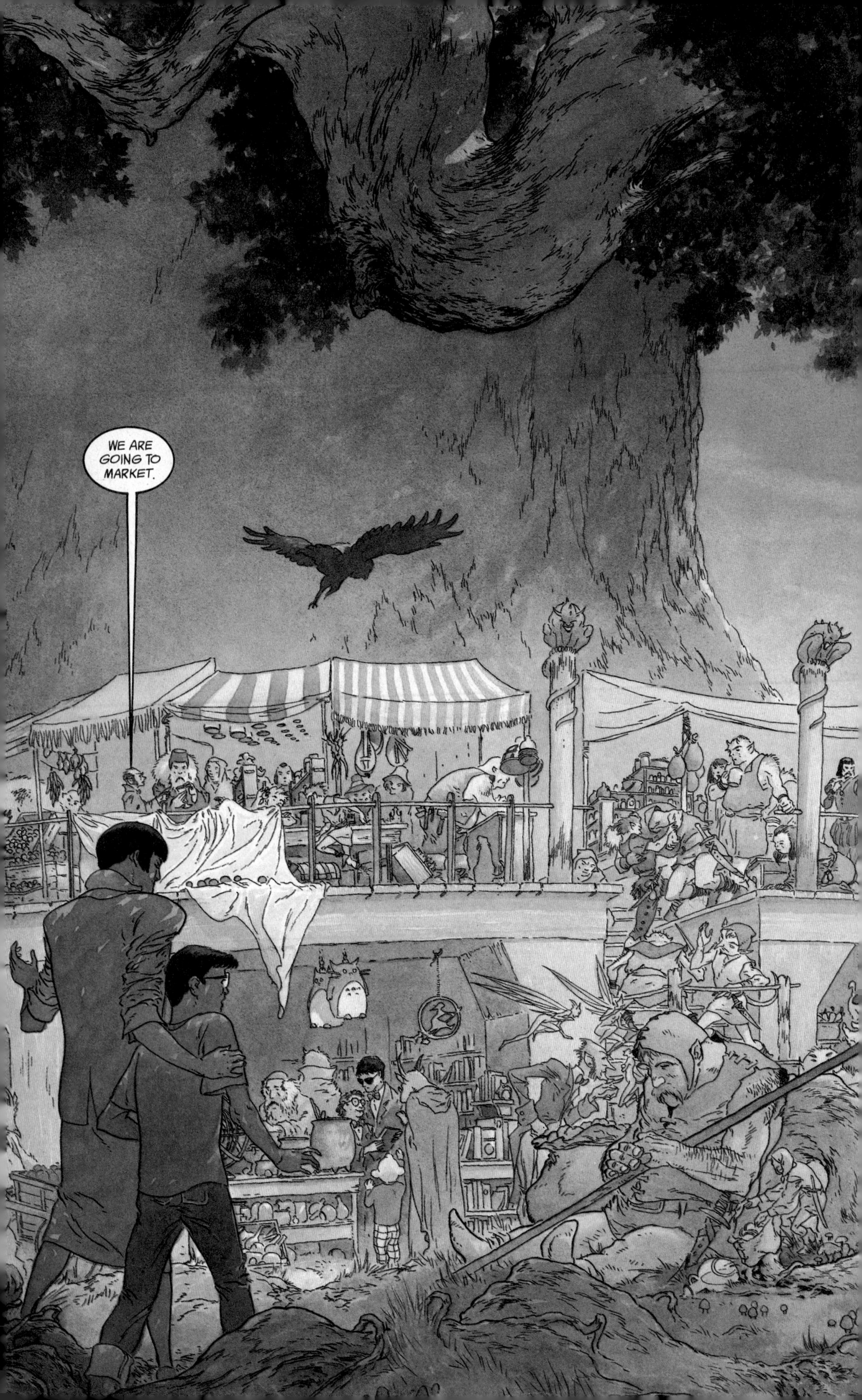
WE ARE GOING TO MARKET.

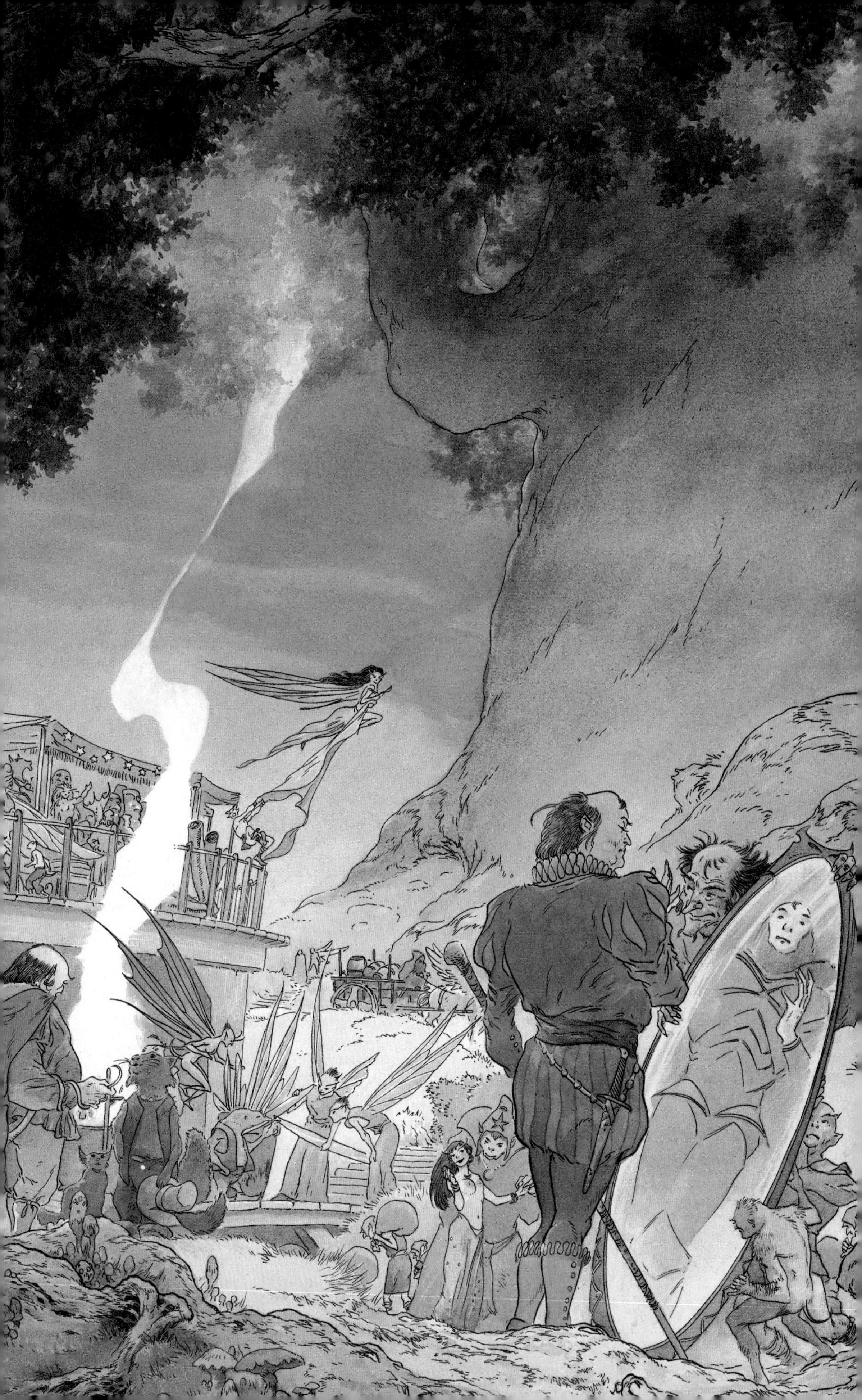

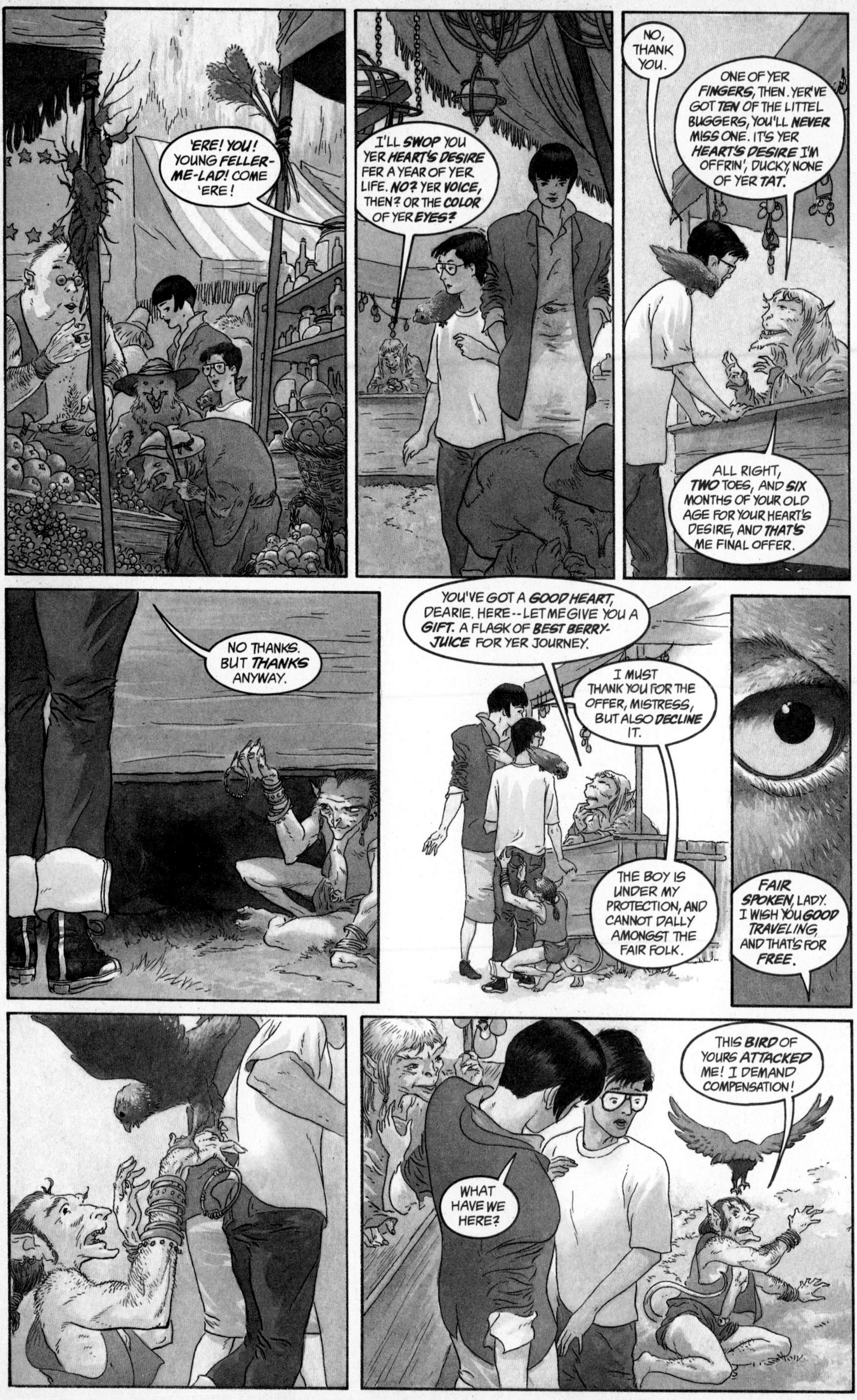
'ERE! YOU! YOUNG FELLER-ME-LAD! COME 'ERE!
I'LL SWOP YOU YER HEART'S DESIRE FER A YEAR OF YER LIFE. NO? YER VOICE, THEN? OR THE COLOR OF YER EYES?
NO, THANK YOU.
ONE OF YER FINGERS, THEN. YER'VE GOT TEN OF THE LITTEL BUGGERS, YOU'LL NEVER MISS ONE. IT'S YER HEART'S DESIRE I'M OFFRIN', DUCKY, NONE OF YER TAT.
ALL RIGHT, TWO TOES, AND SIX MONTHS OF YOUR OLD AGE FOR YOUR HEART'S DESIRE, AND THAT'S ME FINAL OFFER.
NO THANKS. BUT THANKS ANYWAY.
YOU'VE GOT A GOOD HEART, DEARIE. HERE--LET ME GIVE YOU A GIFT. A FLASK OF BEST BERRY-JUICE FOR YER JOURNEY.
I MUST THANK YOU FOR THE OFFER, MISTRESS, BUT ALSO DECLINE IT.
THE BOY IS UNDER MY PROTECTION, AND CANNOT DALLY AMONGST THE FAIR FOLK.
FAIR SPOKEN, LADY. I WISH YOU GOOD TRAVELING, AND THAT'S FOR FREE.
WHAT HAVE WE HERE?
THIS BIRD OF YOURS ATTACKED ME! I DEMAND COMPENSATION!

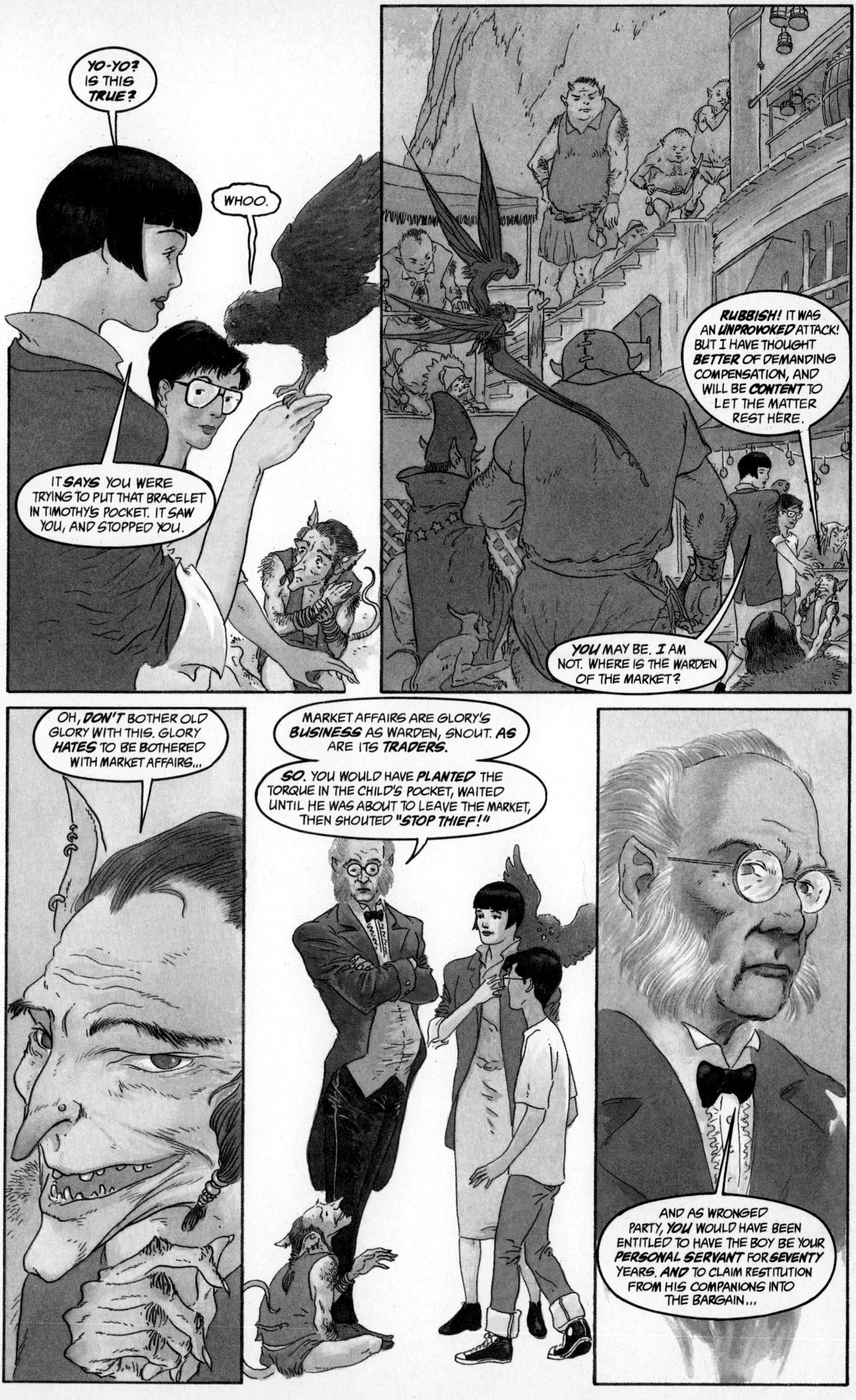
YO-YO? IS THIS TRUE?
WHOO.
IT SAYS YOU WERE TRYING TO PUT THAT BRACELET IN TIMOTHY'S POCKET. IT SAW YOU, AND STOPPED YOU.
RUBBISH! IT WAS AN UNPROVOKED ATTACK! BUT I HAVE THOUGHT BETTER OF DEMANDING COMPENSATION, AND WILL BE CONTENT TO LET THE MATTER REST HERE.
YOU MAY BE. I AM NOT. WHERE IS THE WARDEN OF THE MARKET?
OH, DON'T BOTHER OLD GLORY WITH THIS. GLORY HATES TO BE BOTHERED WITH MARKET AFFAIRS...
MARKET AFFAIRS ARE GLORY'S BUSINESS AS WARDEN, SNOUT. AS ARE ITS TRADERS.
SO. YOU WOULD HAVE PLANTED THE TORQUE IN THE CHILD'S POCKET, WAITED UNTIL HE WAS ABOUT TO LEAVE THE MARKET, THEN SHOUTED "STOP THIEF!"
AND AS WRONGED PARTY, YOU WOULD HAVE BEEN ENTITLED TO HAVE THE BOY BE YOUR PERSONAL SERVANT FOR SEVENTY YEARS. AND TO CLAIM RESTITUTION FROM HIS COMPANIONS INTO THE BARGAIN...

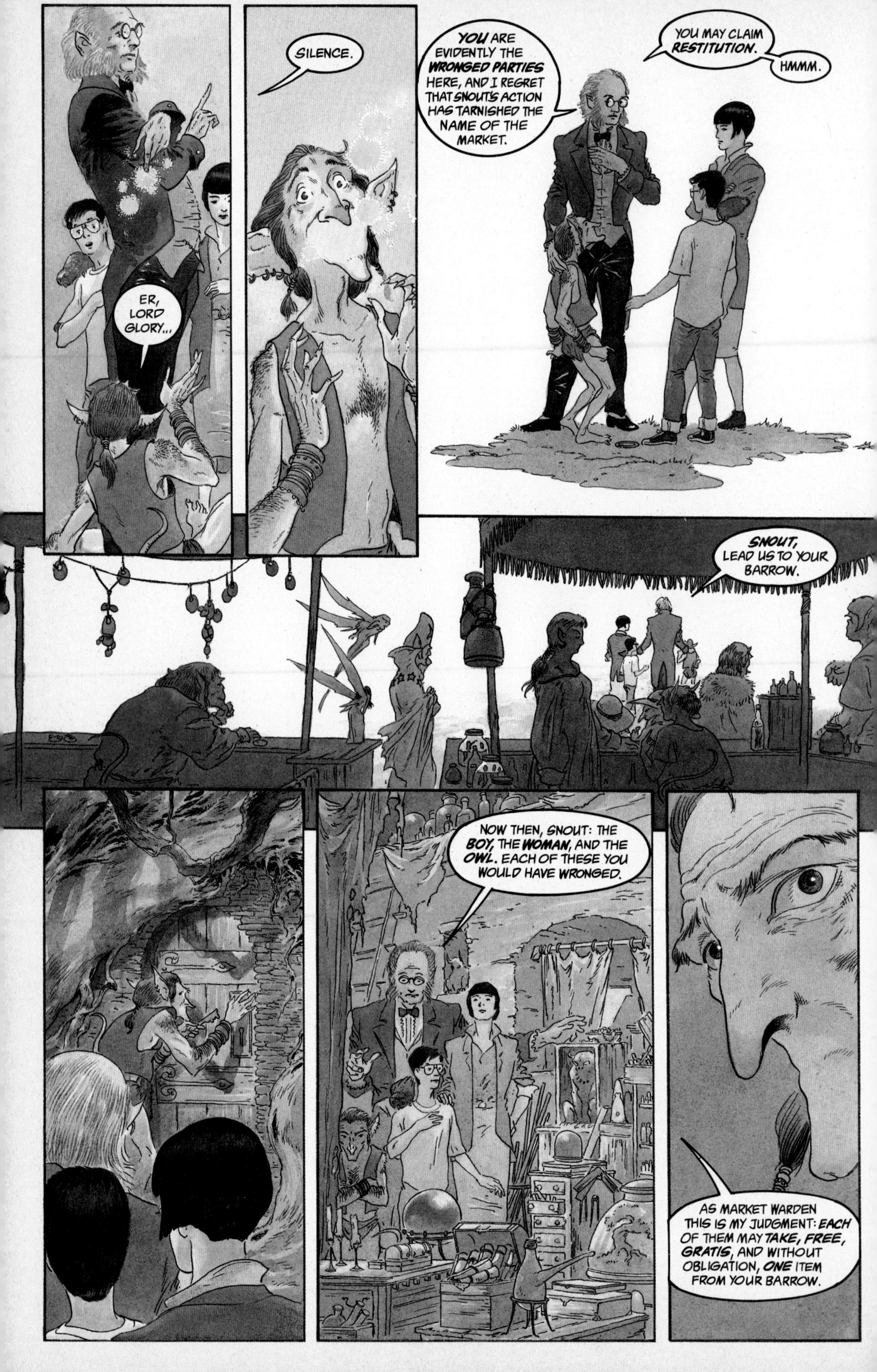
ER, LORD GLORY...
SILENCE.
YOU ARE EVIDENTLY THE WRONGED PARTIES HERE, AND I REGRET THAT SNOUT'S ACTION HAS TARNISHED THE NAME OF THE MARKET.
YOU MAY CLAIM RESTITUTION.
HMMM.
SNOUT, LEAD US TO YOUR BARROW.
NOW THEN, SNOUT: THE BOY, THE WOMAN, AND THE OWL. EACH OF THESE YOU WOULD HAVE WRONGED.
AS MARKET WARDEN THIS IS MY JUDGMENT: EACH OF THEM MAY TAKE, FREE, GRATIS, AND WITHOUT OBLIGATION, ONE ITEM FROM YOUR BARROW.

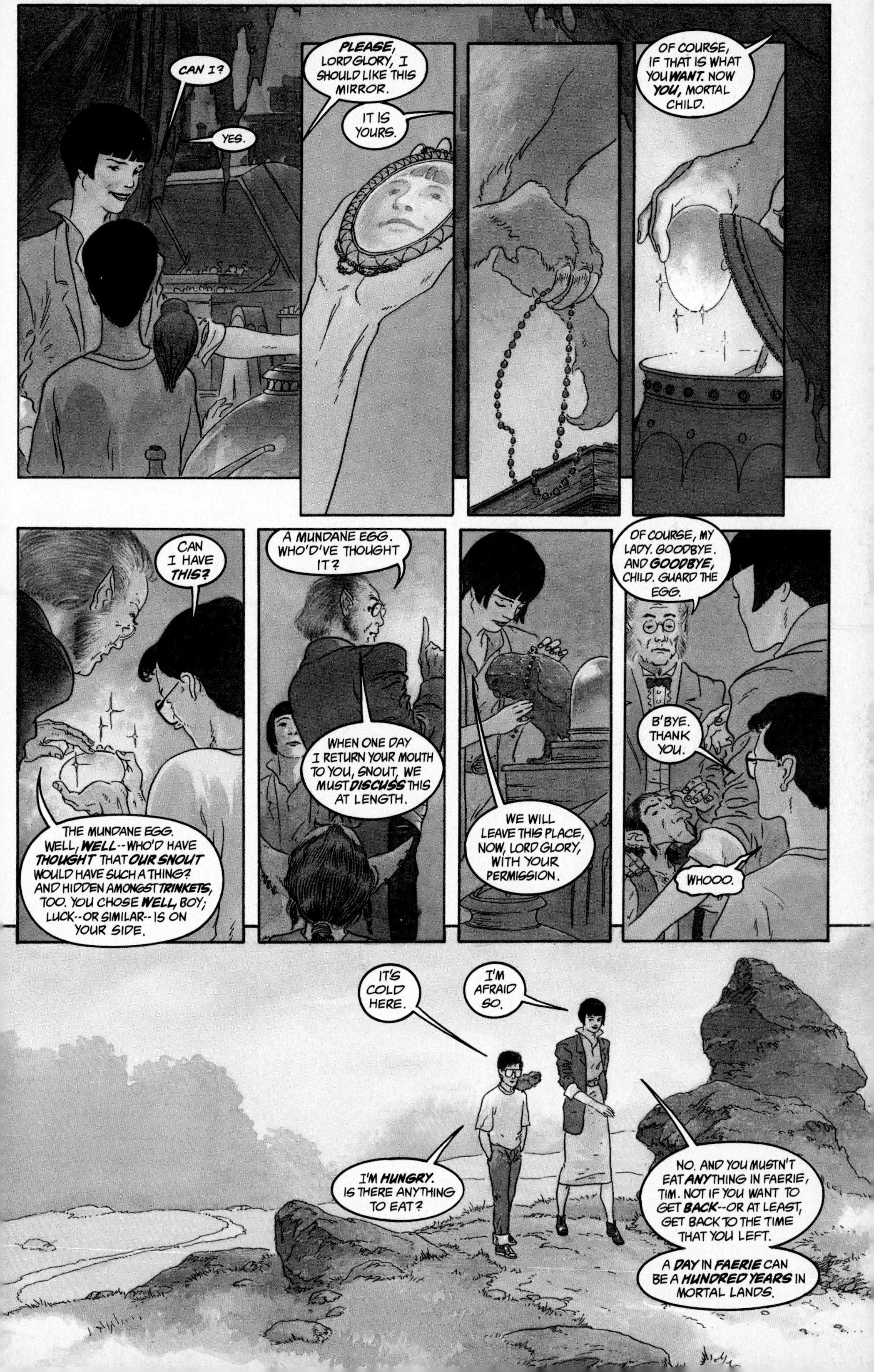
CAN I?
YES.
PLEASE, LORD GLORY, I SHOULD LIKE THIS MIRROR.
IT IS YOURS.
OF COURSE, IF THAT IS WHAT YOU WANT. NOW YOU, MORTAL CHILD.
CAN I HAVE THIS?
THE MUNDANE EGG. WELL, WELL--WHO'D HAVE THOUGHT THAT OUR SNOUT WOULD HAVE SUCH A THING? AND HIDDEN AMONGST TRINKETS, TOO. YOU CHOSE WELL, BOY; LUCK--OR SIMILAR--IS ON YOUR SIDE.
A MUNDANE EGG. WHO'D'VE THOUGHT IT?
WHEN ONE DAY I RETURN YOUR MOUTH TO YOU, SNOUT, WE MUST DISCUSS THIS AT LENGTH.
WE WILL LEAVE THIS PLACE, NOW, LORD GLORY, WITH YOUR PERMISSION.
OF COURSE, MY LADY. GOODBYE. AND GOODBYE, CHILD. GUARD THE EGG.
B'BYE. THANK YOU.
WHOOO.
IT'S COLD HERE.
I'M AFRAID SO.
I'M HUNGRY. IS THERE ANYTHING TO EAT?
NO. AND YOU MUSTN'T EAT ANYTHING IN FAERIE, TIM. NOT IF YOU WANT TO GET BACK--OR AT LEAST, GET BACK TO THE TIME THAT YOU LEFT.
A DAY IN FAERIE CAN BE A HUNDRED YEARS IN MORTAL LANDS.

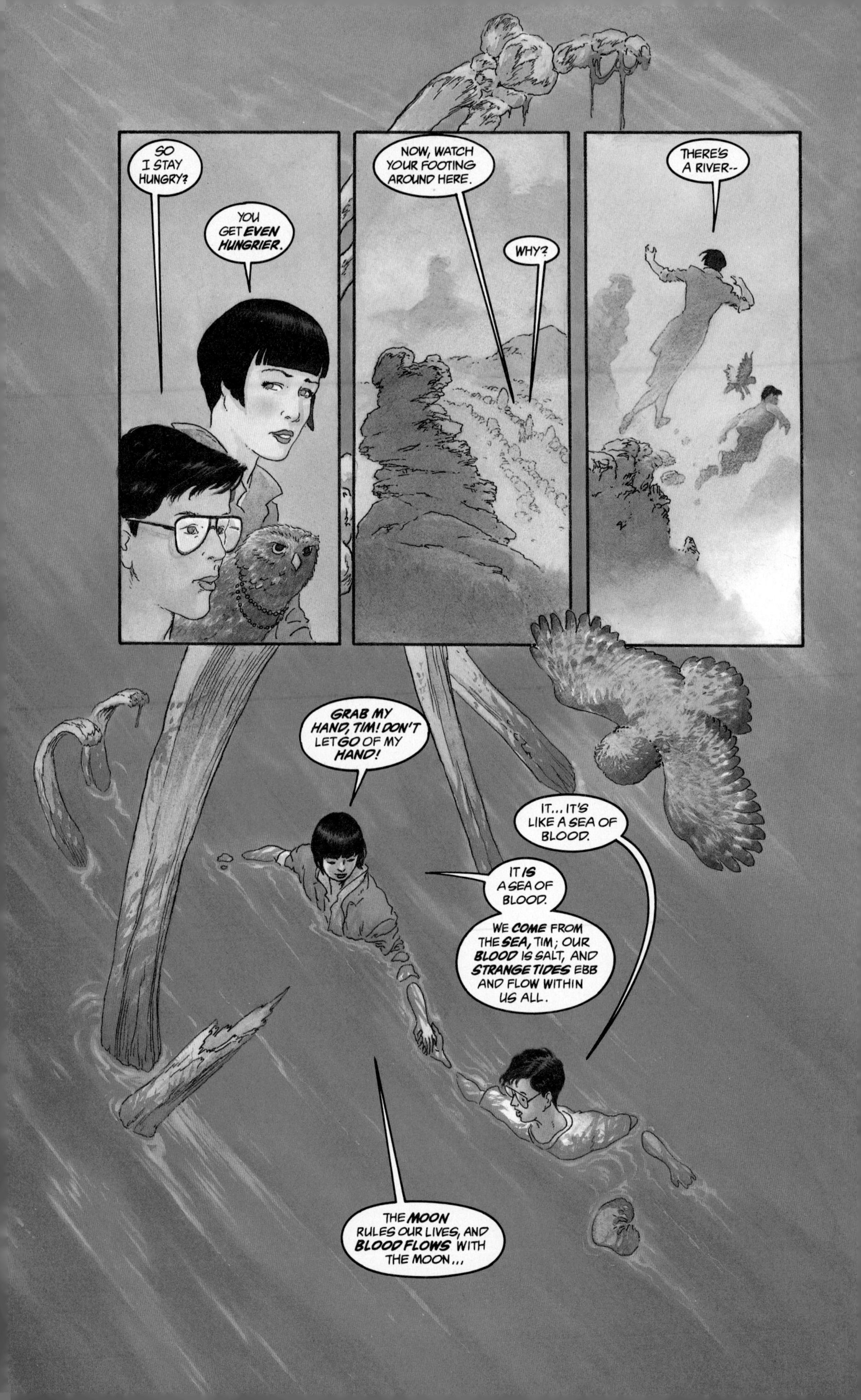
SO I STAY HUNGRY?
YOU GET EVEN HUNGRIER.
NOW, WATCH YOUR FOOTING AROUND HERE.
WHY?
THERE'S A RIVER--
GRAB MY HAND, TIM! DON'T LET GO OF MY HAND!
IT... IT'S LIKE A SEA OF BLOOD.
IT IS A SEA OF BLOOD.
WE COME FROM THE SEA, TIM; OUR BLOOD IS SALT, AND STRANGE TIDES EBB AND FLOW WITHIN US ALL.
THE MOON RULES OUR LIVES, AND BLOOD FLOWS WITH THE MOON...

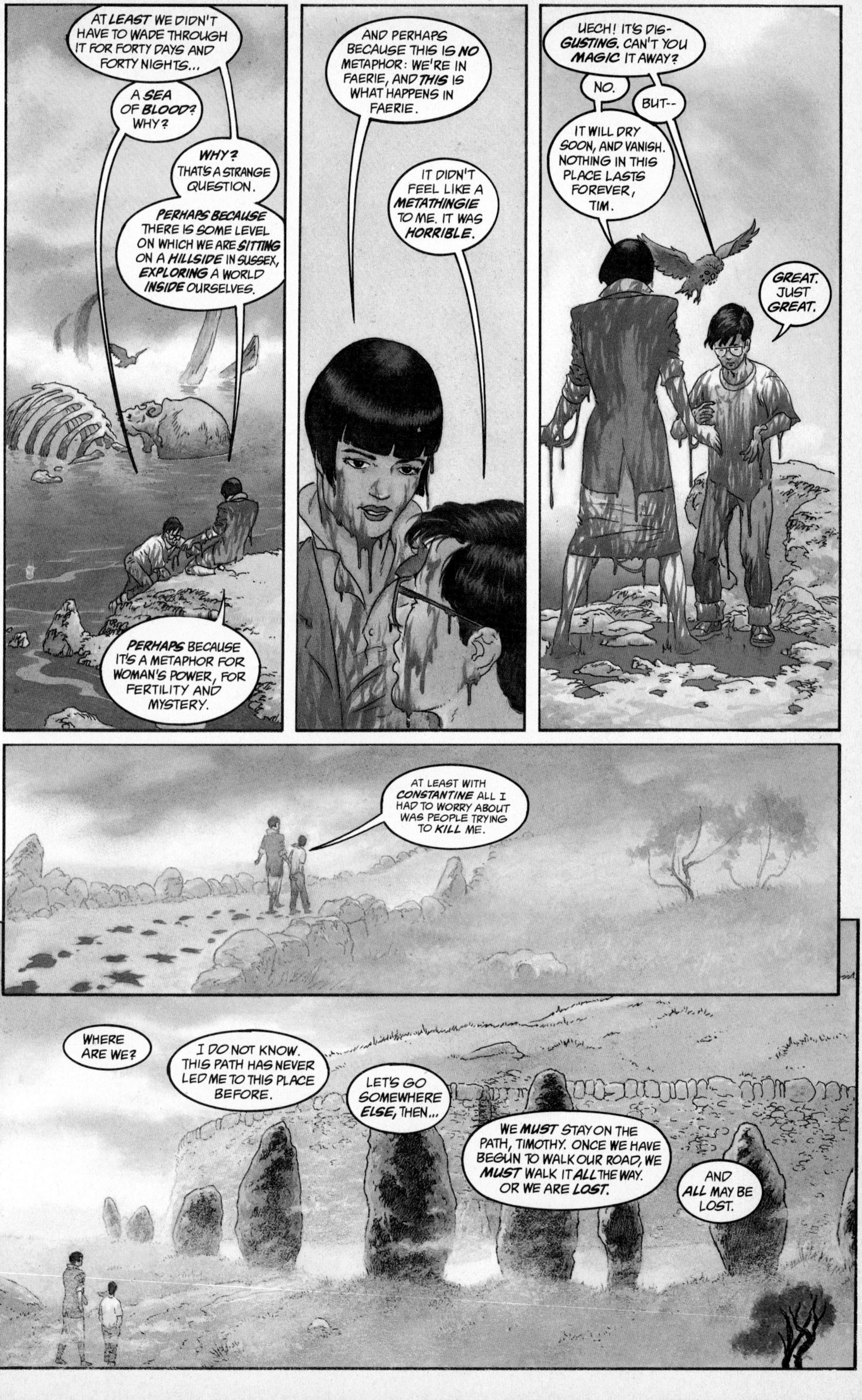
AT LEAST WE DIDN'T HAVE TO WADE THROUGH IT FOR FORTY DAYS AND FORTY NIGHTS...
A SEA OF BLOOD? WHY?
WHY? THAT'S A STRANGE QUESTION.
PERHAPS BECAUSE THERE IS SOME LEVEL ON WHICH WE ARE SITTING ON A HILLSIDE IN SUSSEX, EXPLORING A WORLD INSIDE OURSELVES.
PERHAPS BECAUSE IT'S A METAPHOR FOR WOMAN'S POWER, FOR FERTILITY AND MYSTERY.
AND PERHAPS BECAUSE THIS IS NO METAPHOR: WE'RE IN FAERIE, AND THIS IS WHAT HAPPENS IN FAERIE.
IT DIDN'T FEEL LIKE A METATHINGIE TO ME. IT WAS HORRIBLE.
UECH! IT'S DISGUSTING. CAN'T YOU MAGIC IT AWAY?
NO.
BUT--
IT WILL DRY SOON, AND VANISH. NOTHING IN THIS PLACE LASTS FOREVER, TIM.
GREAT. JUST GREAT.
AT LEAST WITH CONSTANTINE ALL I HAD TO WORRY ABOUT WAS PEOPLE TRYING TO KILL ME.
WHERE ARE WE?
I DO NOT KNOW. THIS PATH HAS NEVER LED ME TO THIS PLACE BEFORE.
LET'S GO SOMEWHERE ELSE, THEN...
WE MUST STAY ON THE PATH, TIMOTHY. ONCE WE HAVE BEGUN TO WALK OUR ROAD, WE MUST WALK IT ALL THE WAY. OR WE ARE LOST.
AND ALL MAY BE LOST.

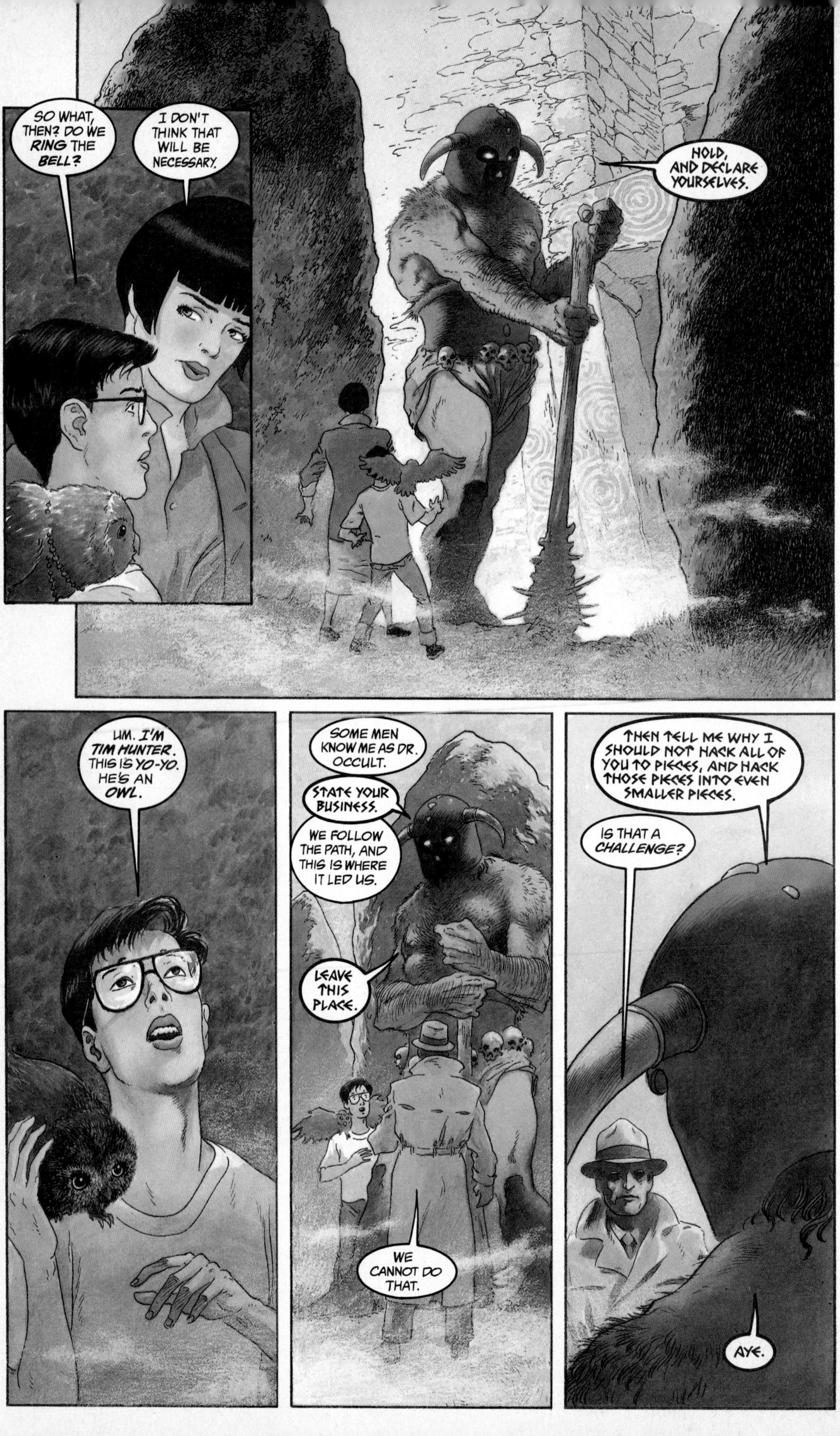
SO WHAT, THEN? DO WE RING THE BELL?
I DON'T THINK THAT WILL BE NECESSARY.
HOLD, AND DECLARE YOURSELVES.
UM. I'M TIM HUNTER. THIS IS YO-YO. HE'S AN OWL.
SOME MEN KNOW ME AS DR. OCCULT.
STATE YOUR BUSINESS.
WE FOLLOW THE PATH, AND THIS IS WHERE IT LED US.
LEAVE THIS PLACE.
WE CANNOT DO THAT.
THEN TELL ME WHY I SHOULD NOT HACK ALL OF YOU TO PIECES, AND HACK THOSE PIECES INTO EVEN SMALLER PIECES.
IS THAT A CHALLENGE?
AYE.

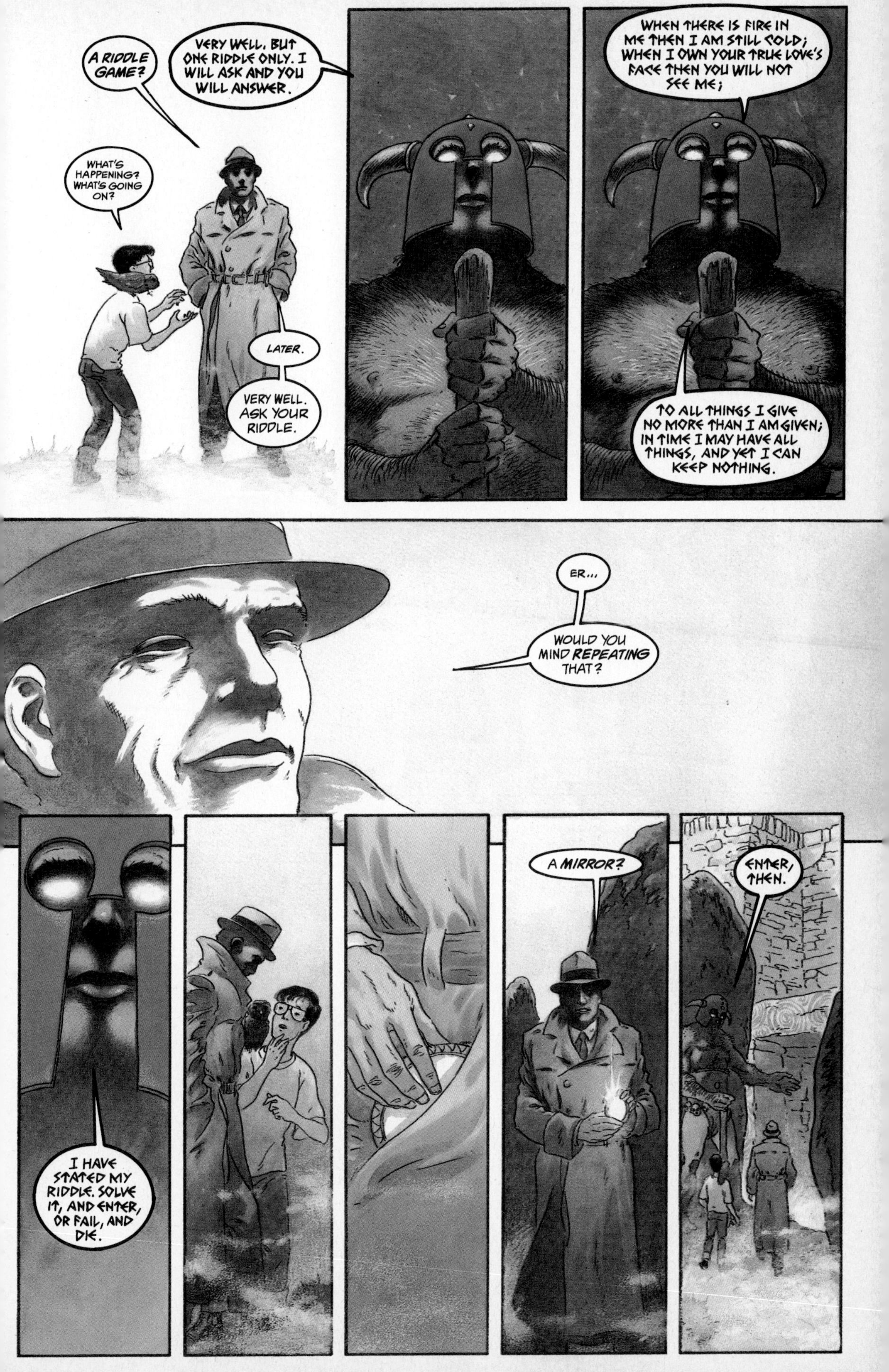
A RIDDLE GAME?
VERY WELL. BUT ONE RIDDLE ONLY. I WILL ASK AND YOU WILL ANSWER.
WHAT'S HAPPENING? WHAT'S GOING ON?
LATER.
VERY WELL. ASK YOUR RIDDLE.
WHEN THERE IS FIRE IN ME THEN I AM STILL COLD; WHEN I OWN YOUR TRUE LOVE'S FACE THEN YOU WILL NOT SEE ME;
TO ALL THINGS I GIVE NO MORE THAN I AM GIVEN; IN TIME I MAY HAVE ALL THINGS, AND YET I CAN KEEP NOTHING.
ER...
WOULD YOU MIND REPEATING THAT?
I HAVE STATED MY RIDDLE. SOLVE IT, AND ENTER, OR FAIL, AND DIE.
A MIRROR?
ENTER, THEN.

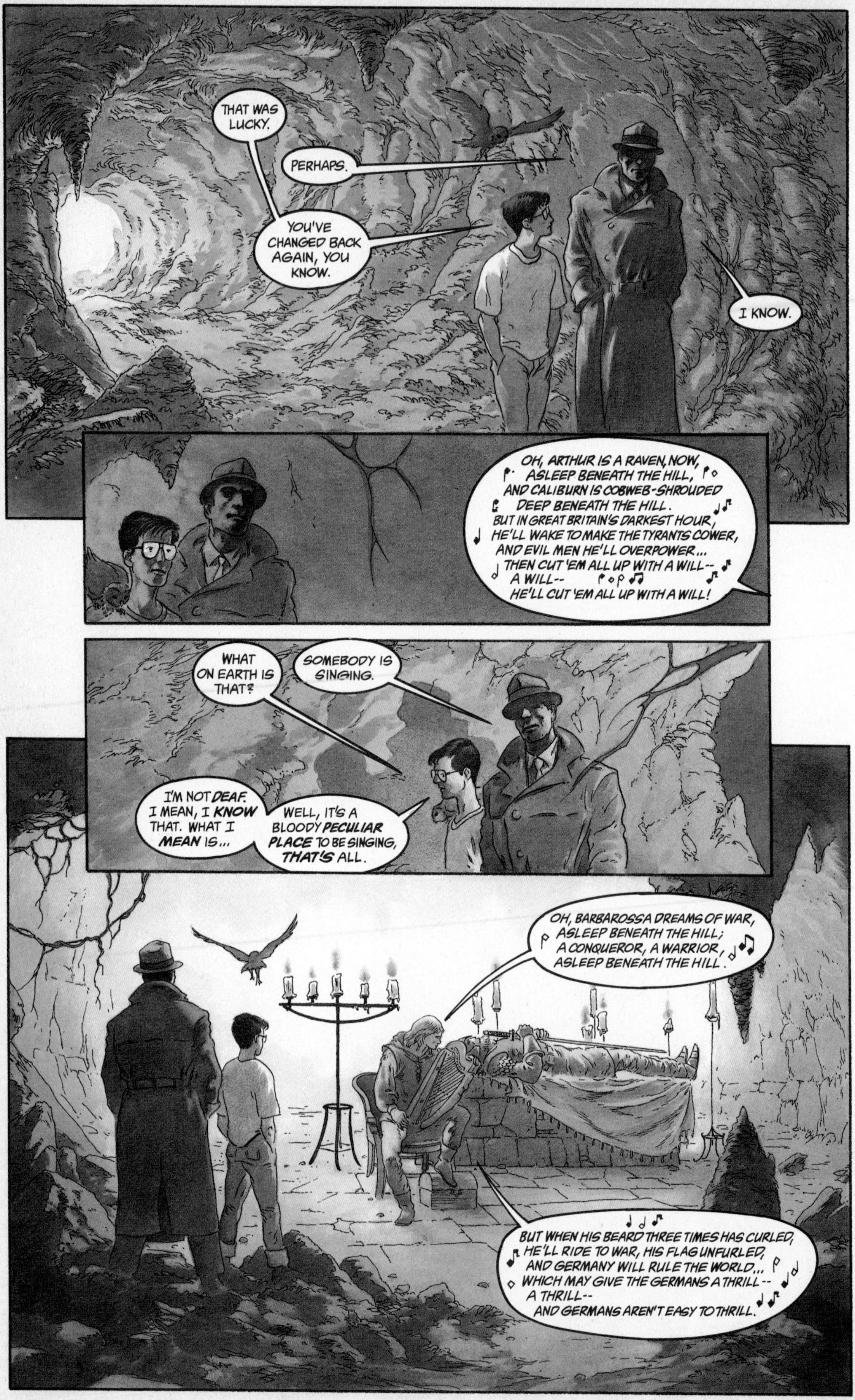
THAT WAS LUCKY.
PERHAPS.
YOU'VE CHANGED BACK AGAIN, YOU KNOW.
I KNOW.
OH, ARTHUR IS A RAVEN, NOW, ASLEEP BENEATH THE HILL, AND CALIBURN IS COBWEB-SHROUDED DEEP BENEATH THE HILL. BUT IN GREAT BRITAIN'S DARKEST HOUR, HE'LL WAKE TO MAKE THE TYRANTS COWER, AND EVIL MEN HE'LL OVERPOWER... THEN CUT 'EM ALL UP WITH A WILL-- A WILL-- HE'LL CUT 'EM ALL UP WITH A WILL!
WHAT ON EARTH IS THAT?
SOMEBODY IS SINGING.
I'M NOT DEAF. I MEAN, I KNOW THAT. WHAT I MEAN IS...
WELL, IT'S A BLOODY PECULIAR PLACE TO BE SINGING, THAT'S ALL.
OH, BARBAROSSA DREAMS OF WAR, ASLEEP BENEATH THE HILL; A CONQUEROR, A WARRIOR, ASLEEP BENEATH THE HILL.
BUT WHEN HIS BEARD THREE TIMES HAS CURLED, HE'LL RIDE TO WAR, HIS FLAG UNFURLED, AND GERMANY WILL RULE THE WORLD... WHICH MAY GIVE THE GERMANS A THRILL-- A THRILL-- AND GERMANS AREN'T EASY TO THRILL.

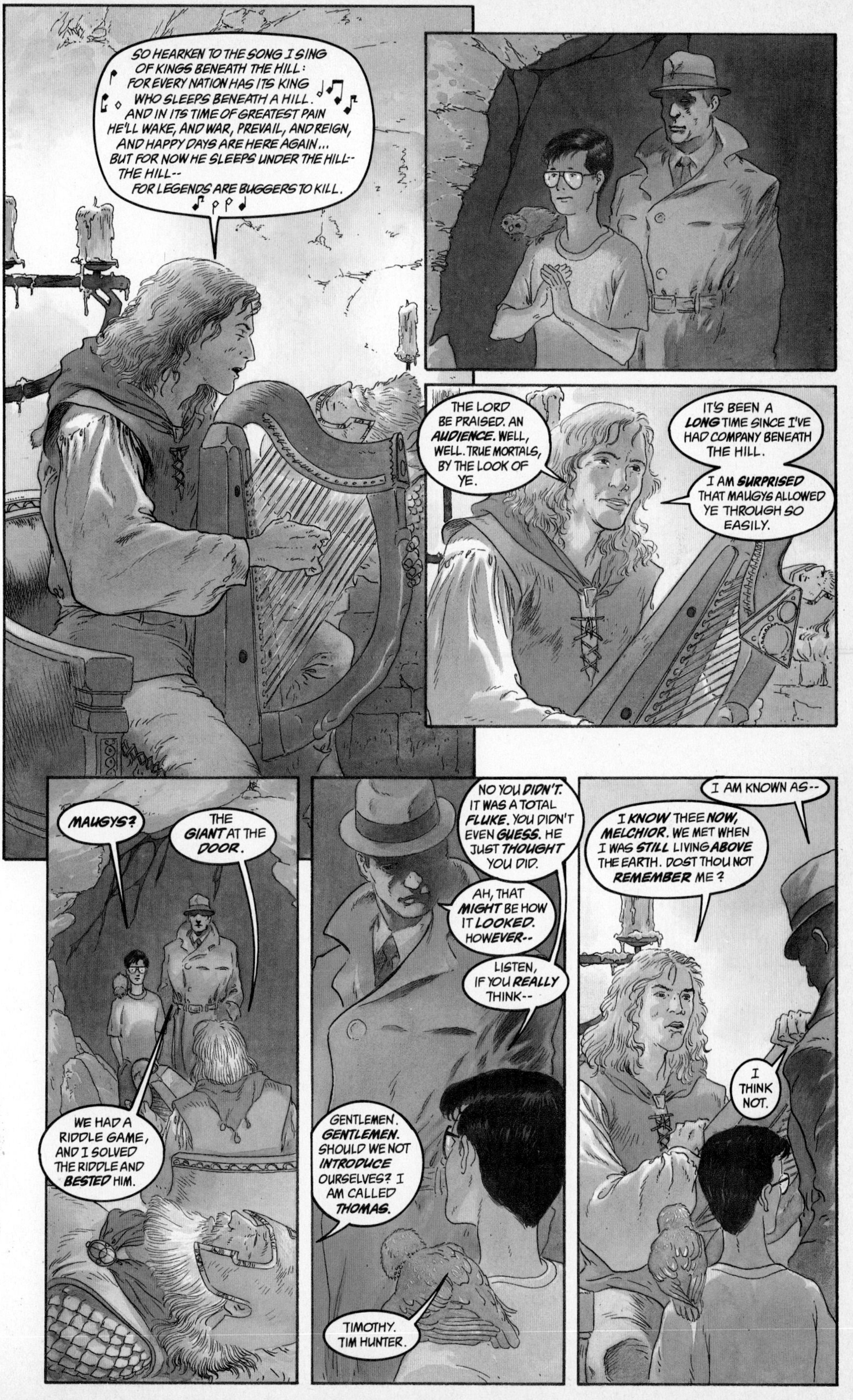

SO HEARKEN TO THE SONG I SING OF KINGS BENEATH THE HILL: FOR EVERY NATION HAS ITS KING WHO SLEEPS BENEATH A HILL. AND IN ITS TIME OF GREATEST PAIN HE'LL WAKE, AND WAR, PREVAIL, AND REIGN, AND HAPPY DAYS ARE HERE AGAIN... BUT FOR NOW HE SLEEPS UNDER THE HILL-- THE HILL-- FOR LEGENDS ARE BUGGERS TO KILL.
THE LORD BE PRAISED. AN AUDIENCE. WELL, WELL. TRUE MORTALS, BY THE LOOK OF YE.
IT'S BEEN A LONG TIME SINCE I'VE HAD COMPANY BENEATH THE HILL.
I AM SURPRISED THAT MAUGYS ALLOWED YE THROUGH SO EASILY.
MAUGYS?
THE GIANT AT THE DOOR.
WE HAD A RIDDLE GAME, AND I SOLVED THE RIDDLE AND BESTED HIM.
NO YOU DIDN'T. IT WAS A TOTAL FLUKE. YOU DIDN'T EVEN GUESS. HE JUST THOUGHT YOU DID.
AH, THAT MIGHT BE HOW IT LOOKED. HOWEVER--
LISTEN, IF YOU REALLY THINK--
GENTLEMEN. GENTLEMEN. SHOULD WE NOT INTRODUCE OURSELVES? I AM CALLED THOMAS.
TIMOTHY. TIM HUNTER.
I AM KNOWN AS--
I KNOW THEE NOW, MELCHIOR. WE MET WHEN I WAS STILL LIVING ABOVE THE EARTH. DOST THOU NOT REMEMBER ME?
I THINK NOT.

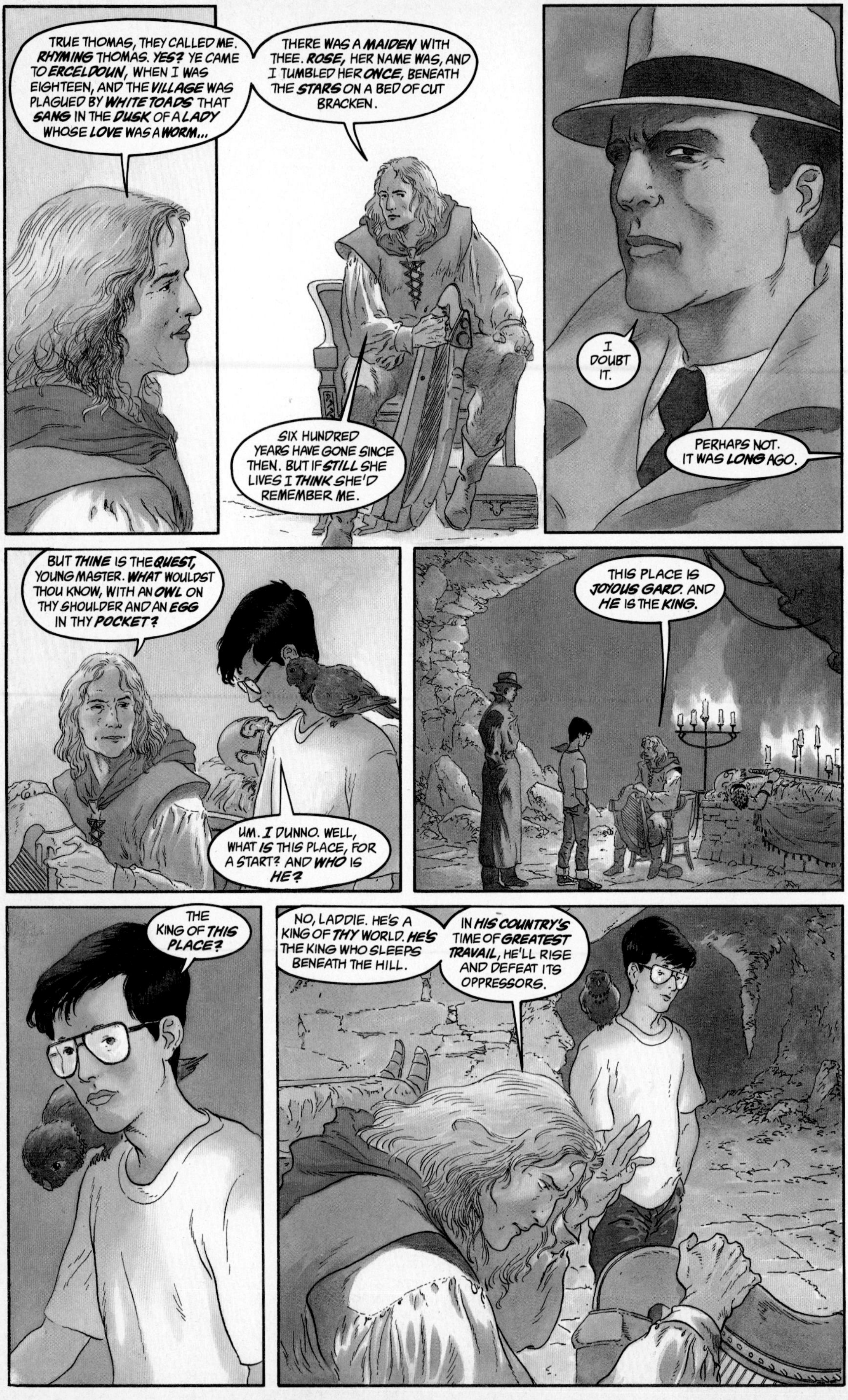
TRUE THOMAS, THEY CALLED ME. RHYMING THOMAS. YES? YE CAME TO ERCELDOUN, WHEN I WAS EIGHTEEN, AND THE VILLAGE WAS PLAGUED BY WHITE TOADS THAT SANG IN THE DUSK OF A LADY WHOSE LOVE WAS A WORM...
THERE WAS A MAIDEN WITH THEE. ROSE, HER NAME WAS, AND I TUMBLED HER ONCE, BENEATH THE STARS ON A BED OF CUT BRACKEN.
SIX HUNDRED YEARS HAVE GONE SINCE THEN. BUT IF STILL SHE LIVES I THINK SHE'D REMEMBER ME.
I DOUBT IT.
PERHAPS NOT. IT WAS LONG AGO.
BUT THINE IS THE QUEST, YOUNG MASTER. WHAT WOULDST THOU KNOW, WITH AN OWL ON THY SHOULDER AND AN EGG IN THY POCKET?
UM. I DUNNO. WELL, WHAT IS THIS PLACE, FOR A START? AND WHO IS HE?
THIS PLACE IS JOYOUS GARD. AND HE IS THE KING.
THE KING OF THIS PLACE?
NO, LADDIE. HE'S A KING OF THY WORLD. HE'S THE KING WHO SLEEPS BENEATH THE HILL.
IN HIS COUNTRY'S TIME OF GREATEST TRAVAIL, HE'LL RISE AND DEFEAT ITS OPPRESSORS.

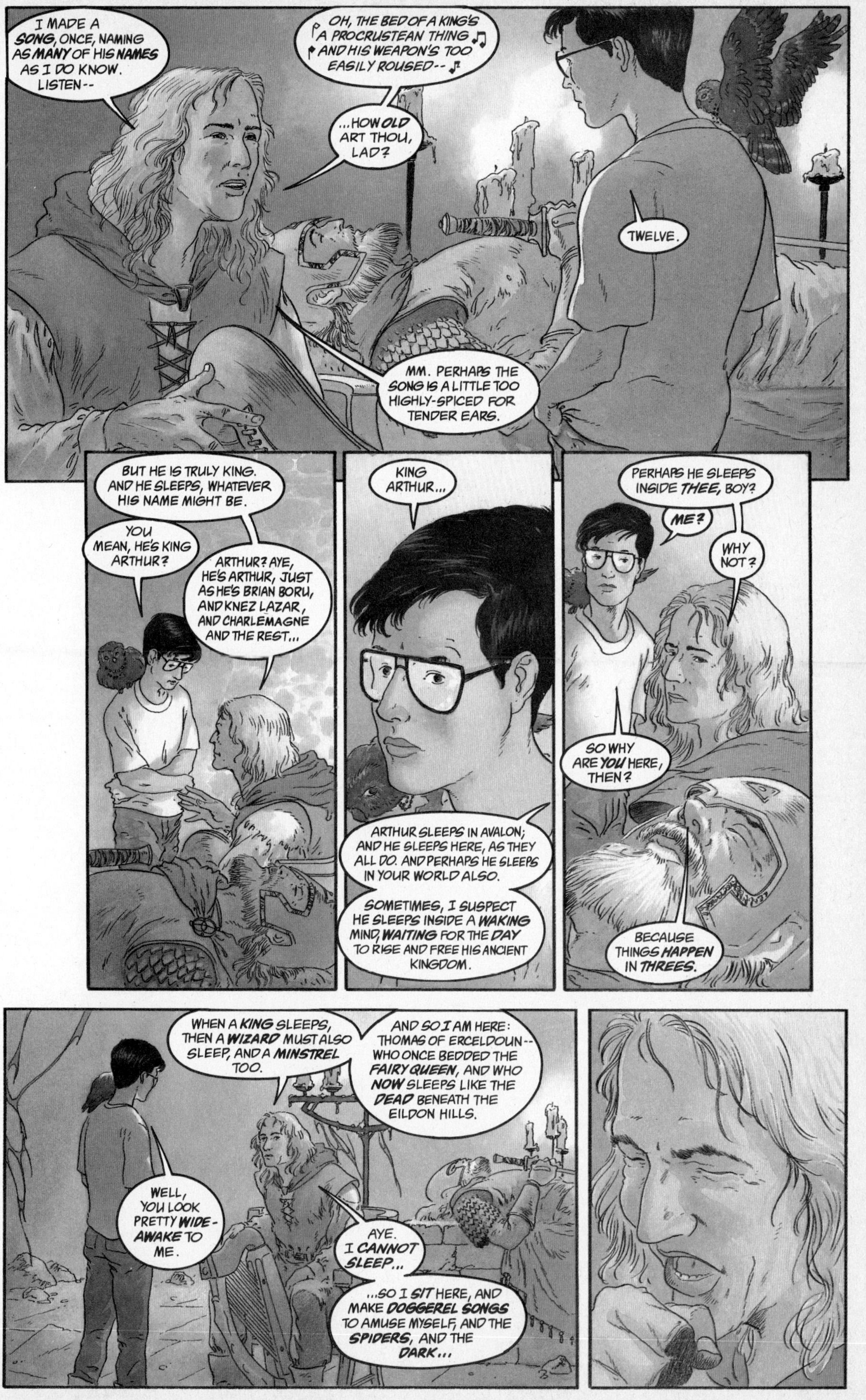

I MADE A SONG, ONCE, NAMING AS MANY OF HIS NAMES AS I DO KNOW. LISTEN--
OH, THE BED OF A KING'S A PROCRUSTEAN THING AND HIS WEAPON'S TOO EASILY ROUSED--
...HOW OLD ART THOU, LAD?
TWELVE.
MM. PERHAPS THE SONG IS A LITTLE TOO HIGHLY-SPICED FOR TENDER EARS.
BUT HE IS TRULY KING. AND HE SLEEPS, WHATEVER HIS NAME MIGHT BE.
YOU MEAN, HE'S KING ARTHUR?
ARTHUR? AYE, HE'S ARTHUR, JUST AS HE'S BRIAN BORU, AND KNEZ LAZAR, AND CHARLEMAGNE AND THE REST...
KING ARTHUR...
ARTHUR SLEEPS IN AVALON; AND HE SLEEPS HERE, AS THEY ALL DO. AND PERHAPS HE SLEEPS IN YOUR WORLD ALSO.
SOMETIMES, I SUSPECT HE SLEEPS INSIDE A WAKING MIND, WAITING FOR THE DAY TO RISE AND FREE HIS ANCIENT KINGDOM.
PERHAPS HE SLEEPS INSIDE THEE, BOY?
ME?
WHY NOT?
SO WHY ARE YOU HERE, THEN?
BECAUSE THINGS HAPPEN IN THREES.
WHEN A KING SLEEPS, THEN A WIZARD MUST ALSO SLEEP, AND A MINSTREL TOO.
AND SO I AM HERE: THOMAS OF ERCELDOUN--WHO ONCE BEDDED THE FAIRY QUEEN, AND WHO NOW SLEEPS LIKE THE DEAD BENEATH THE EILDON HILLS.
WELL, YOU LOOK PRETTY WIDE-AWAKE TO ME.
AYE. I CANNOT SLEEP...
...SO I SIT HERE, AND MAKE DOGGEREL SONGS TO AMUSE MYSELF, AND THE SPIDERS, AND THE DARK...

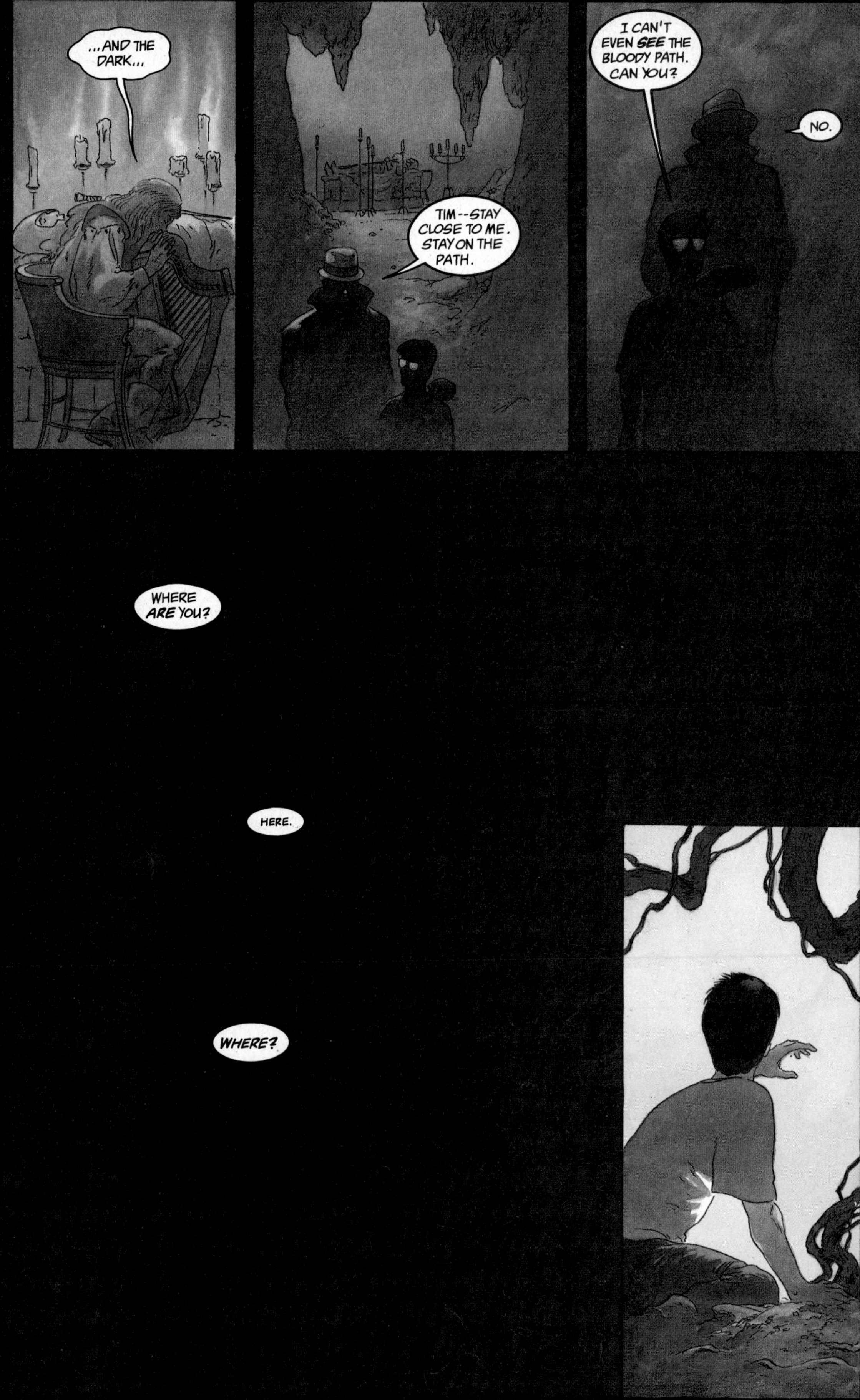
...AND THE DARK...
TIM--STAY CLOSE TO ME. STAY ON THE PATH.
I CAN'T EVEN SEE THE BLOODY PATH. CAN YOU?
NO.
WHERE ARE YOU?
HERE.
WHERE?

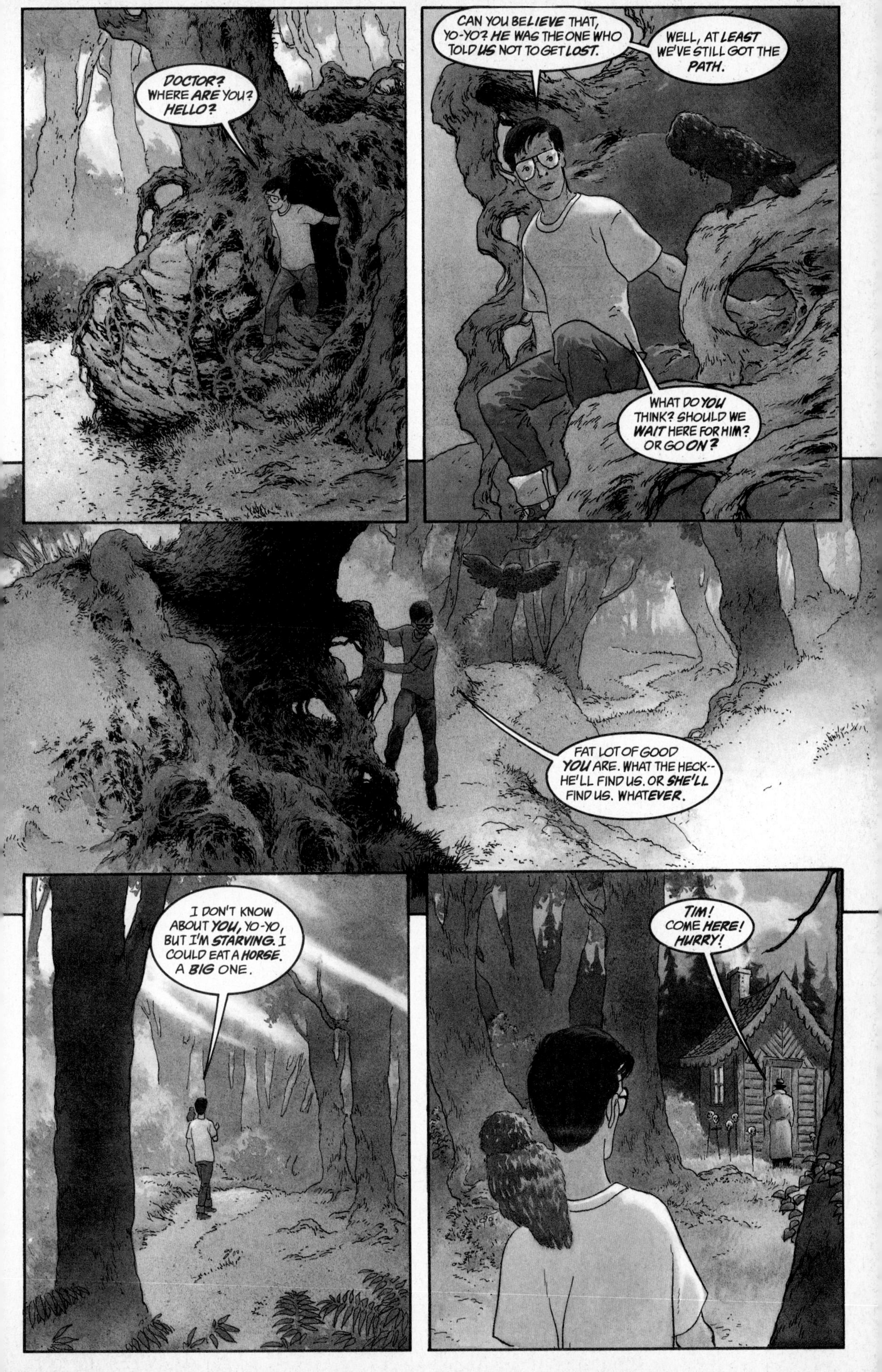
DOCTOR? WHERE ARE YOU? HELLO?
CAN YOU BELIEVE THAT, YO-YO? HE WAS THE ONE WHO TOLD US NOT TO GET LOST.
WELL, AT LEAST WE'VE STILL GOT THE PATH.
WHAT DO YOU THINK? SHOULD WE WAIT HERE FOR HIM? OR GO ON?
FAT LOT OF GOOD YOU ARE. WHAT THE HECK-- HE'LL FIND US. OR SHE'LL FIND US. WHATEVER.
I DON'T KNOW ABOUT YOU, YO-YO, BUT I'M STARVING. I COULD EAT A HORSE. A BIG ONE.
TIM! COME HERE! HURRY!

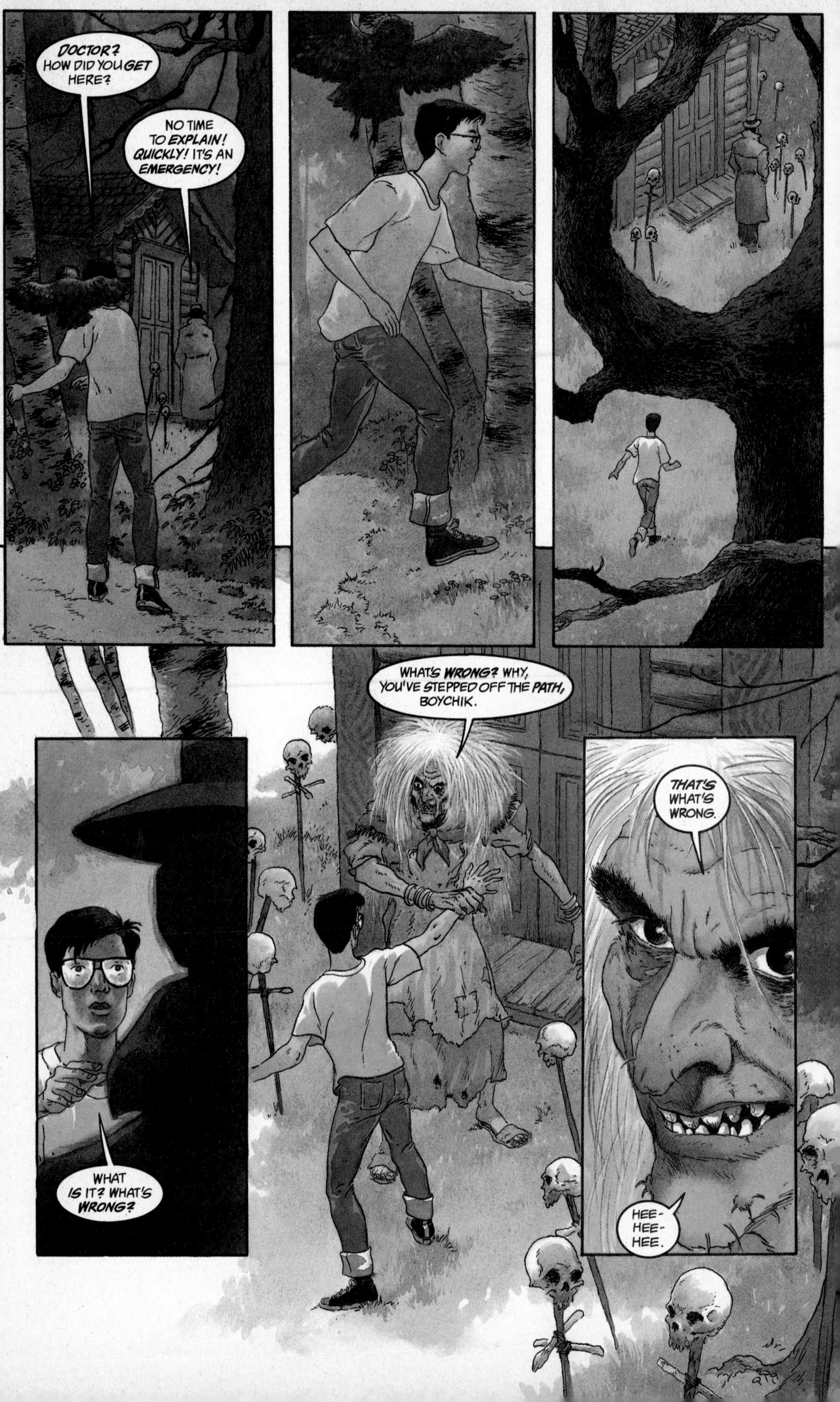
DOCTOR? HOW DID YOU GET HERE?
NO TIME TO EXPLAIN! QUICKLY! IT'S AN EMERGENCY!
WHAT IS IT? WHAT'S WRONG?
WHAT'S WRONG? WHY, YOU'VE STEPPED OFF THE PATH, BOYCHIK.
THAT'S WHAT'S WRONG.
HEE-HEE-HEE.

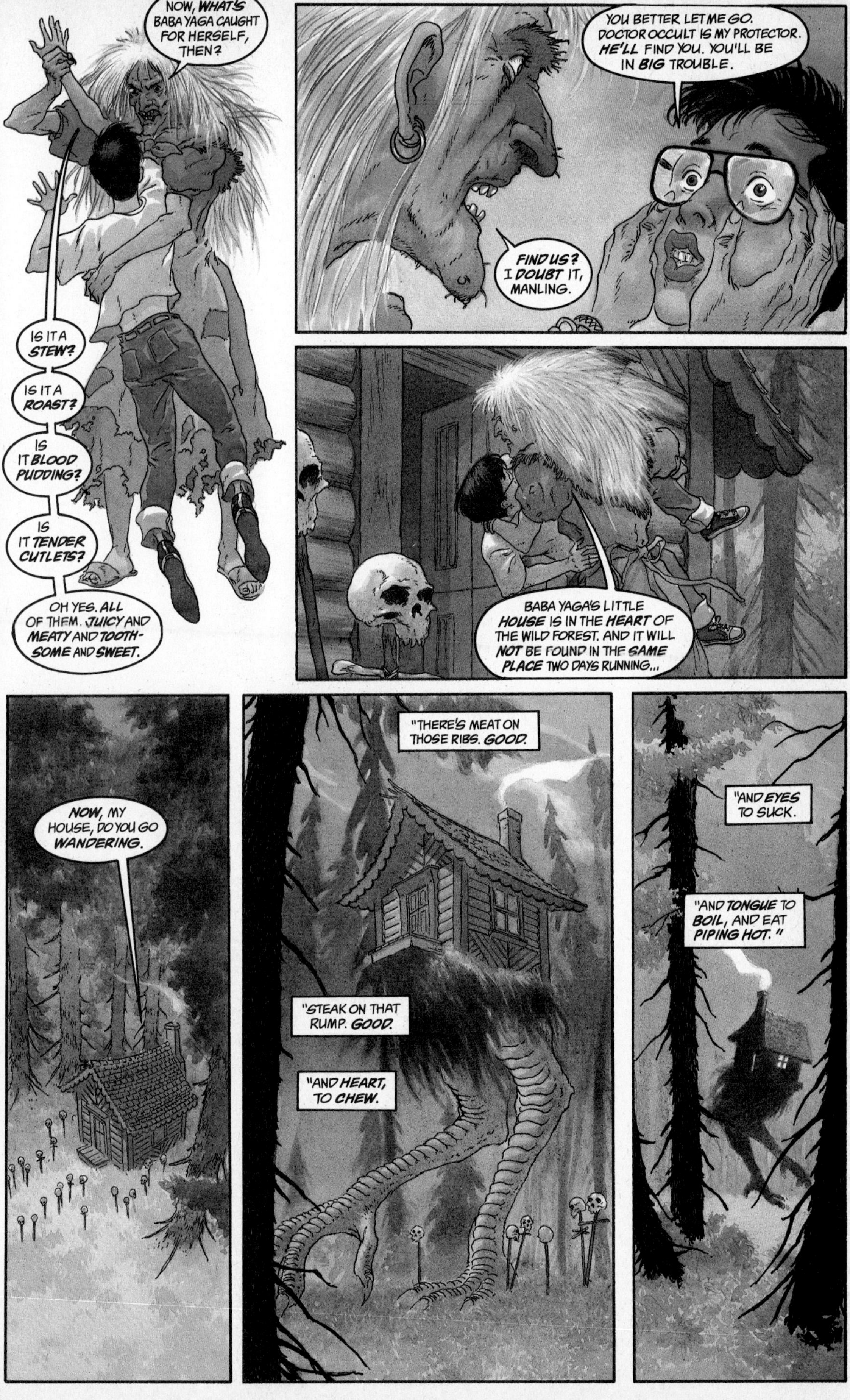

NOW, WHAT'S BABA YAGA CAUGHT FOR HERSELF, THEN?
IS IT A STEW?
IS IT A ROAST?
IS IT BLOOD PUDDING?
IS IT TENDER CUTLETS?
OH YES. ALL OF THEM. JUICY AND MEATY AND TOOTH-SOME AND SWEET.
YOU BETTER LET ME GO. DOCTOR OCCULT IS MY PROTECTOR. HE'LL FIND YOU. YOU'LL BE IN BIG TROUBLE.
FIND US? I DOUBT IT, MANLING.
BABA YAGA'S LITTLE HOUSE IS IN THE HEART OF THE WILD FOREST. AND IT WILL NOT BE FOUND IN THE SAME PLACE TWO DAYS RUNNING...
NOW, MY HOUSE, DO YOU GO WANDERING.
"THERE'S MEAT ON THOSE RIBS. GOOD.
"STEAK ON THAT RUMP. GOOD.
"AND HEART, TO CHEW.
"AND EYES TO SUCK.
"AND TONGUE TO BOIL, AND EAT PIPING HOT."

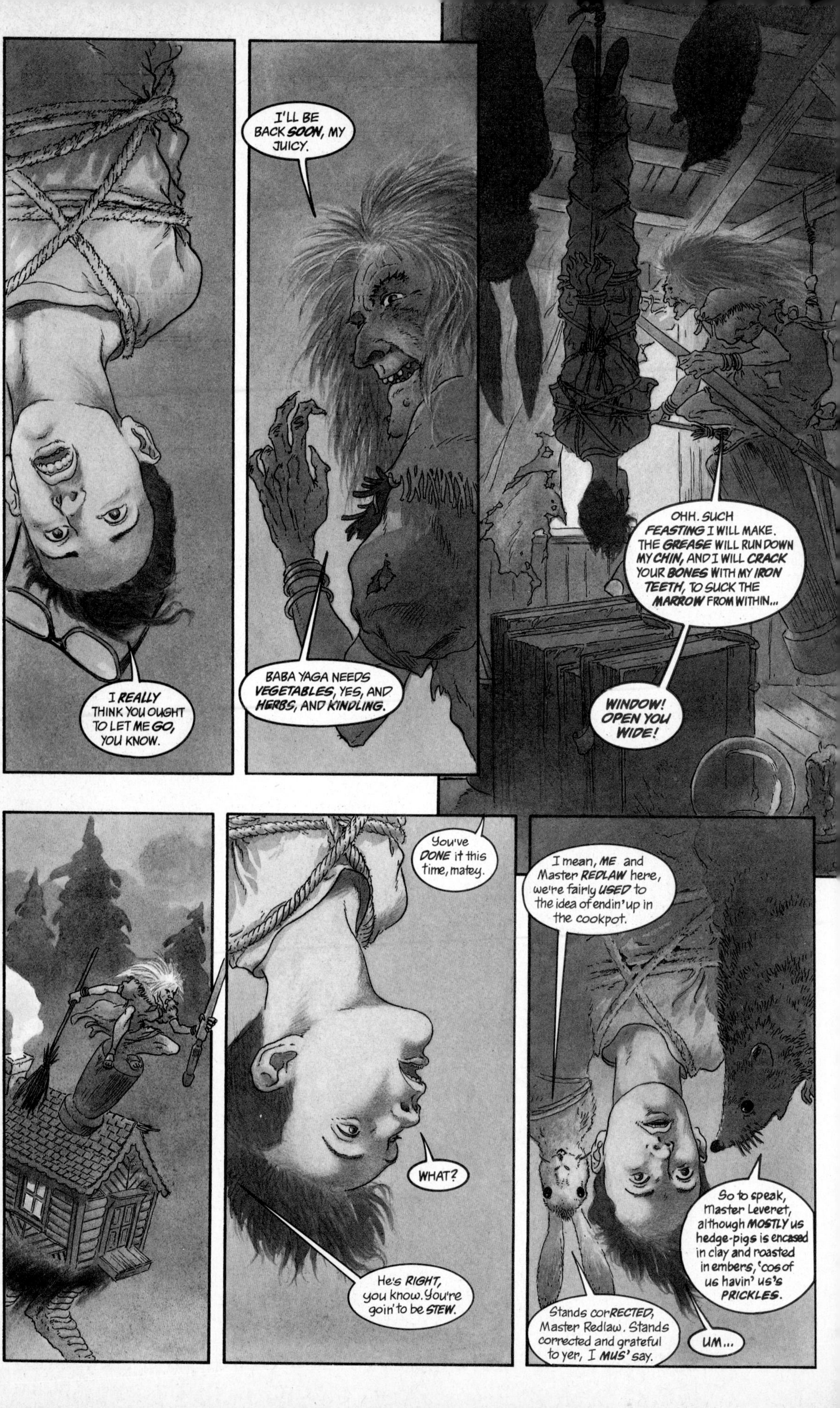

I REALLY THINK YOU OUGHT TO LET ME GO, YOU KNOW.
I'LL BE BACK SOON, MY JUICY.
BABA YAGA NEEDS VEGETABLES, YES, AND HERBS, AND KINDLING.
OHH. SUCH FEASTING I WILL MAKE. THE GREASE WILL RUN DOWN MY CHIN, AND I WILL CRACK YOUR BONES WITH MY IRON TEETH, TO SUCK THE MARROW FROM WITHIN...
WINDOW! OPEN YOU WIDE!
You've DONE it this time, matey.
WHAT?
He's RIGHT, you know. You're goin' to be STEW.
I mean, ME and Master REDLAW here, we're fairly USED to the idea of endin' up in the cookpot.
So to speak, Master Leveret, although MOSTLY us hedge-pigs is encased in clay and roasted in embers, 'cos of us havin' us's PRICKLES.
Stands corRECTED, Master Redlaw. Stands corrected and grateful to yer, I MUS' say.
UM...

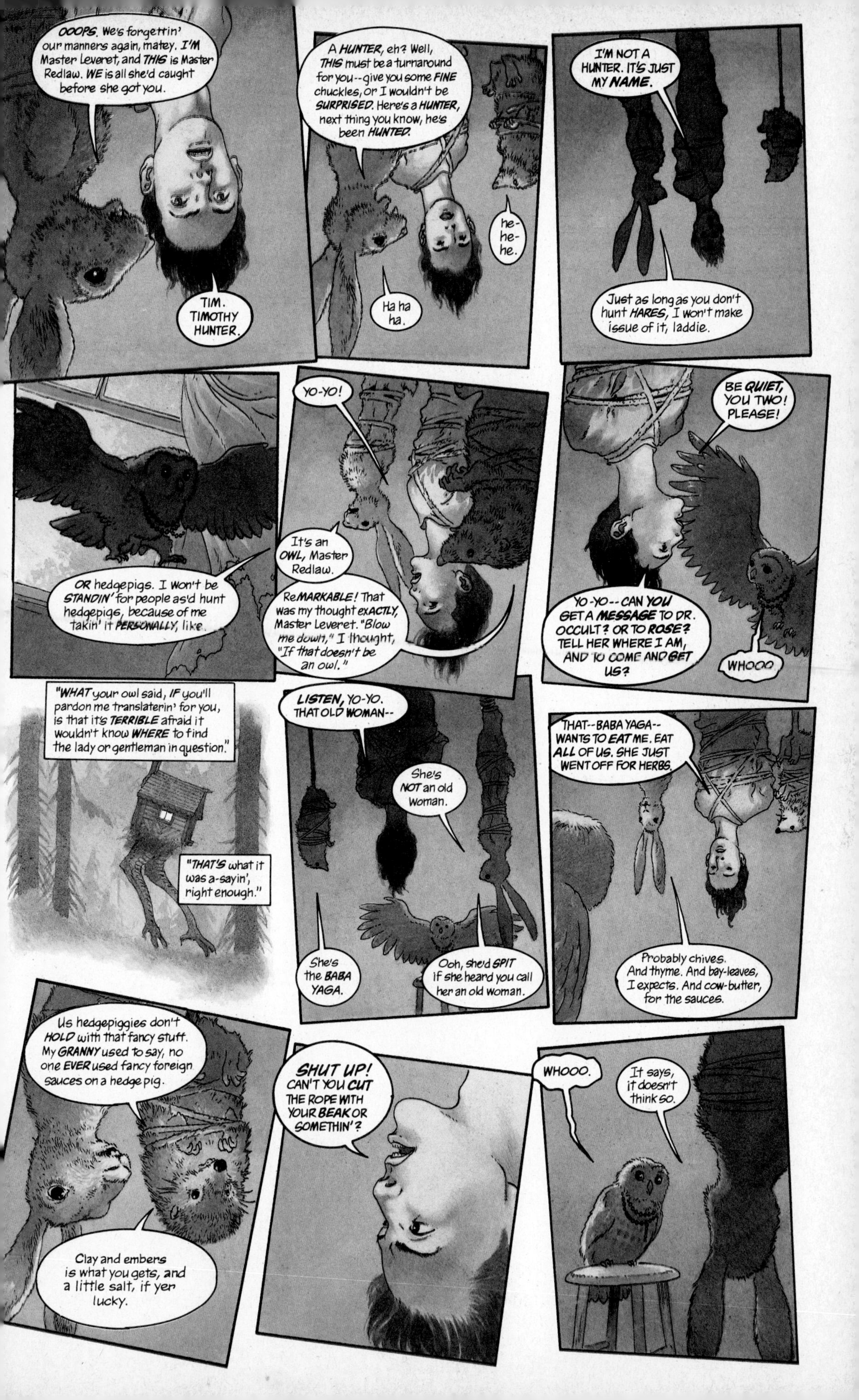
OOOPS. We's forgettin' our manners again, matey. I'M Master Leveret, and THIS is Master Redlaw. WE is all she'd caught before she got you.
TIM. TIMOTHY HUNTER.
A HUNTER, eh? Well, THIS must be a turnaround for you--give you some FINE chuckles, or I wouldn't be SURPRISED. Here's a HUNTER, next thing you know, he's been HUNTED.
Ha ha ha.
he-he-he.
I'M NOT A HUNTER. IT'S JUST MY NAME.
Just as long as you don't hunt HARES, I won't make issue of it, laddie.
OR hedgepigs. I won't be STANDIN' for people as'd hunt hedgepigs, because of me takin' it PERSONALLY, like.
YO-YO!
It's an OWL, Master Redlaw.
ReMARKABLE! That was my thought exACTLY, Master Leveret. "Blow me down," I thought, "If that doesn't be an owl."
BE QUIET, YOU TWO! PLEASE!
YO-YO--CAN YOU GET A MESSAGE TO DR. OCCULT? OR TO ROSE? TELL HER WHERE I AM, AND TO COME AND GET US?
WHOOO.
"WHAT your owl said, IF you'll pardon me translaterin' for you, is that it's TERRIBLE afraid it wouldn't know WHERE to find the lady or gentleman in question."
"THAT'S what it was a-sayin', right enough."
LISTEN, YO-YO. THAT OLD WOMAN--
She's NOT an old woman.
She's the BABA YAGA.
Ooh, she'd SPIT if she heard you call her an old woman.
THAT--BABA YAGA--WANTS TO EAT ME. EAT ALL OF US. SHE JUST WENT OFF FOR HERBS.
Probably chives. And thyme. And bay-leaves, I expects. And cow-butter, for the sauces.
Us hedgepiggies don't HOLD with that fancy stuff. My GRANNY used to say, no one EVER used fancy foreign sauces on a hedge pig.
Clay and embers is what you gets, and a little salt, if yer lucky.
SHUT UP! CAN'T YOU CUT THE ROPE WITH YOUR BEAK OR SOMETHIN'?
WHOOO.
It says, it doesn't think so.

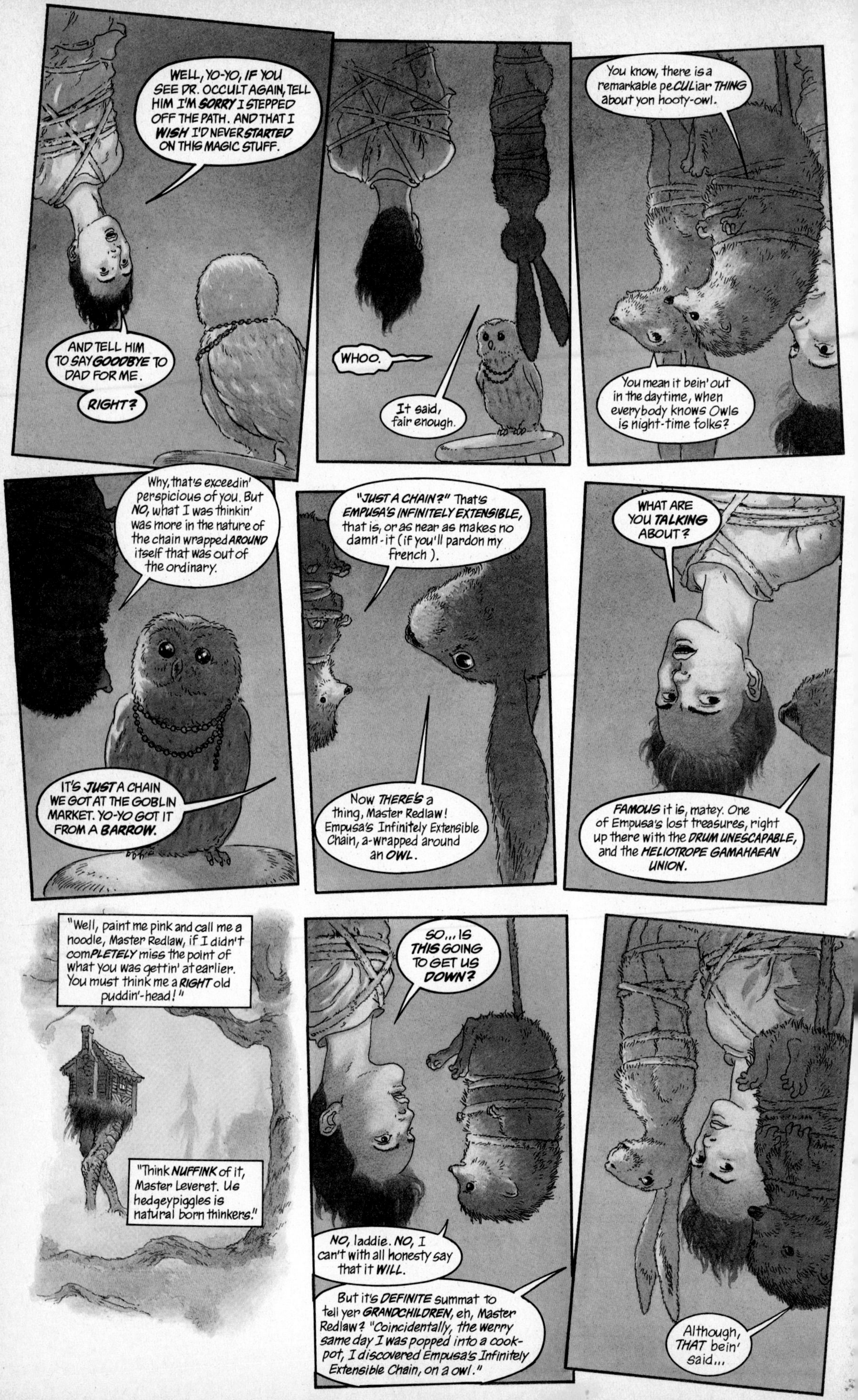
WELL, YO-YO, IF YOU SEE DR. OCCULT AGAIN, TELL HIM I'M SORRY I STEPPED OFF THE PATH. AND THAT I WISH I'D NEVER STARTED ON THIS MAGIC STUFF.
AND TELL HIM TO SAY GOODBYE TO DAD FOR ME.
RIGHT?
WHOO.
It said, fair enough.
You know, there is a remarkable peCULiar THING about yon hooty-owl.
You mean it bein' out in the daytime, when everybody knows Owls is night-time folks?
Why, that's exceedin' perspicious of you. But NO, what I was thinkin' was more in the nature of the chain wrapped AROUND itself that was out of the ordinary.
IT'S JUST A CHAIN WE GOT AT THE GOBLIN MARKET. YO-YO GOT IT FROM A BARROW.
"JUST A CHAIN?" That's EMPUSA'S INFINITELY EXTENSIBLE, that is, or as near as makes no damn-it (if you'll pardon my french).
Now THERE'S a thing, Master Redlaw! Empusa's Infinitely Extensible Chain, a-wrapped around an OWL.
WHAT ARE YOU TALKING ABOUT?
FAMOUS it is, matey. One of Empusa's lost treasures, right up there with the DRUM UNESCAPABLE, and the HELIOTROPE GAMAHAEAN UNION.
"Well, paint me pink and call me a noodle, Master Redlaw, if I didn't comPLETELY miss the point of what you was gettin' at earlier. You must think me a RIGHT old puddin'-head!"
"Think NUFFINK of it, Master Leveret. Us hedgeypiggles is natural born thinkers."
SO... IS THIS GOING TO GET US DOWN?
NO, laddie. NO, I can't with all honesty say that it WILL.
But it's DEFINITE summat to tell yer GRANDCHILDREN, eh, Master Redlaw? "Coincidentally, the werry same day I was popped into a cook-pot, I discovered Empusa's Infinitely Extensible Chain, on a owl."
Although, THAT bein' said...

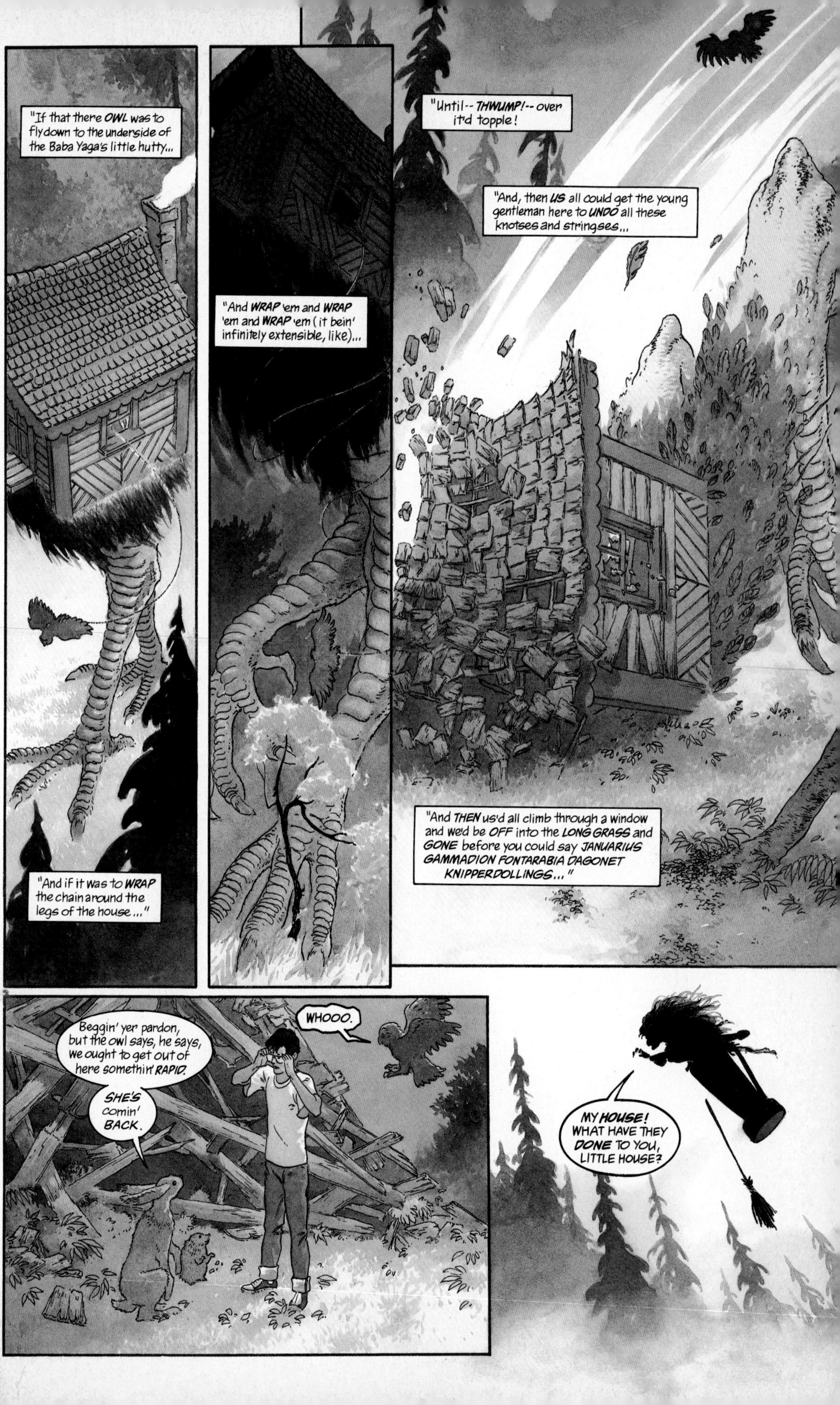
"If that there OWL was to flydown to the underside of the Baba Yaga's little hutty...
"And if it was to WRAP the chain around the legs of the house..."
"And WRAP 'em and WRAP 'em and WRAP 'em (it bein' infinitely extensible, like)...
"Until-- THWUMP!-- over it'd topple!
"And, then US all could get the young gentleman here to UNDO all these knotses and stringses...
"And THEN us'd all climb through a window and we'd be OFF into the LONG GRASS and GONE before you could say JANUARIUS GAMMADION FONTARABIA DAGONET KNIPPERDOLLINGS..."
Beggin' yer pardon, but the owl says, he says, we ought to get out of here somethin' RAPID.
WHOOO.
SHE'S comin' BACK.
MY HOUSE! WHAT HAVE THEY DONE TO YOU, LITTLE HOUSE?

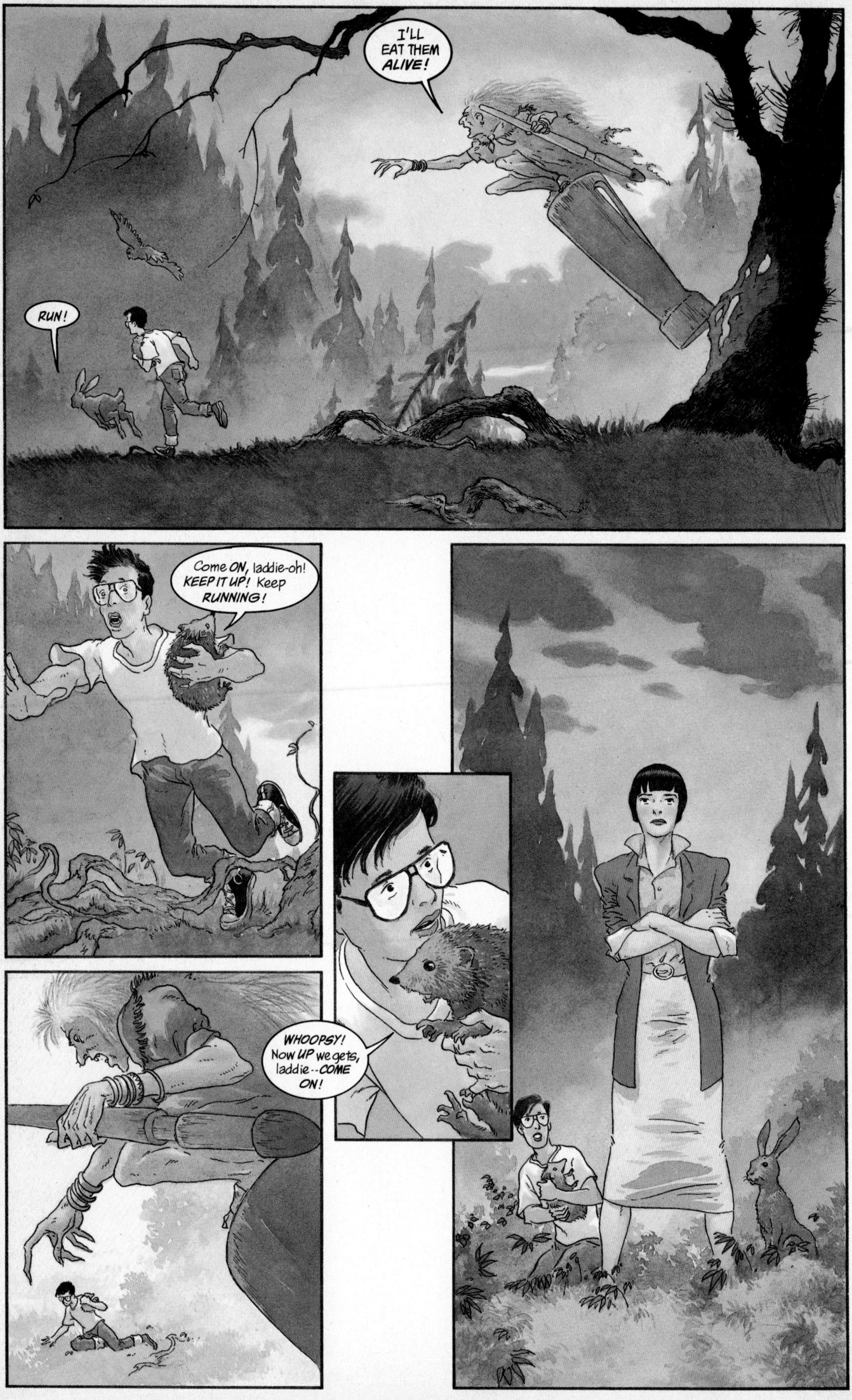
I'LL EAT THEM ALIVE!
RUN!
Come ON, laddie-oh! KEEP IT UP! Keep RUNNING!
WHOOPSY! Now UP we gets, laddie--COME ON!

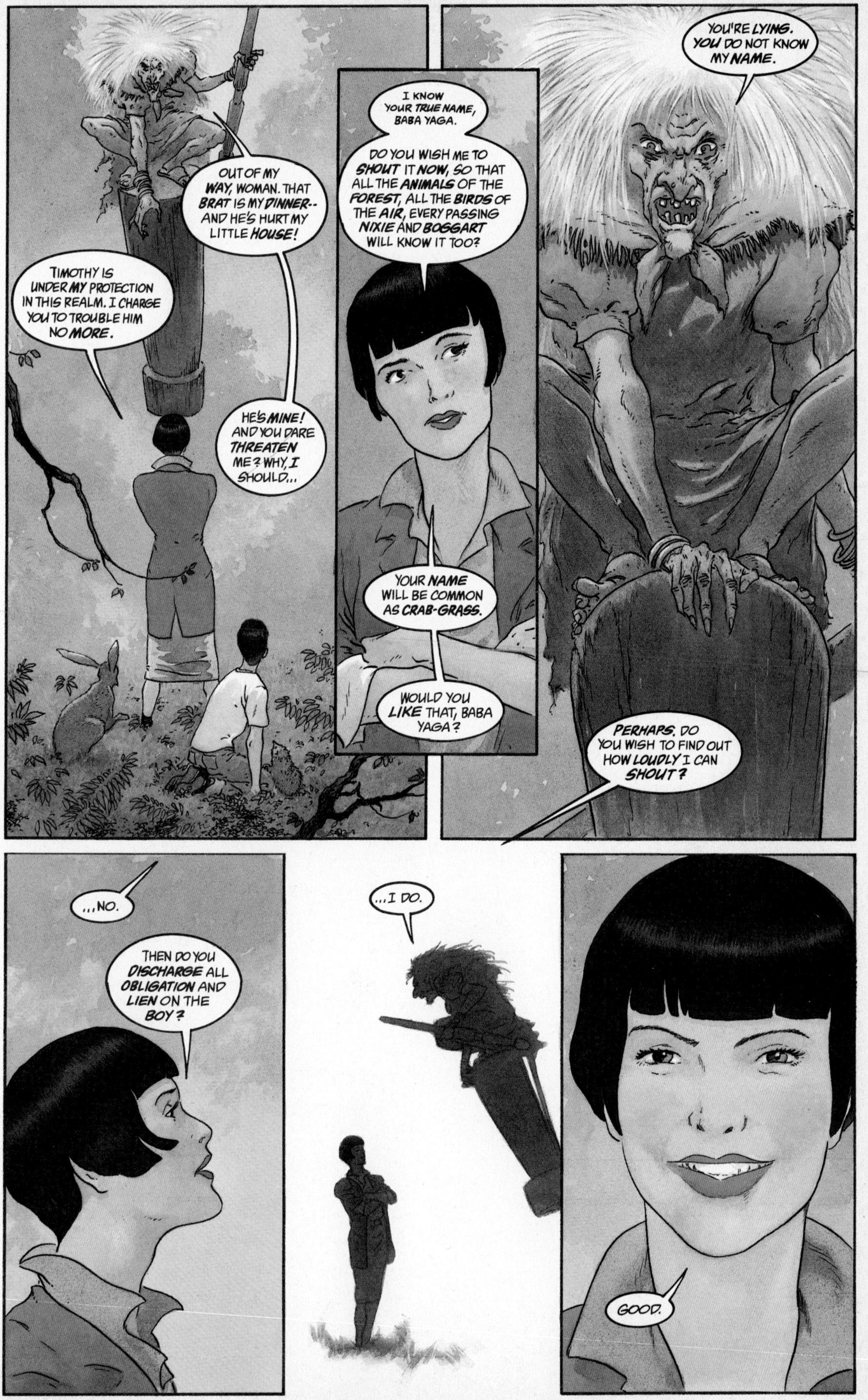
OUT OF MY WAY, WOMAN. THAT BRAT IS MY DINNER-- AND HE'S HURT MY LITTLE HOUSE!
TIMOTHY IS UNDER MY PROTECTION IN THIS REALM. I CHARGE YOU TO TROUBLE HIM NO MORE.
HE'S MINE! AND YOU DARE THREATEN ME? WHY, I SHOULD...
I KNOW YOUR TRUE NAME, BABA YAGA.
DO YOU WISH ME TO SHOUT IT NOW, SO THAT ALL THE ANIMALS OF THE FOREST, ALL THE BIRDS OF THE AIR, EVERY PASSING NIXIE AND BOGGART WILL KNOW IT TOO?
YOUR NAME WILL BE COMMON AS CRAB-GRASS.
WOULD YOU LIKE THAT, BABA YAGA?
YOU'RE LYING. YOU DO NOT KNOW MY NAME.
PERHAPS. DO YOU WISH TO FIND OUT HOW LOUDLY I CAN SHOUT?
...NO.
THEN DO YOU DISCHARGE ALL OBLIGATION AND LIEN ON THE BOY?
...I DO.
GOOD.

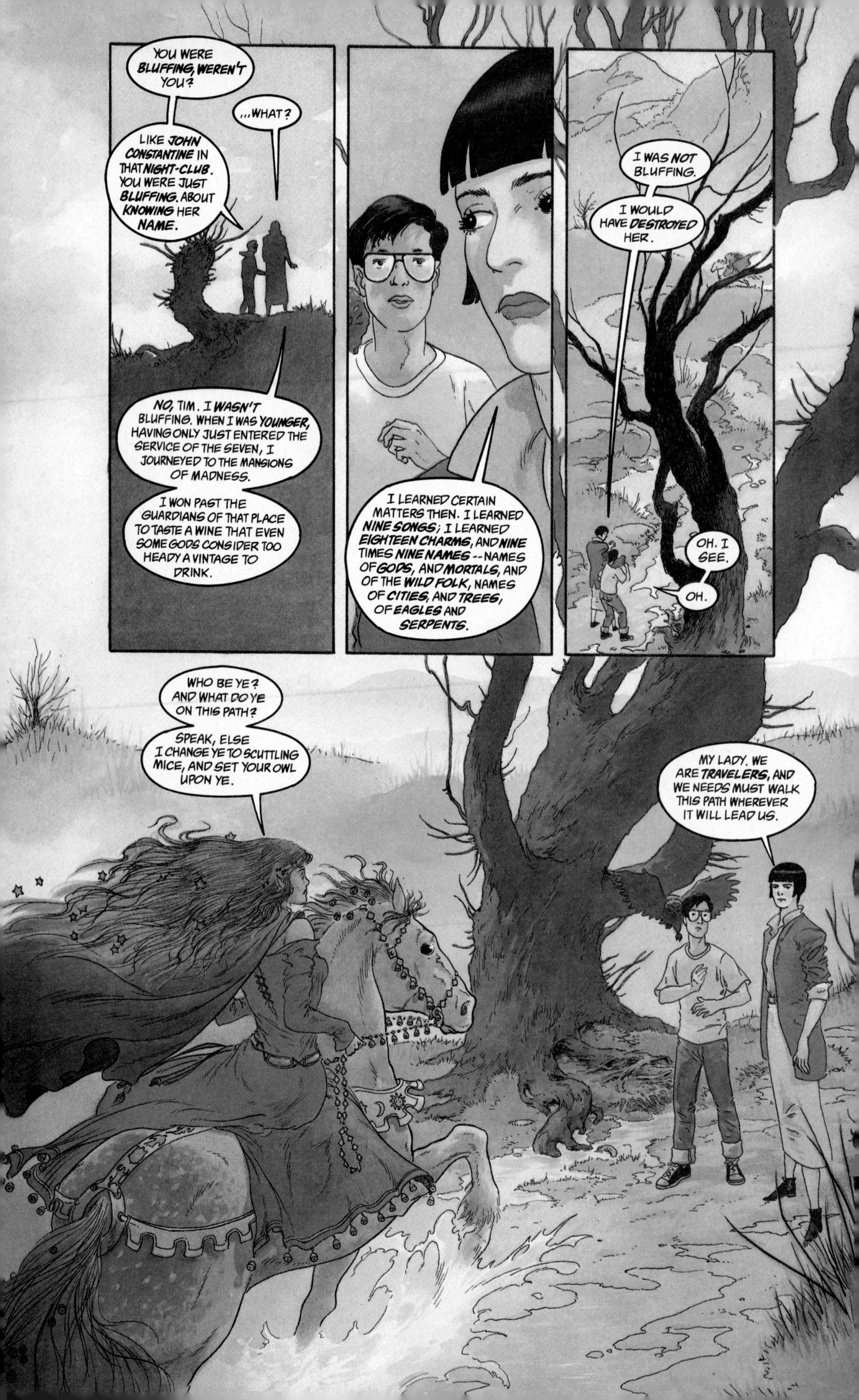
YOU WERE BLUFFING, WEREN'T YOU?
...WHAT?
LIKE JOHN CONSTANTINE IN THAT NIGHT-CLUB. YOU WERE JUST BLUFFING. ABOUT KNOWING HER NAME.
NO, TIM. I WASN'T BLUFFING. WHEN I WAS YOUNGER, HAVING ONLY JUST ENTERED THE SERVICE OF THE SEVEN, I JOURNEYED TO THE MANSIONS OF MADNESS.
I WON PAST THE GUARDIANS OF THAT PLACE TO TASTE A WINE THAT EVEN SOME GODS CONSIDER TOO HEADY A VINTAGE TO DRINK.
I LEARNED CERTAIN MATTERS THEN. I LEARNED NINE SONGS; I LEARNED EIGHTEEN CHARMS, AND NINE TIMES NINE NAMES--NAMES OF GODS, AND MORTALS, AND OF THE WILD FOLK, NAMES OF CITIES, AND TREES, OF EAGLES AND SERPENTS.
I WAS NOT BLUFFING.
I WOULD HAVE DESTROYED HER.
OH. I SEE.
OH.
WHO BE YE? AND WHAT DO YE ON THIS PATH?
SPEAK, ELSE I CHANGE YE TO SCUTTLING MICE, AND SET YOUR OWL UPON YE.
MY LADY. WE ARE TRAVELERS, AND WE NEEDS MUST WALK THIS PATH WHEREVER IT WILL LEAD US.

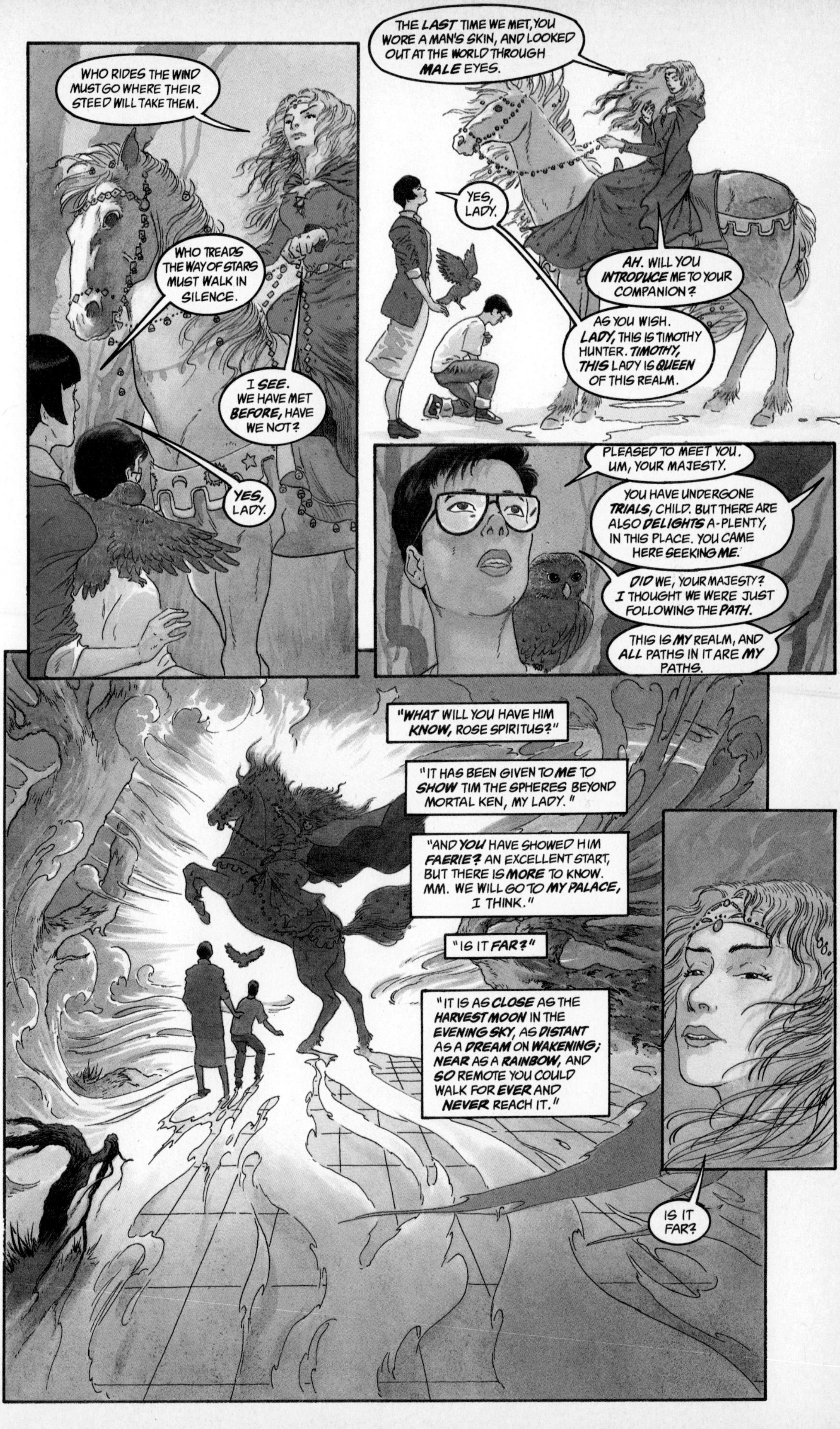
WHO RIDES THE WIND MUST GO WHERE THEIR STEED WILL TAKE THEM.
WHO TREADS THE WAY OF STARS MUST WALK IN SILENCE.
I SEE. WE HAVE MET BEFORE, HAVE WE NOT?
YES, LADY.
THE LAST TIME WE MET, YOU WORE A MAN'S SKIN, AND LOOKED OUT AT THE WORLD THROUGH MALE EYES.
YES, LADY.
AH. WILL YOU INTRODUCE ME TO YOUR COMPANION?
AS YOU WISH. LADY, THIS IS TIMOTHY HUNTER. TIMOTHY, THIS LADY IS QUEEN OF THIS REALM.
PLEASED TO MEET YOU. UM, YOUR MAJESTY.
YOU HAVE UNDERGONE TRIALS, CHILD. BUT THERE ARE ALSO DELIGHTS A-PLENTY, IN THIS PLACE. YOU CAME HERE SEEKING ME.
DID WE, YOUR MAJESTY? I THOUGHT WE WERE JUST FOLLOWING THE PATH.
THIS IS MY REALM, AND ALL PATHS IN IT ARE MY PATHS.
"WHAT WILL YOU HAVE HIM KNOW, ROSE SPIRITUS?"
"IT HAS BEEN GIVEN TO ME TO SHOW TIM THE SPHERES BEYOND MORTAL KEN, MY LADY."
"AND YOU HAVE SHOWED HIM FAERIE? AN EXCELLENT START, BUT THERE IS MORE TO KNOW. MM. WE WILL GO TO MY PALACE, I THINK."
"IS IT FAR?"
"IT IS AS CLOSE AS THE HARVEST MOON IN THE EVENING SKY, AS DISTANT AS A DREAM ON WAKENING; NEAR AS A RAINBOW, AND SO REMOTE YOU COULD WALK FOR EVER AND NEVER REACH IT."
IS IT FAR?

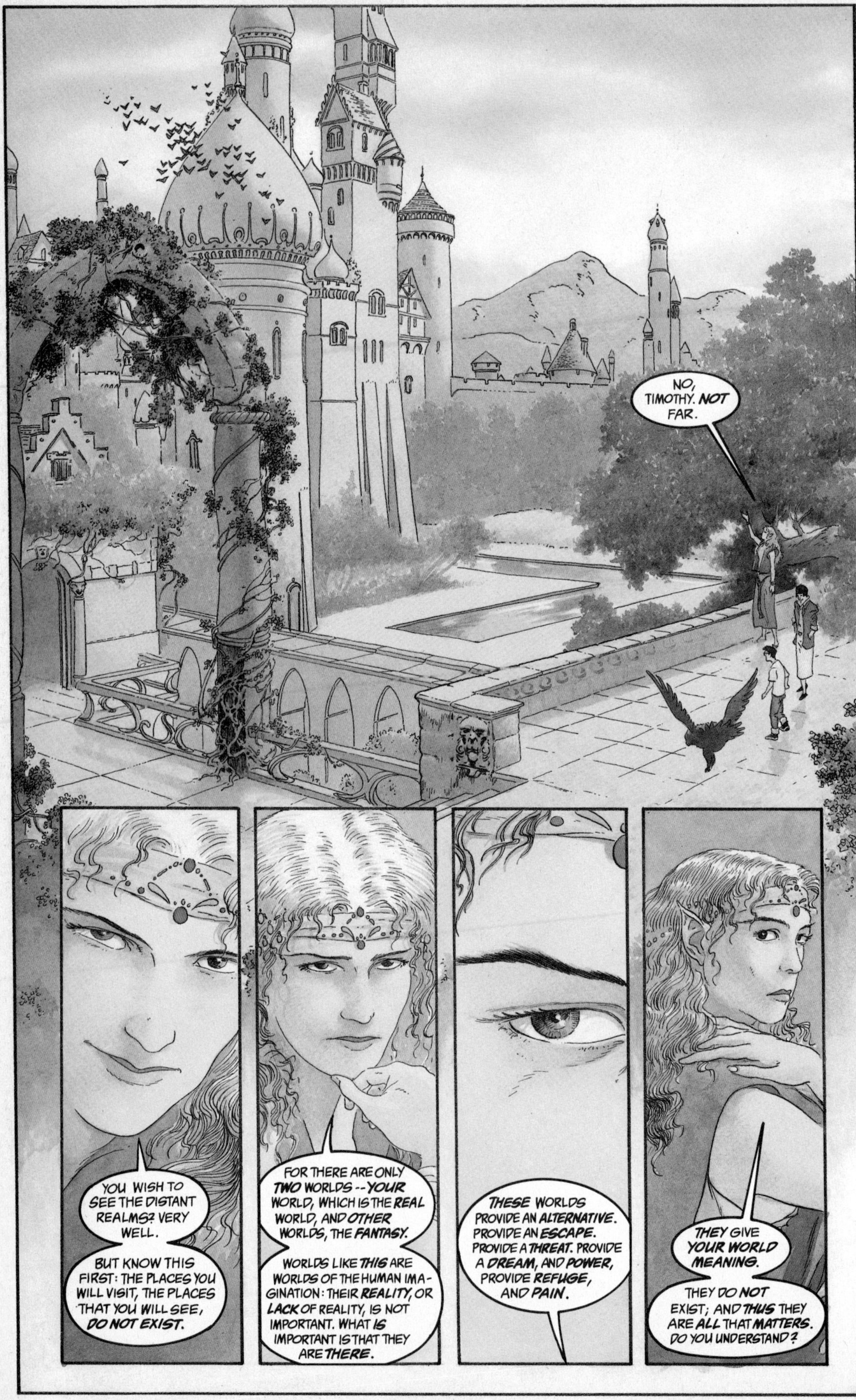
NO, TIMOTHY. NOT FAR.
YOU WISH TO SEE THE DISTANT REALMS? VERY WELL.
BUT KNOW THIS FIRST: THE PLACES YOU WILL VISIT, THE PLACES THAT YOU WILL SEE, DO NOT EXIST.
FOR THERE ARE ONLY TWO WORLDS -- YOUR WORLD, WHICH IS THE REAL WORLD, AND OTHER WORLDS, THE FANTASY.
WORLDS LIKE THIS ARE WORLDS OF THE HUMAN IMAGINATION: THEIR REALITY, OR LACK OF REALITY, IS NOT IMPORTANT. WHAT IS IMPORTANT IS THAT THEY ARE THERE.
THESE WORLDS PROVIDE AN ALTERNATIVE. PROVIDE AN ESCAPE. PROVIDE A THREAT. PROVIDE A DREAM, AND POWER, PROVIDE REFUGE, AND PAIN.
THEY GIVE YOUR WORLD MEANING.
THEY DO NOT EXIST; AND THUS THEY ARE ALL THAT MATTERS. DO YOU UNDERSTAND?

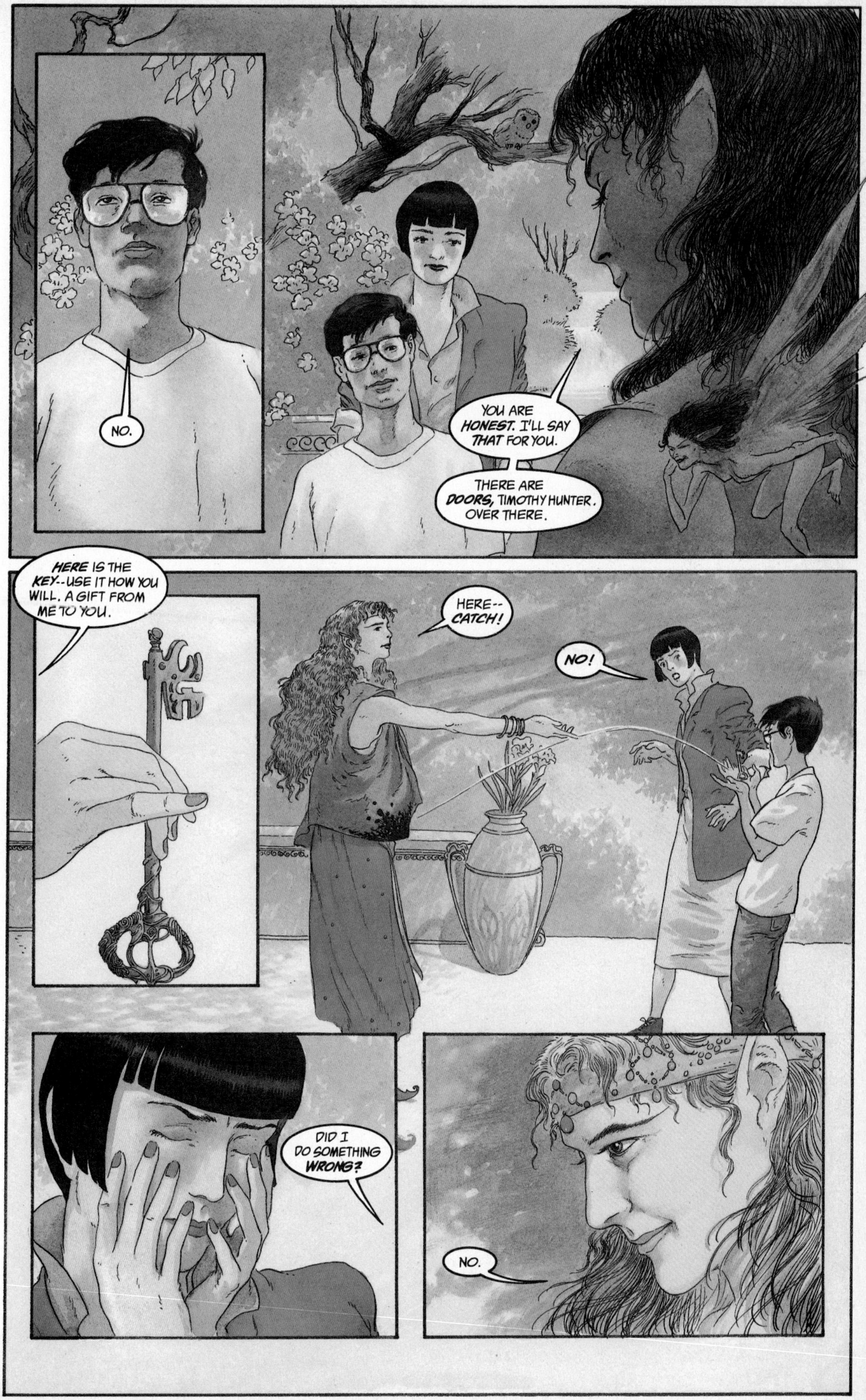
NO.
YOU ARE HONEST. I'LL SAY THAT FOR YOU.
THERE ARE DOORS, TIMOTHY HUNTER. OVER THERE.
HERE IS THE KEY--USE IT HOW YOU WILL. A GIFT FROM ME TO YOU.
HERE-- CATCH!
NO!
DID I DO SOMETHING WRONG?
NO.

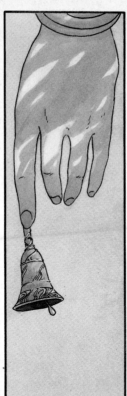

HAMNET? A STRAWBERRY CORDIAL, PLEASE.

YES, YOUR MAJESTY.

WELL, GO ON, CHILD. YOU TOO, ROSE. SHOW HIM THE WORLDS BEYOND REASON.

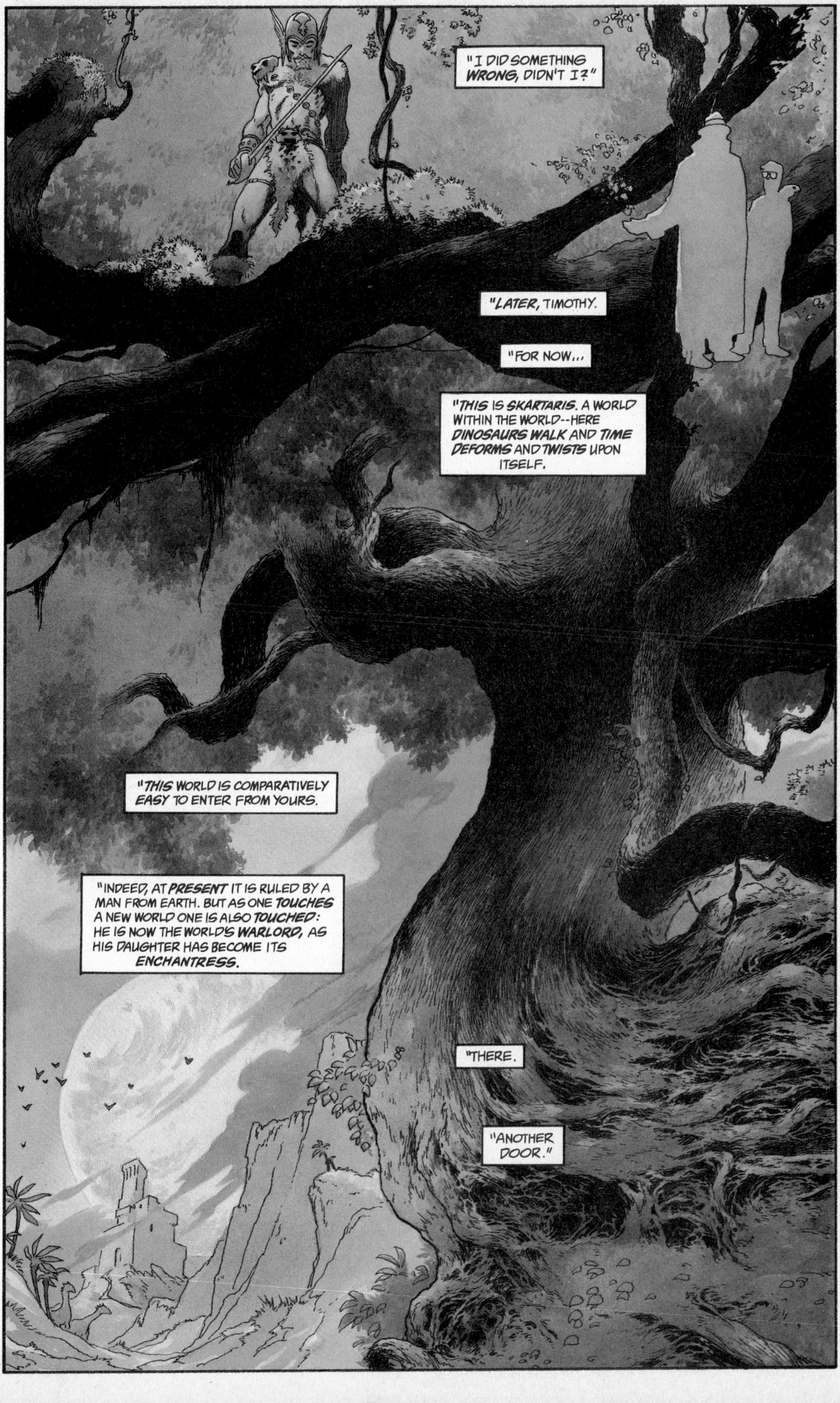
"I DID SOMETHING WRONG, DIDN'T I?"
"LATER, TIMOTHY.
"FOR NOW...
"THIS IS SKARTARIS. A WORLD WITHIN THE WORLD--HERE DINOSAURS WALK AND TIME DEFORMS AND TWISTS UPON ITSELF.
"THIS WORLD IS COMPARATIVELY EASY TO ENTER FROM YOURS.
"INDEED, AT PRESENT IT IS RULED BY A MAN FROM EARTH. BUT AS ONE TOUCHES A NEW WORLD ONE IS ALSO TOUCHED: HE IS NOW THE WORLD'S WARLORD, AS HIS DAUGHTER HAS BECOME ITS ENCHANTRESS.
"THERE.
"ANOTHER DOOR."

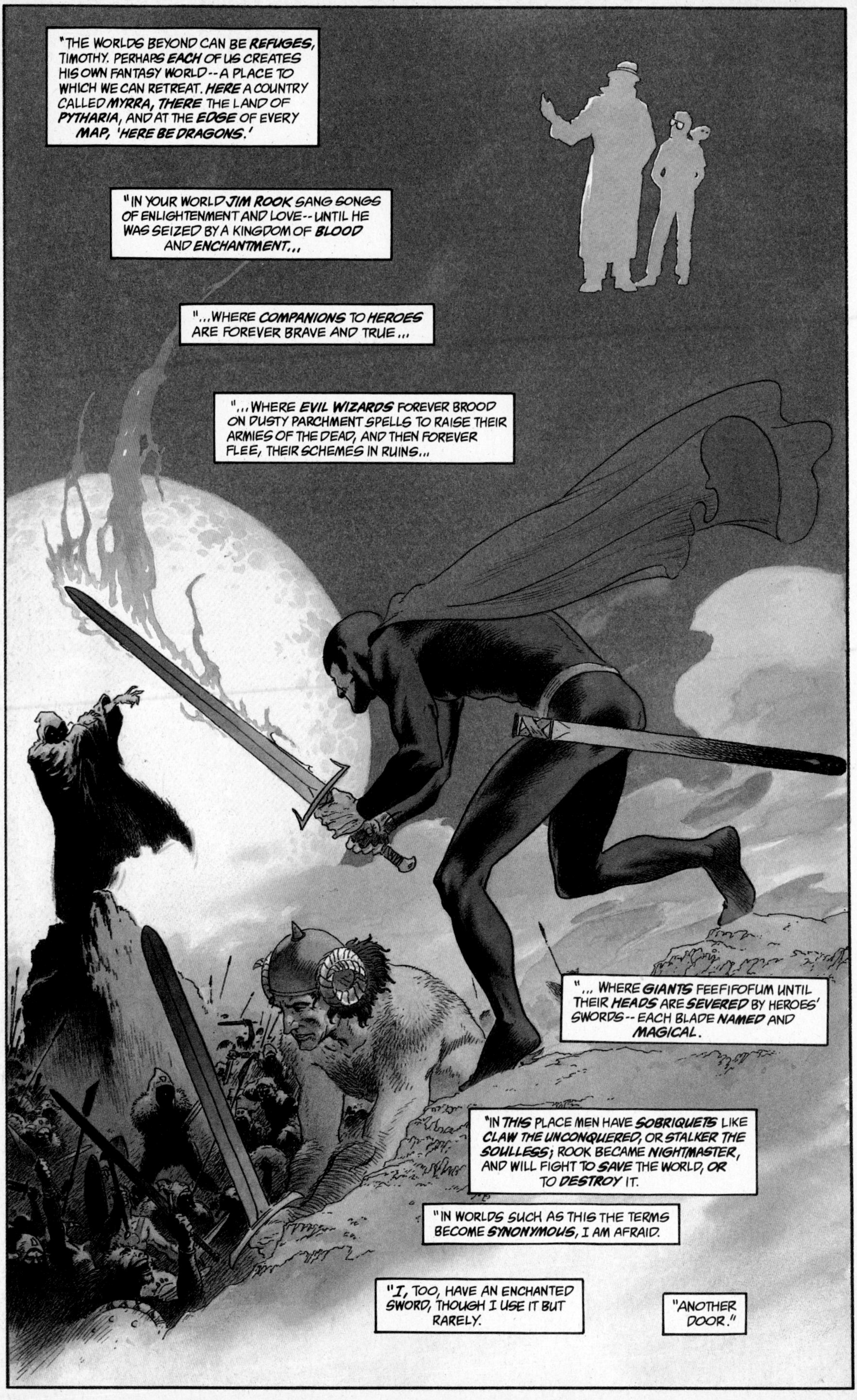
"THE WORLDS BEYOND CAN BE REFUGES, TIMOTHY. PERHAPS EACH OF US CREATES HIS OWN FANTASY WORLD--A PLACE TO WHICH WE CAN RETREAT. HERE A COUNTRY CALLED MYRRA, THERE THE LAND OF PYTHARIA, AND AT THE EDGE OF EVERY MAP, 'HERE BE DRAGONS.'
"IN YOUR WORLD JIM ROOK SANG SONGS OF ENLIGHTENMENT AND LOVE--UNTIL HE WAS SEIZED BY A KINGDOM OF BLOOD AND ENCHANTMENT...
"...WHERE COMPANIONS TO HEROES ARE FOREVER BRAVE AND TRUE...
"...WHERE EVIL WIZARDS FOREVER BROOD ON DUSTY PARCHMENT SPELLS TO RAISE THEIR ARMIES OF THE DEAD, AND THEN FOREVER FLEE, THEIR SCHEMES IN RUINS...
"... WHERE GIANTS FEEFIFOFUM UNTIL THEIR HEADS ARE SEVERED BY HEROES' SWORDS--EACH BLADE NAMED AND MAGICAL.
"IN THIS PLACE MEN HAVE SOBRIQUETS LIKE CLAW THE UNCONQUERED, OR STALKER THE SOULLESS; ROOK BECAME NIGHTMASTER, AND WILL FIGHT TO SAVE THE WORLD, OR TO DESTROY IT.
"IN WORLDS SUCH AS THIS THE TERMS BECOME SYNONYMOUS, I AM AFRAID.
"I, TOO, HAVE AN ENCHANTED SWORD, THOUGH I USE IT BUT RARELY.
"ANOTHER DOOR."

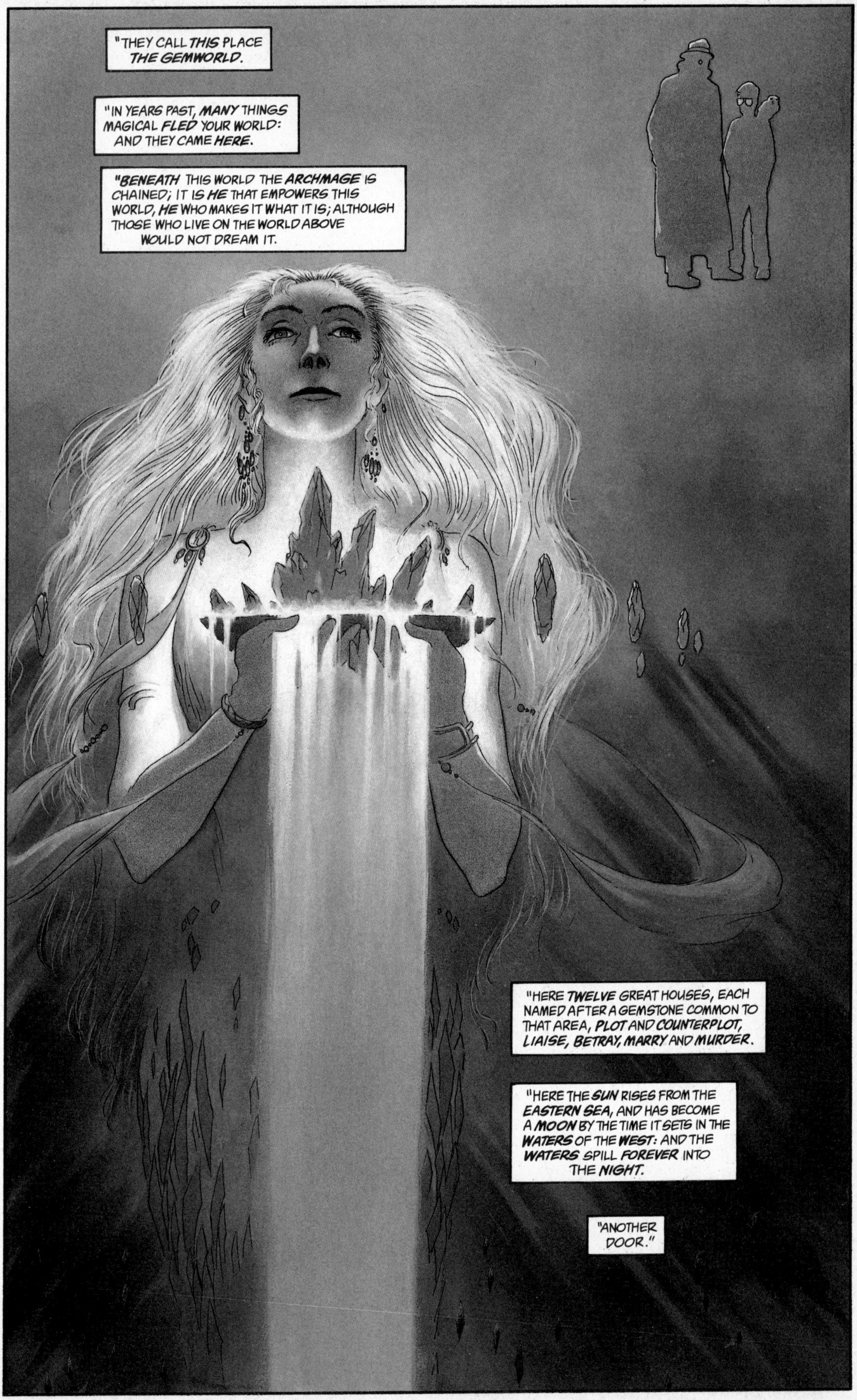
"THEY CALL THIS PLACE THE GEMWORLD.
"IN YEARS PAST, MANY THINGS MAGICAL FLED YOUR WORLD: AND THEY CAME HERE.
"BENEATH THIS WORLD THE ARCHMAGE IS CHAINED; IT IS HE THAT EMPOWERS THIS WORLD, HE WHO MAKES IT WHAT IT IS; ALTHOUGH THOSE WHO LIVE ON THE WORLD ABOVE WOULD NOT DREAM IT.
"HERE TWELVE GREAT HOUSES, EACH NAMED AFTER A GEMSTONE COMMON TO THAT AREA, PLOT AND COUNTERPLOT, LIAISE, BETRAY, MARRY AND MURDER.
"HERE THE SUN RISES FROM THE EASTERN SEA, AND HAS BECOME A MOON BY THE TIME IT SETS IN THE WATERS OF THE WEST: AND THE WATERS SPILL FOREVER INTO THE NIGHT.
"ANOTHER DOOR."

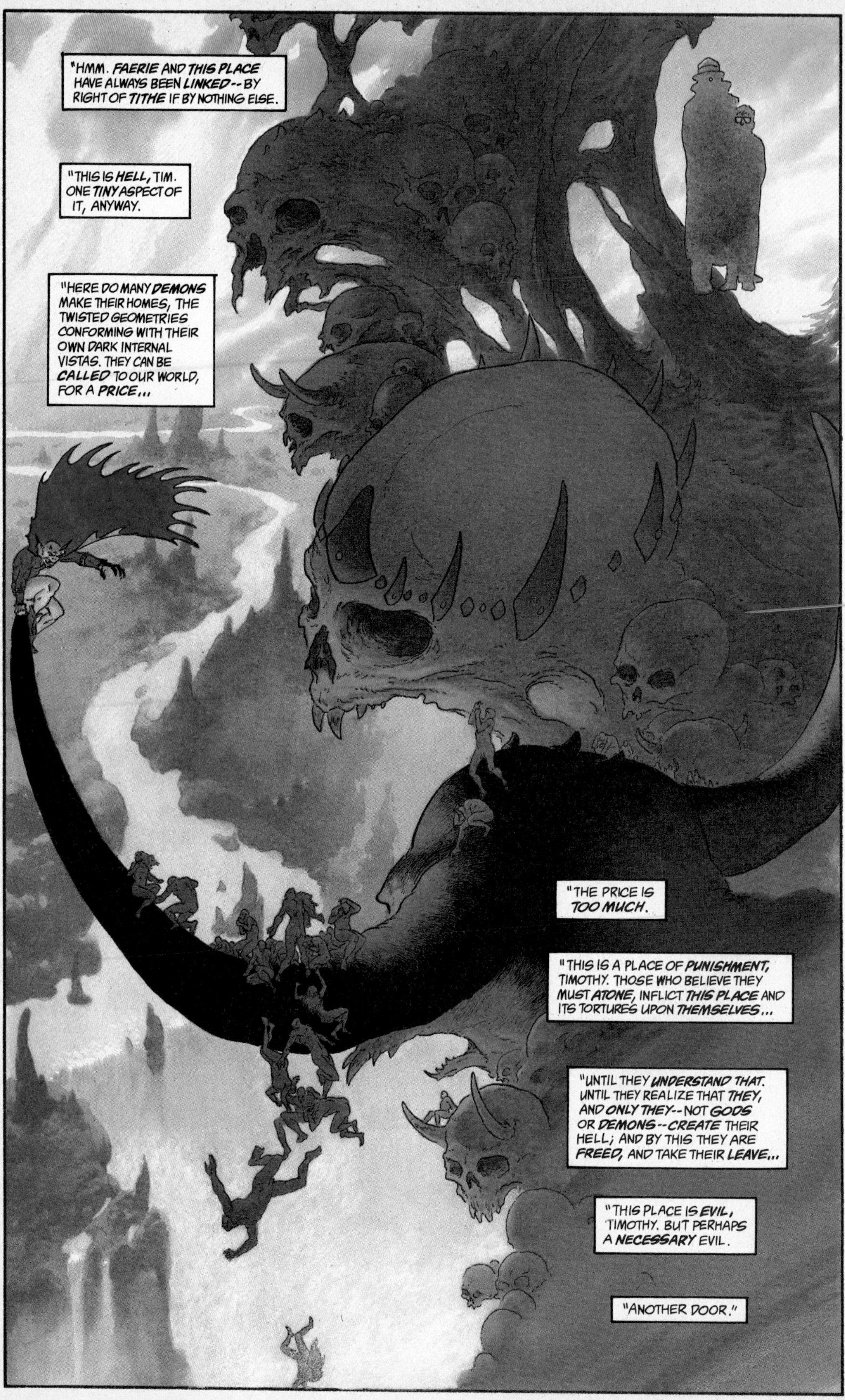
"HMM. FAERIE AND THIS PLACE HAVE ALWAYS BEEN LINKED-- BY RIGHT OF TITHE IF BY NOTHING ELSE.
"THIS IS HELL, TIM. ONE TINY ASPECT OF IT, ANYWAY.
"HERE DO MANY DEMONS MAKE THEIR HOMES, THE TWISTED GEOMETRIES CONFORMING WITH THEIR OWN DARK INTERNAL VISTAS. THEY CAN BE CALLED TO OUR WORLD, FOR A PRICE...
"THE PRICE IS TOO MUCH.
"THIS IS A PLACE OF PUNISHMENT, TIMOTHY. THOSE WHO BELIEVE THEY MUST ATONE, INFLICT THIS PLACE AND ITS TORTURES UPON THEMSELVES...
"UNTIL THEY UNDERSTAND THAT. UNTIL THEY REALIZE THAT THEY, AND ONLY THEY-- NOT GODS OR DEMONS--CREATE THEIR HELL; AND BY THIS THEY ARE FREED, AND TAKE THEIR LEAVE...
"THIS PLACE IS EVIL, TIMOTHY. BUT PERHAPS A NECESSARY EVIL.
"ANOTHER DOOR."

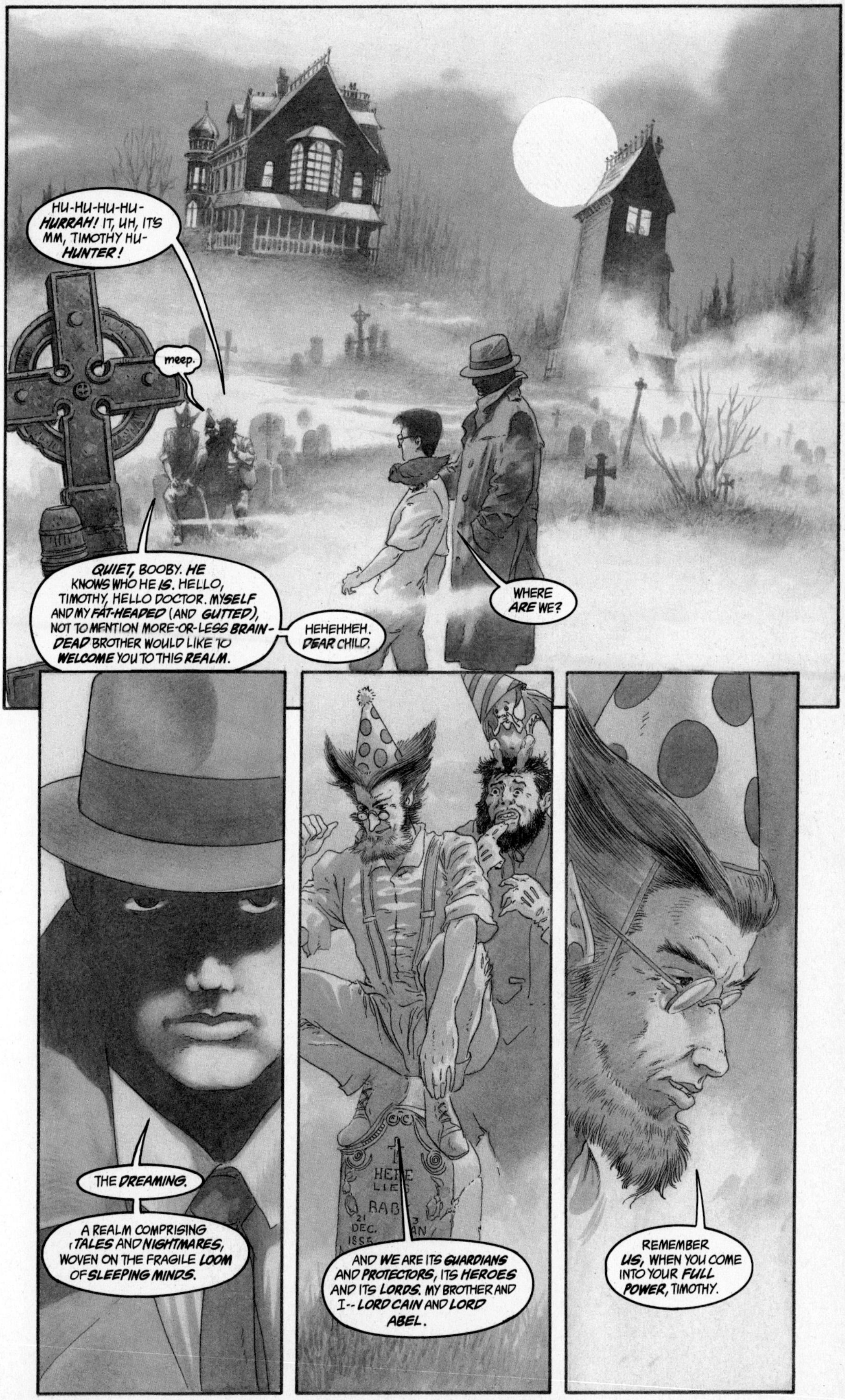
HU-HU-HU-HU-HURRAH! IT, UH, IT'S MM, TIMOTHY HU-HUNTER!
meep.
QUIET, BOOBY. HE KNOWS WHO HE IS. HELLO, TIMOTHY, HELLO DOCTOR. MYSELF AND MY FAT-HEADED (AND GUTTED), NOT TO MENTION MORE-OR-LESS BRAIN-DEAD BROTHER WOULD LIKE TO WELCOME YOU TO THIS REALM.
HEHEHHEH. DEAR CHILD.
WHERE ARE WE?
THE DREAMING.
A REALM COMPRISING TALES AND NIGHTMARES, WOVEN ON THE FRAGILE LOOM OF SLEEPING MINDS.
HERE LIES
AND WE ARE ITS GUARDIANS AND PROTECTORS, ITS HEROES AND ITS LORDS. MY BROTHER AND I-- LORD CAIN AND LORD ABEL.
REMEMBER US, WHEN YOU COME INTO YOUR FULL POWER, TIMOTHY.

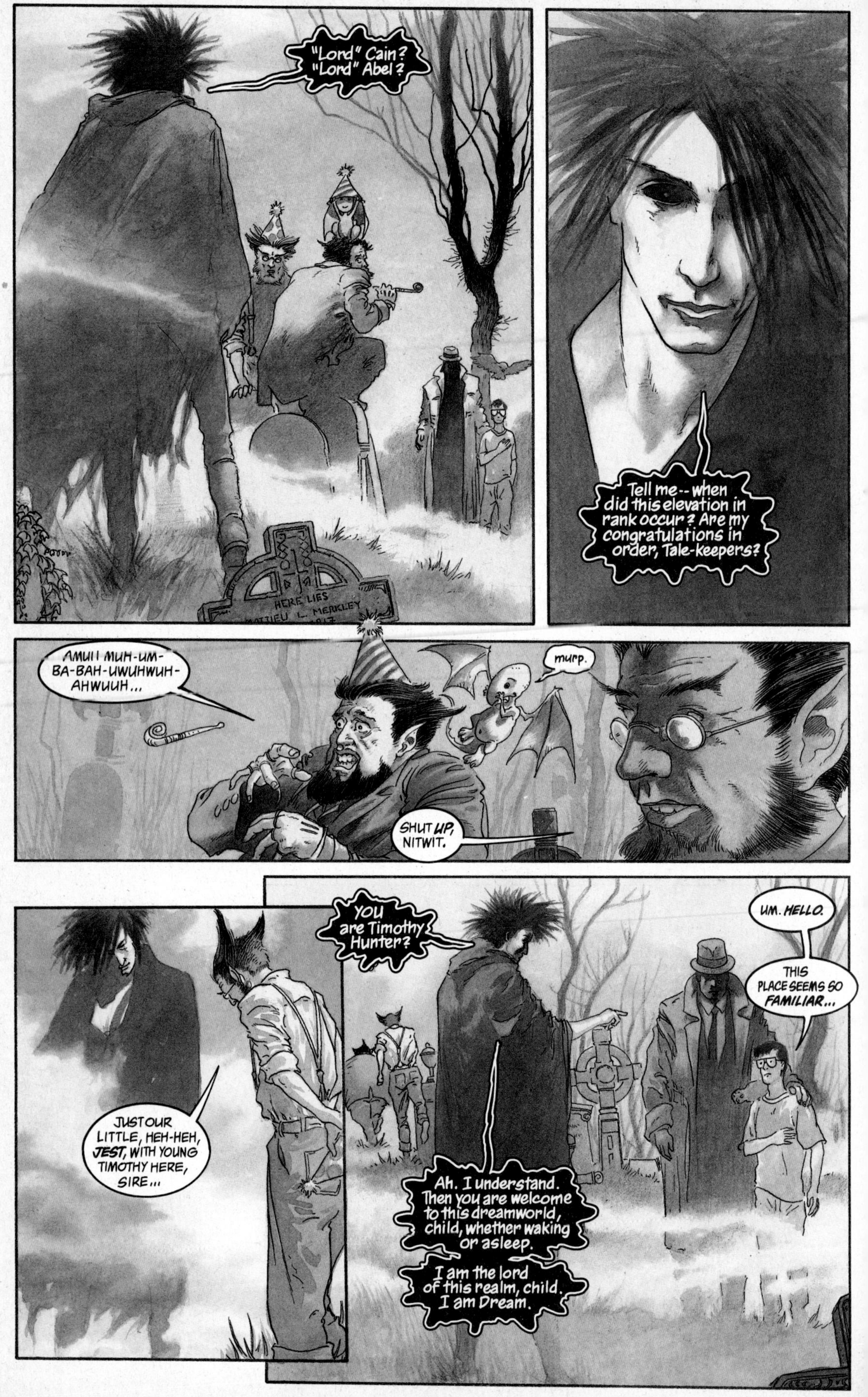
"Lord" Cain? "Lord" Abel?
HERE LIES
MERKLEY
Tell me -- when did this elevation in rank occur? Are my congratulations in order, Tale-keepers?
AMUII MUH-UM-BA-BAH-UWUHWUH-AHWUUH...
murp.
SHUT *UP*, NITWIT.
JUST OUR LITTLE, HEH-HEH, ***JEST***, WITH YOUNG TIMOTHY HERE, SIRE...
YOU are Timothy Hunter?
UM. ***HELLO***.
THIS PLACE SEEMS SO ***FAMILIAR***...
Ah. I understand. Then you are welcome to this dreamworld, child, whether waking or asleep.
I am the lord of this realm, child. I am Dream.

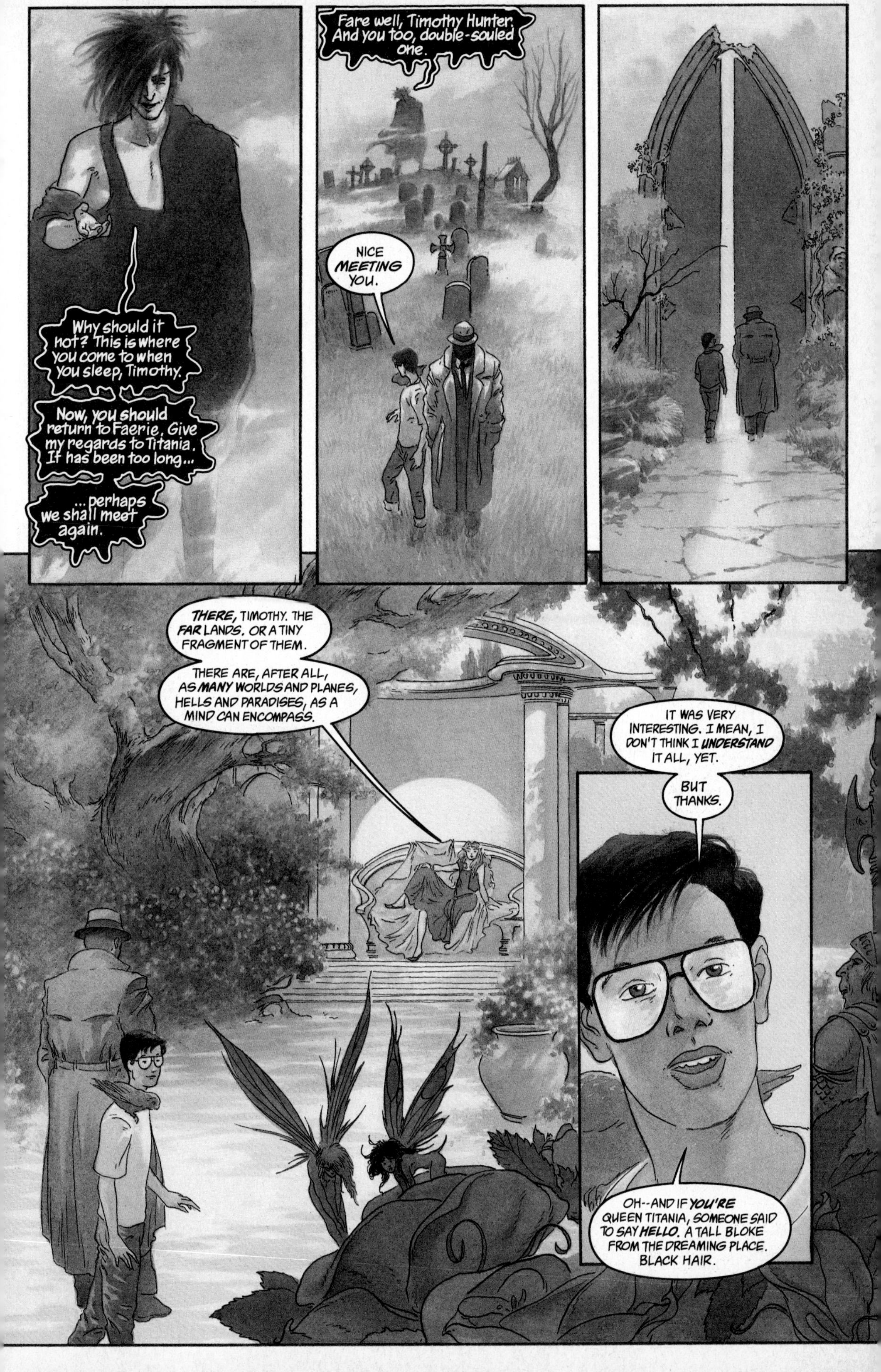

Why should it not? This is where you come to when you sleep, Timothy.
Now, you should return to Faerie. Give my regards to Titania. It has been too long...
...perhaps we shall meet again.
Fare well, Timothy Hunter. And you too, double-souled one.
NICE MEETING YOU.
THERE, TIMOTHY. THE FAR LANDS. OR A TINY FRAGMENT OF THEM.
THERE ARE, AFTER ALL, AS MANY WORLDS AND PLANES, HELLS AND PARADISES, AS A MIND CAN ENCOMPASS.
IT WAS VERY INTERESTING. I MEAN, I DON'T THINK I UNDERSTAND IT ALL, YET.
BUT THANKS.
OH--AND IF YOU'RE QUEEN TITANIA, SOMEONE SAID TO SAY HELLO. A TALL BLOKE FROM THE DREAMING PLACE. BLACK HAIR.

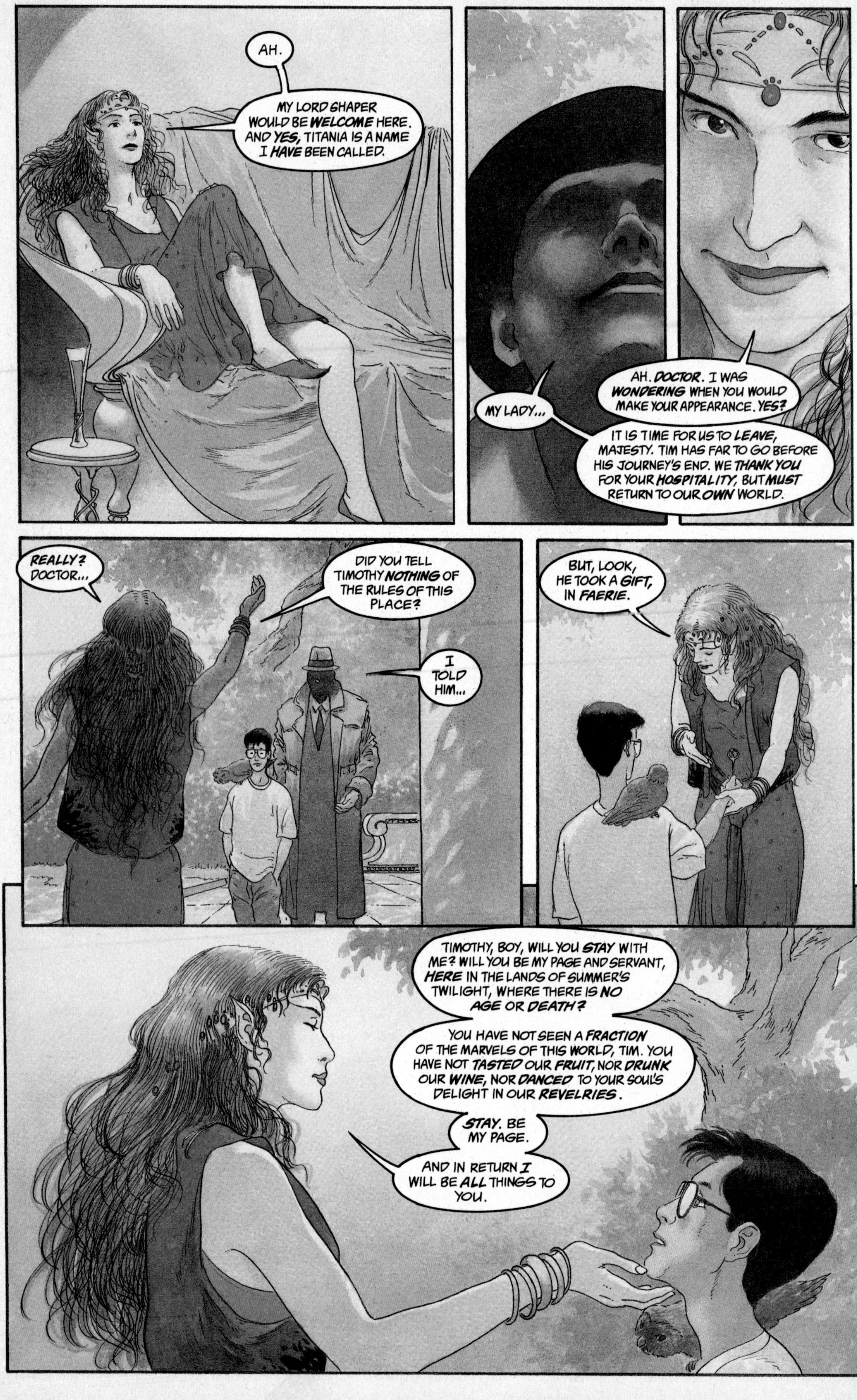
AH.
MY LORD SHAPER WOULD BE WELCOME HERE. AND YES, TITANIA IS A NAME I HAVE BEEN CALLED.
MY LADY...
AH. DOCTOR. I WAS WONDERING WHEN YOU WOULD MAKE YOUR APPEARANCE. YES?
IT IS TIME FOR US TO LEAVE, MAJESTY. TIM HAS FAR TO GO BEFORE HIS JOURNEY'S END. WE THANK YOU FOR YOUR HOSPITALITY, BUT MUST RETURN TO OUR OWN WORLD.
REALLY? DOCTOR...
DID YOU TELL TIMOTHY NOTHING OF THE RULES OF THIS PLACE?
I TOLD HIM...
BUT, LOOK, HE TOOK A GIFT, IN FAERIE.
TIMOTHY, BOY, WILL YOU STAY WITH ME? WILL YOU BE MY PAGE AND SERVANT, HERE IN THE LANDS OF SUMMER'S TWILIGHT, WHERE THERE IS NO AGE OR DEATH?
YOU HAVE NOT SEEN A FRACTION OF THE MARVELS OF THIS WORLD, TIM. YOU HAVE NOT TASTED OUR FRUIT, NOR DRUNK OUR WINE, NOR DANCED TO YOUR SOUL'S DELIGHT IN OUR REVELRIES.
STAY. BE MY PAGE.
AND IN RETURN I WILL BE ALL THINGS TO YOU.

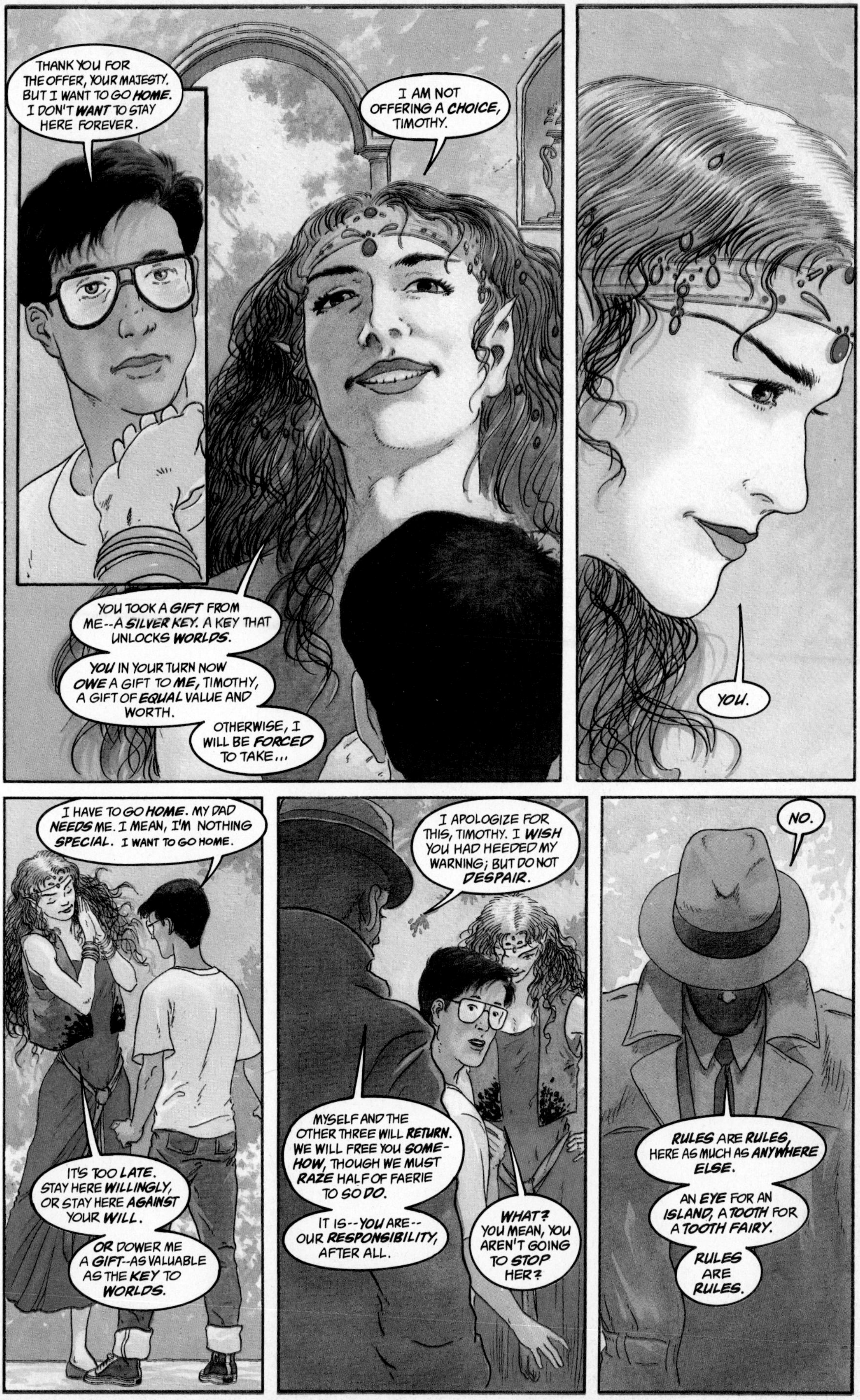
THANK YOU FOR THE OFFER, YOUR MAJESTY. BUT I WANT TO GO HOME. I DON'T WANT TO STAY HERE FOREVER.
I AM NOT OFFERING A CHOICE, TIMOTHY.
YOU TOOK A GIFT FROM ME--A SILVER KEY. A KEY THAT UNLOCKS WORLDS.
YOU IN YOUR TURN NOW OWE A GIFT TO ME, TIMOTHY, A GIFT OF EQUAL VALUE AND WORTH.
OTHERWISE, I WILL BE FORCED TO TAKE...
YOU.
I HAVE TO GO HOME. MY DAD NEEDS ME. I MEAN, I'M NOTHING SPECIAL. I WANT TO GO HOME.
IT'S TOO LATE. STAY HERE WILLINGLY, OR STAY HERE AGAINST YOUR WILL.
OR DOWER ME A GIFT--AS VALUABLE AS THE KEY TO WORLDS.
I APOLOGIZE FOR THIS, TIMOTHY. I WISH YOU HAD HEEDED MY WARNING; BUT DO NOT DESPAIR.
MYSELF AND THE OTHER THREE WILL RETURN. WE WILL FREE YOU SOME-HOW, THOUGH WE MUST RAZE HALF OF FAERIE TO SO DO.
IT IS--YOU ARE--OUR RESPONSIBILITY, AFTER ALL.
WHAT? YOU MEAN, YOU AREN'T GOING TO STOP HER?
NO.
RULES ARE RULES, HERE AS MUCH AS ANYWHERE ELSE.
AN EYE FOR AN ISLAND, A TOOTH FOR A TOOTH FAIRY.
RULES ARE RULES.

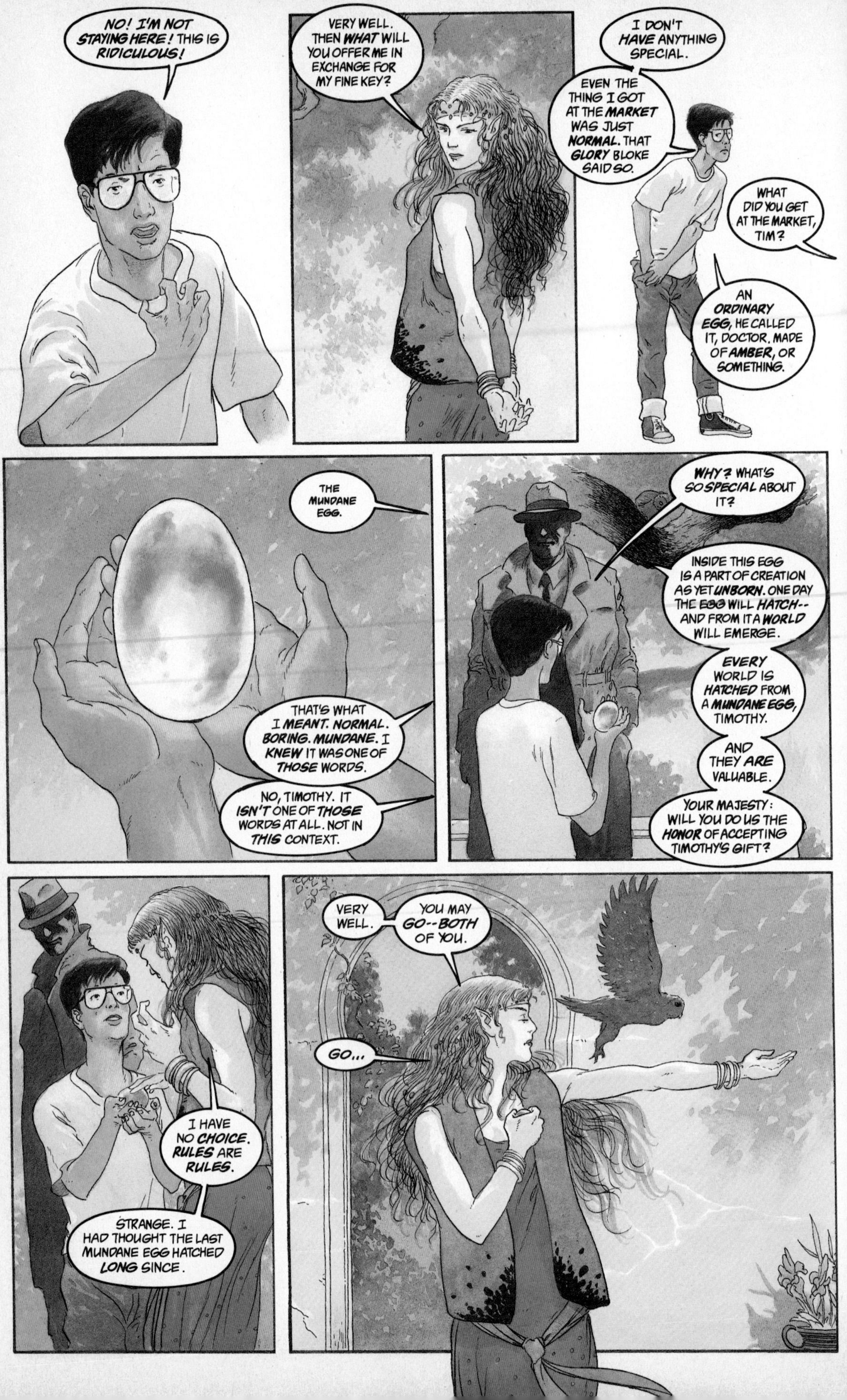
NO! I'M NOT STAYING HERE! THIS IS RIDICULOUS!
VERY WELL. THEN WHAT WILL YOU OFFER ME IN EXCHANGE FOR MY FINE KEY?
I DON'T HAVE ANYTHING SPECIAL.
EVEN THE THING I GOT AT THE MARKET WAS JUST NORMAL. THAT GLORY BLOKE SAID SO.
WHAT DID YOU GET AT THE MARKET, TIM?
AN ORDINARY EGG, HE CALLED IT, DOCTOR. MADE OF AMBER, OR SOMETHING.
THE MUNDANE EGG.
THAT'S WHAT I MEANT. NORMAL. BORING. MUNDANE. I KNEW IT WAS ONE OF THOSE WORDS.
NO, TIMOTHY. IT ISN'T ONE OF THOSE WORDS AT ALL. NOT IN THIS CONTEXT.
WHY? WHAT'S SO SPECIAL ABOUT IT?
INSIDE THIS EGG IS A PART OF CREATION AS YET UNBORN. ONE DAY THE EGG WILL HATCH-- AND FROM IT A WORLD WILL EMERGE.
EVERY WORLD IS HATCHED FROM A MUNDANE EGG, TIMOTHY.
AND THEY ARE VALUABLE.
YOUR MAJESTY: WILL YOU DO US THE HONOR OF ACCEPTING TIMOTHY'S GIFT?
I HAVE NO CHOICE. RULES ARE RULES.
STRANGE. I HAD THOUGHT THE LAST MUNDANE EGG HATCHED LONG SINCE.
VERY WELL.
YOU MAY GO--BOTH OF YOU.
GO...

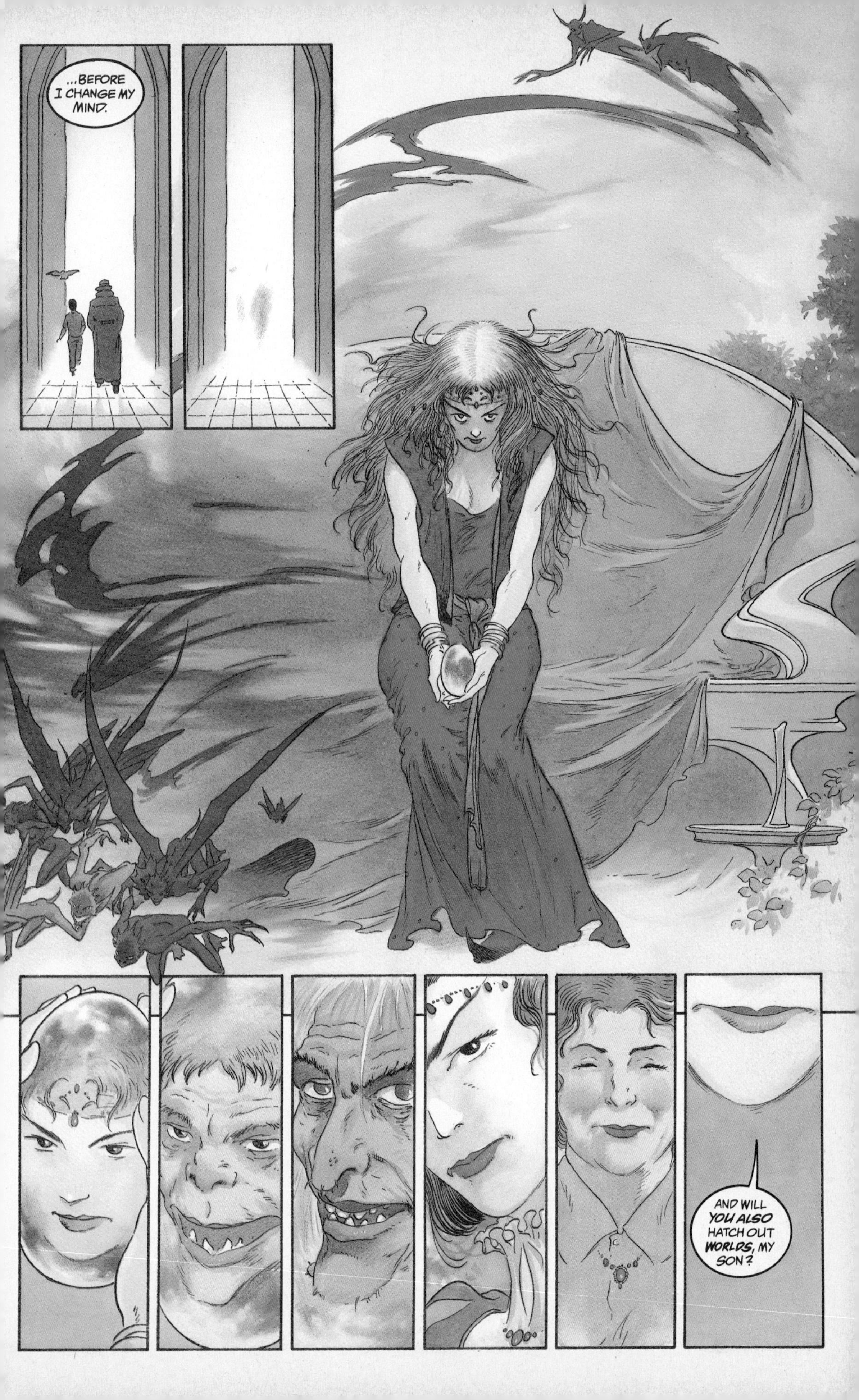
...BEFORE I CHANGE MY MIND.
AND WILL YOU ALSO HATCH OUT WORLDS, MY SON?

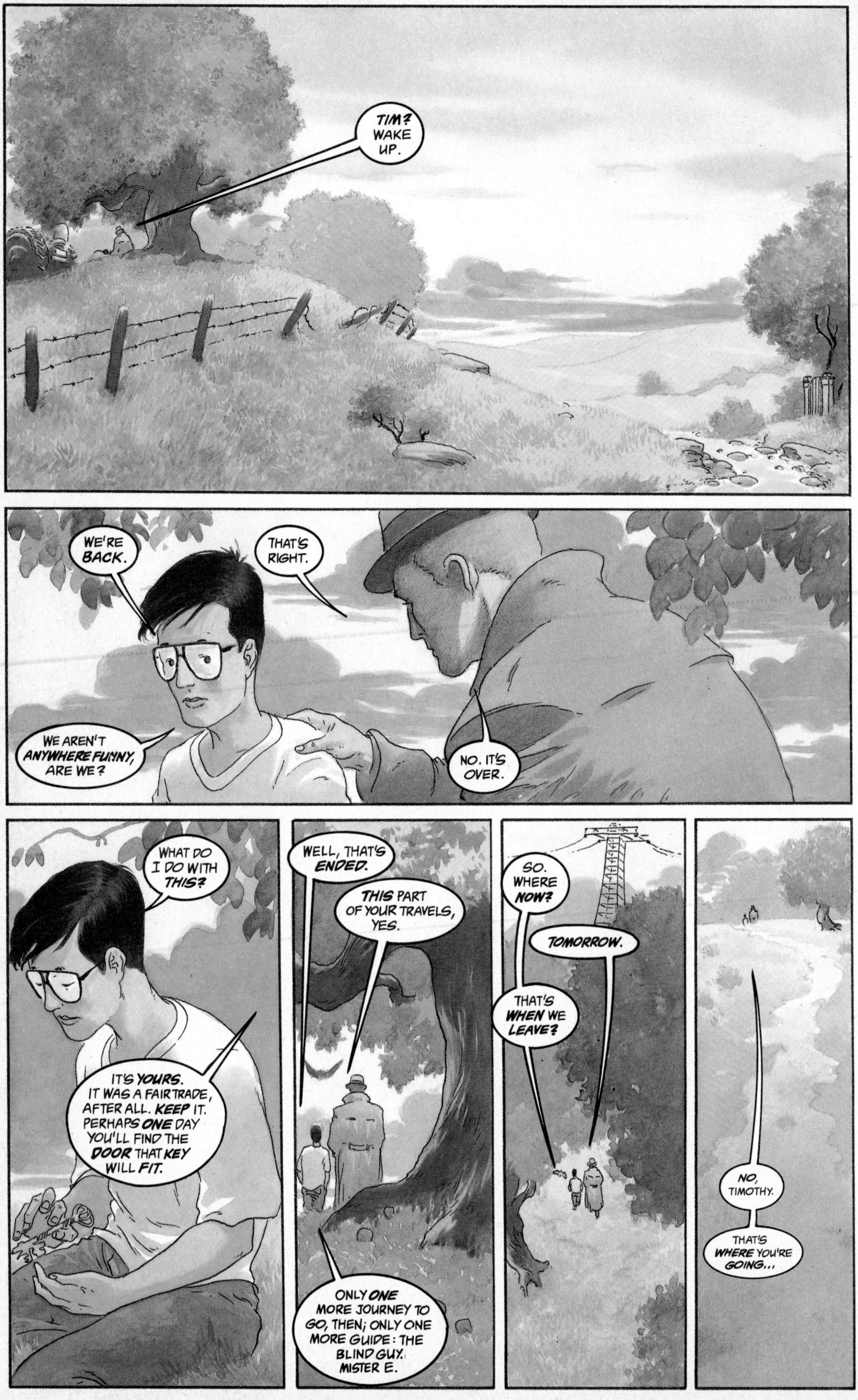
TIM? WAKE UP.
WE'RE BACK.
THAT'S RIGHT.
WE AREN'T ANYWHERE FUNNY, ARE WE?
NO. IT'S OVER.
WHAT DO I DO WITH THIS?
IT'S YOURS. IT WAS A FAIR TRADE, AFTER ALL. KEEP IT. PERHAPS ONE DAY YOU'LL FIND THE DOOR THAT KEY WILL FIT.
WELL, THAT'S ENDED.
THIS PART OF YOUR TRAVELS, YES.
ONLY ONE MORE JOURNEY TO GO, THEN; ONLY ONE MORE GUIDE: THE BLIND GUY. MISTER E.
SO. WHERE NOW?
TOMORROW.
THAT'S WHEN WE LEAVE?
NO, TIMOTHY.
THAT'S WHERE YOU'RE GOING...

IV

The Road to Nowhere

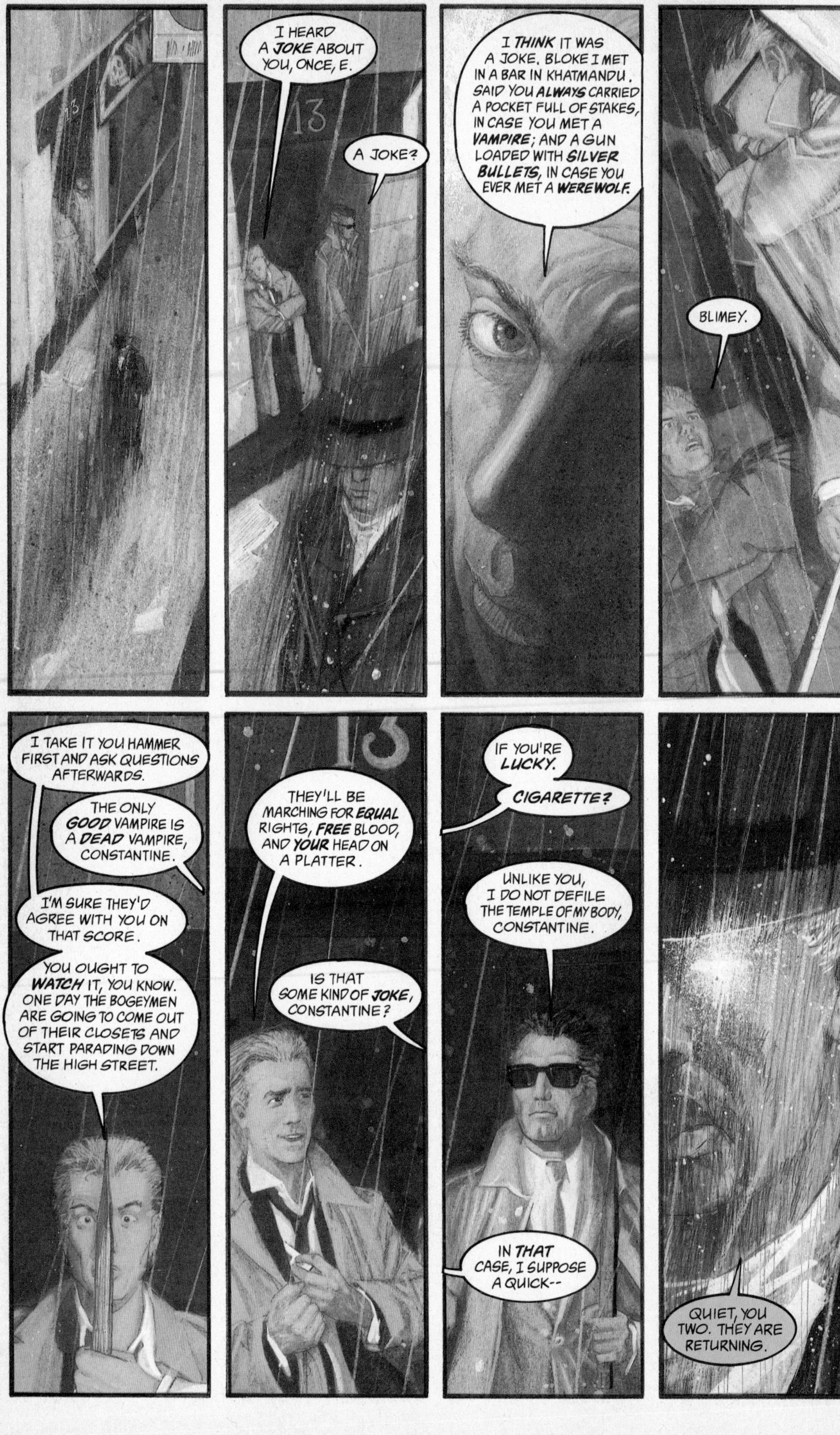

I HEARD A JOKE ABOUT YOU, ONCE, E.
A JOKE?
I THINK IT WAS A JOKE. BLOKE I MET IN A BAR IN KHATMANDU. SAID YOU ALWAYS CARRIED A POCKET FULL OF STAKES, IN CASE YOU MET A VAMPIRE; AND A GUN LOADED WITH SILVER BULLETS, IN CASE YOU EVER MET A WEREWOLF.
BLIMEY.
I TAKE IT YOU HAMMER FIRST AND ASK QUESTIONS AFTERWARDS.
THE ONLY GOOD VAMPIRE IS A DEAD VAMPIRE, CONSTANTINE.
I'M SURE THEY'D AGREE WITH YOU ON THAT SCORE.
YOU OUGHT TO WATCH IT, YOU KNOW. ONE DAY THE BOGEYMEN ARE GOING TO COME OUT OF THEIR CLOSETS AND START PARADING DOWN THE HIGH STREET.
THEY'LL BE MARCHING FOR EQUAL RIGHTS, FREE BLOOD, AND YOUR HEAD ON A PLATTER.
IS THAT SOME KIND OF JOKE, CONSTANTINE?
IF YOU'RE LUCKY.
CIGARETTE?
UNLIKE YOU, I DO NOT DEFILE THE TEMPLE OF MY BODY, CONSTANTINE.
IN THAT CASE, I SUPPOSE A QUICK--
QUIET, YOU TWO. THEY ARE RETURNING.

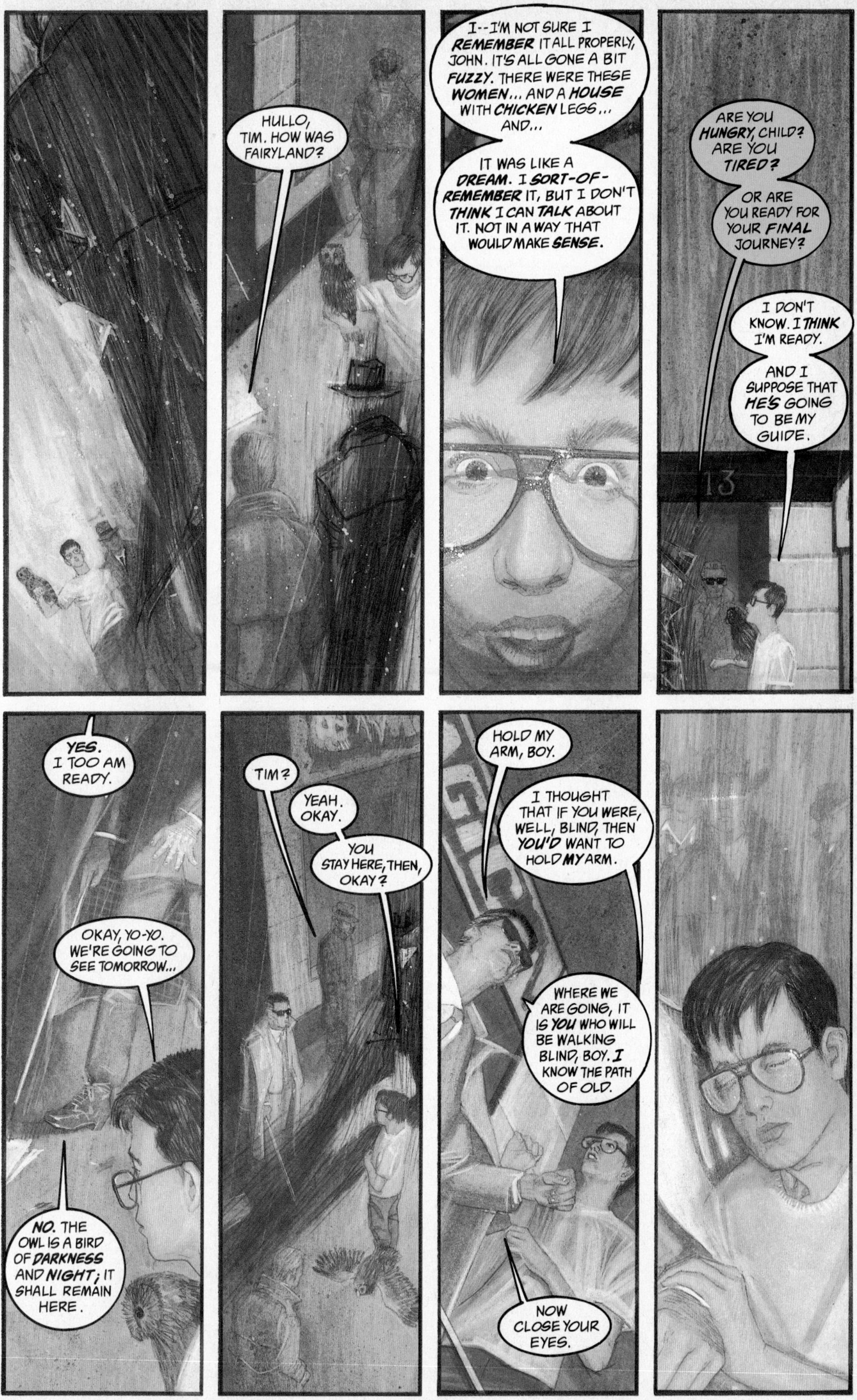
HULLO, TIM. HOW WAS FAIRYLAND?
I--I'M NOT SURE I REMEMBER IT ALL PROPERLY, JOHN. IT'S ALL GONE A BIT FUZZY. THERE WERE THESE WOMEN... AND A HOUSE WITH CHICKEN LEGS... AND...
IT WAS LIKE A DREAM. I SORT-OF-REMEMBER IT, BUT I DON'T THINK I CAN TALK ABOUT IT. NOT IN A WAY THAT WOULD MAKE SENSE.
ARE YOU HUNGRY, CHILD? ARE YOU TIRED?
OR ARE YOU READY FOR YOUR FINAL JOURNEY?
I DON'T KNOW. I THINK I'M READY.
AND I SUPPOSE THAT HE'S GOING TO BE MY GUIDE.
13
YES. I TOO AM READY.
OKAY, YO-YO. WE'RE GOING TO SEE TOMORROW...
NO. THE OWL IS A BIRD OF DARKNESS AND NIGHT; IT SHALL REMAIN HERE.
TIM?
YEAH. OKAY.
YOU STAY HERE, THEN, OKAY?
HOLD MY ARM, BOY.
I THOUGHT THAT IF YOU WERE, WELL, BLIND, THEN YOU'D WANT TO HOLD MY ARM.
WHERE WE ARE GOING, IT IS YOU WHO WILL BE WALKING BLIND, BOY. I KNOW THE PATH OF OLD.
NOW CLOSE YOUR EYES.

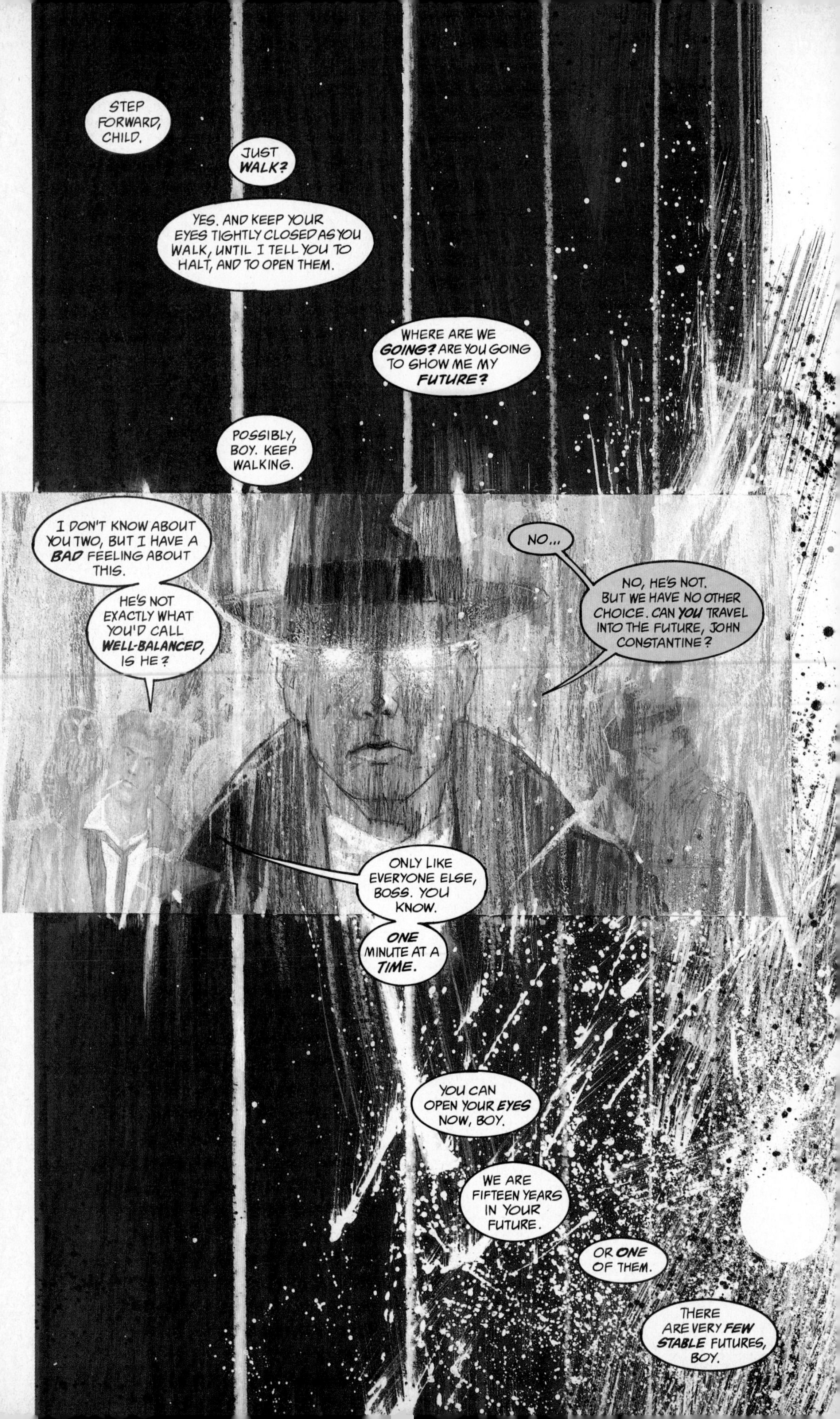
STEP FORWARD, CHILD.
JUST WALK?
YES. AND KEEP YOUR EYES TIGHTLY CLOSED AS YOU WALK, UNTIL I TELL YOU TO HALT, AND TO OPEN THEM.
WHERE ARE WE GOING? ARE YOU GOING TO SHOW ME MY FUTURE?
POSSIBLY, BOY. KEEP WALKING.
I DON'T KNOW ABOUT YOU TWO, BUT I HAVE A BAD FEELING ABOUT THIS.
HE'S NOT EXACTLY WHAT YOU'D CALL WELL-BALANCED, IS HE?
NO...
NO, HE'S NOT. BUT WE HAVE NO OTHER CHOICE. CAN YOU TRAVEL INTO THE FUTURE, JOHN CONSTANTINE?
ONLY LIKE EVERYONE ELSE, BOSS. YOU KNOW.
ONE MINUTE AT A TIME.
YOU CAN OPEN YOUR EYES NOW, BOY.
WE ARE FIFTEEN YEARS IN YOUR FUTURE.
OR ONE OF THEM.
THERE ARE VERY FEW STABLE FUTURES, BOY.

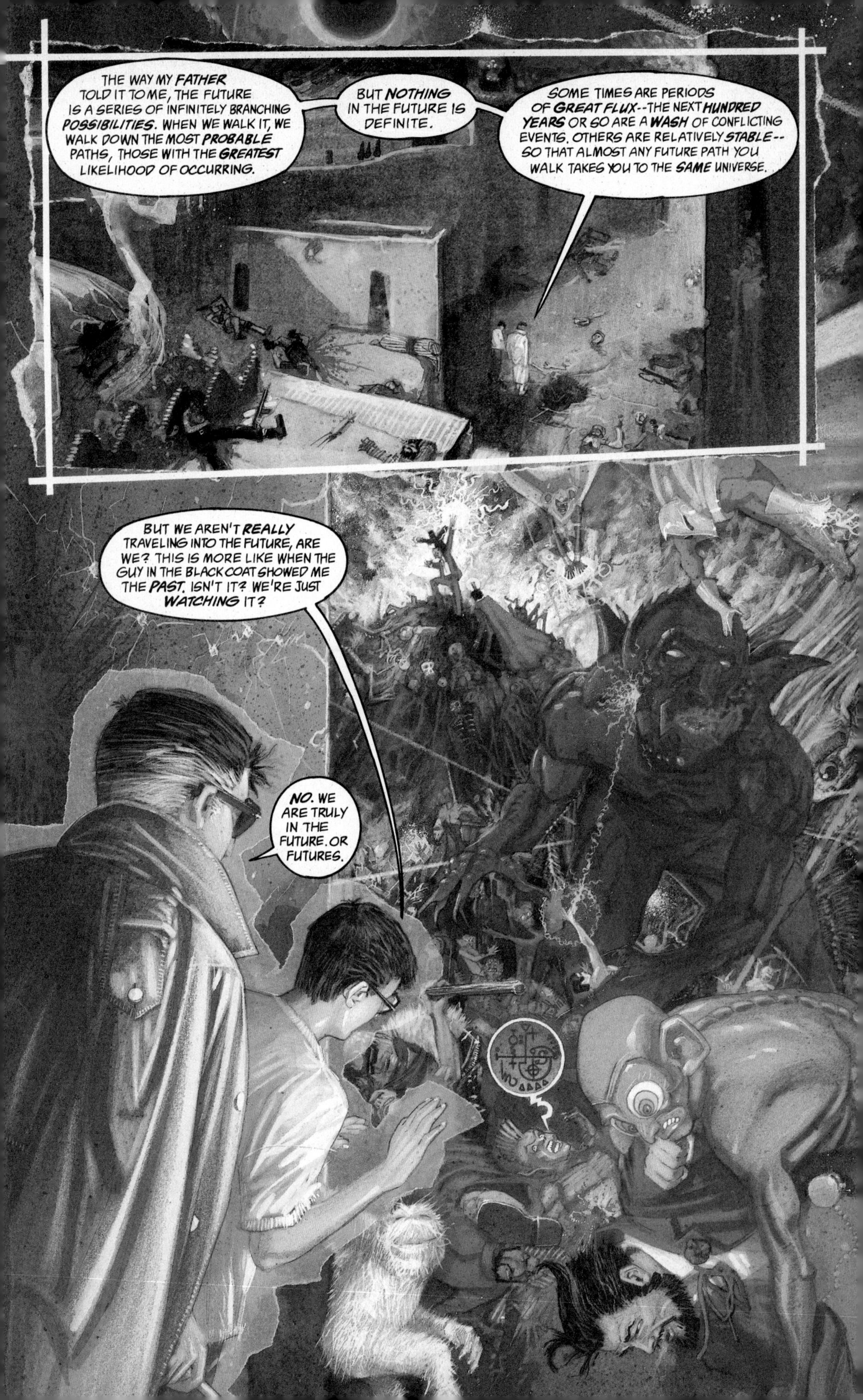
THE WAY MY FATHER TOLD IT TO ME, THE FUTURE IS A SERIES OF INFINITELY BRANCHING POSSIBILITIES. WHEN WE WALK IT, WE WALK DOWN THE MOST PROBABLE PATHS, THOSE WITH THE GREATEST LIKELIHOOD OF OCCURRING.
BUT NOTHING IN THE FUTURE IS DEFINITE.
SOME TIMES ARE PERIODS OF GREAT FLUX--THE NEXT HUNDRED YEARS OR SO ARE A WASH OF CONFLICTING EVENTS. OTHERS ARE RELATIVELY STABLE--SO THAT ALMOST ANY FUTURE PATH YOU WALK TAKES YOU TO THE SAME UNIVERSE.
BUT WE AREN'T REALLY TRAVELING INTO THE FUTURE, ARE WE? THIS IS MORE LIKE WHEN THE GUY IN THE BLACK COAT SHOWED ME THE PAST, ISN'T IT? WE'RE JUST WATCHING IT?
NO. WE ARE TRULY IN THE FUTURE. OR FUTURES.

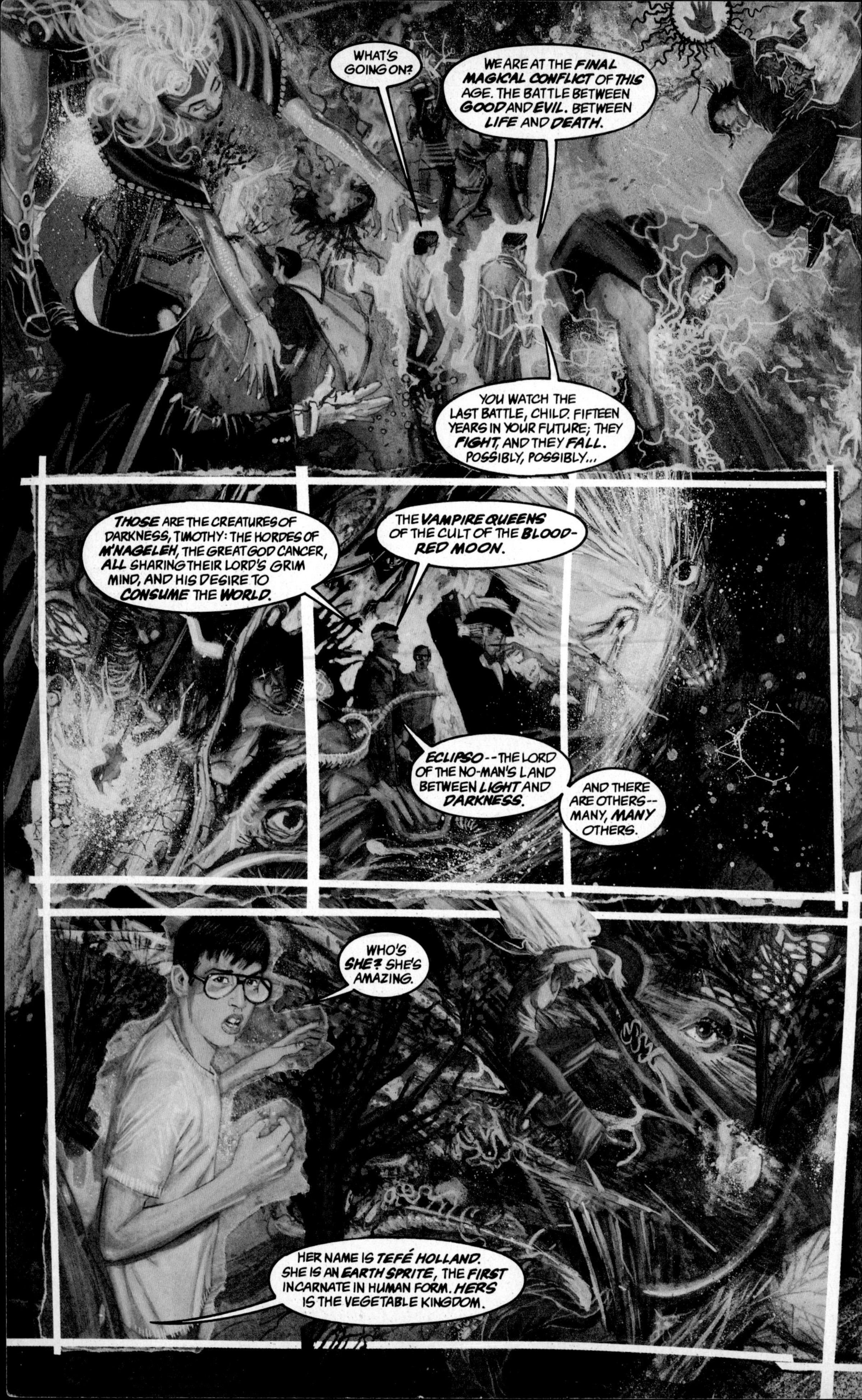
WHAT'S GOING ON?
WE ARE AT THE FINAL MAGICAL CONFLICT OF THIS AGE. THE BATTLE BETWEEN GOOD AND EVIL. BETWEEN LIFE AND DEATH.
YOU WATCH THE LAST BATTLE, CHILD. FIFTEEN YEARS IN YOUR FUTURE; THEY FIGHT, AND THEY FALL. POSSIBLY, POSSIBLY...
THOSE ARE THE CREATURES OF DARKNESS, TIMOTHY: THE HORDES OF M'NAGELEH, THE GREAT GOD CANCER, ALL SHARING THEIR LORD'S GRIM MIND, AND HIS DESIRE TO CONSUME THE WORLD.
THE VAMPIRE QUEENS OF THE CULT OF THE BLOOD-RED MOON.
ECLIPSO--THE LORD OF THE NO-MAN'S LAND BETWEEN LIGHT AND DARKNESS.
AND THERE ARE OTHERS--MANY, MANY OTHERS.
WHO'S SHE? SHE'S AMAZING.
HER NAME IS TEFÉ HOLLAND. SHE IS AN EARTH SPRITE, THE FIRST INCARNATE IN HUMAN FORM. HERS IS THE VEGETABLE KINGDOM.

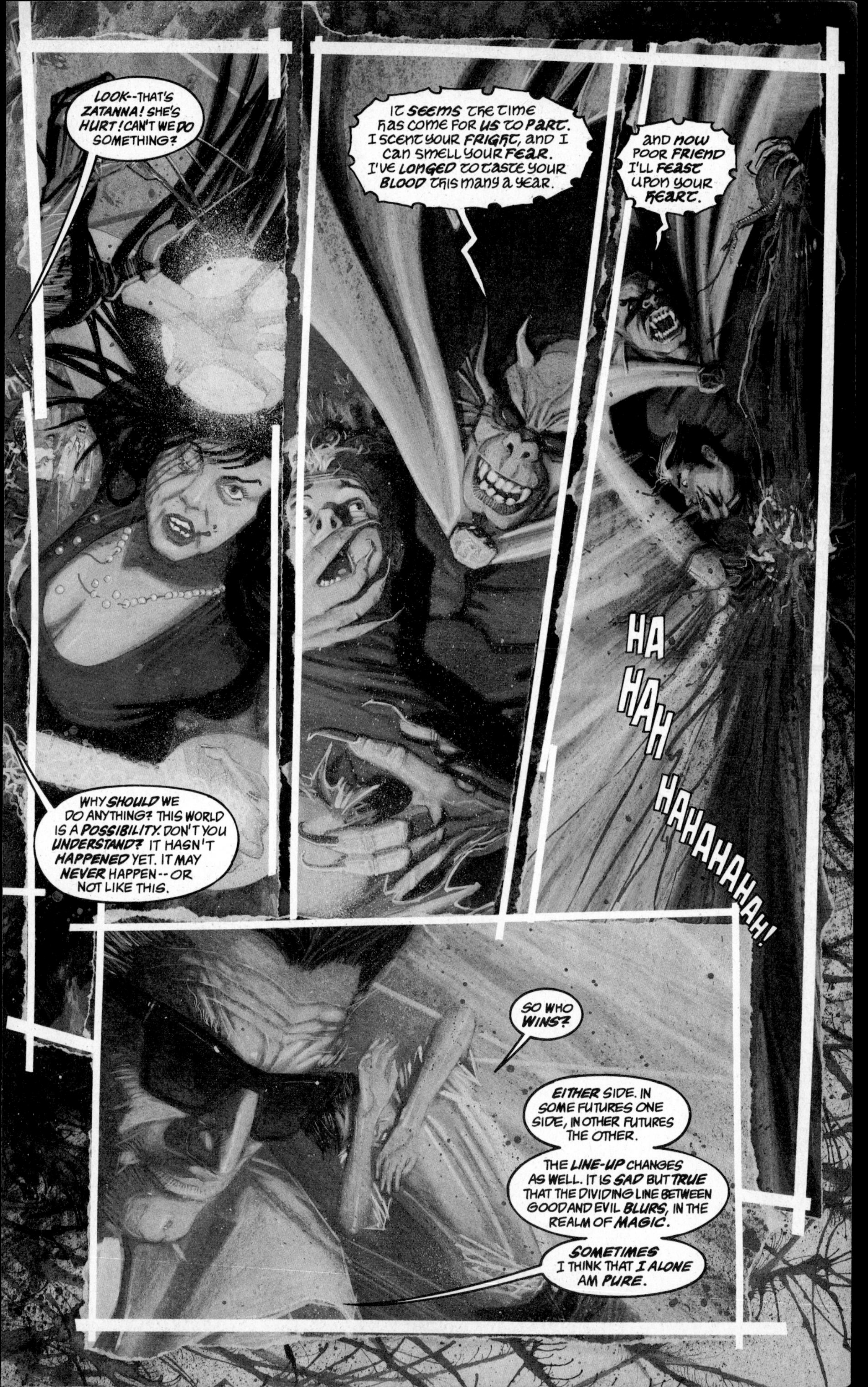
LOOK--THAT'S ZATANNA! SHE'S HURT! CAN'T WE DO SOMETHING?
IT SEEMS THE TIME HAS COME FOR US TO PART. I SCENT YOUR FRIGHT, AND I CAN SMELL YOUR FEAR. I'VE LONGED TO TASTE YOUR BLOOD THIS MANY A YEAR.
AND NOW POOR FRIEND I'LL FEAST UPON YOUR HEART.
HA HAH HAH HAHAHAHAHAH!
WHY SHOULD WE DO ANYTHING? THIS WORLD IS A POSSIBILITY. DON'T YOU UNDERSTAND? IT HASN'T HAPPENED YET. IT MAY NEVER HAPPEN--OR NOT LIKE THIS.
SO WHO WINS?
EITHER SIDE. IN SOME FUTURES ONE SIDE, IN OTHER FUTURES THE OTHER.
THE LINE-UP CHANGES AS WELL. IT IS SAD BUT TRUE THAT THE DIVIDING LINE BETWEEN GOOD AND EVIL BLURS, IN THE REALM OF MAGIC.
SOMETIMES I THINK THAT I ALONE AM PURE.

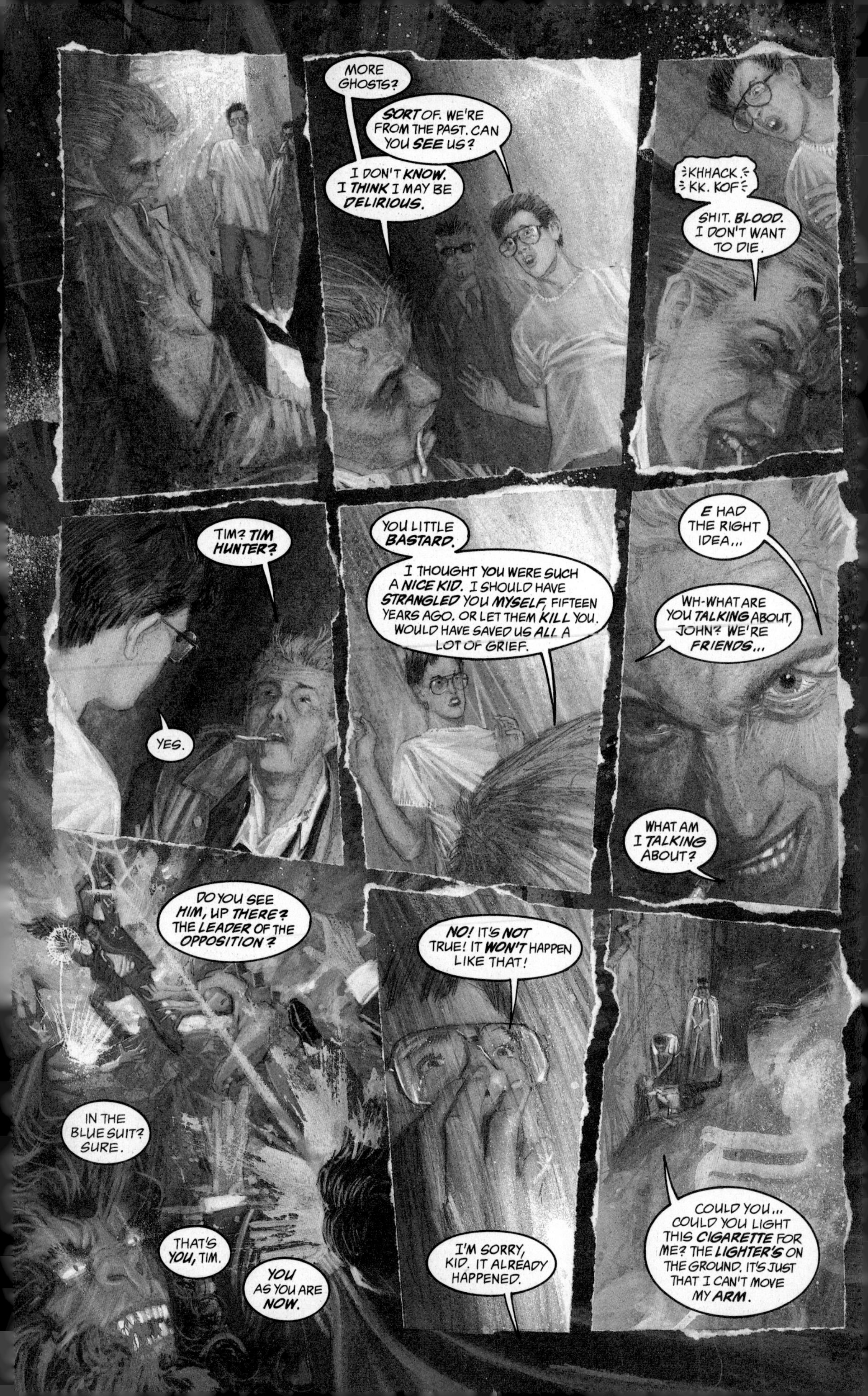
MORE GHOSTS?
SORT OF. WE'RE FROM THE PAST. CAN YOU SEE US?
I DON'T KNOW. I THINK I MAY BE DELIRIOUS.
KHHACK KK. KOF
SHIT. BLOOD. I DON'T WANT TO DIE.
TIM? TIM HUNTER?
YES.
YOU LITTLE BASTARD.
I THOUGHT YOU WERE SUCH A NICE KID. I SHOULD HAVE STRANGLED YOU MYSELF, FIFTEEN YEARS AGO. OR LET THEM KILL YOU. WOULD HAVE SAVED US ALL A LOT OF GRIEF.
E HAD THE RIGHT IDEA...
WH-WHAT ARE YOU TALKING ABOUT, JOHN? WE'RE FRIENDS...
WHAT AM I TALKING ABOUT?
DO YOU SEE HIM, UP THERE? THE LEADER OF THE OPPOSITION?
IN THE BLUE SUIT? SURE.
THAT'S YOU, TIM.
YOU AS YOU ARE NOW.
NO! IT'S NOT TRUE! IT WON'T HAPPEN LIKE THAT!
I'M SORRY, KID. IT ALREADY HAPPENED.
COULD YOU... COULD YOU LIGHT THIS CIGARETTE FOR ME? THE LIGHTER'S ON THE GROUND. IT'S JUST THAT I CAN'T MOVE MY ARM.

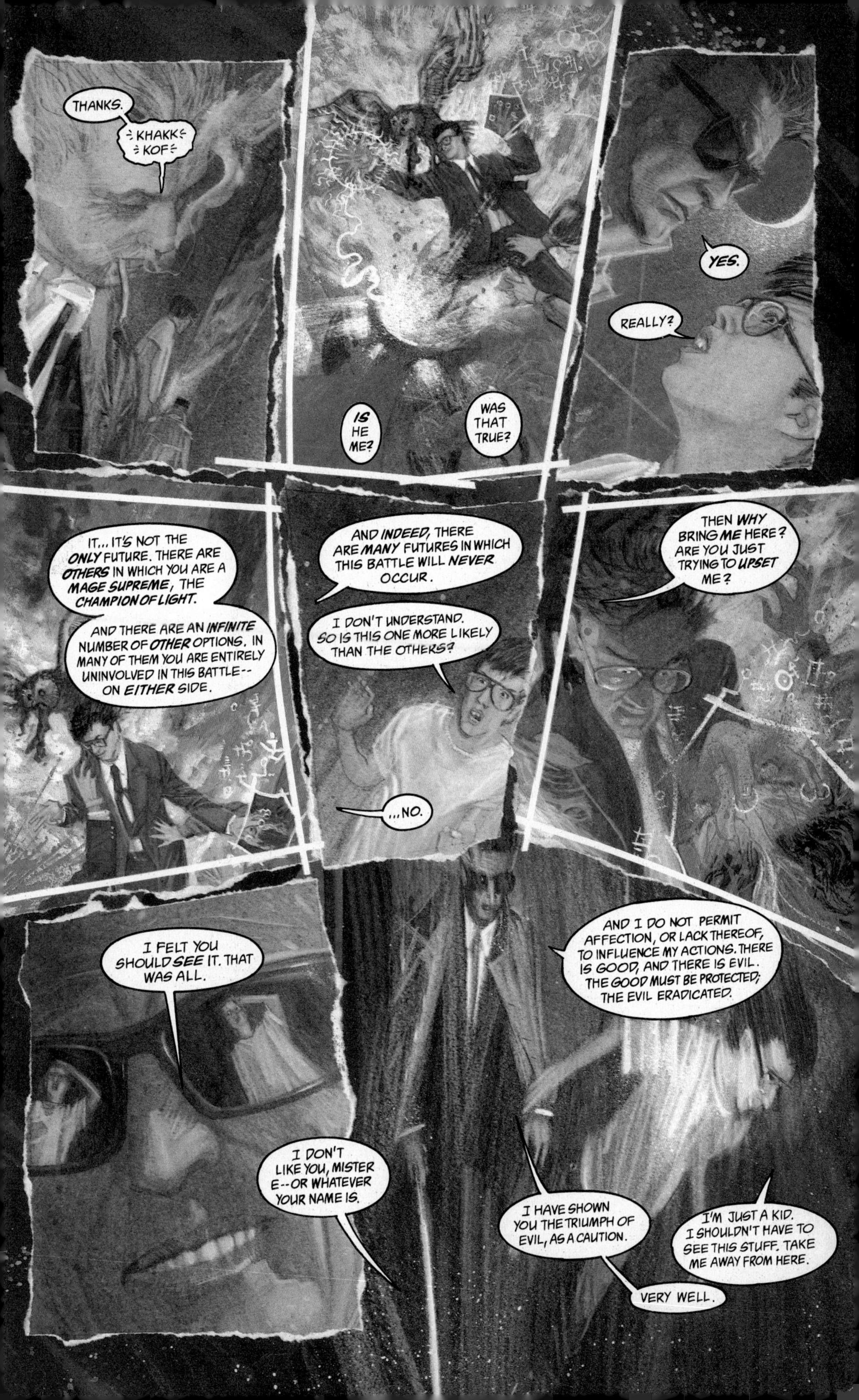
THANKS.
KHAKK KOF
IS HE ME?
WAS THAT TRUE?
YES.
REALLY?
IT... IT'S NOT THE ONLY FUTURE. THERE ARE OTHERS IN WHICH YOU ARE A MAGE SUPREME, THE CHAMPION OF LIGHT.
AND THERE ARE AN INFINITE NUMBER OF OTHER OPTIONS. IN MANY OF THEM YOU ARE ENTIRELY UNINVOLVED IN THIS BATTLE-- ON EITHER SIDE.
AND INDEED, THERE ARE MANY FUTURES IN WHICH THIS BATTLE WILL NEVER OCCUR.
I DON'T UNDERSTAND. SO IS THIS ONE MORE LIKELY THAN THE OTHERS?
...NO.
THEN WHY BRING ME HERE? ARE YOU JUST TRYING TO UPSET ME?
I FELT YOU SHOULD SEE IT. THAT WAS ALL.
AND I DO NOT PERMIT AFFECTION, OR LACK THEREOF, TO INFLUENCE MY ACTIONS. THERE IS GOOD, AND THERE IS EVIL. THE GOOD MUST BE PROTECTED; THE EVIL ERADICATED.
I DON'T LIKE YOU, MISTER E--OR WHATEVER YOUR NAME IS.
I HAVE SHOWN YOU THE TRIUMPH OF EVIL, AS A CAUTION.
I'M JUST A KID. I SHOULDN'T HAVE TO SEE THIS STUFF. TAKE ME AWAY FROM HERE.
VERY WELL.

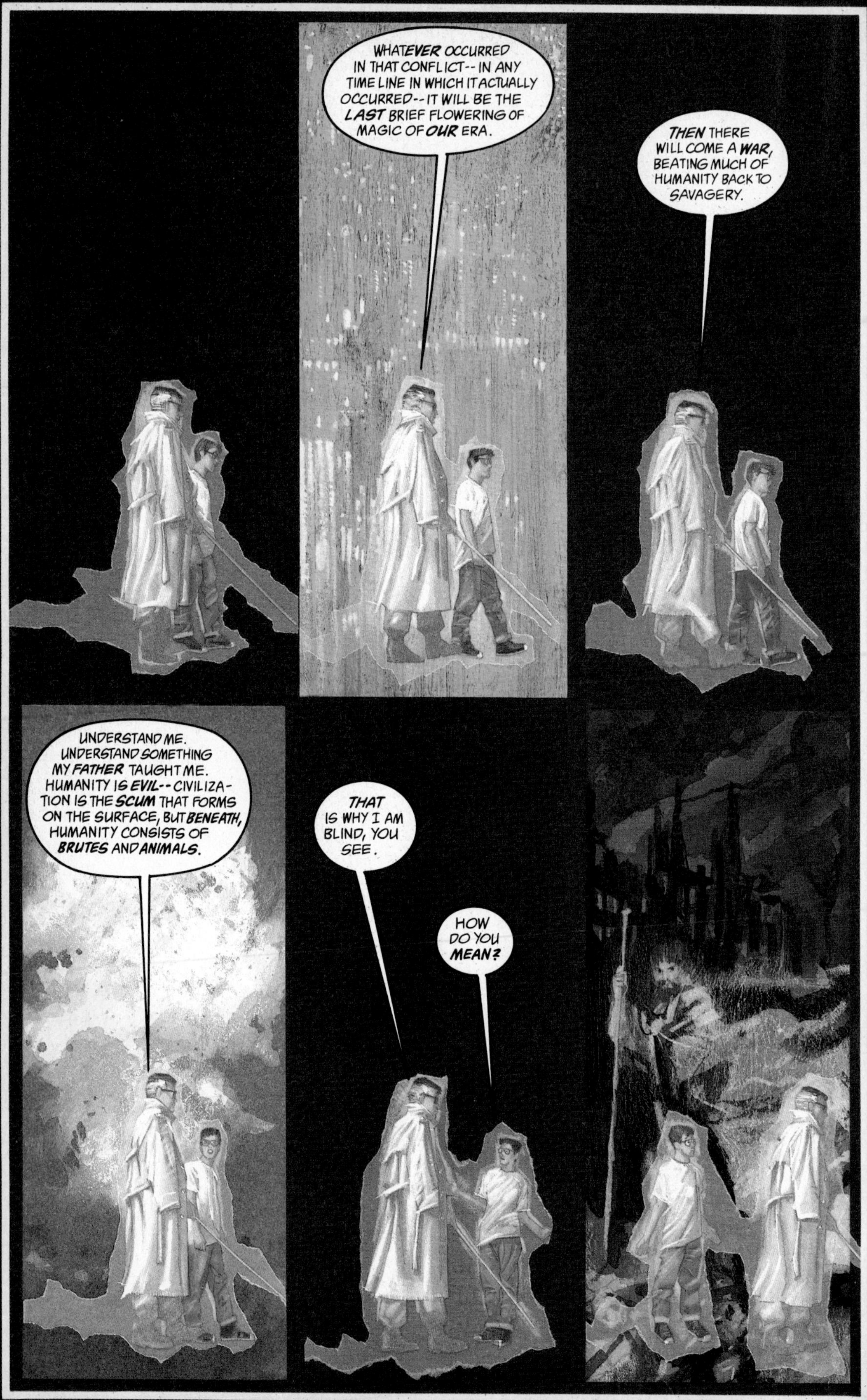

WHATEVER OCCURRED IN THAT CONFLICT-- IN ANY TIME LINE IN WHICH IT ACTUALLY OCCURRED-- IT WILL BE THE LAST BRIEF FLOWERING OF MAGIC OF OUR ERA.
THEN THERE WILL COME A WAR, BEATING MUCH OF HUMANITY BACK TO SAVAGERY.
UNDERSTAND ME. UNDERSTAND SOMETHING MY FATHER TAUGHT ME. HUMANITY IS EVIL-- CIVILIZATION IS THE SCUM THAT FORMS ON THE SURFACE, BUT BENEATH, HUMANITY CONSISTS OF BRUTES AND ANIMALS.
THAT IS WHY I AM BLIND, YOU SEE.
HOW DO YOU MEAN?

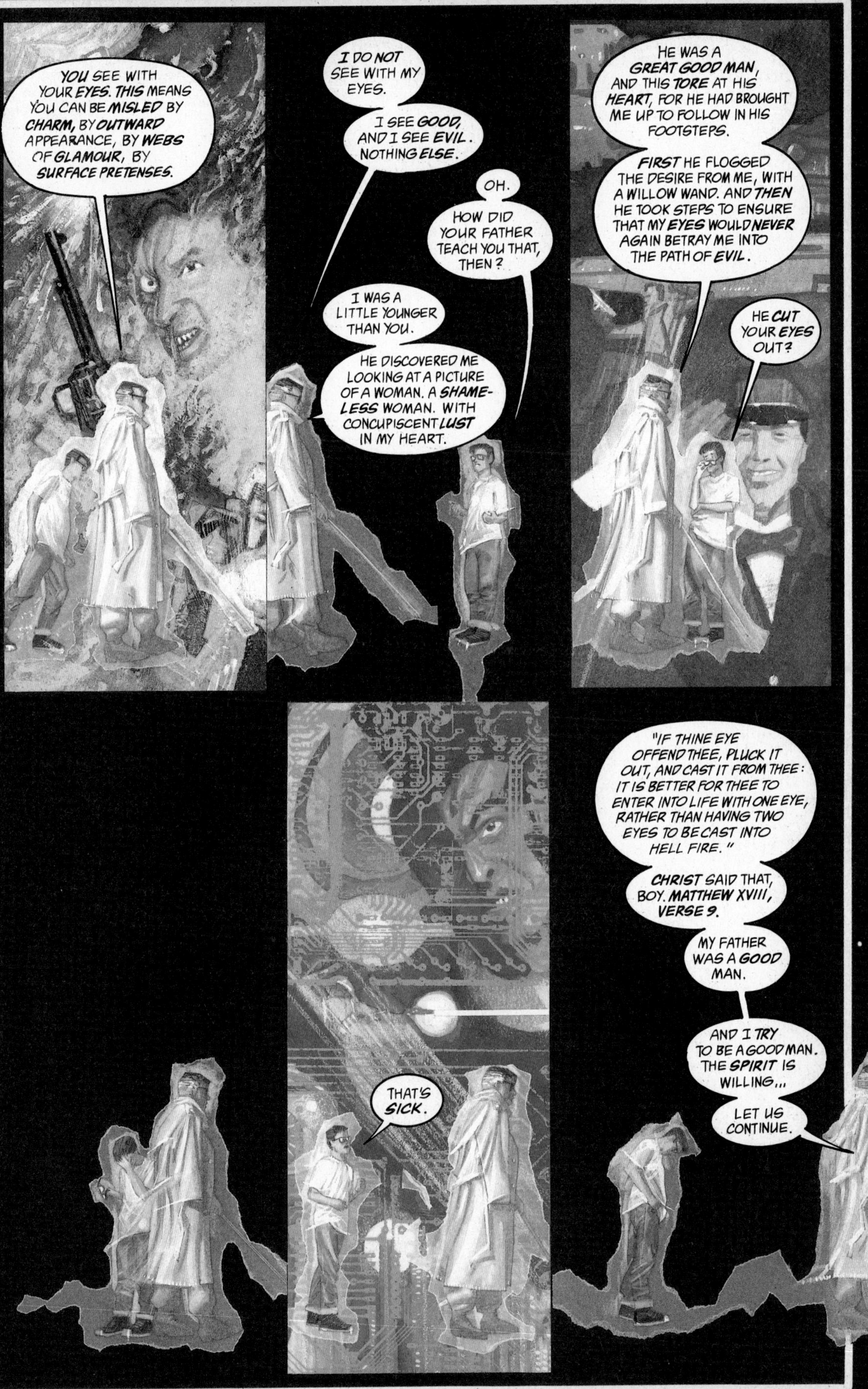
YOU SEE WITH YOUR EYES. THIS MEANS YOU CAN BE MISLED BY CHARM, BY OUTWARD APPEARANCE, BY WEBS OF GLAMOUR, BY SURFACE PRETENSES.
I DO NOT SEE WITH MY EYES.
I SEE GOOD, AND I SEE EVIL. NOTHING ELSE.
OH.
HOW DID YOUR FATHER TEACH YOU THAT, THEN?
I WAS A LITTLE YOUNGER THAN YOU.
HE DISCOVERED ME LOOKING AT A PICTURE OF A WOMAN. A SHAMELESS WOMAN. WITH CONCUPISCENT LUST IN MY HEART.
HE WAS A GREAT GOOD MAN, AND THIS TORE AT HIS HEART, FOR HE HAD BROUGHT ME UP TO FOLLOW IN HIS FOOTSTEPS.
FIRST HE FLOGGED THE DESIRE FROM ME, WITH A WILLOW WAND. AND THEN HE TOOK STEPS TO ENSURE THAT MY EYES WOULD NEVER AGAIN BETRAY ME INTO THE PATH OF EVIL.
HE CUT YOUR EYES OUT?
"IF THINE EYE OFFEND THEE, PLUCK IT OUT, AND CAST IT FROM THEE: IT IS BETTER FOR THEE TO ENTER INTO LIFE WITH ONE EYE, RATHER THAN HAVING TWO EYES TO BE CAST INTO HELL FIRE."
CHRIST SAID THAT, BOY. MATTHEW XVIII, VERSE 9.
MY FATHER WAS A GOOD MAN.
THAT'S SICK.
AND I TRY TO BE A GOOD MAN. THE SPIRIT IS WILLING...
LET US CONTINUE.

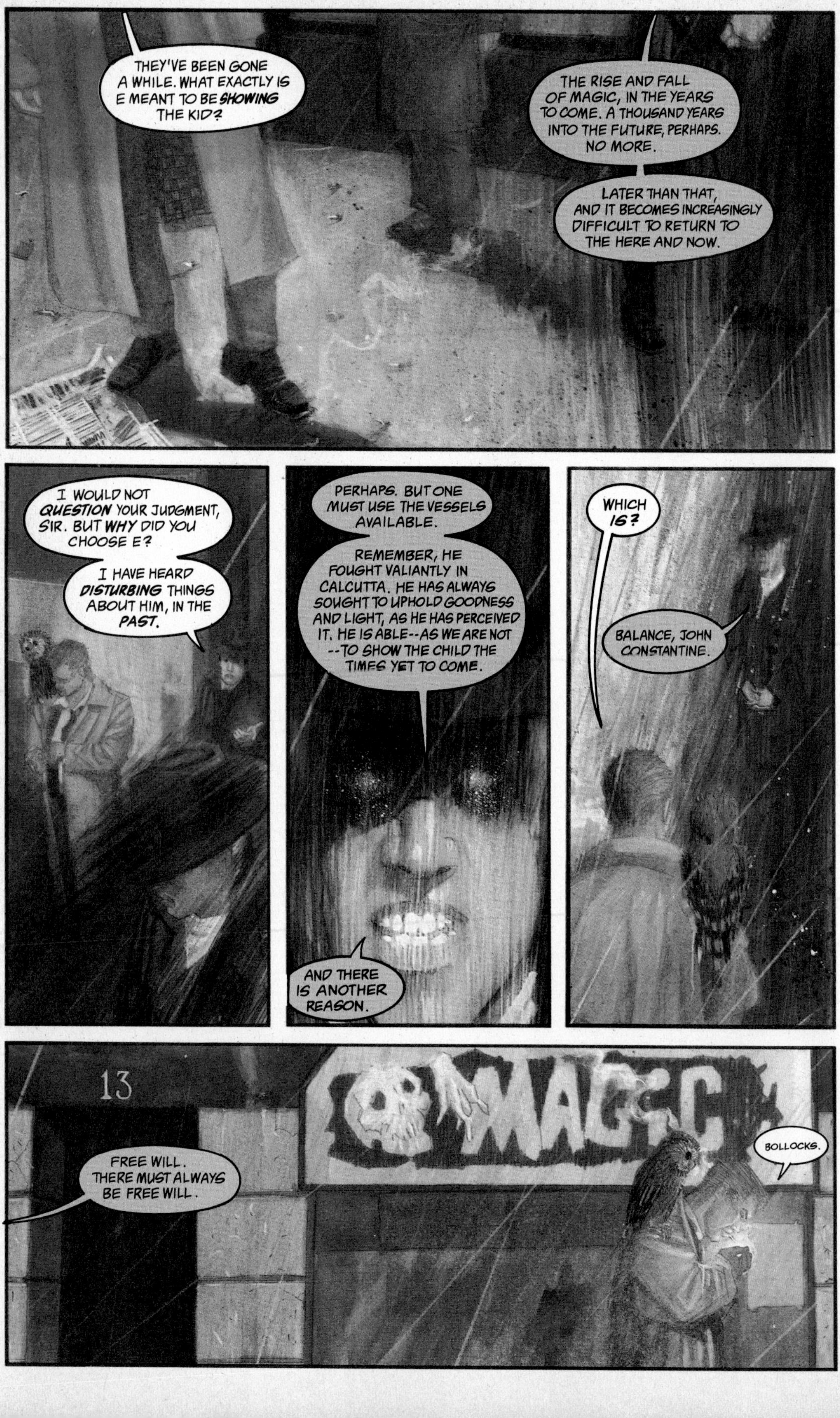
THEY'VE BEEN GONE A WHILE. WHAT EXACTLY IS E MEANT TO BE SHOWING THE KID?
THE RISE AND FALL OF MAGIC, IN THE YEARS TO COME. A THOUSAND YEARS INTO THE FUTURE, PERHAPS. NO MORE.
LATER THAN THAT, AND IT BECOMES INCREASINGLY DIFFICULT TO RETURN TO THE HERE AND NOW.
I WOULD NOT QUESTION YOUR JUDGMENT, SIR. BUT WHY DID YOU CHOOSE E?
I HAVE HEARD DISTURBING THINGS ABOUT HIM, IN THE PAST.
PERHAPS. BUT ONE MUST USE THE VESSELS AVAILABLE.
REMEMBER, HE FOUGHT VALIANTLY IN CALCUTTA. HE HAS ALWAYS SOUGHT TO UPHOLD GOODNESS AND LIGHT, AS HE HAS PERCEIVED IT. HE IS ABLE--AS WE ARE NOT --TO SHOW THE CHILD THE TIMES YET TO COME.
AND THERE IS ANOTHER REASON.
WHICH IS?
BALANCE, JOHN CONSTANTINE.
13
MAGIC
FREE WILL. THERE MUST ALWAYS BE FREE WILL.
BOLLOCKS.

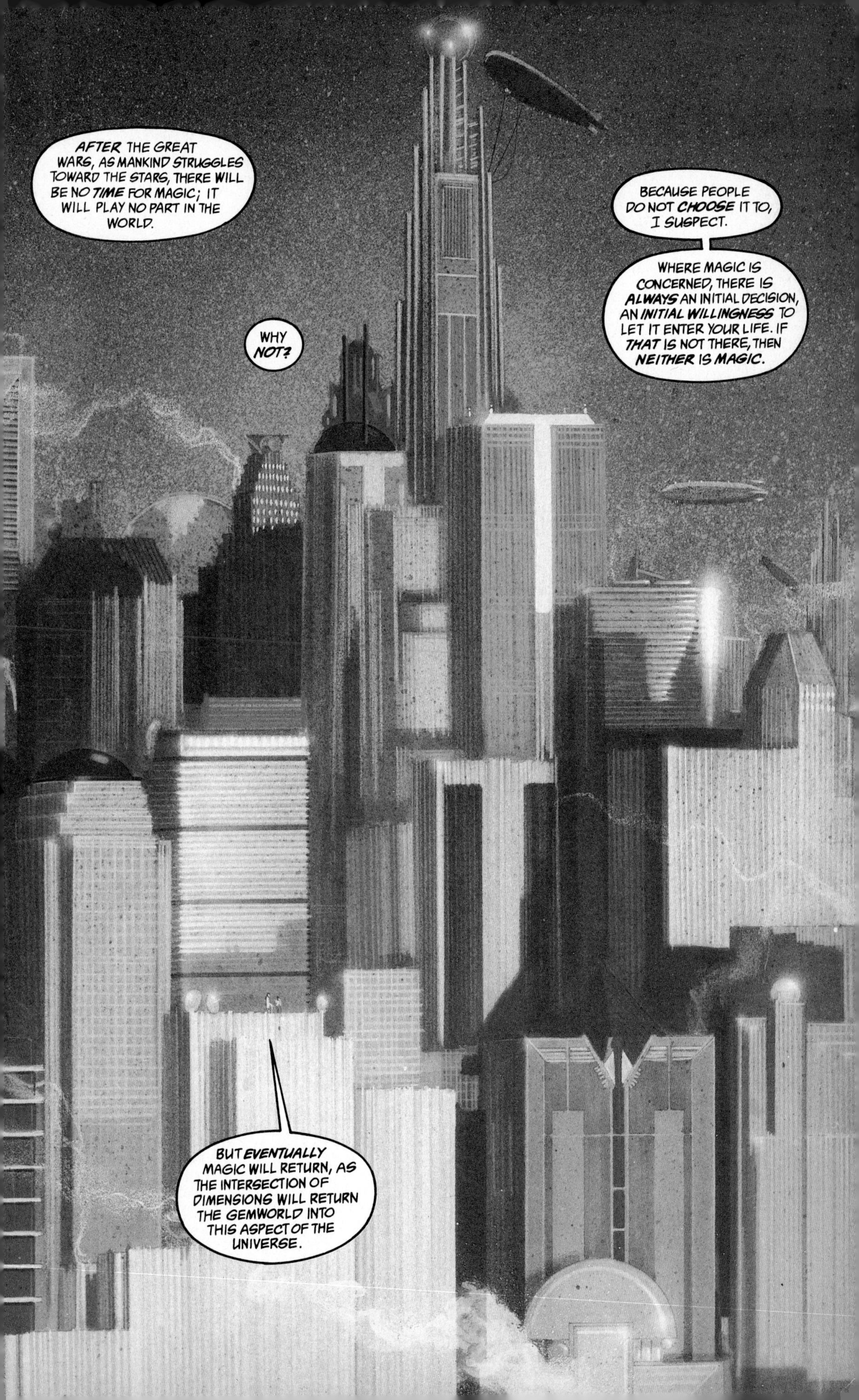
AFTER THE GREAT WARS, AS MANKIND STRUGGLES TOWARD THE STARS, THERE WILL BE NO TIME FOR MAGIC; IT WILL PLAY NO PART IN THE WORLD.
WHY NOT?
BECAUSE PEOPLE DO NOT CHOOSE IT TO, I SUSPECT.
WHERE MAGIC IS CONCERNED, THERE IS ALWAYS AN INITIAL DECISION, AN INITIAL WILLINGNESS TO LET IT ENTER YOUR LIFE. IF THAT IS NOT THERE, THEN NEITHER IS MAGIC.
BUT EVENTUALLY MAGIC WILL RETURN, AS THE INTERSECTION OF DIMENSIONS WILL RETURN THE GEMWORLD INTO THIS ASPECT OF THE UNIVERSE.

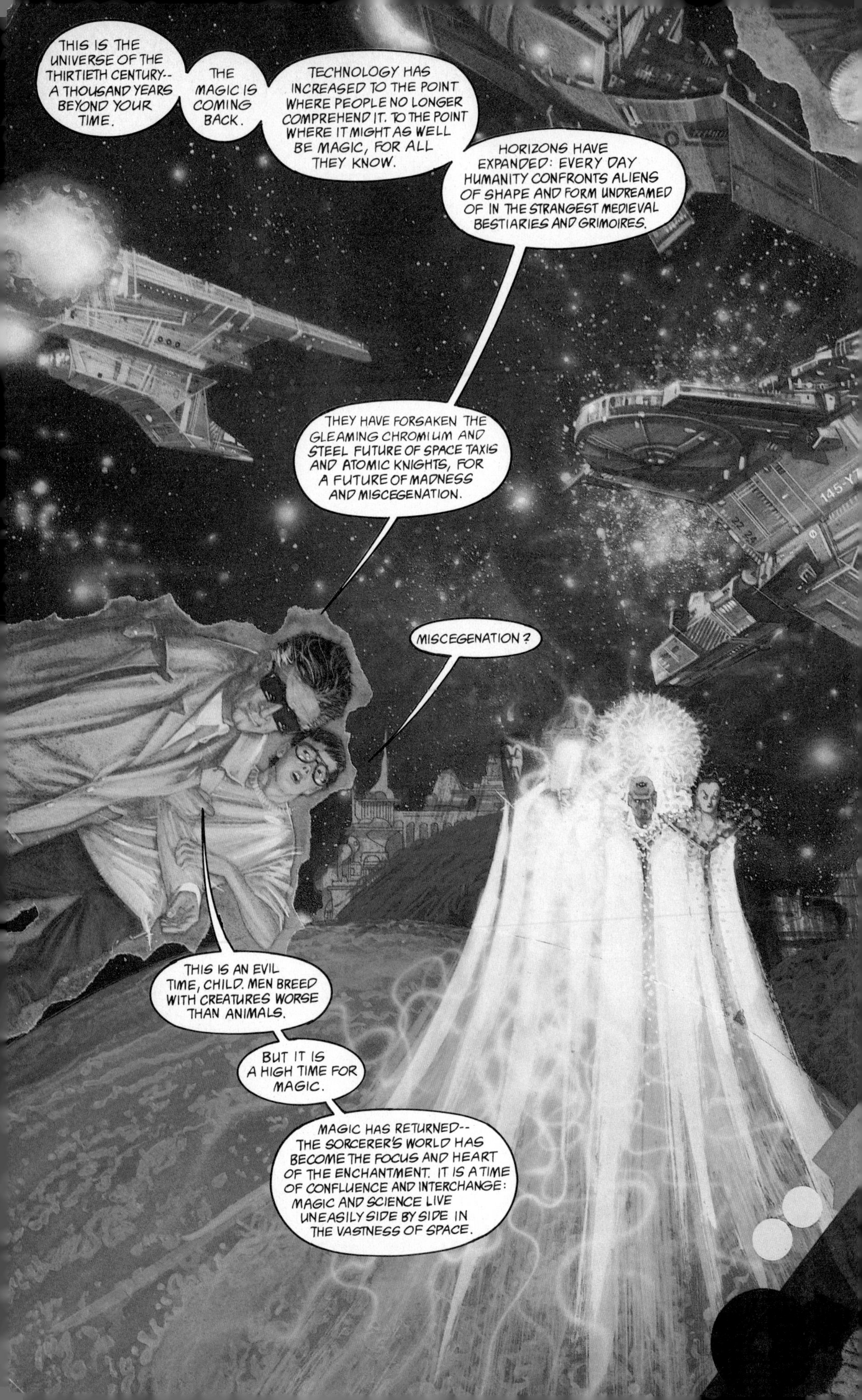
THIS IS THE UNIVERSE OF THE THIRTIETH CENTURY-- A THOUSAND YEARS BEYOND YOUR TIME.
THE MAGIC IS COMING BACK.
TECHNOLOGY HAS INCREASED TO THE POINT WHERE PEOPLE NO LONGER COMPREHEND IT. TO THE POINT WHERE IT MIGHT AS WELL BE MAGIC, FOR ALL THEY KNOW.
HORIZONS HAVE EXPANDED: EVERY DAY HUMANITY CONFRONTS ALIENS OF SHAPE AND FORM UNDREAMED OF IN THE STRANGEST MEDIEVAL BESTIARIES AND GRIMOIRES.
THEY HAVE FORSAKEN THE GLEAMING CHROMIUM AND STEEL FUTURE OF SPACE TAXIS AND ATOMIC KNIGHTS, FOR A FUTURE OF MADNESS AND MISCEGENATION.
MISCEGENATION?
THIS IS AN EVIL TIME, CHILD. MEN BREED WITH CREATURES WORSE THAN ANIMALS.
BUT IT IS A HIGH TIME FOR MAGIC.
MAGIC HAS RETURNED-- THE SORCERER'S WORLD HAS BECOME THE FOCUS AND HEART OF THE ENCHANTMENT. IT IS A TIME OF CONFLUENCE AND INTERCHANGE: MAGIC AND SCIENCE LIVE UNEASILY SIDE BY SIDE IN THE VASTNESS OF SPACE.
145-Y7

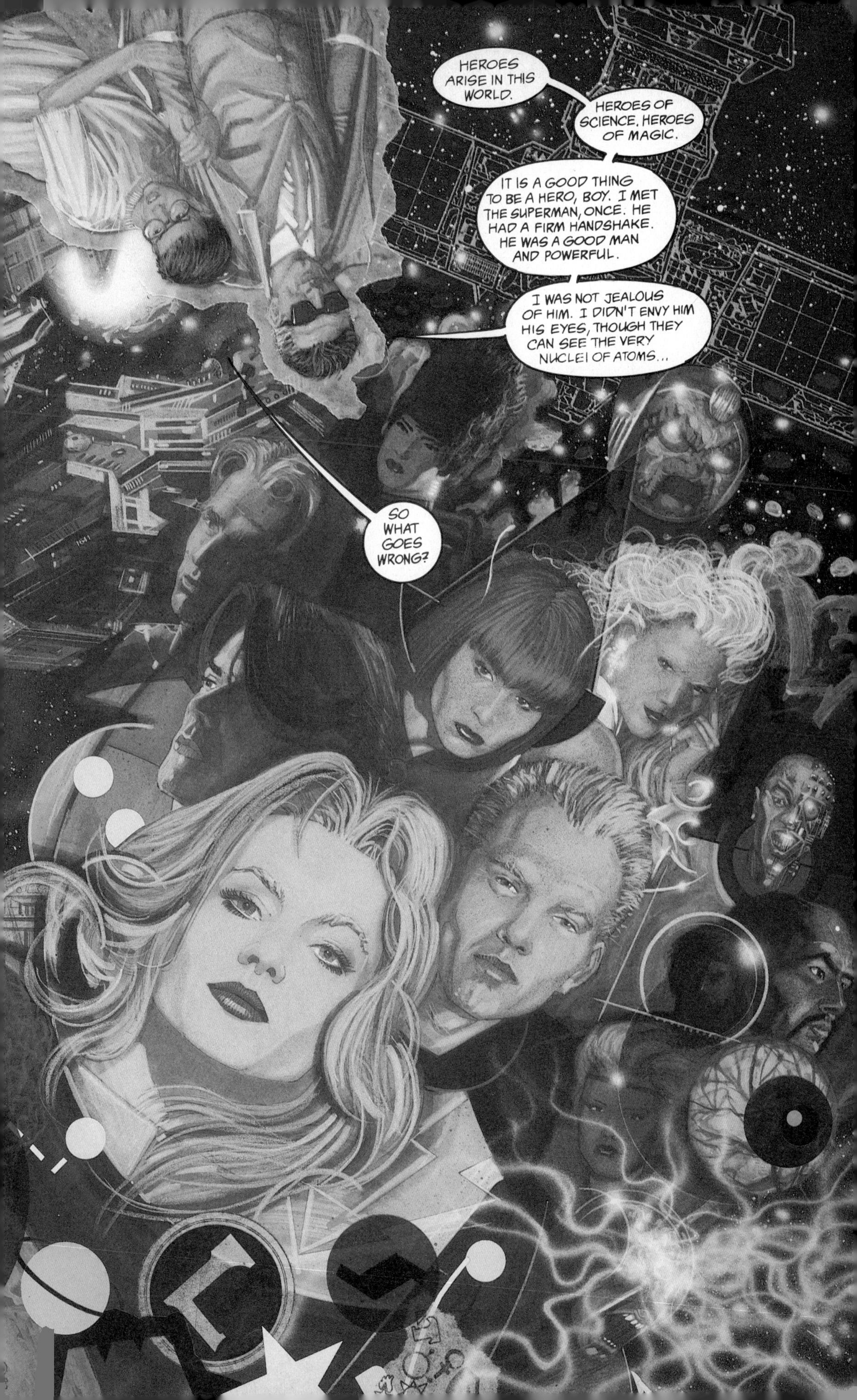
HEROES ARISE IN THIS WORLD.
HEROES OF SCIENCE. HEROES OF MAGIC.
IT IS A GOOD THING TO BE A HERO, BOY. I MET THE SUPERMAN, ONCE. HE HAD A FIRM HANDSHAKE. HE WAS A GOOD MAN AND POWERFUL.
I WAS NOT JEALOUS OF HIM. I DIDN'T ENVY HIM HIS EYES, THOUGH THEY CAN SEE THE VERY NUCLEI OF ATOMS...
SO WHAT GOES WRONG?

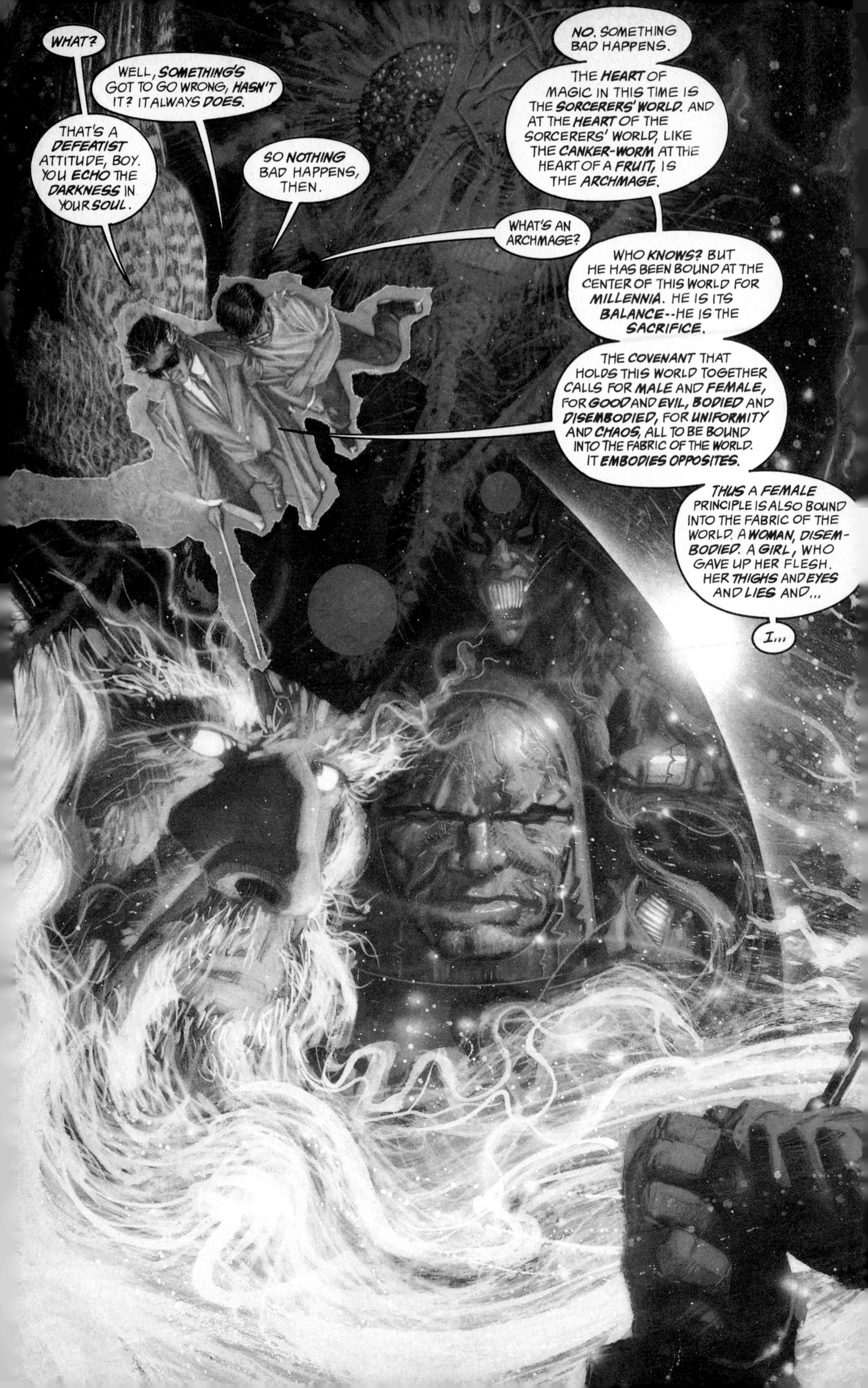
WHAT?
WELL, SOMETHING'S GOT TO GO WRONG, HASN'T IT? IT ALWAYS DOES.
THAT'S A DEFEATIST ATTITUDE, BOY. YOU ECHO THE DARKNESS IN YOUR SOUL.
SO NOTHING BAD HAPPENS, THEN.
NO. SOMETHING BAD HAPPENS.
THE HEART OF MAGIC IN THIS TIME IS THE SORCERERS' WORLD. AND AT THE HEART OF THE SORCERERS' WORLD, LIKE THE CANKER-WORM AT THE HEART OF A FRUIT, IS THE ARCHMAGE.
WHAT'S AN ARCHMAGE?
WHO KNOWS? BUT HE HAS BEEN BOUND AT THE CENTER OF THIS WORLD FOR MILLENNIA. HE IS ITS BALANCE--HE IS THE SACRIFICE.
THE COVENANT THAT HOLDS THIS WORLD TOGETHER CALLS FOR MALE AND FEMALE, FOR GOOD AND EVIL, BODIED AND DISEMBODIED, FOR UNIFORMITY AND CHAOS, ALL TO BE BOUND INTO THE FABRIC OF THE WORLD. IT EMBODIES OPPOSITES.
THUS A FEMALE PRINCIPLE IS ALSO BOUND INTO THE FABRIC OF THE WORLD. A WOMAN, DISEMBODIED. A GIRL, WHO GAVE UP HER FLESH. HER THIGHS AND EYES AND LIES AND...
I...

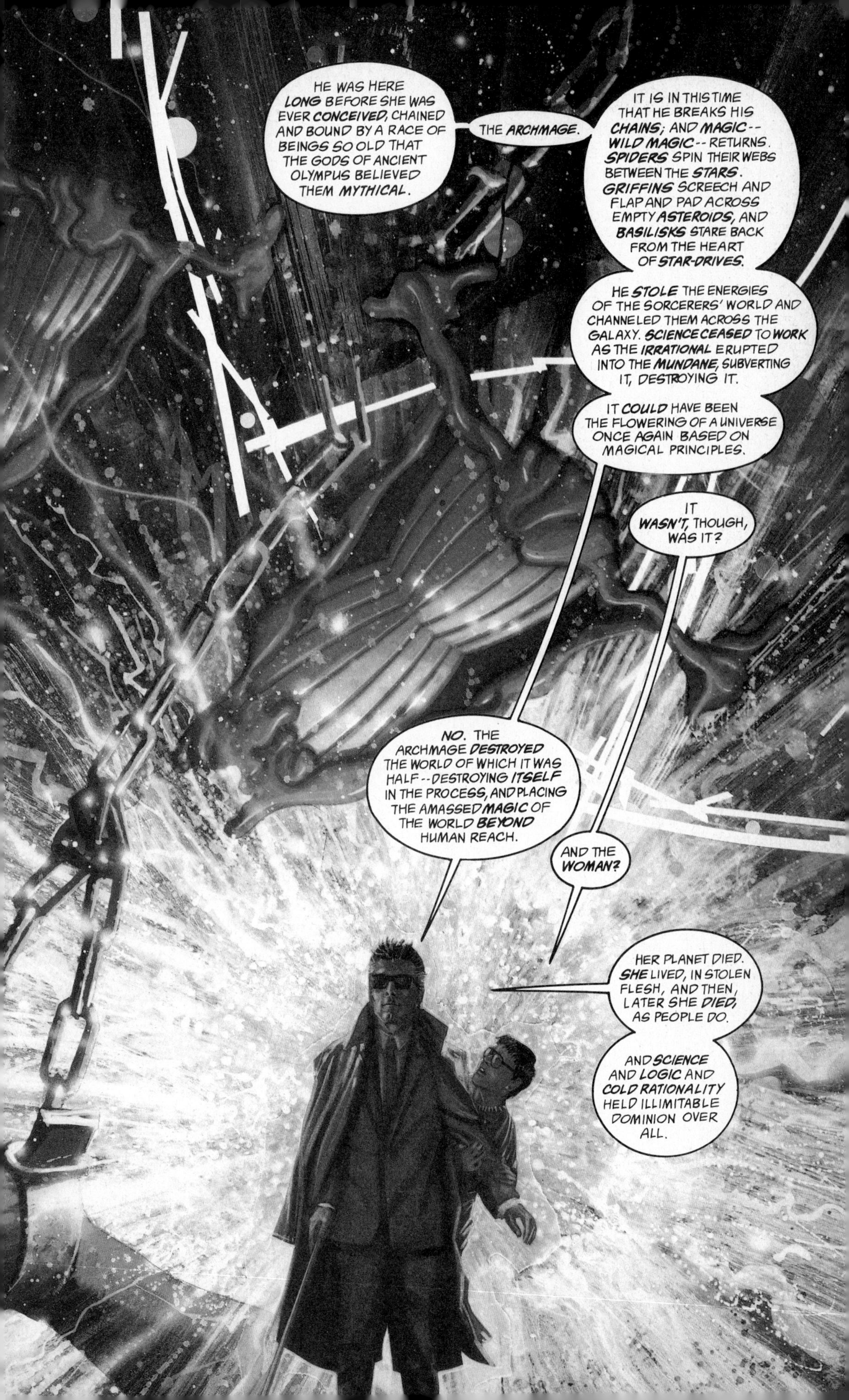
HE WAS HERE LONG BEFORE SHE WAS EVER CONCEIVED, CHAINED AND BOUND BY A RACE OF BEINGS SO OLD THAT THE GODS OF ANCIENT OLYMPUS BELIEVED THEM MYTHICAL.
THE ARCHMAGE.
IT IS IN THIS TIME THAT HE BREAKS HIS CHAINS; AND MAGIC -- WILD MAGIC -- RETURNS. SPIDERS SPIN THEIR WEBS BETWEEN THE STARS. GRIFFINS SCREECH AND FLAP AND PAD ACROSS EMPTY ASTEROIDS, AND BASILISKS STARE BACK FROM THE HEART OF STAR-DRIVES.
HE STOLE THE ENERGIES OF THE SORCERERS' WORLD AND CHANNELED THEM ACROSS THE GALAXY. SCIENCE CEASED TO WORK AS THE IRRATIONAL ERUPTED INTO THE MUNDANE, SUBVERTING IT, DESTROYING IT.
IT COULD HAVE BEEN THE FLOWERING OF A UNIVERSE ONCE AGAIN BASED ON MAGICAL PRINCIPLES.
IT WASN'T, THOUGH, WAS IT?
NO. THE ARCHMAGE DESTROYED THE WORLD OF WHICH IT WAS HALF -- DESTROYING ITSELF IN THE PROCESS, AND PLACING THE AMASSED MAGIC OF THE WORLD BEYOND HUMAN REACH.
AND THE WOMAN?
HER PLANET DIED. SHE LIVED, IN STOLEN FLESH, AND THEN, LATER SHE DIED, AS PEOPLE DO.
AND SCIENCE AND LOGIC AND COLD RATIONALITY HELD ILLIMITABLE DOMINION OVER ALL.

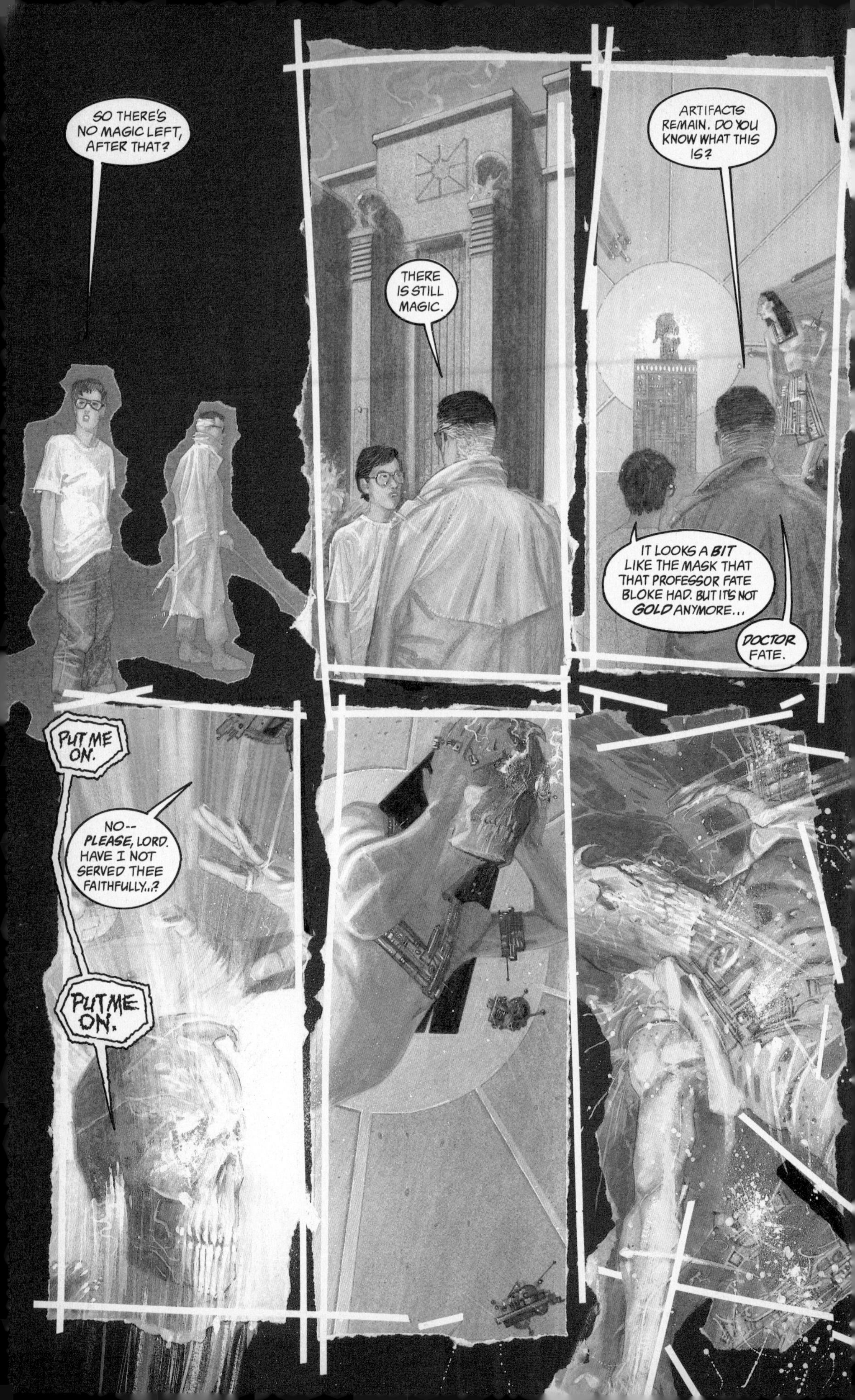
SO THERE'S NO MAGIC LEFT, AFTER THAT?
THERE IS STILL MAGIC.
ARTIFACTS REMAIN. DO YOU KNOW WHAT THIS IS?
IT LOOKS A BIT LIKE THE MASK THAT THAT PROFESSOR FATE BLOKE HAD. BUT IT'S NOT GOLD ANYMORE...
DOCTOR FATE.
PUT ME ON.
NO-- PLEASE, LORD. HAVE I NOT SERVED THEE FAITHFULLY...?
PUT ME ON.

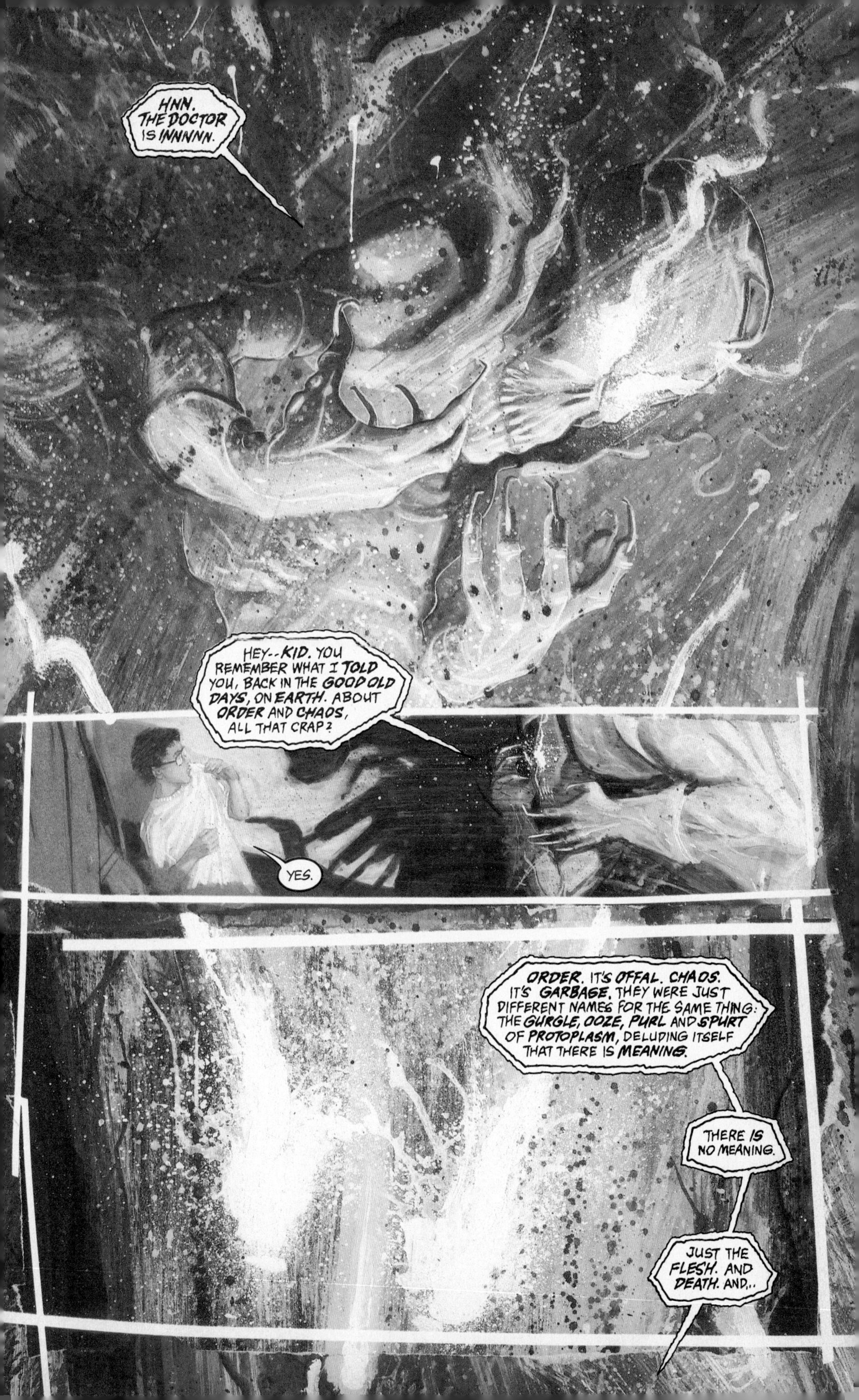
HNN. THE DOCTOR IS INNNNN.
HEY--KID. YOU REMEMBER WHAT I TOLD YOU, BACK IN THE GOOD OLD DAYS, ON EARTH. ABOUT ORDER AND CHAOS, ALL THAT CRAP?
YES.
ORDER. IT'S OFFAL. CHAOS. IT'S GARBAGE. THEY WERE JUST DIFFERENT NAMES FOR THE SAME THING: THE GURGLE, OOZE, PURL AND SPURT OF PROTOPLASM, DELUDING ITSELF THAT THERE IS MEANING.
THERE IS NO MEANING.
JUST THE FLESH. AND DEATH. AND...

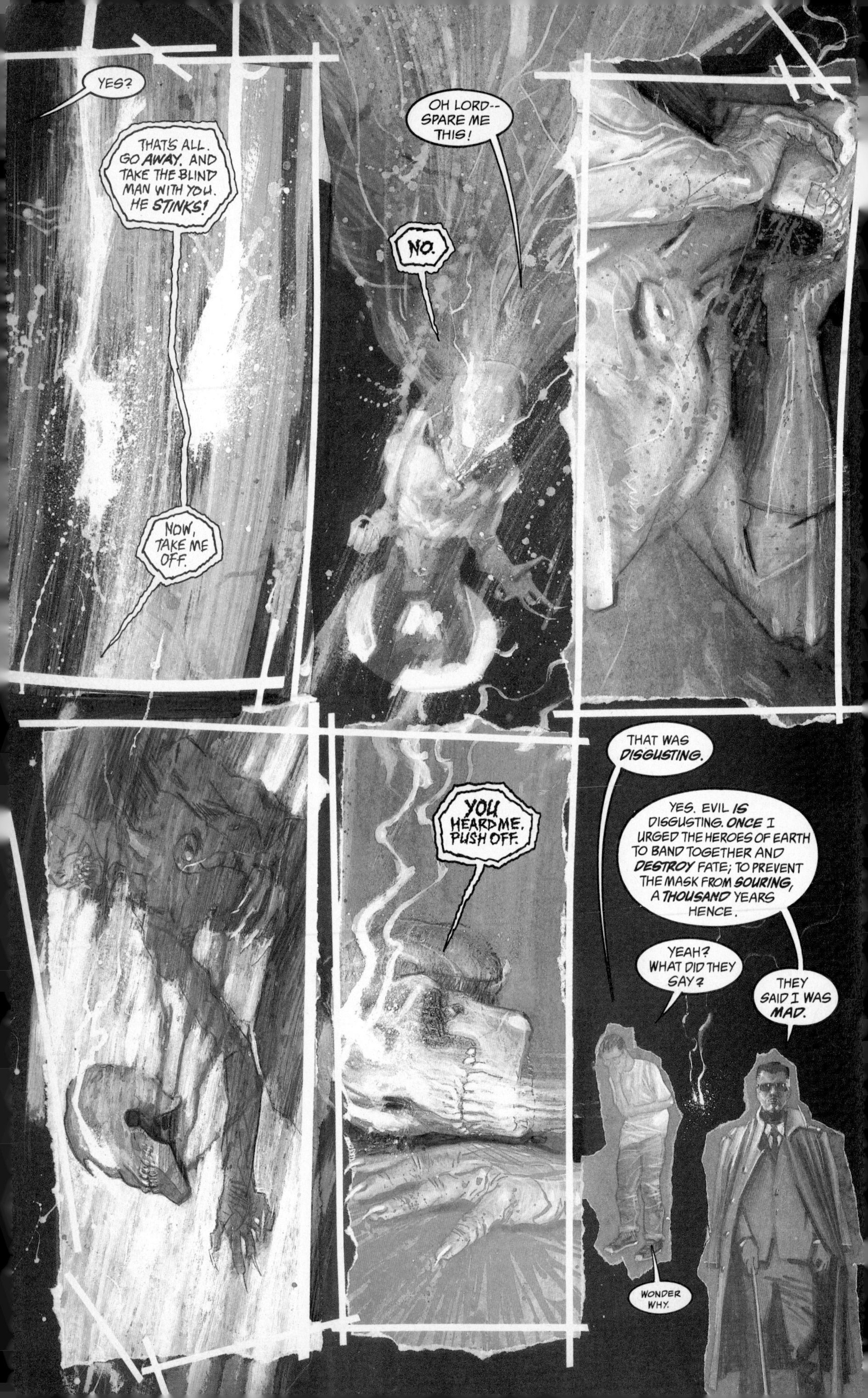
YES?
THAT'S ALL. GO AWAY. AND TAKE THE BLIND MAN WITH YOU. HE STINKS!
NOW, TAKE ME OFF.
OH LORD-- SPARE ME THIS!
NO.
YOU HEARD ME. PUSH OFF.
THAT WAS DISGUSTING.
YES. EVIL IS DISGUSTING. ONCE I URGED THE HEROES OF EARTH TO BAND TOGETHER AND DESTROY FATE; TO PREVENT THE MASK FROM SOURING, A THOUSAND YEARS HENCE.
YEAH? WHAT DID THEY SAY?
THEY SAID I WAS MAD.
WONDER WHY.

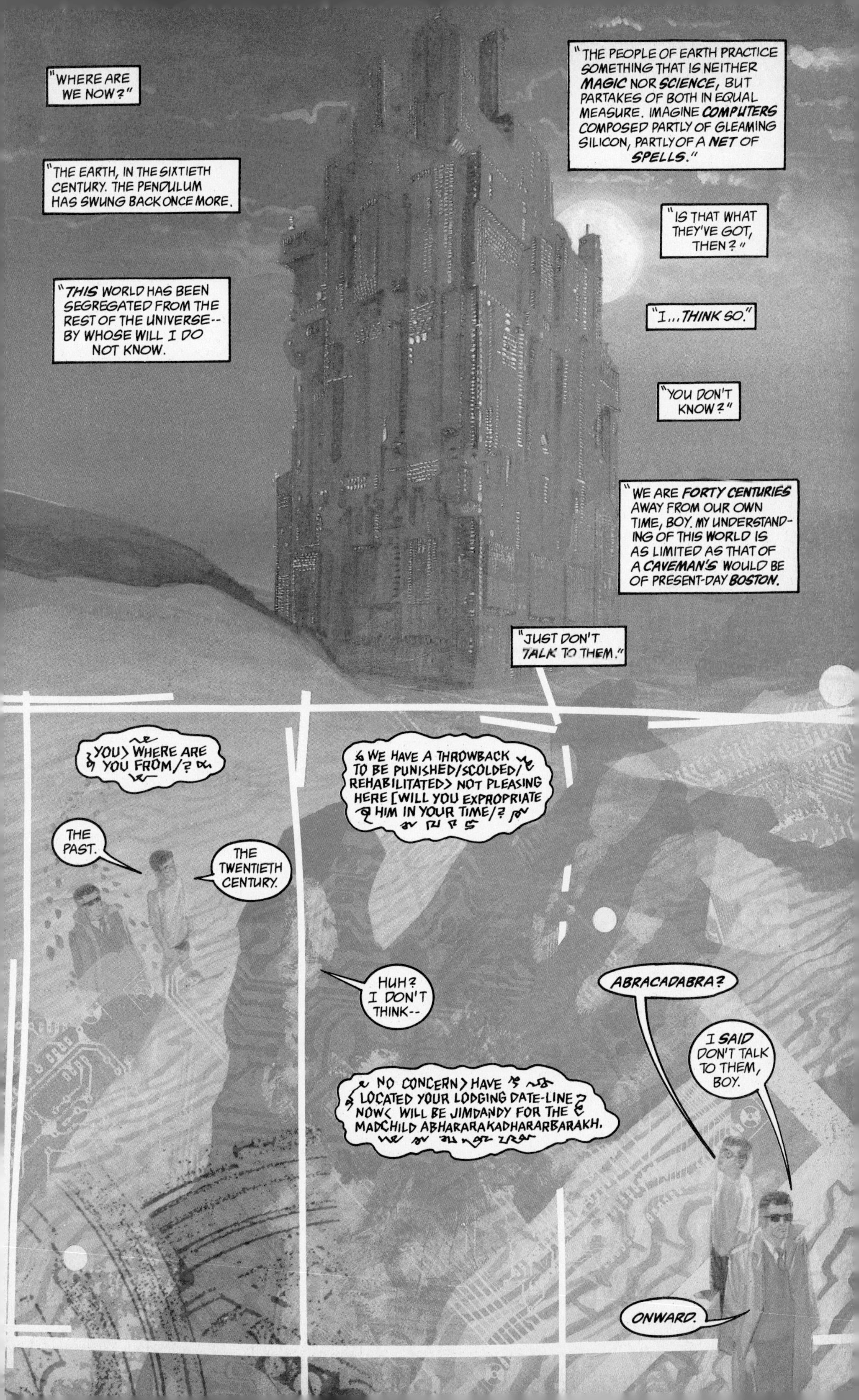
"WHERE ARE WE NOW?"
"THE EARTH, IN THE SIXTIETH CENTURY. THE PENDULUM HAS SWUNG BACK ONCE MORE.
"THIS WORLD HAS BEEN SEGREGATED FROM THE REST OF THE UNIVERSE-- BY WHOSE WILL I DO NOT KNOW.
"THE PEOPLE OF EARTH PRACTICE SOMETHING THAT IS NEITHER MAGIC NOR SCIENCE, BUT PARTAKES OF BOTH IN EQUAL MEASURE. IMAGINE COMPUTERS COMPOSED PARTLY OF GLEAMING SILICON, PARTLY OF A NET OF SPELLS."
"IS THAT WHAT THEY'VE GOT, THEN?"
"I... THINK SO."
"YOU DON'T KNOW?"
"WE ARE FORTY CENTURIES AWAY FROM OUR OWN TIME, BOY. MY UNDERSTANDING OF THIS WORLD IS AS LIMITED AS THAT OF A CAVEMAN'S WOULD BE OF PRESENT-DAY BOSTON.
"JUST DON'T TALK TO THEM."
YOU> WHERE ARE YOU FROM/?
THE PAST.
THE TWENTIETH CENTURY.
WE HAVE A THROWBACK TO BE PUNISHED/SCOLDED/REHABILITATED> NOT PLEASING HERE [WILL YOU EXPROPRIATE HIM IN YOUR TIME/?
HUH? I DON'T THINK--
NO CONCERN> HAVE LOCATED YOUR LODGING DATE-LINE NOW< WILL BE JIMDANDY FOR THE MADCHILD ABHARARAKADHARARBARAKH.
ABRACADABRA?
I SAID DON'T TALK TO THEM, BOY.
ONWARD.

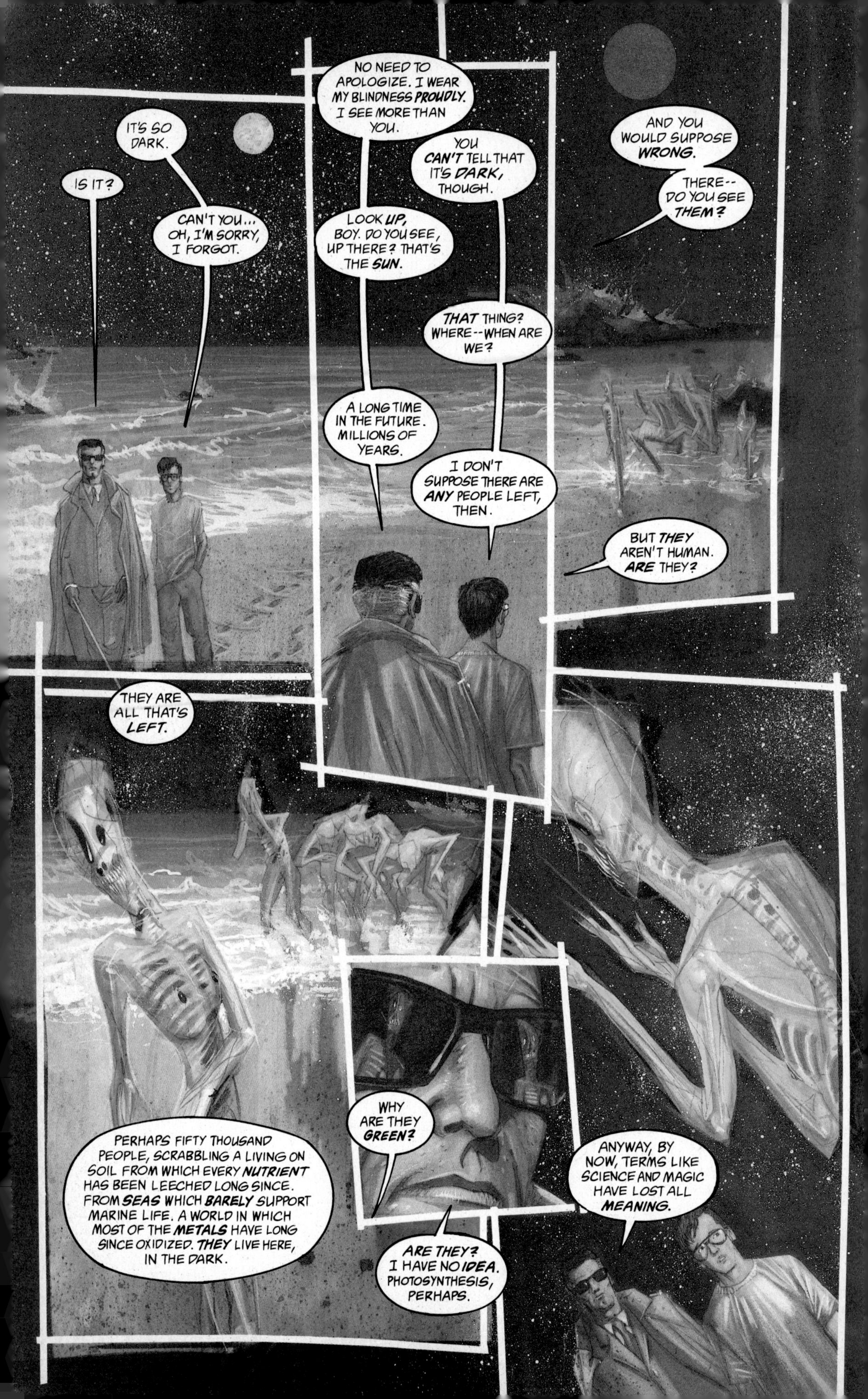

IT'S SO DARK.
IS IT?
CAN'T YOU... OH, I'M SORRY, I FORGOT.
NO NEED TO APOLOGIZE. I WEAR MY BLINDNESS PROUDLY. I SEE MORE THAN YOU.
YOU CAN'T TELL THAT IT'S DARK, THOUGH.
LOOK UP, BOY. DO YOU SEE, UP THERE? THAT'S THE SUN.
THAT THING? WHERE--WHEN ARE WE?
A LONG TIME IN THE FUTURE. MILLIONS OF YEARS.
I DON'T SUPPOSE THERE ARE ANY PEOPLE LEFT, THEN.
AND YOU WOULD SUPPOSE WRONG.
THERE-- DO YOU SEE THEM?
BUT THEY AREN'T HUMAN. ARE THEY?
THEY ARE ALL THAT'S LEFT.
PERHAPS FIFTY THOUSAND PEOPLE, SCRABBLING A LIVING ON SOIL FROM WHICH EVERY NUTRIENT HAS BEEN LEECHED LONG SINCE. FROM SEAS WHICH BARELY SUPPORT MARINE LIFE. A WORLD IN WHICH MOST OF THE METALS HAVE LONG SINCE OXIDIZED. THEY LIVE HERE, IN THE DARK.
WHY ARE THEY GREEN?
ARE THEY? I HAVE NO IDEA. PHOTOSYNTHESIS, PERHAPS.
ANYWAY, BY NOW, TERMS LIKE SCIENCE AND MAGIC HAVE LOST ALL MEANING.

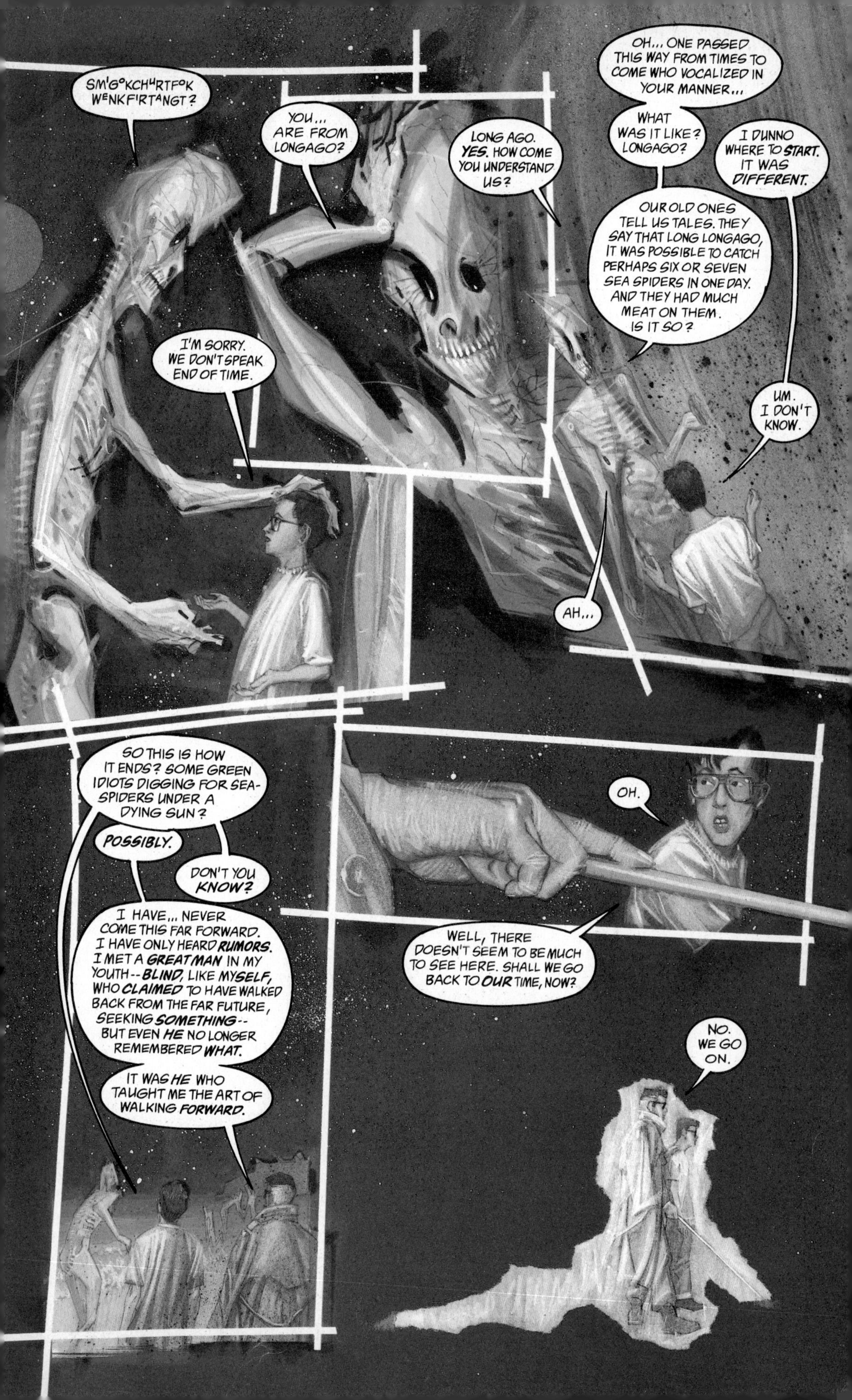
SM'G°KCHURTF°K WENKF'RTANGT?
YOU... ARE FROM LONGAGO?
LONG AGO. YES. HOW COME YOU UNDERSTAND US?
OH... ONE PASSED THIS WAY FROM TIMES TO COME WHO VOCALIZED IN YOUR MANNER...
WHAT WAS IT LIKE? LONGAGO?
I DUNNO WHERE TO START. IT WAS DIFFERENT.
OUR OLD ONES TELL US TALES. THEY SAY THAT LONG LONGAGO, IT WAS POSSIBLE TO CATCH PERHAPS SIX OR SEVEN SEA SPIDERS IN ONE DAY. AND THEY HAD MUCH MEAT ON THEM. IS IT SO?
I'M SORRY. WE DON'T SPEAK END OF TIME.
UM. I DON'T KNOW.
AH...
SO THIS IS HOW IT ENDS? SOME GREEN IDIOTS DIGGING FOR SEA-SPIDERS UNDER A DYING SUN?
POSSIBLY.
DON'T YOU KNOW?
I HAVE... NEVER COME THIS FAR FORWARD. I HAVE ONLY HEARD RUMORS. I MET A GREAT MAN IN MY YOUTH--BLIND, LIKE MYSELF, WHO CLAIMED TO HAVE WALKED BACK FROM THE FAR FUTURE, SEEKING SOMETHING--BUT EVEN HE NO LONGER REMEMBERED WHAT.
IT WAS HE WHO TAUGHT ME THE ART OF WALKING FORWARD.
OH.
WELL, THERE DOESN'T SEEM TO BE MUCH TO SEE HERE. SHALL WE GO BACK TO OUR TIME, NOW?
NO. WE GO ON.

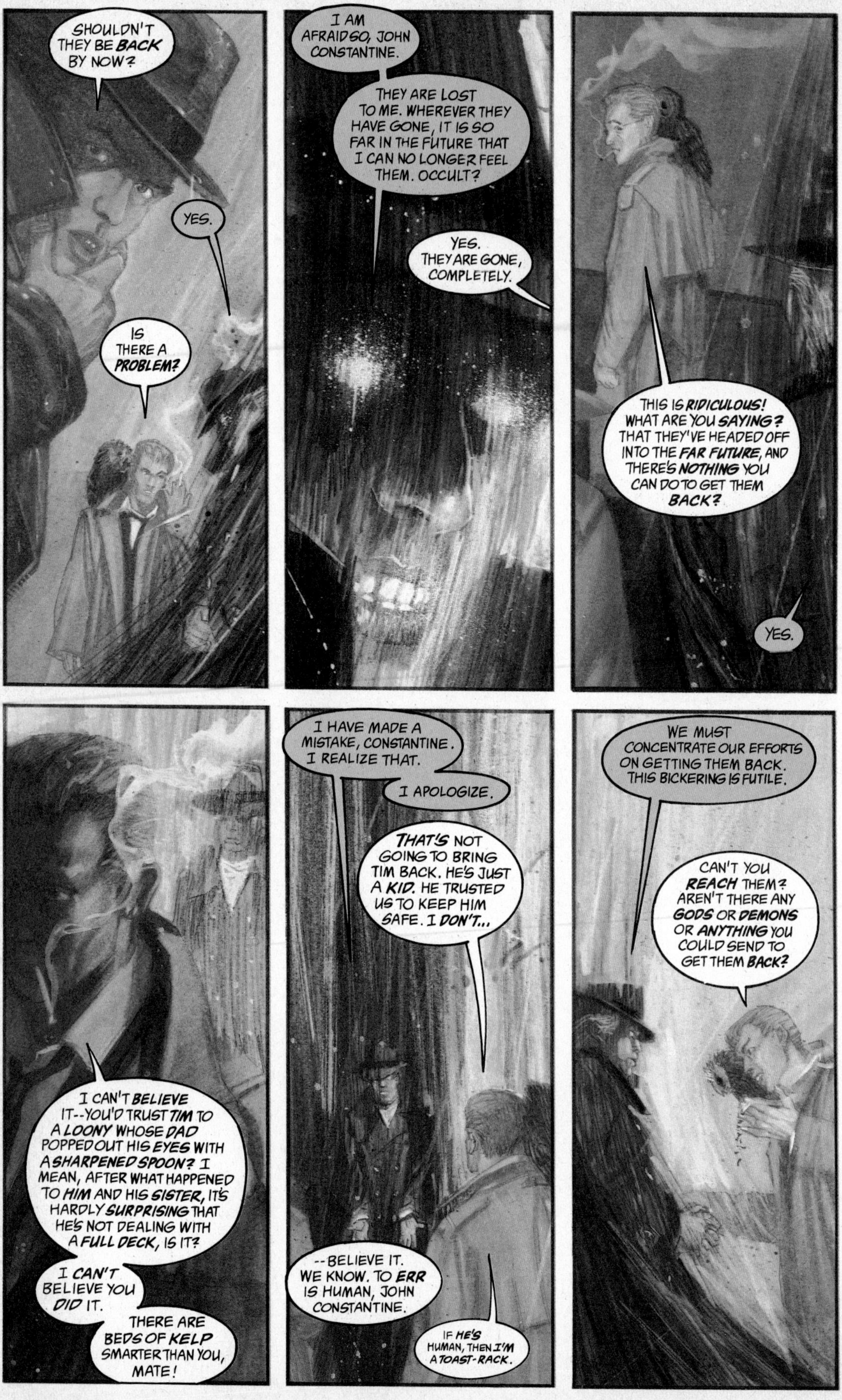
SHOULDN'T THEY BE BACK BY NOW?
YES.
IS THERE A PROBLEM?
I AM AFRAID SO, JOHN CONSTANTINE.
THEY ARE LOST TO ME. WHEREVER THEY HAVE GONE, IT IS SO FAR IN THE FUTURE THAT I CAN NO LONGER FEEL THEM. OCCULT?
YES. THEY ARE GONE, COMPLETELY.
THIS IS RIDICULOUS! WHAT ARE YOU SAYING? THAT THEY'VE HEADED OFF INTO THE FAR FUTURE, AND THERE'S NOTHING YOU CAN DO TO GET THEM BACK?
YES.
I CAN'T BELIEVE IT--YOU'D TRUST TIM TO A LOONY WHOSE DAD POPPED OUT HIS EYES WITH A SHARPENED SPOON? I MEAN, AFTER WHAT HAPPENED TO HIM AND HIS SISTER, IT'S HARDLY SURPRISING THAT HE'S NOT DEALING WITH A FULL DECK, IS IT?
I CAN'T BELIEVE YOU DID IT.
THERE ARE BEDS OF KELP SMARTER THAN YOU, MATE!
I HAVE MADE A MISTAKE, CONSTANTINE. I REALIZE THAT.
I APOLOGIZE.
THAT'S NOT GOING TO BRING TIM BACK. HE'S JUST A KID. HE TRUSTED US TO KEEP HIM SAFE. I DON'T...
--BELIEVE IT. WE KNOW. TO ERR IS HUMAN, JOHN CONSTANTINE.
IF HE'S HUMAN, THEN I'M A TOAST-RACK.
WE MUST CONCENTRATE OUR EFFORTS ON GETTING THEM BACK. THIS BICKERING IS FUTILE.
CAN'T YOU REACH THEM? AREN'T THERE ANY GODS OR DEMONS OR ANYTHING YOU COULD SEND TO GET THEM BACK?

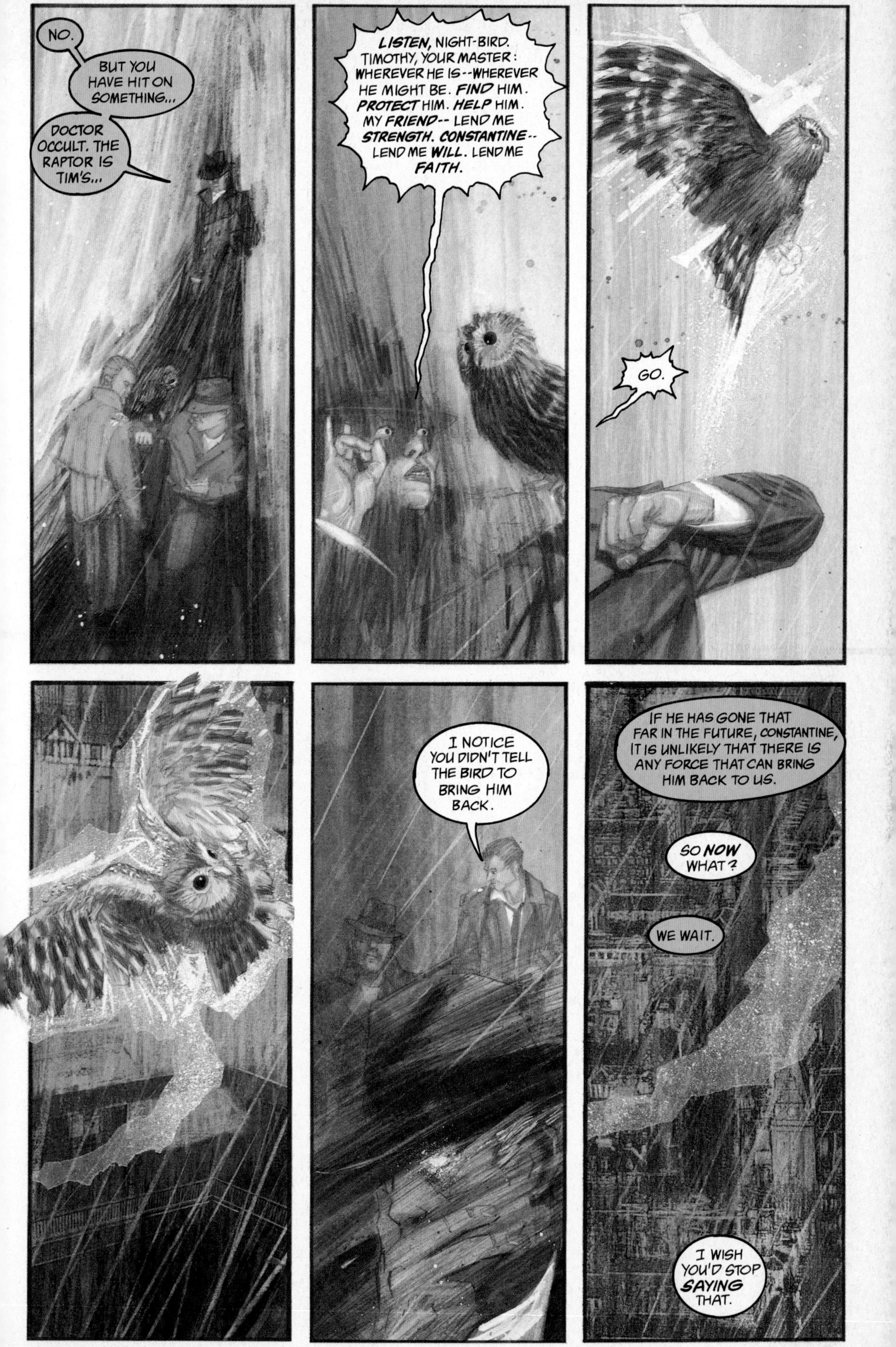
NO.
BUT YOU HAVE HIT ON SOMETHING...
DOCTOR OCCULT. THE RAPTOR IS TIM'S...
LISTEN, NIGHT-BIRD. TIMOTHY, YOUR MASTER: WHEREVER HE IS--WHEREVER HE MIGHT BE. FIND HIM. PROTECT HIM. HELP HIM. MY FRIEND-- LEND ME STRENGTH. CONSTANTINE-- LEND ME WILL. LEND ME FAITH.
GO.
I NOTICE YOU DIDN'T TELL THE BIRD TO BRING HIM BACK.
IF HE HAS GONE THAT FAR IN THE FUTURE, CONSTANTINE, IT IS UNLIKELY THAT THERE IS ANY FORCE THAT CAN BRING HIM BACK TO US.
SO NOW WHAT?
WE WAIT.
I WISH YOU'D STOP SAYING THAT.

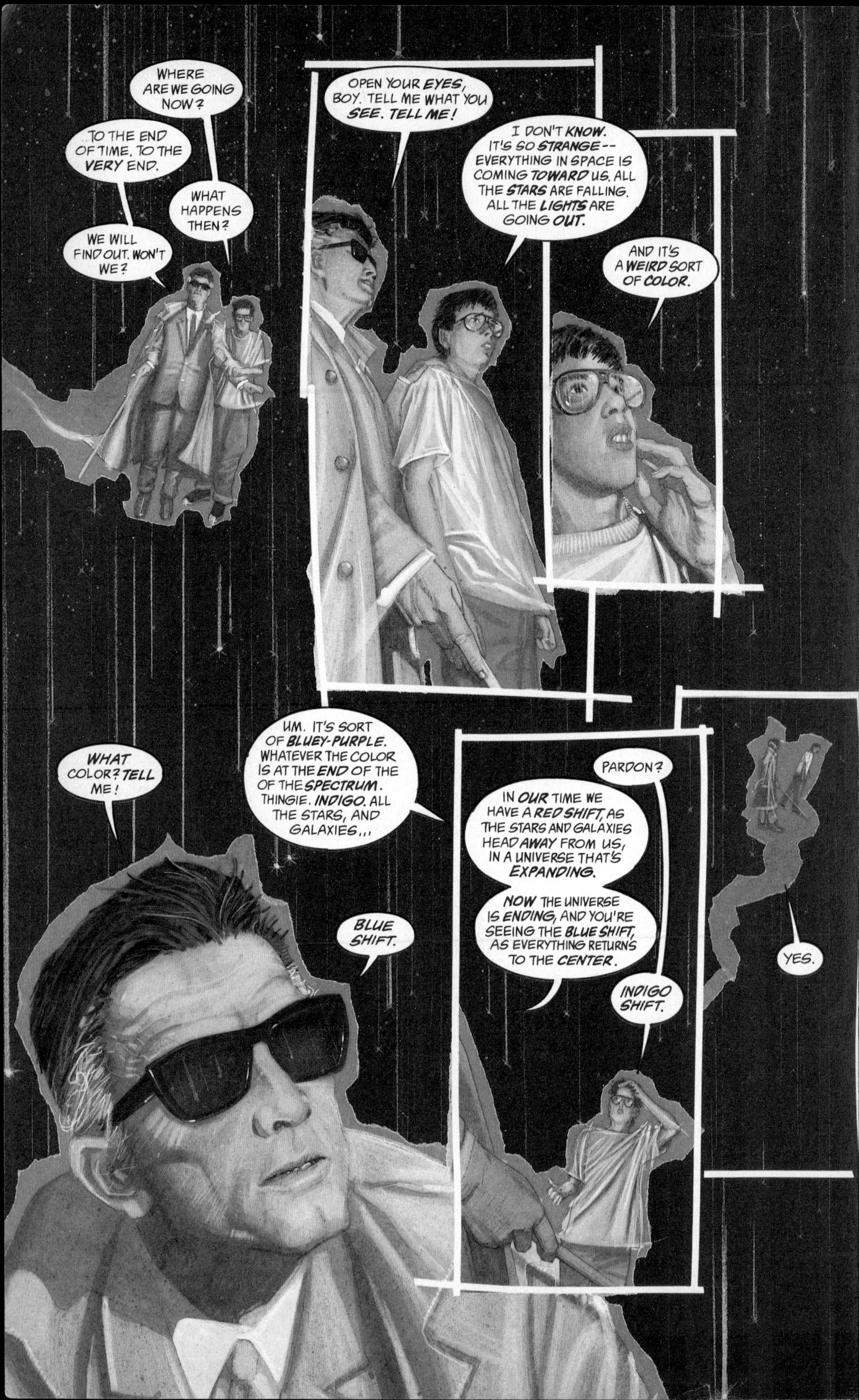
WHERE ARE WE GOING NOW?
...TO THE END OF TIME. TO THE VERY END.
WHAT HAPPENS THEN?
WE WILL FIND OUT. WON'T WE?
OPEN YOUR EYES, BOY. TELL ME WHAT YOU SEE. TELL ME!
I DON'T KNOW. IT'S SO STRANGE-- EVERYTHING IN SPACE IS COMING TOWARD US. ALL THE STARS ARE FALLING. ALL THE LIGHTS ARE GOING OUT.
AND IT'S A WEIRD SORT OF COLOR.
WHAT COLOR? TELL ME!
UM. IT'S SORT OF BLUEY-PURPLE. WHATEVER THE COLOR IS AT THE END OF THE OF THE SPECTRUM. THINGIE. INDIGO. ALL THE STARS, AND GALAXIES...
BLUE SHIFT.
PARDON?
IN OUR TIME WE HAVE A RED SHIFT, AS THE STARS AND GALAXIES HEAD AWAY FROM US, IN A UNIVERSE THAT'S EXPANDING.
NOW THE UNIVERSE IS ENDING, AND YOU'RE SEEING THE BLUE SHIFT, AS EVERYTHING RETURNS TO THE CENTER.
INDIGO SHIFT.
YES.

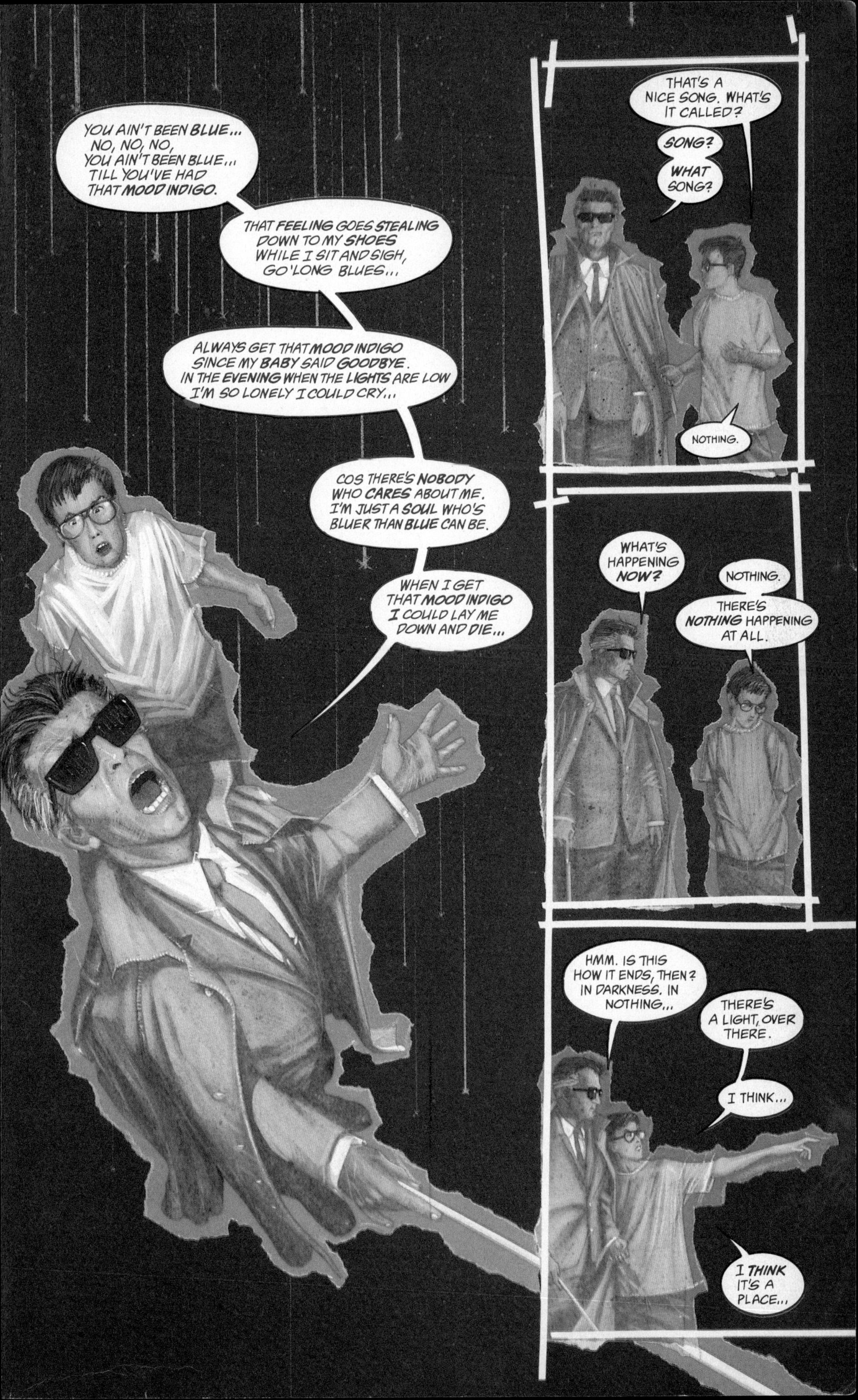
YOU AIN'T BEEN BLUE... NO, NO, NO, YOU AIN'T BEEN BLUE... TILL YOU'VE HAD THAT MOOD INDIGO.
THAT FEELING GOES STEALING DOWN TO MY SHOES WHILE I SIT AND SIGH, GO'LONG BLUES...
ALWAYS GET THAT MOOD INDIGO SINCE MY BABY SAID GOODBYE. IN THE EVENING WHEN THE LIGHTS ARE LOW I'M SO LONELY I COULD CRY...
COS THERE'S NOBODY WHO CARES ABOUT ME. I'M JUST A SOUL WHO'S BLUER THAN BLUE CAN BE.
WHEN I GET THAT MOOD INDIGO I COULD LAY ME DOWN AND DIE...
THAT'S A NICE SONG. WHAT'S IT CALLED?
SONG?
WHAT SONG?
NOTHING.
WHAT'S HAPPENING NOW?
NOTHING.
THERE'S NOTHING HAPPENING AT ALL.
HMM. IS THIS HOW IT ENDS, THEN? IN DARKNESS. IN NOTHING...
THERE'S A LIGHT, OVER THERE.
I THINK...
I THINK IT'S A PLACE...

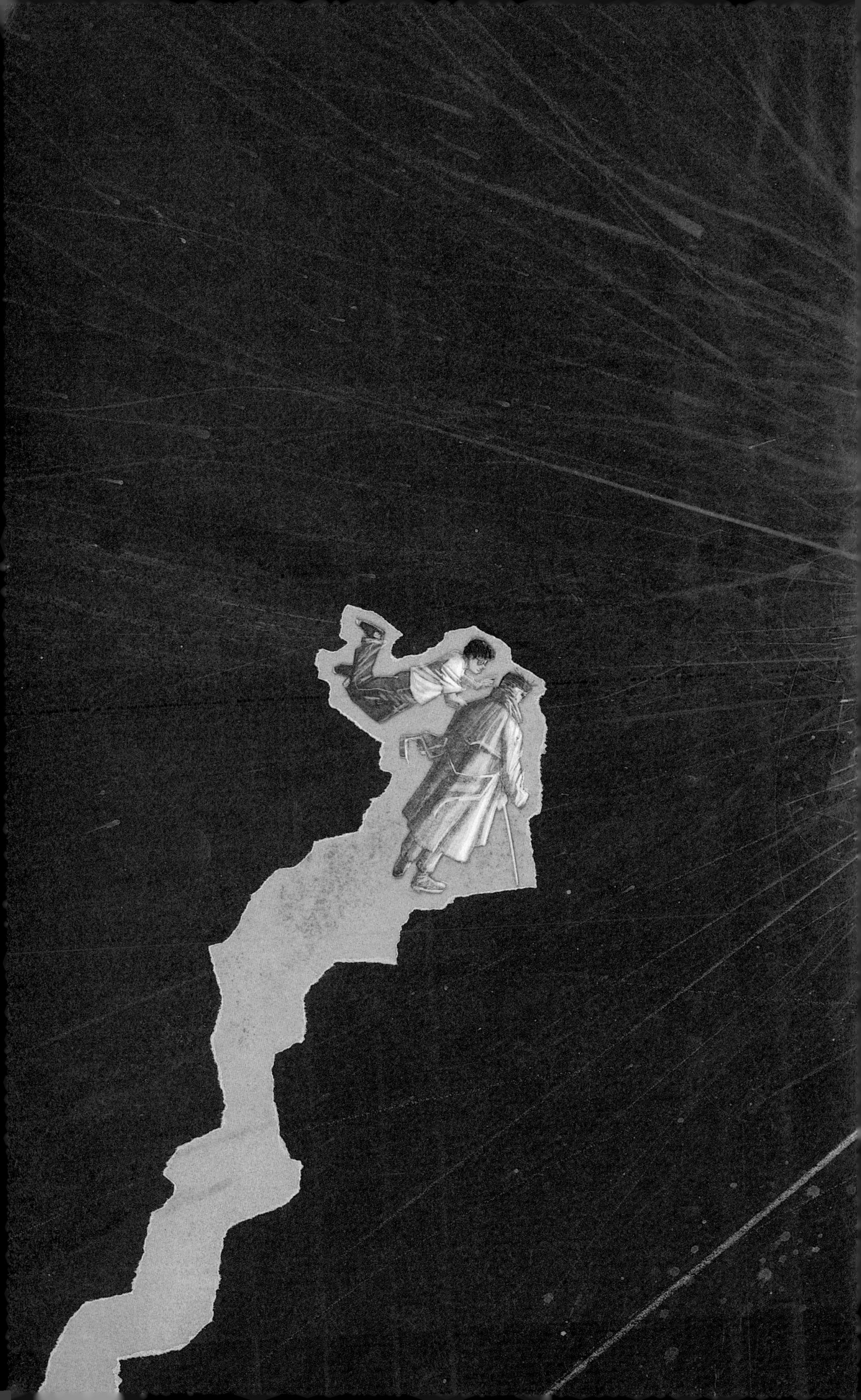

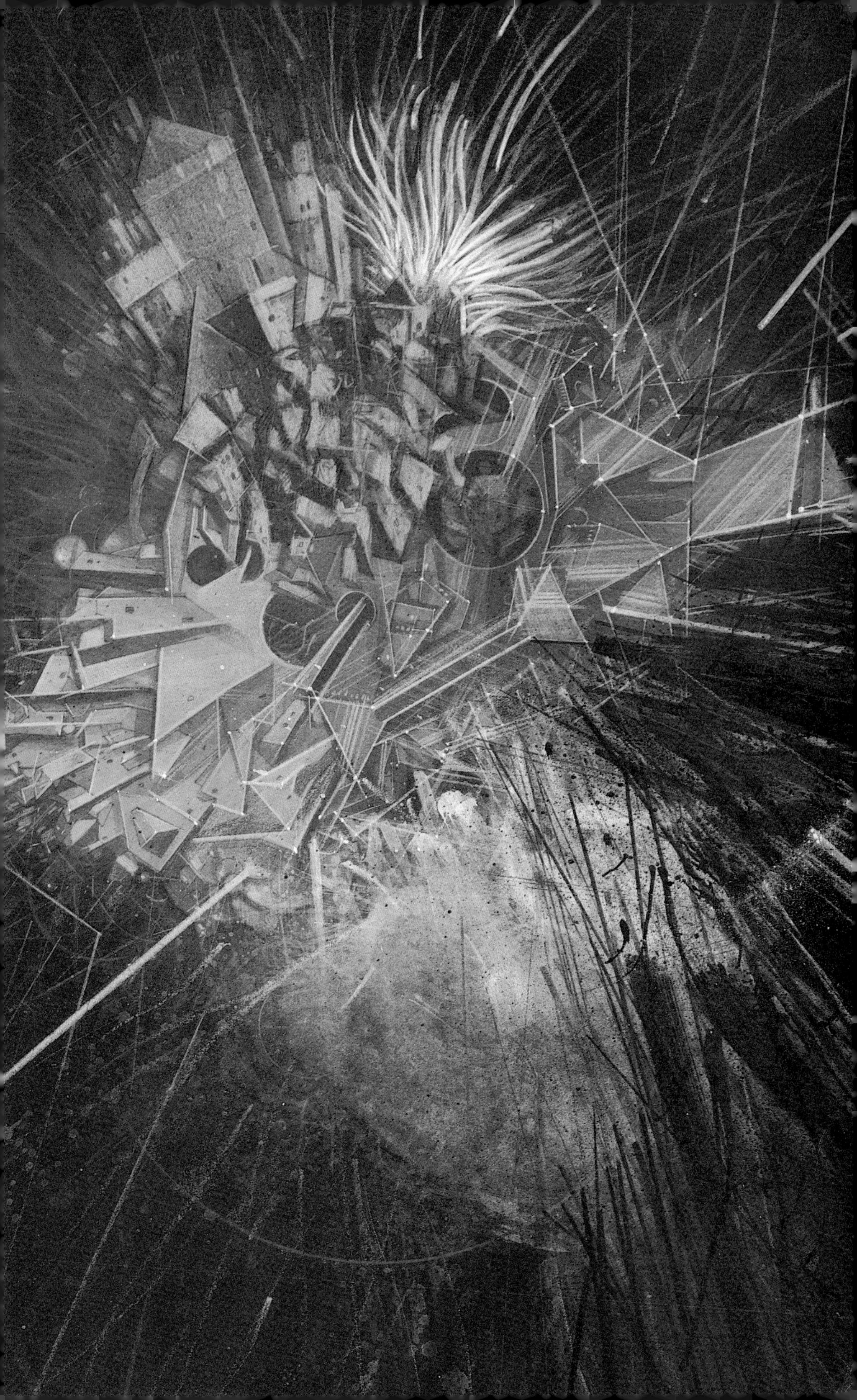

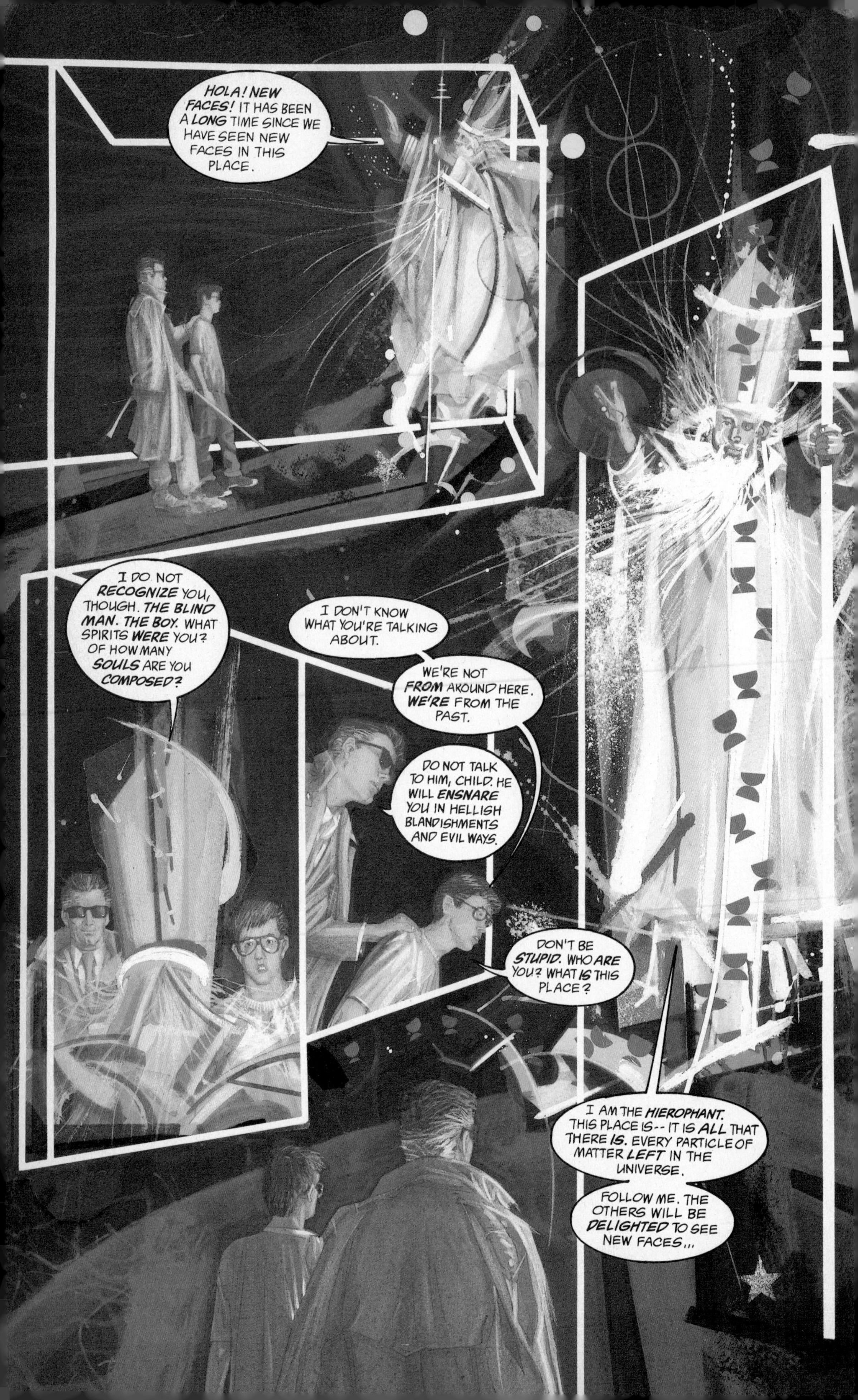
HOLA! NEW FACES! IT HAS BEEN A LONG TIME SINCE WE HAVE SEEN NEW FACES IN THIS PLACE.
I DO NOT RECOGNIZE YOU, THOUGH. THE BLIND MAN. THE BOY. WHAT SPIRITS WERE YOU? OF HOW MANY SOULS ARE YOU COMPOSED?
I DON'T KNOW WHAT YOU'RE TALKING ABOUT.
WE'RE NOT FROM AROUND HERE. WE'RE FROM THE PAST.
DO NOT TALK TO HIM, CHILD. HE WILL ENSNARE YOU IN HELLISH BLANDISHMENTS AND EVIL WAYS.
DON'T BE STUPID. WHO ARE YOU? WHAT IS THIS PLACE?
I AM THE HIEROPHANT. THIS PLACE IS-- IT IS ALL THAT THERE IS. EVERY PARTICLE OF MATTER LEFT IN THE UNIVERSE.
FOLLOW ME. THE OTHERS WILL BE DELIGHTED TO SEE NEW FACES...

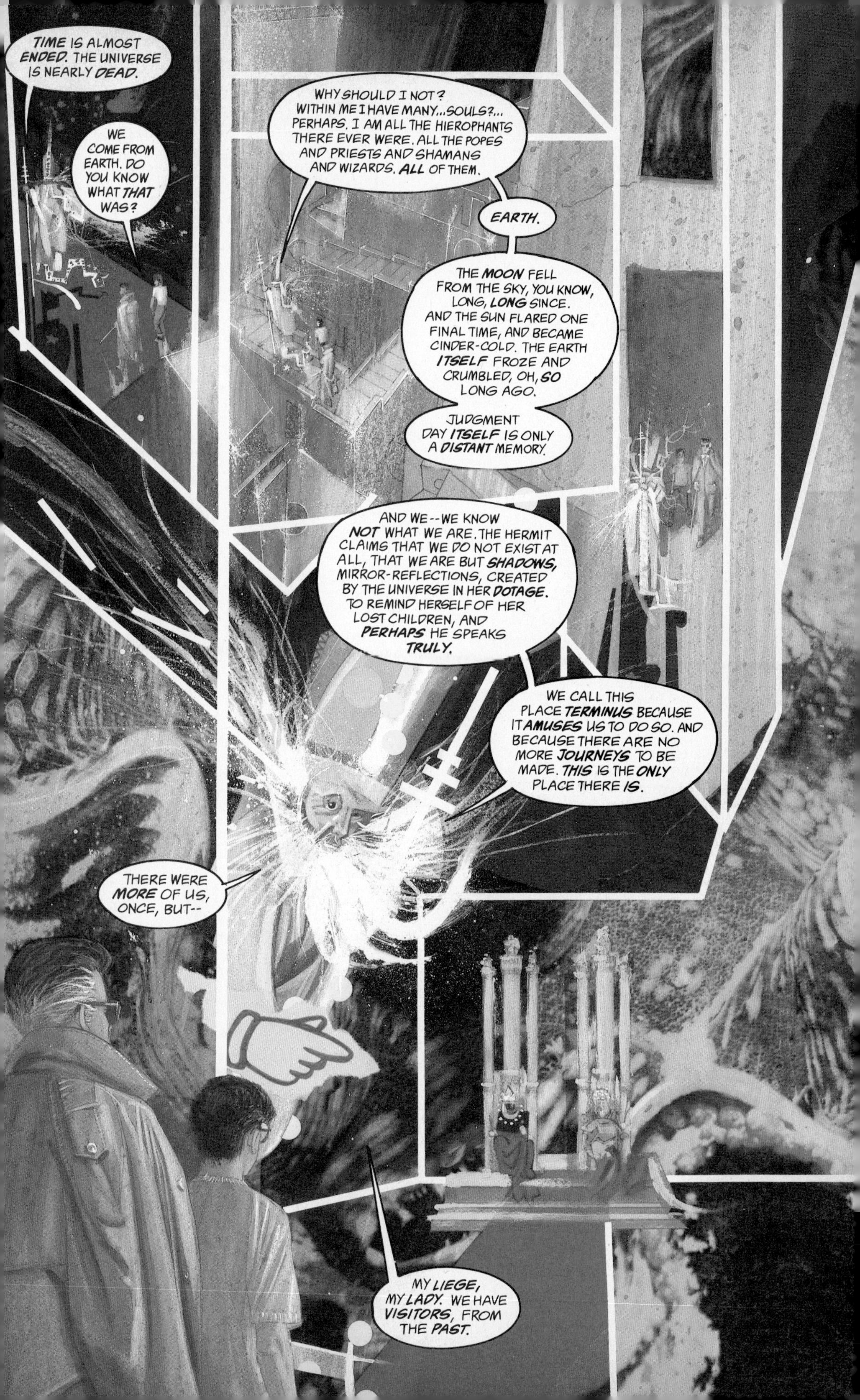

TIME IS ALMOST ENDED. THE UNIVERSE IS NEARLY DEAD.
WE COME FROM EARTH. DO YOU KNOW WHAT THAT WAS?
WHY SHOULD I NOT? WITHIN ME I HAVE MANY...SOULS?... PERHAPS. I AM ALL THE HIEROPHANTS THERE EVER WERE. ALL THE POPES AND PRIESTS AND SHAMANS AND WIZARDS. ALL OF THEM.
EARTH.
THE MOON FELL FROM THE SKY, YOU KNOW, LONG, LONG SINCE. AND THE SUN FLARED ONE FINAL TIME, AND BECAME CINDER-COLD. THE EARTH ITSELF FROZE AND CRUMBLED, OH, SO LONG AGO.
JUDGMENT DAY ITSELF IS ONLY A DISTANT MEMORY.
AND WE--WE KNOW NOT WHAT WE ARE. THE HERMIT CLAIMS THAT WE DO NOT EXIST AT ALL, THAT WE ARE BUT SHADOWS, MIRROR-REFLECTIONS, CREATED BY THE UNIVERSE IN HER DOTAGE. TO REMIND HERSELF OF HER LOST CHILDREN, AND PERHAPS HE SPEAKS TRULY.
WE CALL THIS PLACE TERMINUS BECAUSE IT AMUSES US TO DO SO. AND BECAUSE THERE ARE NO MORE JOURNEYS TO BE MADE. THIS IS THE ONLY PLACE THERE IS.
THERE WERE MORE OF US, ONCE, BUT--
MY LIEGE, MY LADY. WE HAVE VISITORS, FROM THE PAST.

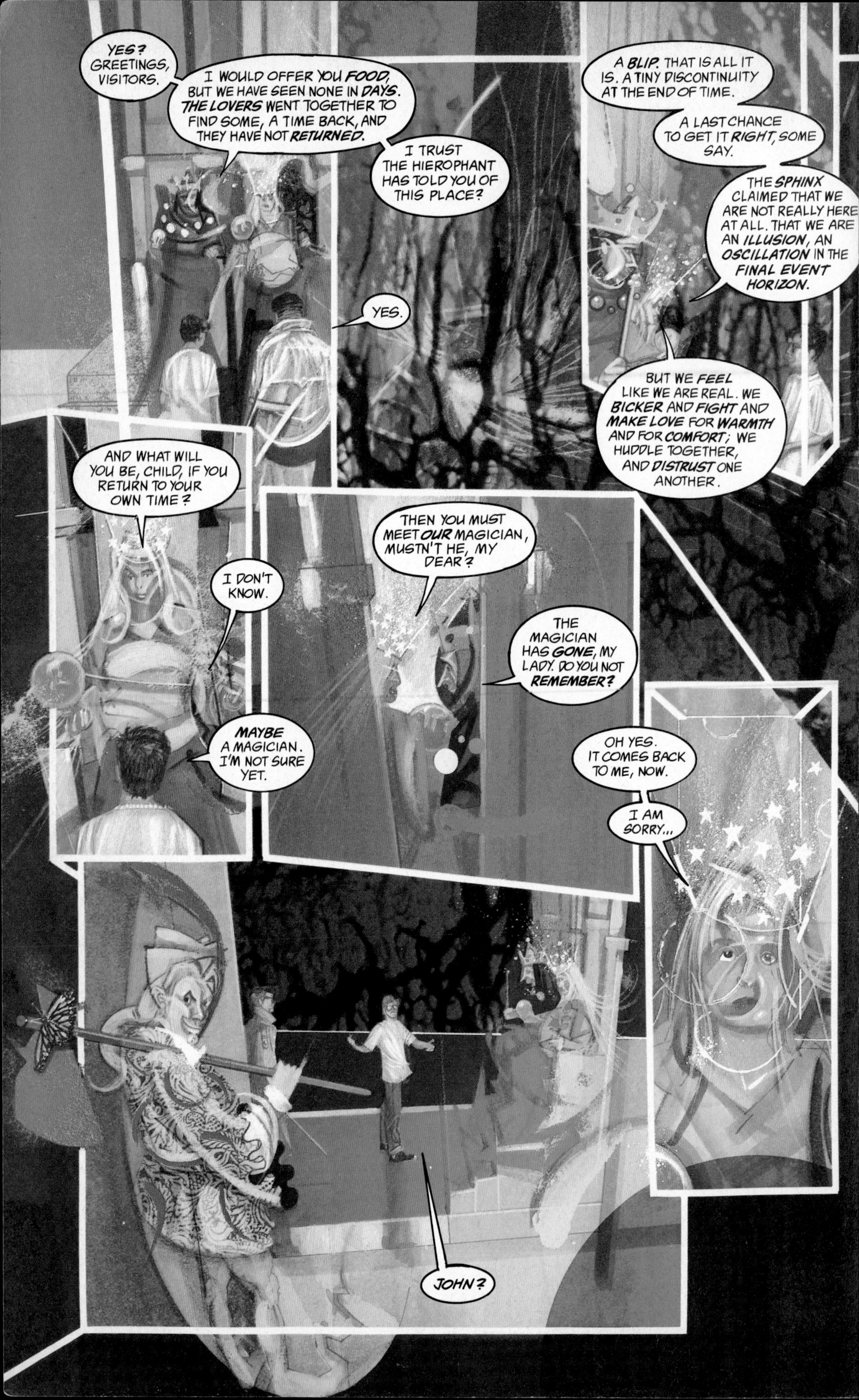
YES? GREETINGS, VISITORS.
I WOULD OFFER YOU FOOD, BUT WE HAVE SEEN NONE IN DAYS. THE LOVERS WENT TOGETHER TO FIND SOME, A TIME BACK, AND THEY HAVE NOT RETURNED.
I TRUST THE HIEROPHANT HAS TOLD YOU OF THIS PLACE?
YES.
A BLIP. THAT IS ALL IT IS. A TINY DISCONTINUITY AT THE END OF TIME.
A LAST CHANCE TO GET IT RIGHT, SOME SAY.
THE SPHINX CLAIMED THAT WE ARE NOT REALLY HERE AT ALL. THAT WE ARE AN ILLUSION, AN OSCILLATION IN THE FINAL EVENT HORIZON.
BUT WE FEEL LIKE WE ARE REAL. WE BICKER AND FIGHT AND MAKE LOVE FOR WARMTH AND FOR COMFORT; WE HUDDLE TOGETHER, AND DISTRUST ONE ANOTHER.
AND WHAT WILL YOU BE, CHILD, IF YOU RETURN TO YOUR OWN TIME?
I DON'T KNOW.
MAYBE A MAGICIAN. I'M NOT SURE YET.
THEN YOU MUST MEET OUR MAGICIAN, MUSTN'T HE, MY DEAR?
THE MAGICIAN HAS GONE, MY LADY. DO YOU NOT REMEMBER?
OH YES. IT COMES BACK TO ME, NOW.
I AM SORRY...
JOHN?

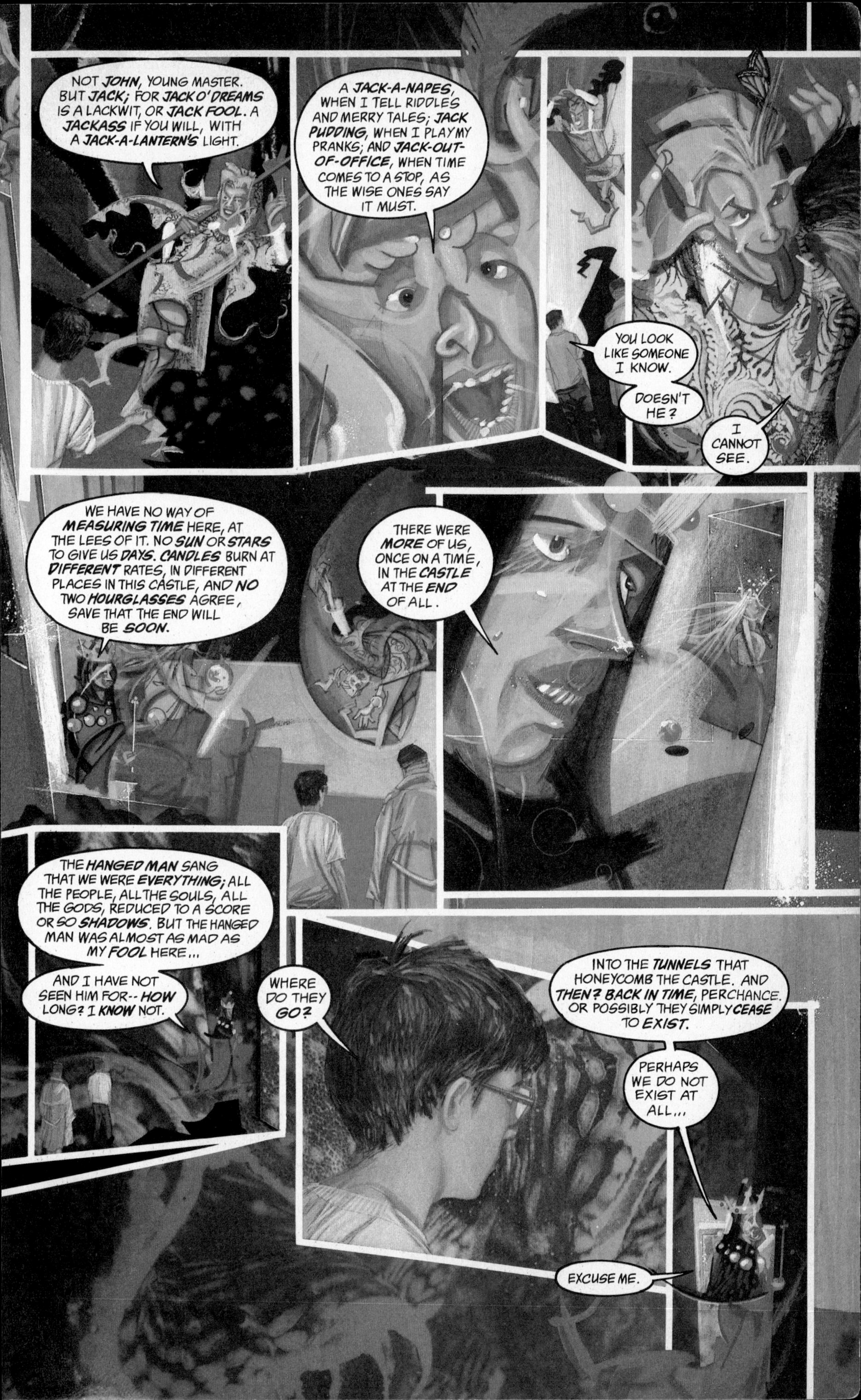
NOT JOHN, YOUNG MASTER. BUT JACK; FOR JACK O' DREAMS IS A LACKWIT, OR JACK FOOL. A JACKASS IF YOU WILL, WITH A JACK-A-LANTERN'S LIGHT.
A JACK-A-NAPES, WHEN I TELL RIDDLES AND MERRY TALES; JACK PUDDING, WHEN I PLAY MY PRANKS; AND JACK-OUT-OF-OFFICE, WHEN TIME COMES TO A STOP, AS THE WISE ONES SAY IT MUST.
YOU LOOK LIKE SOMEONE I KNOW.
DOESN'T HE?
I CANNOT SEE.
WE HAVE NO WAY OF MEASURING TIME HERE, AT THE LEES OF IT. NO SUN OR STARS TO GIVE US DAYS. CANDLES BURN AT DIFFERENT RATES, IN DIFFERENT PLACES IN THIS CASTLE, AND NO TWO HOURGLASSES AGREE, SAVE THAT THE END WILL BE SOON.
THERE WERE MORE OF US, ONCE ON A TIME, IN THE CASTLE AT THE END OF ALL.
THE HANGED MAN SANG THAT WE WERE EVERYTHING; ALL THE PEOPLE, ALL THE SOULS, ALL THE GODS, REDUCED TO A SCORE OR SO SHADOWS. BUT THE HANGED MAN WAS ALMOST AS MAD AS MY FOOL HERE...
AND I HAVE NOT SEEN HIM FOR-- HOW LONG? I KNOW NOT.
WHERE DO THEY GO?
INTO THE TUNNELS THAT HONEYCOMB THE CASTLE. AND THEN? BACK IN TIME, PERCHANCE. OR POSSIBLY THEY SIMPLY CEASE TO EXIST.
PERHAPS WE DO NOT EXIST AT ALL...
EXCUSE ME.

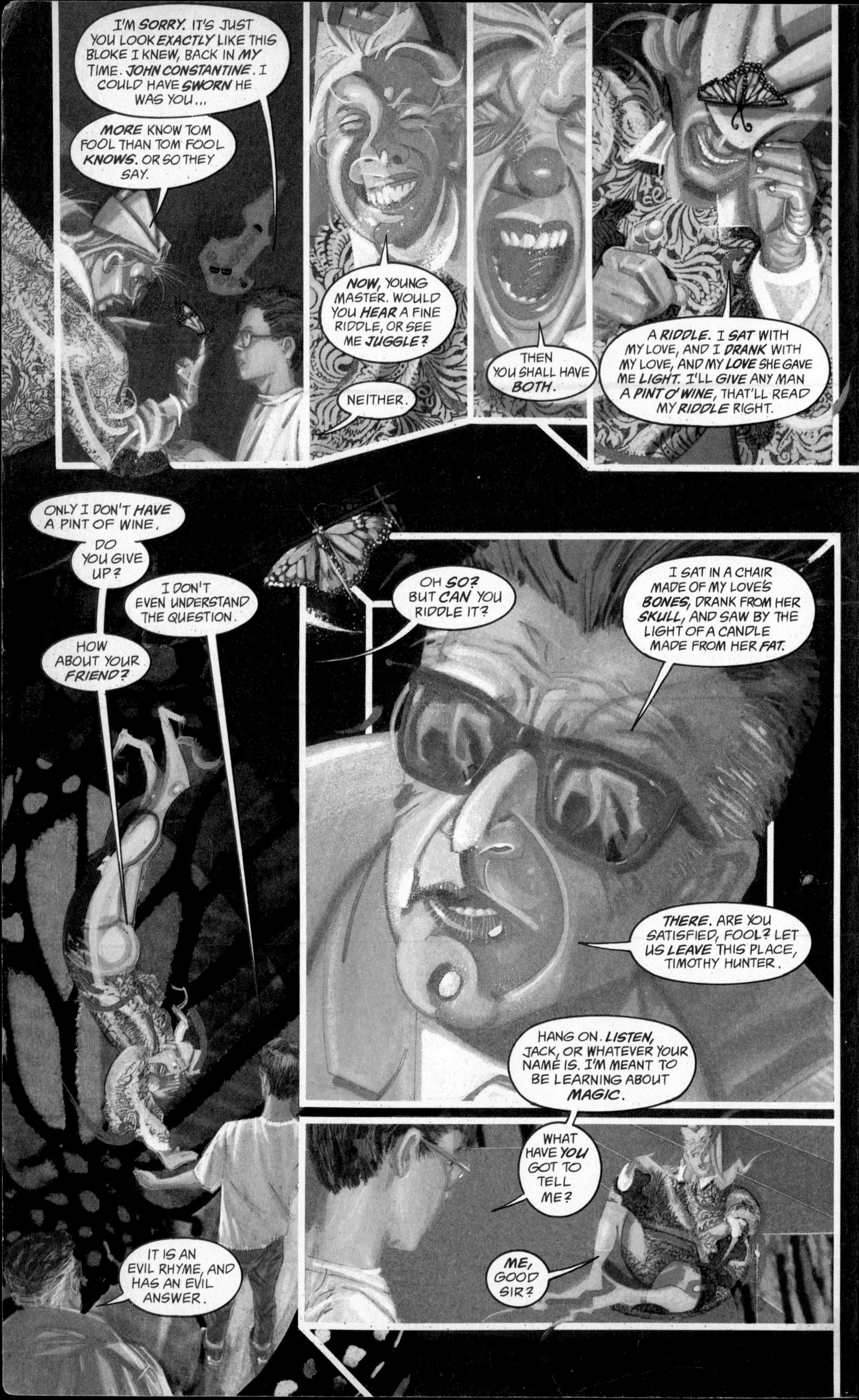
I'M SORRY. IT'S JUST YOU LOOK EXACTLY LIKE THIS BLOKE I KNEW, BACK IN MY TIME. JOHN CONSTANTINE. I COULD HAVE SWORN HE WAS YOU...
MORE KNOW TOM FOOL THAN TOM FOOL KNOWS. OR SO THEY SAY.
NOW, YOUNG MASTER. WOULD YOU HEAR A FINE RIDDLE, OR SEE ME JUGGLE?
NEITHER.
THEN YOU SHALL HAVE BOTH.
A RIDDLE. I SAT WITH MY LOVE, AND I DRANK WITH MY LOVE, AND MY LOVE SHE GAVE ME LIGHT. I'LL GIVE ANY MAN A PINT O' WINE, THAT'LL READ MY RIDDLE RIGHT.
ONLY I DON'T HAVE A PINT OF WINE.
DO YOU GIVE UP?
I DON'T EVEN UNDERSTAND THE QUESTION.
HOW ABOUT YOUR FRIEND?
OH SO? BUT CAN YOU RIDDLE IT?
I SAT IN A CHAIR MADE OF MY LOVE'S BONES, DRANK FROM HER SKULL, AND SAW BY THE LIGHT OF A CANDLE MADE FROM HER FAT.
THERE. ARE YOU SATISFIED, FOOL? LET US LEAVE THIS PLACE, TIMOTHY HUNTER.
HANG ON. LISTEN, JACK, OR WHATEVER YOUR NAME IS. I'M MEANT TO BE LEARNING ABOUT MAGIC.
WHAT HAVE YOU GOT TO TELL ME?
ME, GOOD SIR?
IT IS AN EVIL RHYME, AND HAS AN EVIL ANSWER.

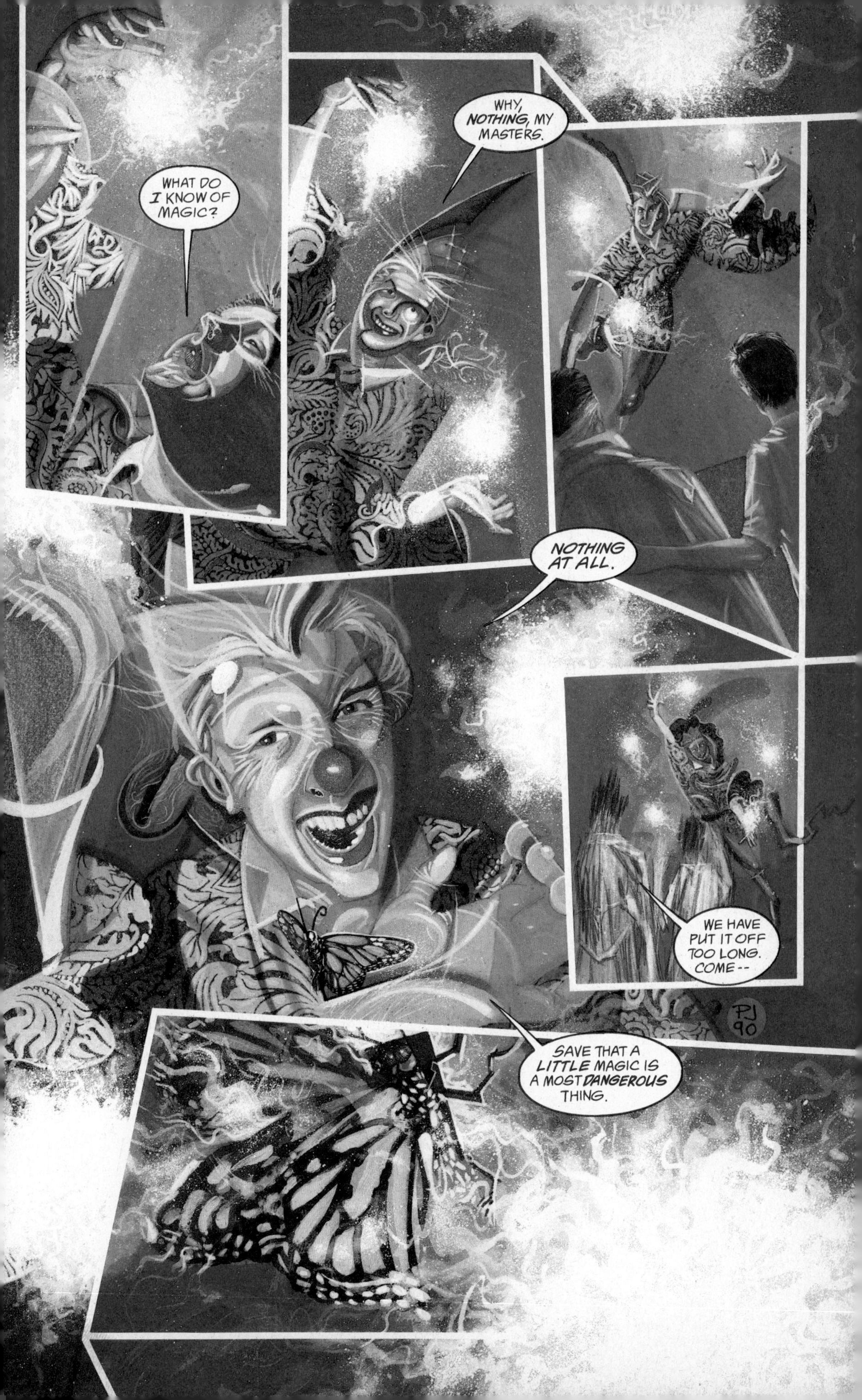
WHAT DO I KNOW OF MAGIC?
WHY, NOTHING, MY MASTERS.
NOTHING AT ALL.
WE HAVE PUT IT OFF TOO LONG. COME --
SAVE THAT A LITTLE MAGIC IS A MOST DANGEROUS THING.
PJ 90

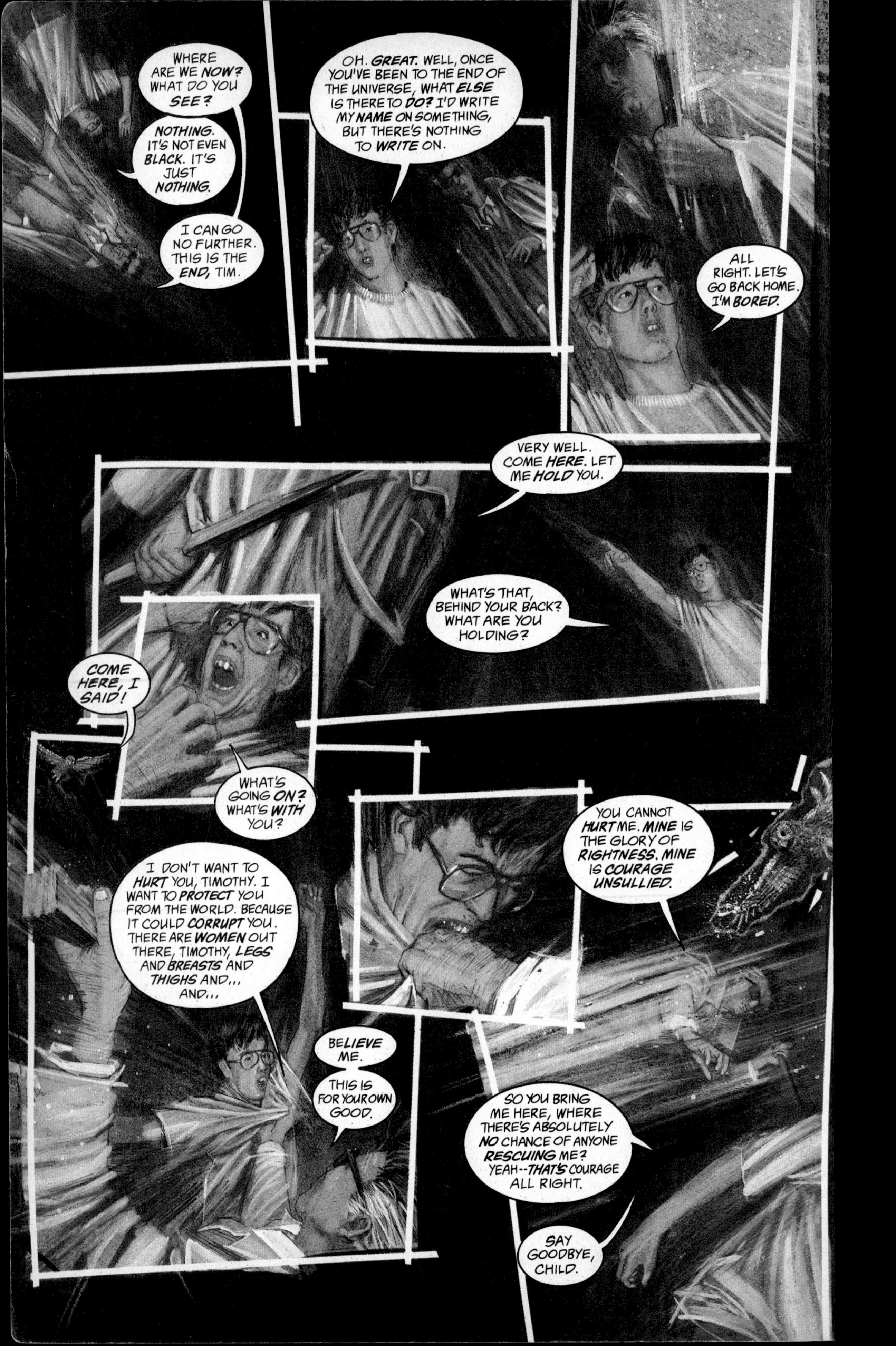
WHERE ARE WE NOW? WHAT DO YOU SEE?
NOTHING. IT'S NOT EVEN BLACK. IT'S JUST NOTHING.
I CAN GO NO FURTHER. THIS IS THE END, TIM.
OH. GREAT. WELL, ONCE YOU'VE BEEN TO THE END OF THE UNIVERSE, WHAT ELSE IS THERE TO DO? I'D WRITE MY NAME ON SOMETHING, BUT THERE'S NOTHING TO WRITE ON.
ALL RIGHT. LET'S GO BACK HOME. I'M BORED.
VERY WELL. COME HERE. LET ME HOLD YOU.
WHAT'S THAT, BEHIND YOUR BACK? WHAT ARE YOU HOLDING?
COME HERE, I SAID!
WHAT'S GOING ON? WHAT'S WITH YOU?
I DON'T WANT TO HURT YOU, TIMOTHY. I WANT TO PROTECT YOU FROM THE WORLD. BECAUSE IT COULD CORRUPT YOU. THERE ARE WOMEN OUT THERE, TIMOTHY, LEGS AND BREASTS AND THIGHS AND... AND...
BELIEVE ME.
THIS IS FOR YOUR OWN GOOD.
YOU CANNOT HURT ME. MINE IS THE GLORY OF RIGHTNESS. MINE IS COURAGE UNSULLIED.
SO YOU BRING ME HERE, WHERE THERE'S ABSOLUTELY NO CHANCE OF ANYONE RESCUING ME? YEAH--THAT'S COURAGE ALL RIGHT.
SAY GOODBYE, CHILD.

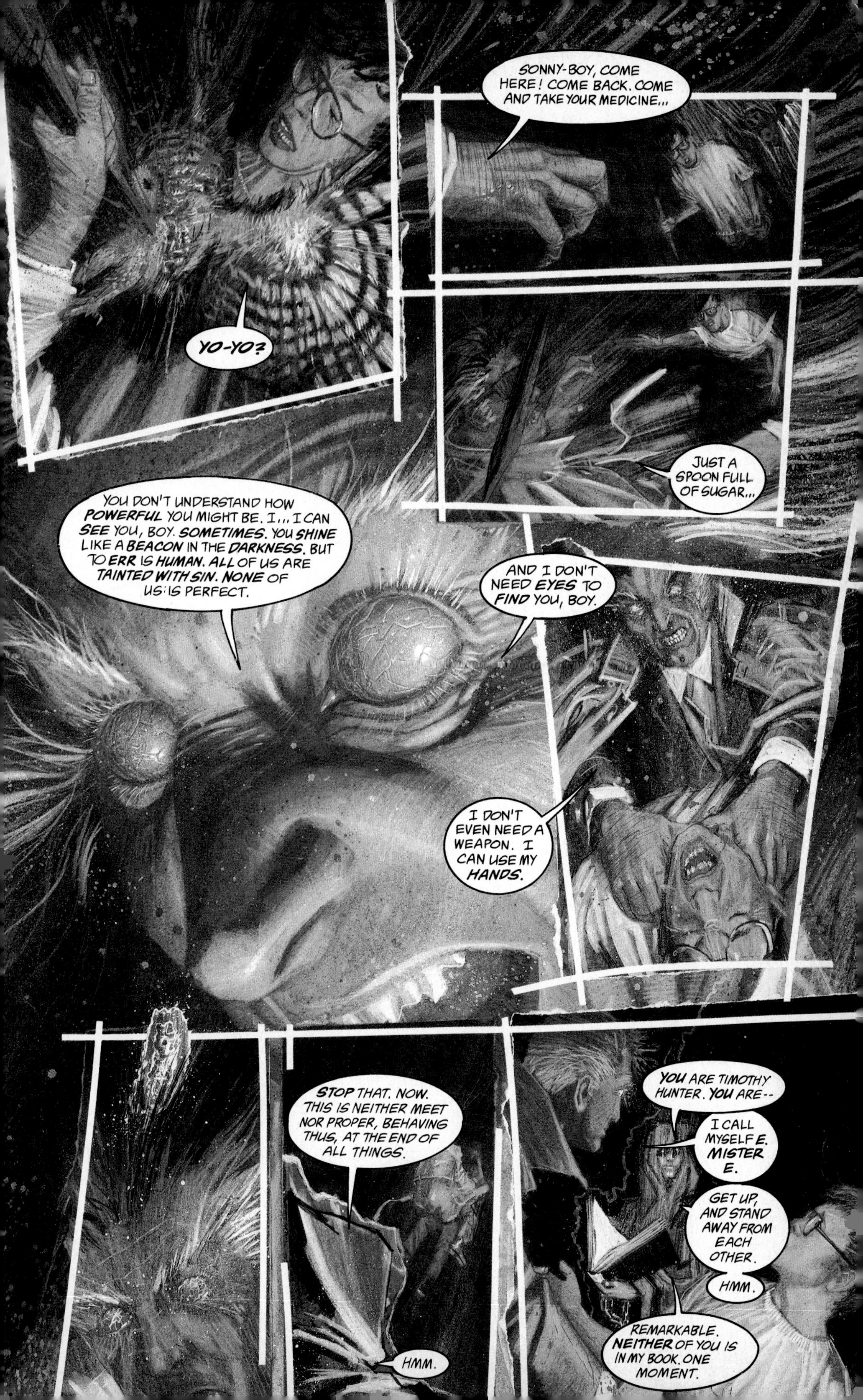
YO-YO?
SONNY-BOY, COME HERE! COME BACK. COME AND TAKE YOUR MEDICINE...
JUST A SPOON FULL OF SUGAR...
YOU DON'T UNDERSTAND HOW POWERFUL YOU MIGHT BE. I... I CAN SEE YOU, BOY. SOMETIMES. YOU SHINE LIKE A BEACON IN THE DARKNESS. BUT TO ERR IS HUMAN. ALL OF US ARE TAINTED WITH SIN. NONE OF US IS PERFECT.
AND I DON'T NEED EYES TO FIND YOU, BOY.
I DON'T EVEN NEED A WEAPON. I CAN USE MY HANDS.
STOP THAT. NOW. THIS IS NEITHER MEET NOR PROPER, BEHAVING THUS, AT THE END OF ALL THINGS.
HMM.
YOU ARE TIMOTHY HUNTER. YOU ARE--
I CALL MYSELF E. MISTER E.
GET UP, AND STAND AWAY FROM EACH OTHER.
HMM.
REMARKABLE. NEITHER OF YOU IS IN MY BOOK. ONE MOMENT.

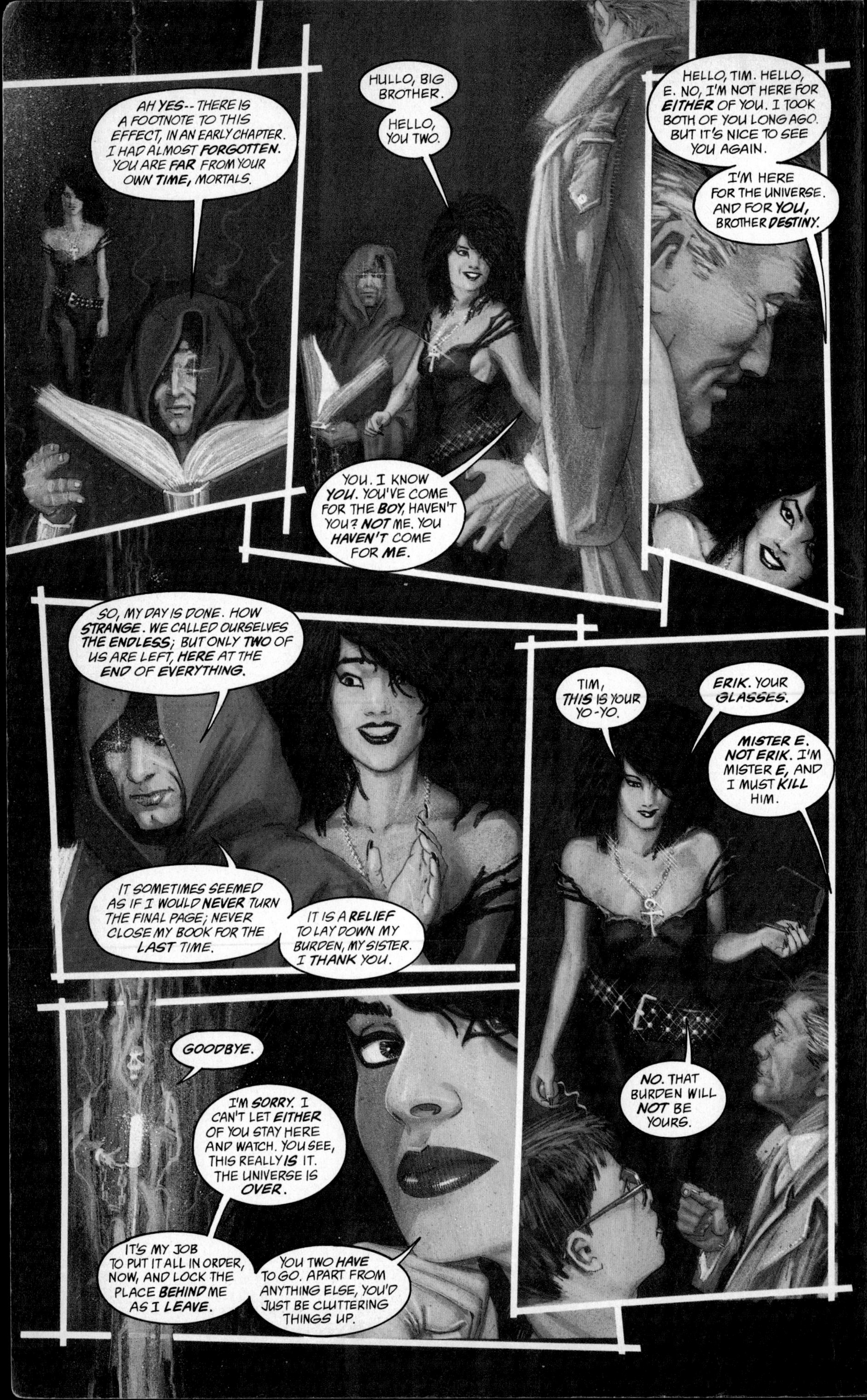
AH YES-- THERE IS A FOOTNOTE TO THIS EFFECT, IN AN EARLY CHAPTER. I HAD ALMOST FORGOTTEN. YOU ARE FAR FROM YOUR OWN TIME, MORTALS.
HULLO, BIG BROTHER.
HELLO, YOU TWO.
YOU. I KNOW YOU. YOU'VE COME FOR THE BOY, HAVEN'T YOU? NOT ME. YOU HAVEN'T COME FOR ME.
HELLO, TIM. HELLO, E. NO, I'M NOT HERE FOR EITHER OF YOU. I TOOK BOTH OF YOU LONG AGO. BUT IT'S NICE TO SEE YOU AGAIN.
I'M HERE FOR THE UNIVERSE. AND FOR YOU, BROTHER DESTINY.
SO, MY DAY IS DONE. HOW STRANGE. WE CALLED OURSELVES THE ENDLESS; BUT ONLY TWO OF US ARE LEFT, HERE AT THE END OF EVERYTHING.
IT SOMETIMES SEEMED AS IF I WOULD NEVER TURN THE FINAL PAGE; NEVER CLOSE MY BOOK FOR THE LAST TIME.
IT IS A RELIEF TO LAY DOWN MY BURDEN, MY SISTER. I THANK YOU.
TIM, THIS IS YOUR YO-YO.
ERIK. YOUR GLASSES.
MISTER E. NOT ERIK. I'M MISTER E, AND I MUST KILL HIM.
NO. THAT BURDEN WILL NOT BE YOURS.
GOODBYE.
I'M SORRY. I CAN'T LET EITHER OF YOU STAY HERE AND WATCH. YOU SEE, THIS REALLY IS IT. THE UNIVERSE IS OVER.
IT'S MY JOB TO PUT IT ALL IN ORDER, NOW, AND LOCK THE PLACE BEHIND ME AS I LEAVE.
YOU TWO HAVE TO GO. APART FROM ANYTHING ELSE, YOU'D JUST BE CLUTTERING THINGS UP.

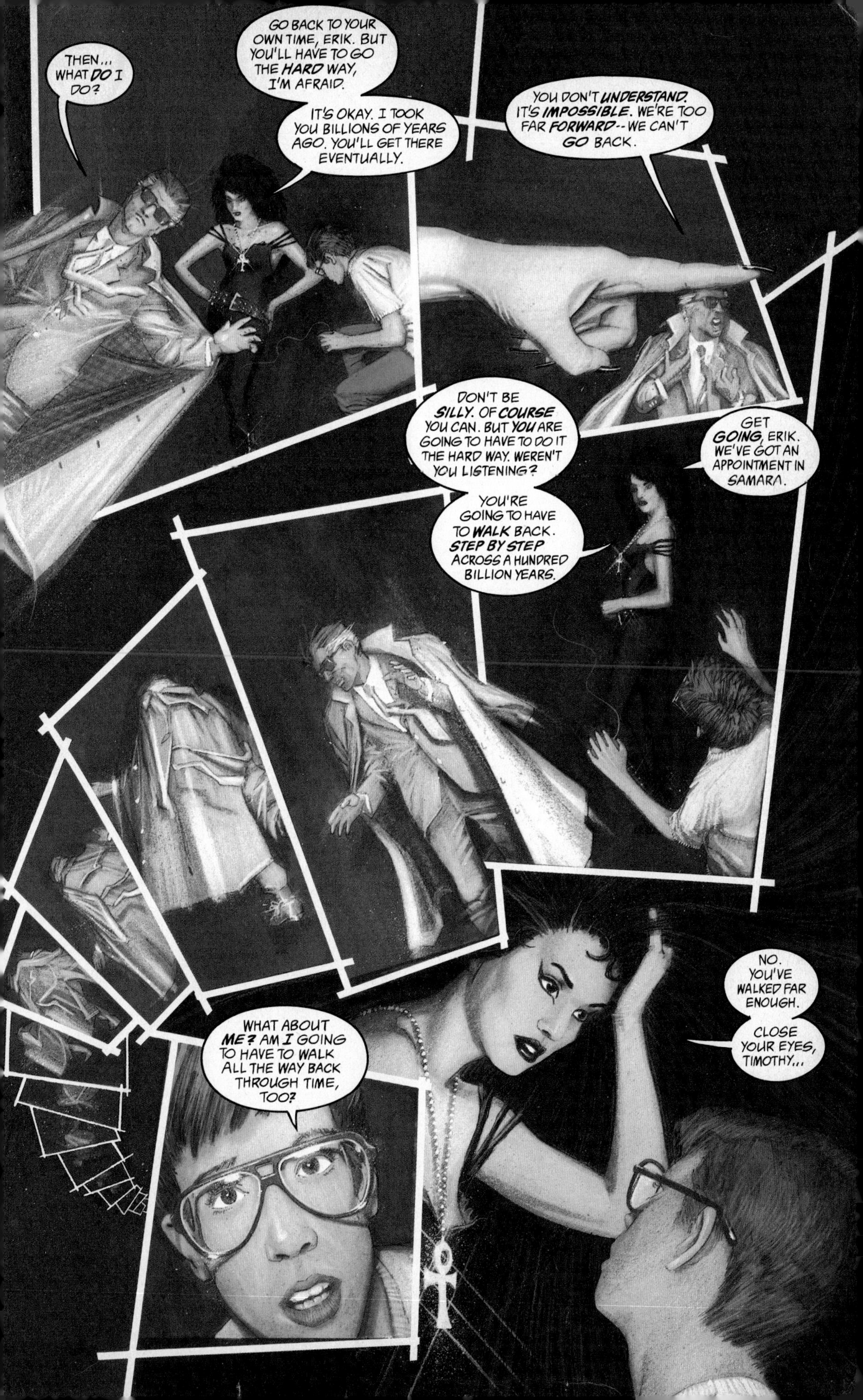

THEN... WHAT DO I DO?
GO BACK TO YOUR OWN TIME, ERIK. BUT YOU'LL HAVE TO GO THE HARD WAY, I'M AFRAID.
IT'S OKAY. I TOOK YOU BILLIONS OF YEARS AGO. YOU'LL GET THERE EVENTUALLY.
YOU DON'T UNDERSTAND. IT'S IMPOSSIBLE. WE'RE TOO FAR FORWARD-- WE CAN'T GO BACK.
DON'T BE SILLY. OF COURSE YOU CAN. BUT YOU ARE GOING TO HAVE TO DO IT THE HARD WAY. WEREN'T YOU LISTENING?
YOU'RE GOING TO HAVE TO WALK BACK. STEP BY STEP ACROSS A HUNDRED BILLION YEARS.
GET GOING, ERIK. WE'VE GOT AN APPOINTMENT IN SAMARA.
WHAT ABOUT ME? AM I GOING TO HAVE TO WALK ALL THE WAY BACK THROUGH TIME, TOO?
NO. YOU'VE WALKED FAR ENOUGH.
CLOSE YOUR EYES, TIMOTHY...

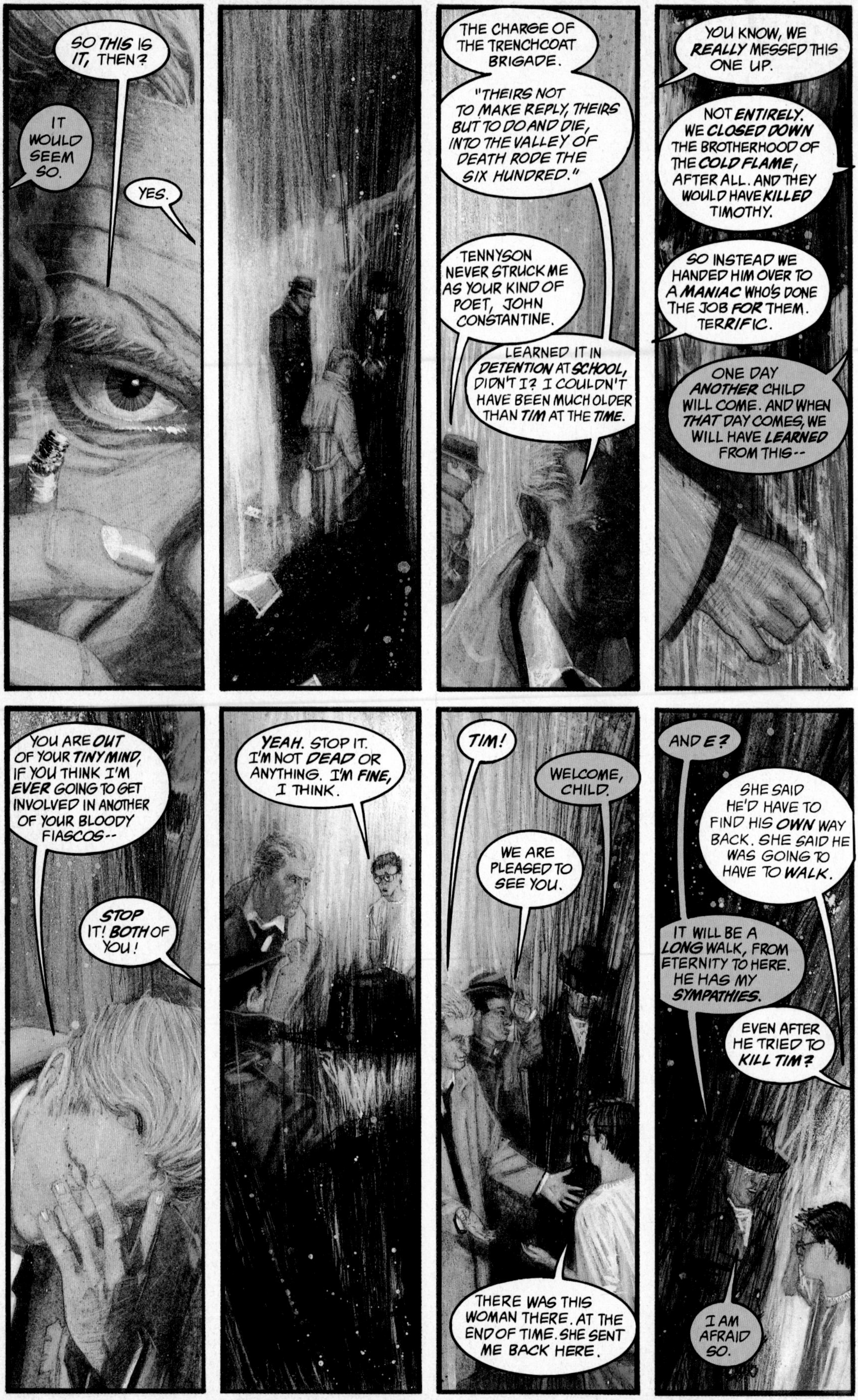
SO THIS IS IT, THEN?
IT WOULD SEEM SO.
YES.
THE CHARGE OF THE TRENCHCOAT BRIGADE.
"THEIRS NOT TO MAKE REPLY, THEIRS BUT TO DO AND DIE, INTO THE VALLEY OF DEATH RODE THE SIX HUNDRED."
TENNYSON NEVER STRUCK ME AS YOUR KIND OF POET, JOHN CONSTANTINE.
LEARNED IT IN DETENTION AT SCHOOL, DIDN'T I? I COULDN'T HAVE BEEN MUCH OLDER THAN TIM AT THE TIME.
YOU KNOW, WE REALLY MESSED THIS ONE UP.
NOT ENTIRELY. WE CLOSED DOWN THE BROTHERHOOD OF THE COLD FLAME, AFTER ALL. AND THEY WOULD HAVE KILLED TIMOTHY.
SO INSTEAD WE HANDED HIM OVER TO A MANIAC WHO'S DONE THE JOB FOR THEM. TERRIFIC.
ONE DAY ANOTHER CHILD WILL COME. AND WHEN THAT DAY COMES, WE WILL HAVE LEARNED FROM THIS--
YOU ARE OUT OF YOUR TINY MIND, IF YOU THINK I'M EVER GOING TO GET INVOLVED IN ANOTHER OF YOUR BLOODY FIASCOS--
STOP IT! BOTH OF YOU!
YEAH. STOP IT. I'M NOT DEAD OR ANYTHING. I'M FINE, I THINK.
TIM!
WELCOME, CHILD.
WE ARE PLEASED TO SEE YOU.
THERE WAS THIS WOMAN THERE. AT THE END OF TIME. SHE SENT ME BACK HERE.
AND E?
SHE SAID HE'D HAVE TO FIND HIS OWN WAY BACK. SHE SAID HE WAS GOING TO HAVE TO WALK.
IT WILL BE A LONG WALK, FROM ETERNITY TO HERE. HE HAS MY SYMPATHIES.
EVEN AFTER HE TRIED TO KILL TIM?
I AM AFRAID SO.

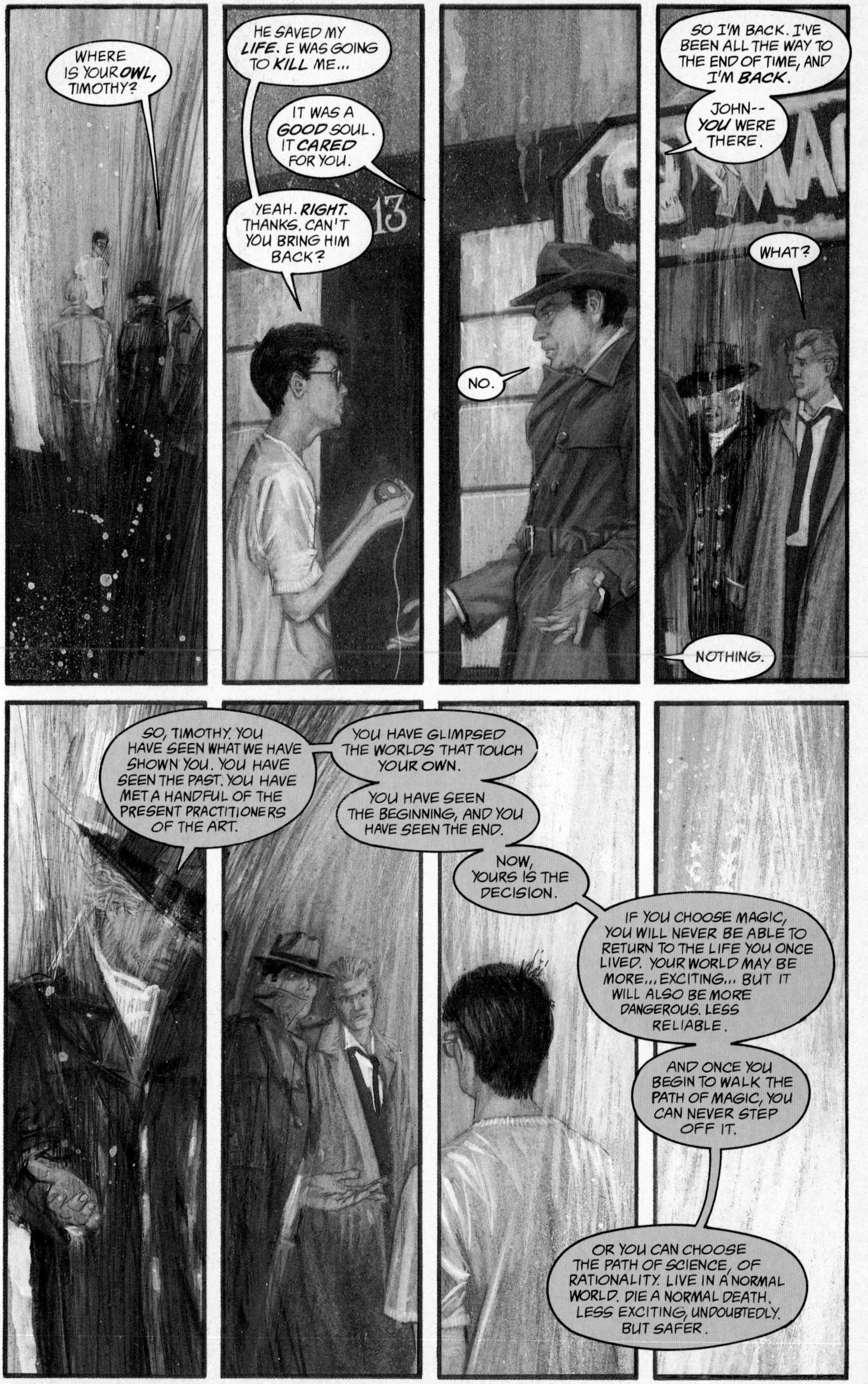
WHERE IS YOUR OWL, TIMOTHY?
HE SAVED MY LIFE. E WAS GOING TO KILL ME...
IT WAS A GOOD SOUL. IT CARED FOR YOU.
YEAH. RIGHT. THANKS. CAN'T YOU BRING HIM BACK?
13
NO.
SO I'M BACK. I'VE BEEN ALL THE WAY TO THE END OF TIME, AND I'M BACK.
JOHN-- YOU WERE THERE.
WHAT?
NOTHING.
SO, TIMOTHY. YOU HAVE SEEN WHAT WE HAVE SHOWN YOU. YOU HAVE SEEN THE PAST. YOU HAVE MET A HANDFUL OF THE PRESENT PRACTITIONERS OF THE ART.
YOU HAVE GLIMPSED THE WORLDS THAT TOUCH YOUR OWN.
YOU HAVE SEEN THE BEGINNING, AND YOU HAVE SEEN THE END.
NOW, YOURS IS THE DECISION.
IF YOU CHOOSE MAGIC, YOU WILL NEVER BE ABLE TO RETURN TO THE LIFE YOU ONCE LIVED. YOUR WORLD MAY BE MORE... EXCITING... BUT IT WILL ALSO BE MORE DANGEROUS. LESS RELIABLE.
AND ONCE YOU BEGIN TO WALK THE PATH OF MAGIC, YOU CAN NEVER STEP OFF IT.
OR YOU CAN CHOOSE THE PATH OF SCIENCE, OF RATIONALITY. LIVE IN A NORMAL WORLD. DIE A NORMAL DEATH. LESS EXCITING, UNDOUBTEDLY. BUT SAFER.

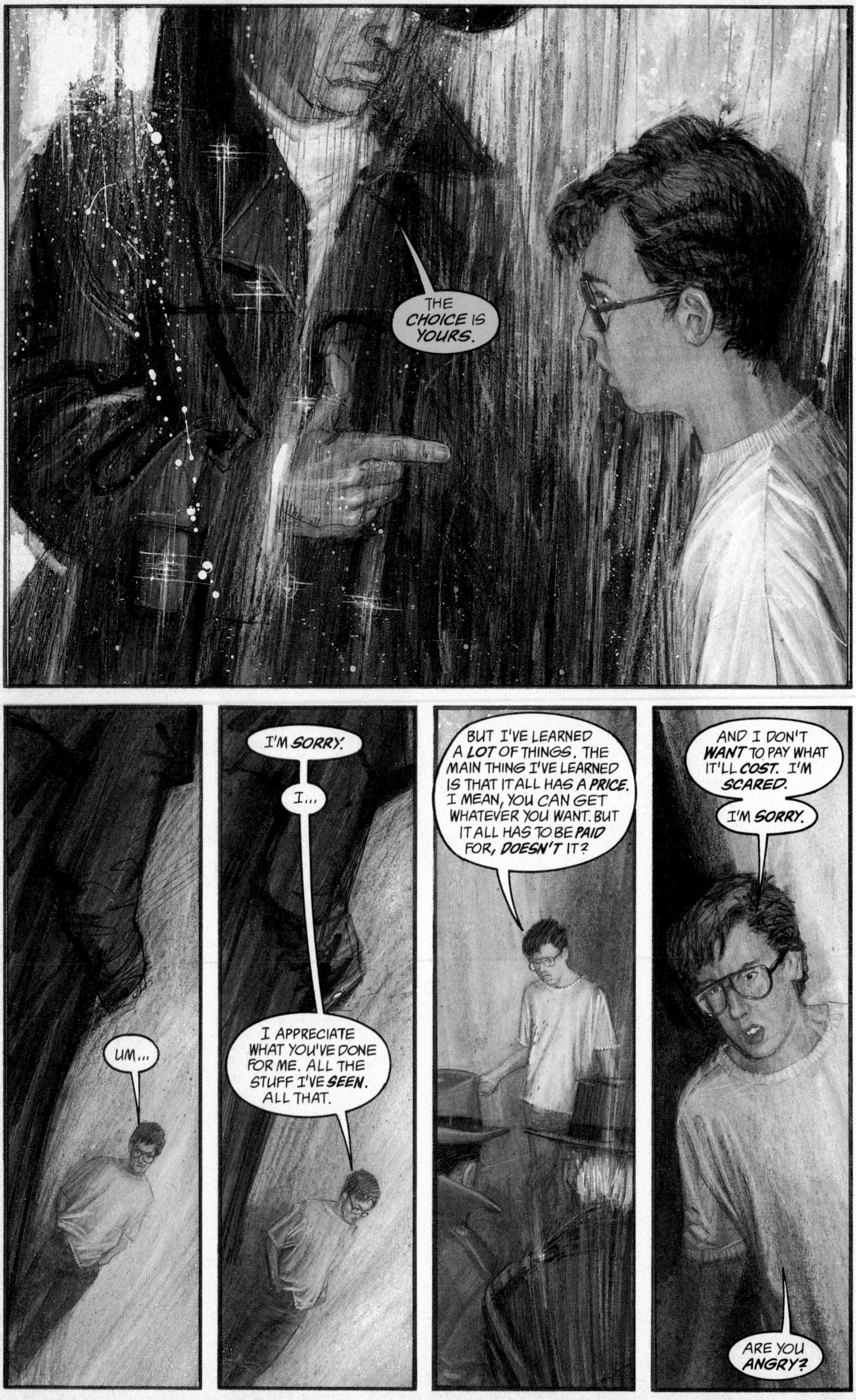
THE CHOICE IS YOURS.
UM...
I'M SORRY.
I...
I APPRECIATE WHAT YOU'VE DONE FOR ME. ALL THE STUFF I'VE SEEN. ALL THAT.
BUT I'VE LEARNED A LOT OF THINGS. THE MAIN THING I'VE LEARNED IS THAT IT ALL HAS A PRICE. I MEAN, YOU CAN GET WHATEVER YOU WANT. BUT IT ALL HAS TO BE PAID FOR, DOESN'T IT?
AND I DON'T WANT TO PAY WHAT IT'LL COST. I'M SCARED.
I'M SORRY.
ARE YOU ANGRY?

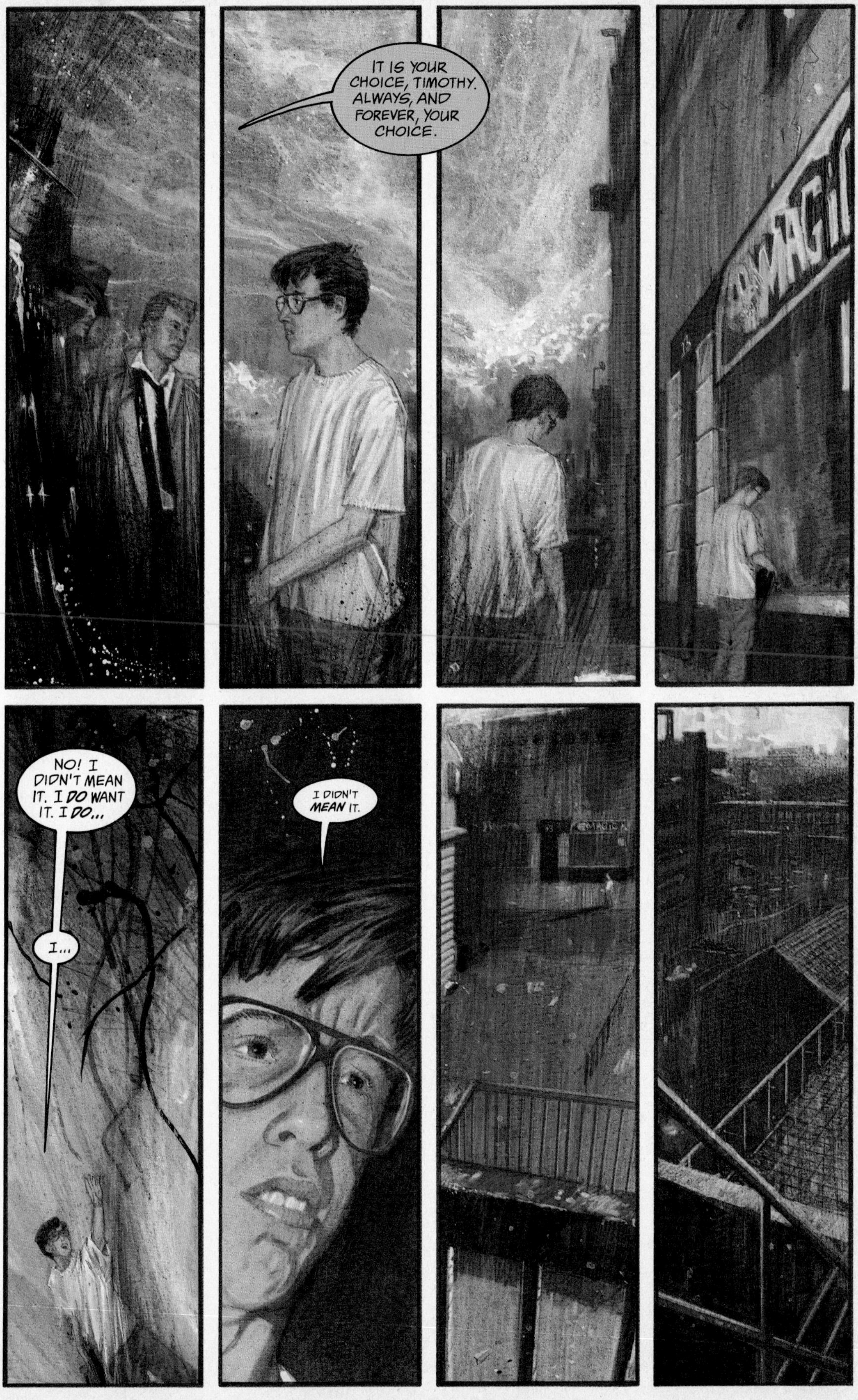
IT IS YOUR CHOICE, TIMOTHY. ALWAYS, AND FOREVER, YOUR CHOICE.
NO! I DIDN'T MEAN IT. I *DO* WANT IT. I *DO*...
I...
I DIDN'T *MEAN* IT.

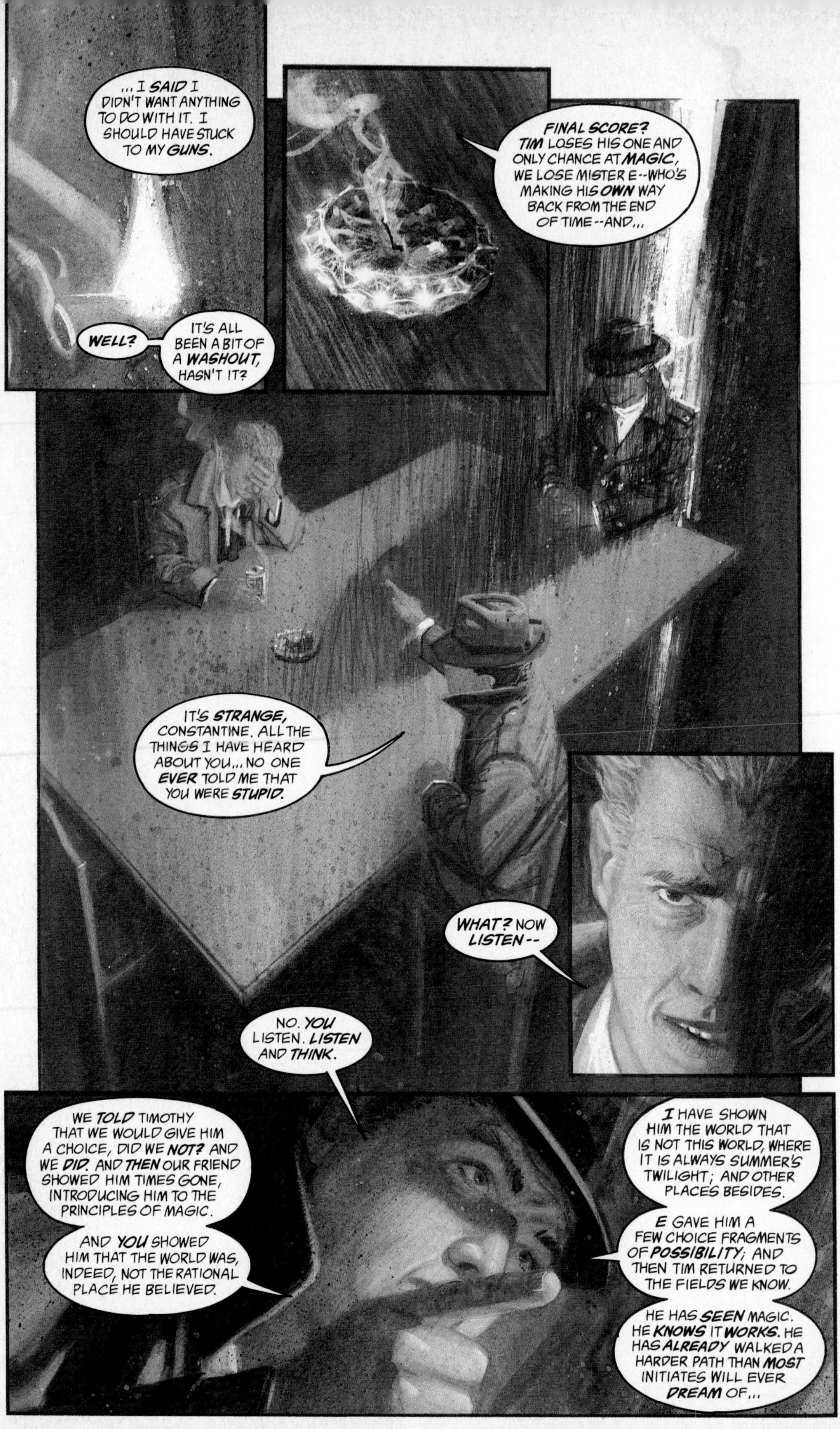
...I SAID I DIDN'T WANT ANYTHING TO DO WITH IT. I SHOULD HAVE STUCK TO MY GUNS.
WELL?
IT'S ALL BEEN A BIT OF A WASHOUT, HASN'T IT?
FINAL SCORE? TIM LOSES HIS ONE AND ONLY CHANCE AT MAGIC, WE LOSE MISTER E--WHO'S MAKING HIS OWN WAY BACK FROM THE END OF TIME--AND...
IT'S STRANGE, CONSTANTINE. ALL THE THINGS I HAVE HEARD ABOUT YOU... NO ONE EVER TOLD ME THAT YOU WERE STUPID.
WHAT? NOW LISTEN--
NO. YOU LISTEN. LISTEN AND THINK.
WE TOLD TIMOTHY THAT WE WOULD GIVE HIM A CHOICE, DID WE NOT? AND WE DID. AND THEN OUR FRIEND SHOWED HIM TIMES GONE, INTRODUCING HIM TO THE PRINCIPLES OF MAGIC.
AND YOU SHOWED HIM THAT THE WORLD WAS, INDEED, NOT THE RATIONAL PLACE HE BELIEVED.
I HAVE SHOWN HIM THE WORLD THAT IS NOT THIS WORLD, WHERE IT IS ALWAYS SUMMER'S TWILIGHT; AND OTHER PLACES BESIDES.
E GAVE HIM A FEW CHOICE FRAGMENTS OF POSSIBILITY; AND THEN TIM RETURNED TO THE FIELDS WE KNOW.
HE HAS SEEN MAGIC. HE KNOWS IT WORKS. HE HAS ALREADY WALKED A HARDER PATH THAN MOST INITIATES WILL EVER DREAM OF...

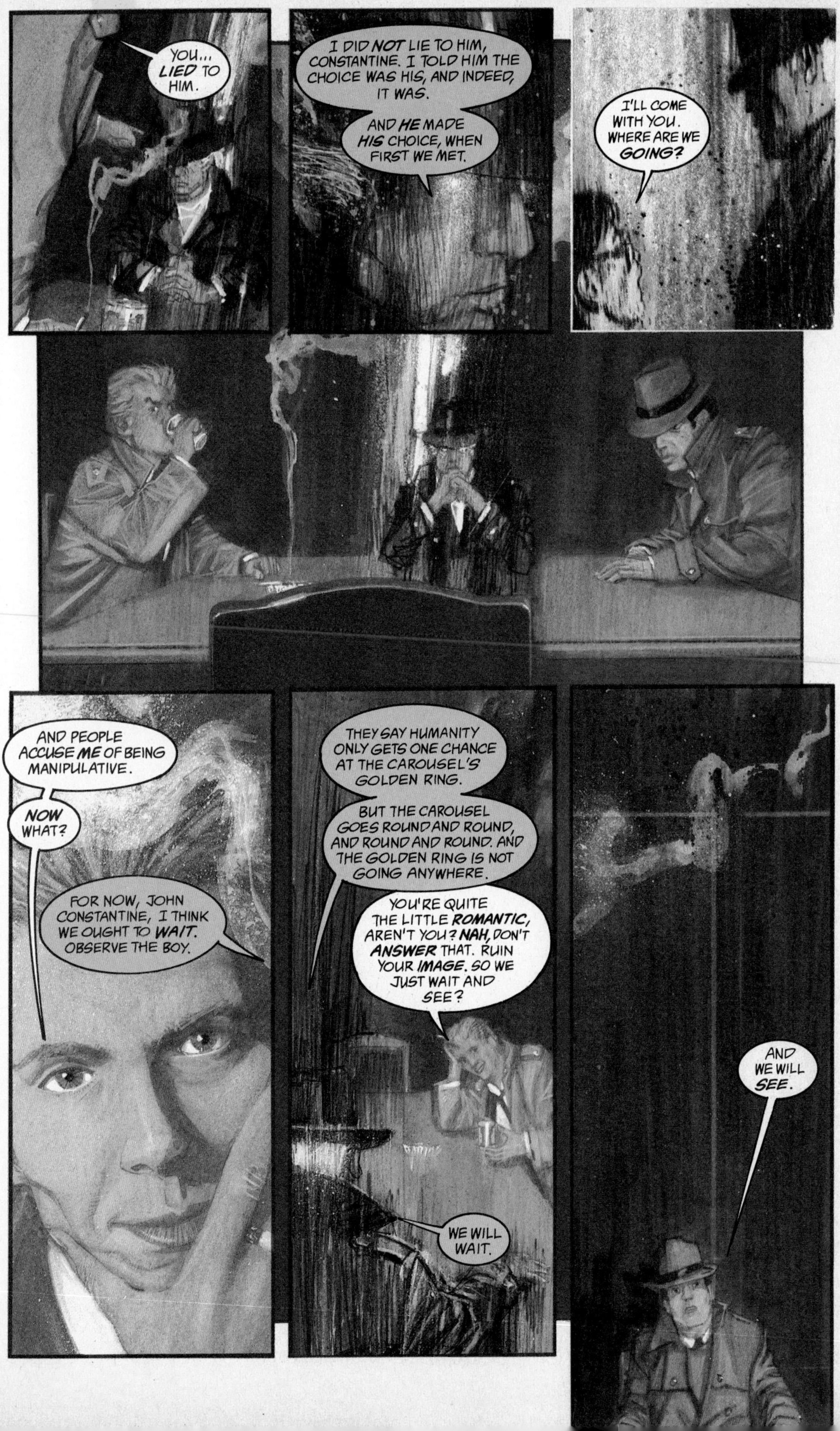
YOU... LIED TO HIM.
I DID NOT LIE TO HIM, CONSTANTINE. I TOLD HIM THE CHOICE WAS HIS, AND INDEED, IT WAS.
AND HE MADE HIS CHOICE, WHEN FIRST WE MET.
I'LL COME WITH YOU. WHERE ARE WE GOING?
AND PEOPLE ACCUSE ME OF BEING MANIPULATIVE.
NOW WHAT?
FOR NOW, JOHN CONSTANTINE, I THINK WE OUGHT TO WAIT. OBSERVE THE BOY.
THEY SAY HUMANITY ONLY GETS ONE CHANCE AT THE CAROUSEL'S GOLDEN RING.
BUT THE CAROUSEL GOES ROUND AND ROUND, AND ROUND AND ROUND. AND THE GOLDEN RING IS NOT GOING ANYWHERE.
YOU'RE QUITE THE LITTLE ROMANTIC, AREN'T YOU? NAH, DON'T ANSWER THAT. RUIN YOUR IMAGE. SO WE JUST WAIT AND SEE?
WE WILL WAIT.
AND WE WILL SEE.

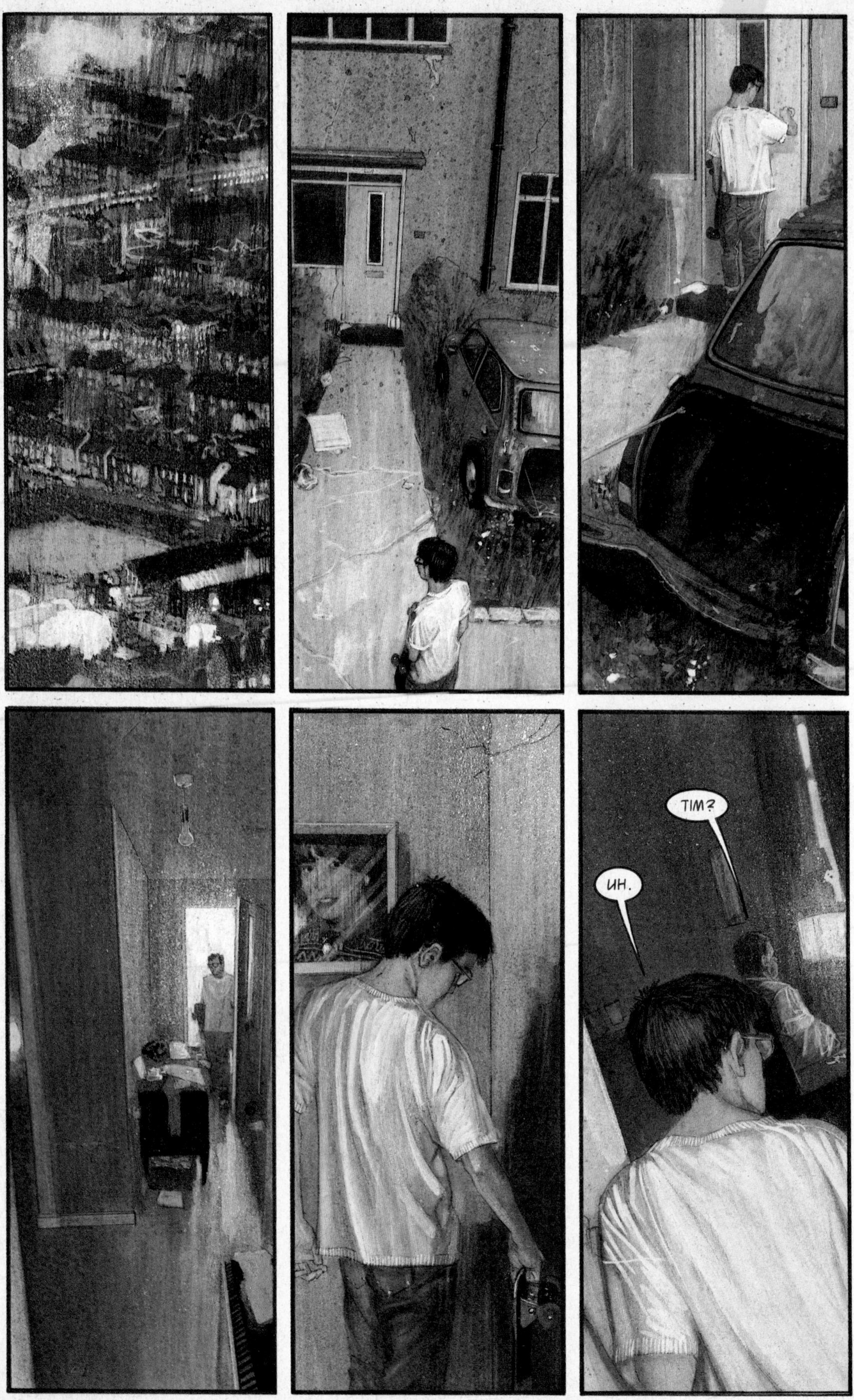
TIM?
UH.

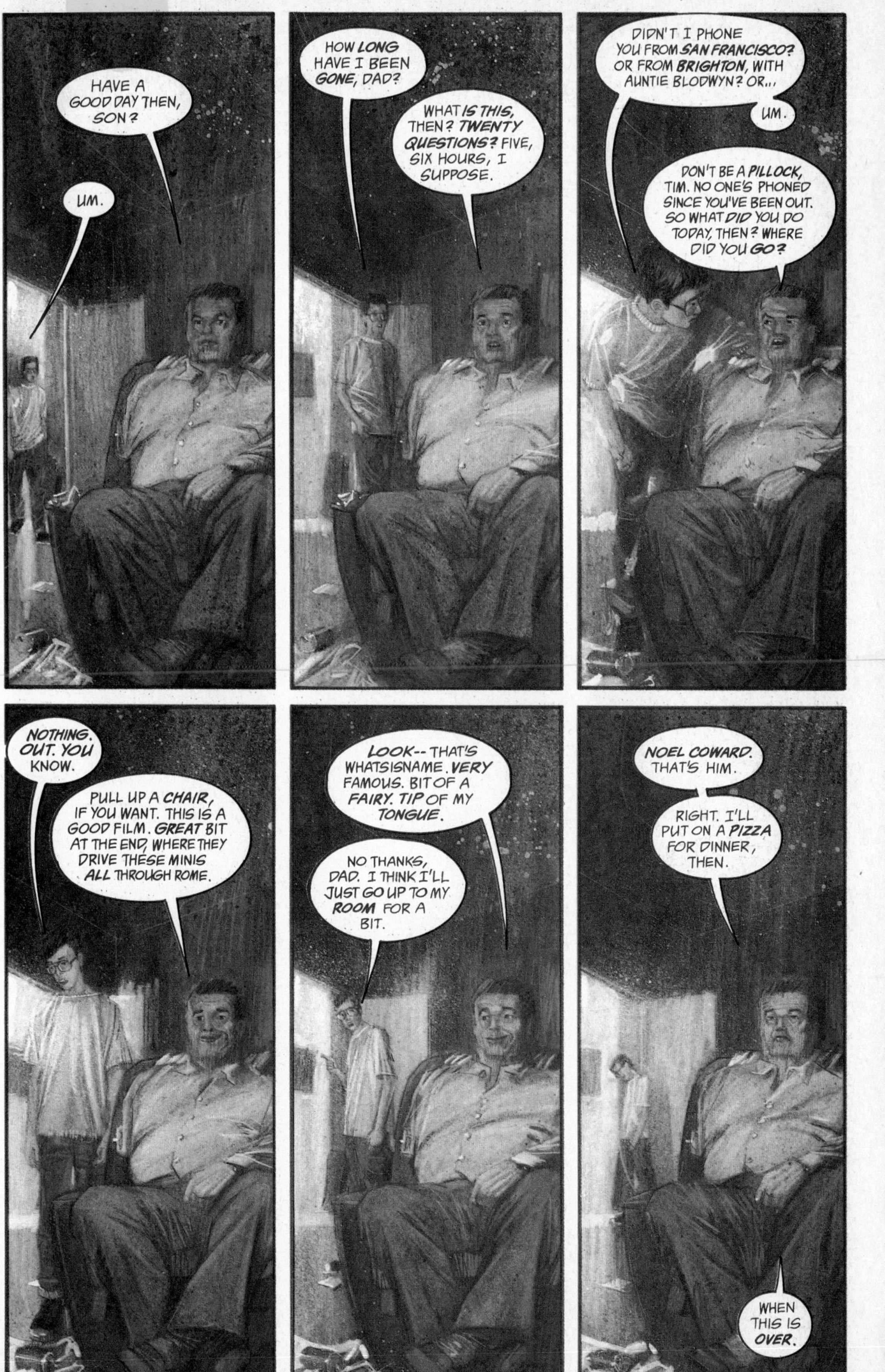
HAVE A GOOD DAY THEN, SON?
UM.
HOW LONG HAVE I BEEN GONE, DAD?
WHAT IS THIS, THEN? TWENTY QUESTIONS? FIVE, SIX HOURS, I SUPPOSE.
DIDN'T I PHONE YOU FROM SAN FRANCISCO? OR FROM BRIGHTON, WITH AUNTIE BLODWYN? OR...
UM.
DON'T BE A PILLOCK, TIM. NO ONE'S PHONED SINCE YOU'VE BEEN OUT. SO WHAT DID YOU DO TODAY, THEN? WHERE DID YOU GO?
NOTHING. OUT. YOU KNOW.
PULL UP A CHAIR, IF YOU WANT. THIS IS A GOOD FILM. GREAT BIT AT THE END, WHERE THEY DRIVE THESE MINIS ALL THROUGH ROME.
LOOK-- THAT'S WHATSISNAME. VERY FAMOUS. BIT OF A FAIRY. TIP OF MY TONGUE.
NO THANKS, DAD. I THINK I'LL JUST GO UP TO MY ROOM FOR A BIT.
NOEL COWARD. THAT'S HIM.
RIGHT. I'LL PUT ON A PIZZA FOR DINNER, THEN.
WHEN THIS IS OVER.

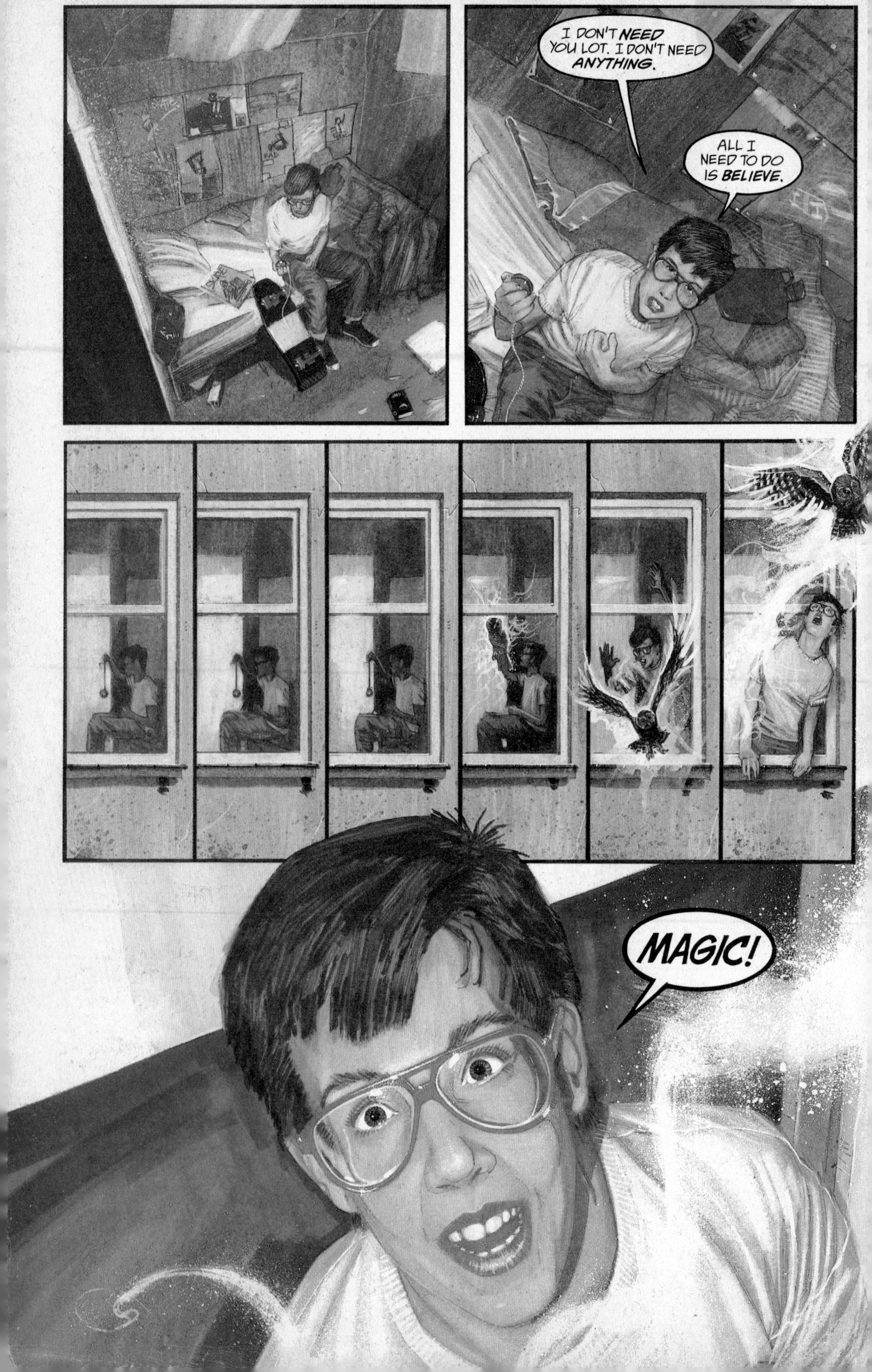
I DON'T NEED YOU LOT. I DON'T NEED ANYTHING.
ALL I NEED TO DO IS BELIEVE.
MAGIC!